THE GO-GO YEARS

THE DRAMA AND CRASHING FINALE
OF WALL STREET'S BULLISH 60S

JOHN BROOKS

Foreword by Michael Lewis

ALLWORTH PRESS
NEW YORK

Published by Allworth Press
An imprint of Allworth Communications
10 East 23rd Street, New York, NY 10010

Cover design by Douglas Designs, New York, NY

Cover photo © 1998 Tad Crawford

Book design by Bob Antler

ISBN: 1-880559-91-9

Library of Congress Catalog Card Number: 98-72178

Contents

Foreword

"This may be, conceivably, one of the last books to be written about 'Wall Street' in its own time." Thus John Brooks concludes his famous portrait of Wall Street in the 1960s. Well, we all know what happened to that prediction. Books about Wall Street in its own time went forth and multiplied. You could fill a small library with the books about Wall Street that have been published since *The Go-Go Years* first appeared in 1973. In the past few years alone I have seen manuscripts, or outlines, or proposals, for books about Goldman Sachs, Morgan Stanley, Merrill Lynch, Bear Stearns, George Soros, Michael Steinhardt, and Michael Milken. One small-time Wall Street dealer, a man named Victor Niederhoffer, published a four hundred plus page tome about himself, called *Education of a Speculator*, then promptly speculated himself out of business. These days, no book about money is considered too trivial, or ill conceived, to publish.

Brooks himself is partly to blame for this state of affairs. He was one of the first journalists to prove that an outsider could walk into Wall Street and emerge with a long and detailed story that a generally educated but specifically ignorant outsider could read with pleasure. *The Go-Go Years* is such a story.

The tendency with books about Wall Street is to put them down with a reassuring sigh and say, the more things change,

v

the more they stay the same. (Or as Brooks would no doubt put it to his old *New Yorker* audience, *plus ça change, plus ça la même chose*.) This book contains plenty in it to justify that response. As the stock market chart races to the roof, a cast of characters familiar to observers of the financial 1990s takes the stage. In 1960s Fidelity-mutual-fund-guru Gerald Tsai there are echoes of 1990s Fidelity-mutual-fund-guru Jeff Vinik. In the detached aloofness of the original hedge fund manager, A. W. Jones, there is at least a trace of the detached aloofness of his successor, George Soros. In the money grubbing of 1960s Market Man there is an echo of the money grubbing of the 1990s Market Man. "In America," writes Brooks, "with its deeply imprinted business ethic, no inherent stabilizer, moral or practical, is sufficiently strong in and of itself to support the turning away of new business when competitors are taking it in. As a people we would rather face chaos making potsfull of short term money than maintain order and sanity by profiting less."

But what is mainly interesting today for readers of John Brooks is how different the market of the 1990s feels from the market of the 1960s. There is no real equivalent in Brooks's account to the technology stocks of today, for instance. There are no foreign markets, no bonds, almost no computers. On the other hand, all those Great White Institutions that these days barely merit a mention in today's books on Wall Street—the SEC, the NYSE, the Establishment—loom large in Brooks's account.

Then there is the moral of the story, or stories. *The Go-Go Years* reduces fairly neatly to a series of morality tales about the most outlandish events of the 1960s: Ross Perot dropping $450 million in one day; Saul Steinberg having the nerve to *consider*—much less to attempt—a takeover of Chemical Bank; Eddie Gilbert seducing some rich people into investing in his ill-starred ventures before vanishing into Brazil with the other stock market losers. How *tame* they now all seem! At least to this reader they have lost their ability to shock. The author clearly considers his subjects engaged in an endless cycle of falls and redemptions. But the modern reader is constantly having to remind himself who has fallen, and why he needs to be redeemed. These are moralist tales in which the moral has at least in part been lost.

This may help to explain the most curious thing about *The Go-Go Years:* its tone of voice. Those lovely, long, multipartite sentences, the glorious arch of the authorial eyebrow, Brooks's palpable feeling that you, gentle reader, are a broadly educated person who instinctively disapproves of these . . . speculators. . . . Brooks's voice is, above all, the voice of the Old Establishment. The reader Brooks imagines himself to be speaking to is the same shockable character who has vanished from the financial world over the past thirty years. Who on Wall Street these days thinks twice about speculation? Who disapproves of large corporate takeovers? No such person exists, or if he does he's living on some island so remote that no word of the market will ever reach him.

In the end, *The Go-Go Years* is not to be read in the usual manner of Wall Street classics. You do not read this book to see our present situations reenacted in the past, with only the names changed. You read it because it is a wonderful description of the way things were in a different time and place. If Brooks's sense that the end of the Old Establishment would mean the end of Wall Street led him occasionally to get things wrong, at least he got them wrong in an interesting way. "Wall Street as a social context is apparently doomed not by reform but by mechanization," he wrote toward the end of the book. "Already in the early nineteen seventies, a significant proportion of stock trading is being conducted not face to face on the floor under a skylight but between men sitting in front of closed circuit television screens in offices hundreds or thousands of miles apart. . . . Wall Street (is heading) toward transforming itself into an impersonal national slot machine—presumably fairer to the investor but of much less interest as a microcosm of America."

The description was dead-on, but the forecast could not have been more wrong. In a mere twenty-five years, Wall Street has become the largest microcosm on earth.

MICHAEL LEWIS

CHAPTER I

Climax

1

On April 22, 1970, Henry Ross Perot of Dallas, Texas, one of the half-dozen richest men in the United States, was so new to wealth, at forty, that he was not listed in *Poor's Register* and had just appeared for the first time in *Who's Who in America*. Only a small fraction of his fellow countrymen had ever heard of him. Many who had met him by happening to sit next to him on airliners had not found him particularly impressive or interesting. Barely five and a half feet tall, with a naïve, straightforward gaze, an unamused smile, a crooked nose, a hillbilly East Texas accent, and a short crewcut tended like a tennis lawn, he was inclined to talk at length and with enthusiasm about things like patriotism and the Boy Scouts of America. More than anything else, he seemed to be a nice, promising young man who was probably selling something.

Yet that day Perot made a landmark in the financial history of the United States and perhaps of the Western world. It was hardly a landmark to be envied, but it was certainly one to be remembered. That day, he suffered a paper stock-market loss of about $450 million. He still had, on paper, almost a billion dollars left afterward, but that wasn't the point. The point was that his one-day loss amounted to more than the total assets of any charitable foundation in the country after the top five; more than the annual welfare budget of any city except New York; and more—not just in figures, but in actual purchasing power —than J. Pierpont Morgan was known to be worth at the time of his death in 1913. It was also quite possibly more in actual purchasing power than any man had ever lost in a single day since the Industrial Revolution brought large private accumulations of money into being.

2

It was Earth Day; the environment had recently become a national mania, especially among the young, and a group of conservationist leaders headed by Senator Gaylord Nelson of Wisconsin had picked April 22 as a day of national dedication to the cause of eliminating pollution in all its forms. (Were preposterously large paper stock-market profits such as Ross Perot had made to be considered a form of pollution? Quite possibly.) In Washington, in front of the Department of the Interior Building, twelve hundred young people milled around shouting "Off the oil!" and "Stop the muck!" to protest government leases to oil producers whose operations were thought to cause pollution. There were antipollution rallies of twenty-five thousand or more (watched by the F.B.I., it became known later) in New York, Chicago, and Philadelphia. In Bloomington, Minnesota, former Vice President Humphrey urged the United Nations to establish an environmental agency to combat pollution around the world, and at Georgetown University in Washington, Senator Birch Bayh of Indiana called for a national agency "to conquer pollution as we have conquered space." Interior Secretary Walter Hickel—an authentic hero of environmentalism, since he was a convert soon to be martyred professionally for his views—was in his home state of Alaska, getting a hero's welcome. In New York City, children rode bicycles to school; huge, lighthearted crowds gamboled on an automobile-free Fifth Avenue; at Seventeenth Street people were offered the opportunity to breath "pure air" from the nozzle of a blocklong polyethylene bubble; and so on, as all the artillery of promotion and public relations was turned, momentarily, in an unfamiliar and uncharacteristic direction. The same day, the novelist Kurt Vonnegut, after alluding to President Nixon's statement that he did not propose to be the first American President to lose a war, commented, "He may be the first American President to lose a planet."

All this resolution and high spirits fought upstream against one of the deepest moods of gloom to darken any American April since the Civil War. The first My Lai revelations were five months old; the dangerous and disturbing New Haven strike in support of the Black Panthers, which would spread quickly to campuses all over the Northeast, was to begin that same day, April 22; the stunningly unpopular invasion of Cambodia was eight days off, the Kent State University killings of students by National Guardsmen twelve days off. The gloom, compounded by signs of an approaching national economic recession, had caused a stock-market panic that, though far from over, was already comparable in a remarkable number of ways to that of October 1929. The Dow-Jones industrial average of common stocks had sunk relentlessly through almost all of 1969; then, after holding fairly firm through the first three months of the new year, it had gone into a sickening collapse that had carried it, by April 22, to a level some 235 points below where it had been at its peak sixteen months earlier. Much worse, the Dow did not begin to tell the whole story. Interest rates were at near-record highs, strangling new housing construction and making most industrial expansion impractical. The dollar was in bad trouble in the international markets, with foreigners holding American currency worth many billions more than the national gold hoard. One hundred or more Wall Street brokerage firms were near failure. As for the Dow, made up as it was of the old blue chips that had long since been deposed as sensitive and accurate market leaders, it was a pale, watered-down reflection of the real stock-market situation. A better indication is to be found in the fact that in May 1970, a portfolio consisting of one share of every stock listed on the Big Board was worth just about half of what it would have been worth at the start of 1969. The high flyers that had led the market of 1967 and 1968 —conglomerates, computer leasers, far-out electronics companies, franchisers—were precipitously down from their peaks. Nor were they down 25 percent, like the Dow, but 80, 90, or 95 percent. This was vintage 1929 stuff, and the prospect of another great depression, this one induced as much by despair as by economic factors as such, was a very real one.

The visible parallels to 1929, in the business and financial spheres, were enough to make a man agree not merely with Santayana, who said that those who forget history are condemned to repeat it, but with Proust, whose whole great book, read one way, seems to say that man's apparent capacity to learn from experience is an illusion.

Before the crash in 1929 the financial sages had insisted repeatedly that there couldn't be another panic like that of 1907 because of the protective role of the Federal Reserve System; before the crash of 1969–70 a later generation observed repeatedly that there couldn't be another panic like that of 1929 because of the protective role of the Federal Reserve System and the Securities and Exchange Commission. In each case a severe market break had taken place about eight years earlier (in 1921 and 1962, respectively), followed by a period of progressively more unfettered speculation. In each case huge, shaky financial pyramids, built on a minimum of cash base, had been erected by financiers eager to take maximum advantage of the public's insatiable appetite for common stocks. Before 1929 they had been called investment trusts and holding companies; now they were called conglomerates. In each case there had been a single market operator to whom the public assigned the star role of official seer. In the 1920s the man to whom the public ascribed almost supernatural power to divine the future prices of stocks had been Jesse L. Livermore. In the middle 1960s, it was Gerald Tsai.

In each case, certain insiders contrived to use privileged information and superior market technique to manipulate stock prices and thus deceive the public; in the 1920s the manipulators had been called pool operators, in the 1960s they were called portfolio managers. (It is curious to note that, while the operations of both the pools of the 1920s and the high-performance funds of the 1960s were obviously unfair if not illegal, there was no public disapproval of either so long as people were making money on them.) In each case, the practice of slack ethics started in the untended underbrush on the fringes of Wall Street and moved, sooner or later, to the very centers of power and respectability. In 1926 (although it wasn't known publicly until over a decade later), the future president of the New York Stock Exchange committed the first of a series of embezzlements of funds entrusted to his care; in 1929 the president of the Chase National Bank made a personal profit of $4 million by selling short the shares of his own bank. No wrongdoing so melodramatic occurred among the Wall Street leaders of the 1960s—or, at least, none has so far been uncovered. But in 1926 a partner of J.P. Morgan and Company shocked the financial world, which believed the Morgans sat on the right hand of God, by openly touting a stock, General Motors, in which his firm was substantially interested; and forty years later, in 1966, a not dissimilar shudder went through the Street when it became known that two years earlier a key vice president of J.P. Morgan and Company's successor firm, Morgan Guaranty Trust Company, had bought or caused to be bought ten thousand shares of Texas Gulf Sulphur in less than half an hour, apparently on the basis of privileged information of a great ore strike in Ontario.

The parallels go down to certain curious details. In each case, the market collapse occurred under a Republican President who had been elected on the crest of the preceding boom, and who had a strong pro-business orientation. In each case, the crisis was marked by carefully planned and publicized Presidential meetings at the White House with Wall Street leaders. Finally, in each case the crash gave rise to an orgy of recrimination and finger-pointing.

Of course, there were tremendous differences, too—not just the fact that the more recent crash did not lead to a catastrophic national depression (though it did lead to a severe one), but differences in style and nuance and social implication that will be the main subject of this chronicle. One might, in comparing 1929 with 1969–70, even find a certain appositeness in Karl Marx's famous observation that history repeats itself the first time as tragedy, the second time as farce.

3

Wall Street, in the geographical sense, was to become an actual battleground that spring, less than three weeks after Earth Day and Ross Perot's Down-to-Earth Day. By Wednesday, May 6, 1970, a week after the Cambodia announcement and two days after the Kent State incident, eighty colleges across the country were closed entirely as a result of student and faculty strikes, and students were boycotting classes at over three hundred more. Most New York City schools and colleges were scheduled to be closed that Friday, May 8, in a gesture of protest, and among the student antiwar demonstrations being planned was one to be held in Wall Street. On Wednesday the sixth, a small group of white-coated students and faculty members from several medical and nursing schools in the city came to Wall Street to demonstrate for peace on their own. There they were greeted warmly by the vigorous, youth-oriented, peace-crusading vicar of Trinity Church, Donald R. Woodward. In the course of the ensuing conversations, the medical people suggested that it might be a good idea, considering the vast daytime population of the Wall Street area, to establish a noon-hour first-aid center at Trinity Church, which, standing as it has since colonial times right at the head of Wall Street, is at the very heart of the financial district in the physical—though scarcely, it often seems, in the spiritual—sense. If Trinity would provide space, the medical people said, they would undertake to set up and man the first-aid center on a volunteer basis. The vicar gratefully and enthusiastically accepted the offer. The first day that the center was in operation was Friday, May 8—a circumstance that in retrospect seems little less than providential.

That Friday morning—a damp, drizzly, bone-chilling morning such as New York can often produce in early May— beginning at about seven-thirty, boys and girls by the hundreds began debouching from Wall Street's two principal subway stations, the Seventh Avenue–Broadway stop at Chase Manhattan Plaza and the Lexington Avenue at Broadway and Wall. Most of them were from New York University, Hunter College, and the city's public high schools, all of those institutions being closed for the day. Eventually something like a thousand strong, they jammed into the financial district's central plaza, the intersection of Broad and Wall, where they milled around under the apprehensive scrutiny of a good-sized cadre of city policemen who had been dispatched there in anticipation of their arrival. But the students seemed to be in no mood to cause the police any trouble. In light rain, under the columns of Federal Hall, where George Washington had once taken the oath of office as the United States' first President, and facing the intimidating entrance to the great marble building from which imperial Morgan had once more or less ruled the nation, they spent the morning rallying their spirits and formulating their demands. The demands, not too surprisingly, turned out to be the same as those agreed upon a few days earlier by a secret convention of radical youth leaders in New Haven, and now being put forth on dozens of northeastern campuses. One: immediate United States withdrawal from Vietnam and Cambodia. Two: release of all "political prisoners" in the nation—a pointed, not to say loaded, reference to the Black Panthers imprisoned on charges of participating in the torture and murder of Alex Rackley, a Panther accused of being a police informer. Three: cessation of all military-oriented research work under the auspices of American universities. Unlike many student demonstrations in the spring of 1970, this one was wholly nonviolent. Indeed, it was positively good-humored, and when, as noon approached, the rain stopped and a warm sun broke through, the mood became even better. Most of the demonstrators sat down on the sidewalk to listen to speakers.

Eleven fifty-five: suddenly, simultaneously from all four approaches to the intersection, like a well-trained raiding force, the hardhats came. They were construction workers, many employed in the huge nearby World Trade Center project, and their brown overalls and orange-and-yellow helmets seemed to be a sort of uniform. Many of them carried American flags; others, it soon became clear, carried construction tools and wore heavy boots that were intended as weapons. Later it was said that their movements appeared to be directed, by means of hand signals, by two unidentified men in gray hats and gray suits. There were perhaps two hundred of them.

As they pushed through the mob of seated students, it became manifest that their two objectives were to place flags at the base of the Washington statue in front of Federal Hall, otherwise known as the Subtreasury Building, and to break up the demonstration, if necessary by violence. As to the first objective, they marched toward the statue shouting "All the way, U.S.A.!" and "Love it or leave it!"; their way was barred on the steps by a thin line of policemen; the policemen, overwhelmed by greater numbers, were brushed aside; and the flags were triumphantly planted under the statue. As to the second objective: construction workers repeatedly struck students with sticks, fists, boots, screwdrivers, and pliers. They chased screaming students of both sexes down the canyons of the financial district, striking to hurt when they came within range. They ripped the Red Cross banner, indicating the presence of the new first-aid station, from the front gates of Trinity. The air was filled with the cries of the enraged and the injured, and the acrid, ominous aroma of a storm-troop putsch. Vicar Woodward, brave and exposed, stood through it all by the Trinity front gates, directing victims to the aid station inside; twice, fearing an actual invasion of the church, he ordered the gates closed.

Inside Trinity, a communion service was in progress—a Mass, as it happened, for peace and in commemoration of the Kent State students and all the war dead in Vietnam. Those in the congregation were first aware of the noise of a rising mob filtering in from the street; then, as the service proceeded, they watched a steady stream of bloodied students walking or being carried down the nave's side aisle to the Sacristy and Clergy Vesting Room where the young doctors and nurses were ready to treat them. In all, about fifty demonstrators were treated at the Trinity first-aid station; another twenty-three were serious enough cases to require attention at Beekman-Downtown Hospital.

For more than a week afterward, Wall Street bristled daily with police as if it were in a fascist state.

To the extent that it had any part in this dispiriting affair —this small but fierce and rancorous struggle that came so close to being a crystallization of the whole nation's tragedy at that moment—professional Wall Street, the Wall Street of finance and law, of power and elegance, seemed to be on the side of the students. Perhaps out of common humanity, or perhaps out of class feeling, the bulls and bears felt more kinship with the doves than with the hawks. At Exchange Place, Robert A. Bernhard, a partner in the aristocratic firm of Lehman Brothers, was himself assaulted and severely cut in the head by a construction worker's heavy pliers, after he had tried to protect a youth who was being beaten. A few blocks north, a young Wall Street lawyer was knocked down, kicked, and beaten when he protested against hardhats who were yelling "Kill the Commie bastards!" But most of the mighty of the Street—Communist bastards or not—had no part in the struggle. They were not on the street. Like the famous, allegedly anarchist bombing on Wall Street in 1920, when thirty persons were killed and hundreds wounded, the riot of 1970 occurred just before noon: not quite lunch time. There was a racket in the street, and everyone above (or everyone privileged to have a window) looked out. The market was unaffected. Most of Wall Street's elite working population watched the carnage from high, safe windows.

Indeed, there was little else they could sensibly have done; no purpose would have been served by their rushing down and joining the fray. Nevertheless, there is an all too symbolic aspect to professional Wall Street's role that day as a bystander, sympathizing, unmistakably, with the underdogs, the unarmed, the peace-lovers, but keeping its hands clean—watching with fascination and horror from its windows that looked out over the lovely (at that perspective) Upper Bay with its still-green islands and its proud passing liners, and down into the canyon from which there now rose, inconveniently, the cries of hurt or frightened children.

4

The event (like the unreal gyrations in the fortunes of Perot) called attention to the relationship, or the lack of one, between Wall Street and the nation in the new times. Did it make sense anymore to live—and live at the top of the heap—by playing games with paper while children screamed under the window? Could not one almost hear the tumbrils to the revolutionary guillotine rattling in the distance? Well, at any rate, if you were a Wall Streeter in 1970 you were at least no longer directly profiting by war. As late as the Eisenhower era the market had adhered to its age-old habit of greeting war news with complacency if not with outright glee, and of greeting peace news— "peace scares" was the local term—with panic and hysteria. But sometime in late 1967 Wall Street had come to decide that the Vietnam war was bad business, and had broken all precedent by turning decisively bearish on war and bullish on peace. The defense contractors were no longer blue chips; one of the biggest, Lockheed, would soon be in danger of bankruptcy. The peace initiatives of early 1968 had caused or contributed to a huge bull market on record volume. An unheard-of phenomenon; an old shame of Wall Street ended, to sighs of relief from financiers with consciences.

Or again: if you were a conscientious Wall Streeter you could tell yourself that you were contributing to progress by financing industrial expansion that would help reduce poverty and would finally abolish it. But now you knew, or had recently been compelled at last to reflect, that industrial expansion was not an unalloyed blessing; that each new factory, however modern and antiseptic, would mean new money for many but might also mean—through pollution—ugliness, suffering, and death.

Wall Street as a political issue was long dead except in those homes of the stuck record, Moscow and Peking. Even the American Old Left had stopped attacking Wall Street long since (and was probably long since in the market itself). "Lackeys of Wall Street" was a phrase to laugh at when Mao or Khrushchev mouthed it—as well say "lackeys of Monte Carlo." Spreading affluence and the rise of corporate and federal power had reduced Wall Street to the status of a national facility without important political influence. The New Left simply ignored it, except in 1967 when Abbie Hoffman and his Yippie friends had the inspired notion of throwing dollar bills from the visitors' gallery onto the Stock Exchange floor. A few months later, the Exchange management did *its* bit for the Yippie cause by installing bulletproof glass around the visitors' gallery, thereby seeming to indicate that it considered thrown-away dollar bills to be lethal weapons. (And maybe, after all, from the Exchange's point of view they were.) In short, a taunt was offered and magnificently accepted. But the taunt was not even to Wall Street; Wall Street had become a convenient metaphor for commercial America. Hoffman was right to crow, "Throwing money onto the floor of the Stock Exchange is pure information. It needs no explanation. It says more than thousands of anticapitalist tracts and essays." And how magnificently bulletproof glass underlines the message! Wall Street, which despises suckers, had been suckered.

And all through the stormy course of 1967 and 1968, when

things had been coming apart and it had seemed that the center really couldn't hold—the rising national economic crisis culminating in a day when the dollar was unredeemable in Paris, the Martin Luther King and Robert Kennedy assassinations, the shame of the Chicago Democratic convention, the rising tempo of student riots—the silly market had gone its merry way, heedlessly soaring upward as if everything were O.K. or would surely come out O.K., as mindlessly, maniacally euphoric as a Japanese beetle in July. Or as a doomed man enjoying his last meal. One could only ask: Did Wall Street, for all its gutter shrewdness, have the slightest idea what was *really* going on?

Beyond that, wasn't Wall Street the very living symbol and embodiment of everything—the Protestant work ethic, Social Darwinism, market orientation, money-madness—that America was only now learning, if not to reject, at least to get into a new and lesser perspective? Wasn't Wall Street backward-looking, a kind of simplified, idealized version of the older and now largely discredited America, unrelated or even antipathetic to the new America that was struggling now to come into being?

Of course, Wall Street itself claimed to be more broadly American than ever before. Even at the height of the 1929 boom, Wall Street could and did point out, there were only 4 or 5 million Americans in the stock market. In the summer of 1970 the Stock Exchange proudly unveiled a survey showing that the country now held over 30 million shareowners. "People's capitalism" had arrived, then, and there were figures to prove it. Yet in another and perhaps more important perspective, the stock market was not more closely related to American life in 1970 than in 1929; in fact, the contrary was true. In 1929, America—the America of history, the one described in books and newspapers and popular magazines and even in the intellectual journals—had been essentially still a small country consisting of people possessing either land or money. Everybody else had been simply considered beneath notice. As the majority consisting of slaves is ignored in the idyllic histories of the democracy of ancient Greece, so the majority of the poor was ignored in the social histories of America *circa* 1929. By 1970, social commentary at all levels had become democratic; minorities, black and other, had become consequently self-conscious, aware of their right to be included and noticed even though they remain as they are rather than remolding themselves in the white Protestant image, as the Jews and the Irish had so largely done in earlier times. Even among the affluent, discussing the stock market at social occasions—a custom not just sanctioned but approved in 1929—had come to be considered generally dull or boorish. In the national context, the 4 or 5 million stockholders of 1929 loomed far larger than the 30 million of 1970. And in 1970, people's capitalism—as almost any black, Mexican, Puerto Rican, Appalachian poor white, unemployed laborer, or hardscrabble farmer would tell you—was still largely a myth.

Wall Street—sometimes so beautifully, so patly metaphorical that it could break a poet's heart—was not only a place sorely in need of physical and spiritual "greening," but had been almost the first place in the nation to be literally ungreened. A print made in 1847, long before the coming of large-scale industrialization, the age of asphalt, hangs in the famous old restaurant Sweets in Fulton Street. It shows almost the whole six-hundred-yard stretch of Wall Street looking toward Trinity Church, and the scene contains exactly one tree. With the physical ungreening went—and goes—the spiritual concomitant, a certain dehumanization. For generations, Wall Street as a social ambiance has tended to represent what is hardest, coldest, and meanest in America. Sneaky, parsimonious, hypocritical old Daniel Drew is not a Wall Street legend for nothing. This is not to say that life there has been (or is) all mean and inhuman. Along with Drew's unprepossessing qualities, in Wall Street there has always been extraordinary enterprise, generosity, courage, villainy on a grand scale, the drama of success and failure, even now and again a certain nobility. In the nineteen sixties Wall Street still had a stimulating tendency, as it had had for a century and more, to project humanity (and specifically American humanity) on a wide screen, larger than life; to be a stage, perhaps one of the last, for high, pure, moral melodrama on the themes of possession, domination, and belonging.

But at a cost. As few plants bloom there, so do few people. While the Wall Street kings play out their classic dramas in the filtered air behind the high windows, the vassals, footmen, and ladies-in-waiting of the Street are short of the little satisfactions that make life bearable. Numbers and machines that they don't understand benumb them. One gets off the subway at Broadway and Wall and begins to feel depressed. Men's faces seem pinched and preoccupied. Pretty women seem flesh without magic. In winter a savage wind curls around the corners of those canyons; in summer the air lies heavy, dank, and sunless. The debaters of theology who cluster outside the Bankers Trust seem disturbingly psychotic, not engagingly zany. Not greed nor avarice, but footling bad temper, is too often the prevailing mood.

In a revolutionary time like 1970, could it be that Wall Street, that summary of so much that is least engaging about our national tradition, was coming to be—in the cliché of the moment—irrelevant?

5

Not to Ross Perot. To him, Wall Street was a Puritan's Hell, dangerous and fascinating, and also, as he well knew, the source of his almost incredible riches. He had entered Hell, conquered it, and remained pure. By environment and temperament he was a perfect Western populist, feeling toward "city slickers," including those in Wall Street, a fear and suspicion not unmixed with envy and contempt. His boyhood in East Texas, as the son of a depression-ridden small-town cotton broker and horse-trader, had set the pattern of his life: he had broken horses for pay before he was ten (and repeatedly broken his nose in the process), become an Eagle Scout, learned the cult of self-reliance and learned to make a holy Calvinist doctrine of the pursuit of the honest dollar by honest effort. In some senses he was an anachronism. He had grown up, before and during World War

II, believing that the frontier not only existed but still dominated American life. What had been physically extinct long before his birth summed up his spiritual reality. He believed that all things were possible in America for the man of enterprise and that the natural habitat of the man of enterprise was the "frontier." Even now, when he had turned the tables and was admired, envied, perhaps hated in Wall Street itself, he instinctively equated "West" with "good" and "East" with "bad"; traveling on airliners—as I learned when I spent three days traveling with him on them, late in 1970—he found that his fellow passengers became more pinched, constricted, snobbish, close-mouthed as a plane moved eastward over the nation, and more generous, open-hearted, and free-thinking as it moved westward.

He was of pioneer stock; his grandfather Perot, son of an immigrant from France to Louisiana before the Civil War, in the true frontier days, had made his way upriver and overland to New Boston, Texas, where he had hacked out a clearing, hewed timber, and built a trading post and general store. Ross Perot, after high school and two years of junior college in nearby Texarkana, had wangled an appointment to the Naval Academy, where he had graduated in 1953 with an average academic record but had been recognized for leadership through election as class president. Already he showed promise as a supersalesman. After four years of active Navy duty he had taken a job as a computer drummer, on commission, for I.B.M. in Dallas. He had soon turned out to be such an overachiever that any promotion to a salaried job would have involved a cut in pay, so the company had taken drastic steps to control his income. It had cut his commission on sales by four-fifths and assigned him an annual sales quota beyond which he would get no commission. For the year 1962, he had made his annual quota by January 19, thus putting himself effectively out of business for the next eleven months and twelve days. After brooding on his dilemma, he quit I.B.M. that June and incorporated his own company—Electronic Data Systems Corp., designers, installers, and operators of computer systems—taking with him a couple of brilliant young I.B.M. colleagues, Milledge A. Hart, III, and Thomas Marquez. He had no investors or backers; his initial investment was $1,000, the minimum required for incorporation under Texas law; his directors, apart from himself, were his wife, his mother, and his sister. Hard times followed for a while. (When E.D.S. put up its own building in Dallas and decorated it with the firm's initials, some local people took the place for a restaurant called "Ed's.") But persistence and salesmanship paid off. In 1965, opportunity knocked for E.D.S. when federal Medicare legislation was passed and E.D.S. quickly got in on the ground floor. Perot actually spent a spell working part-time for Texas Blue Shield, which had a contract with the Social Security Administration to develop a computerized system for paying Medicare bills. Out of this association came a subcontract from Texas Blue Shield to E.D.S. That was only the beginning. Eventually E.D.S. had subcontracts to administer Medicare or Medicaid in eleven states, including Texas, California, and Indiana; the firm derived the major portion of its revenue from these contracts, and was, as *Ramparts* remarked scathingly in 1971, "America's first welfare billionaire." All told, by 1968 E.D.S. had twenty-three contracts for computer systems, 323 full-time employees, about $10 million in assets, annual net profits of over $1.5 million, and a growth curve so fantastic as to make investment bankers' mouths water.

Of such cloth was cut the man who, by early 1970—and by methods that we shall soon see—had beaten every one of the city slickers on their home ground, and become the single biggest winner in what the writer "Adam Smith" called "the money game," emerging with paper assets to his name of almost $1.5 billion. His personal relations with Wall Street and its slickers began early in 1968, when the market was going through the roof and the hungry investment bankers had suddenly realized that Perot's little clutch of refugees from the fur-lined trap of I.B.M. was now ripe for a public sale that might be a bonanza all around. Seventeen investment bankers visited Perot in rapid succession and urged him to put his stock on the market. At first he said, as he had always said previously, that he never would.

He didn't want outside interference in his company's affairs, he just wanted to be left alone to do a job. But the seventeenth banker got to Perot. He was Kenneth Langone of R.W. Pressprich and Company, a respectable enough Wall Street firm. Langone was a youngish, sympathetic, fast-talking stock peddler of urban Italian extraction. In character, temperament, and background he and Perot presented a study in contrasts—in almost everything except that great binding tie, a shared respect for money. Other investment bankers had offered to sell Perot's stock at thirty times current annual earnings, then at fifty times, then at seventy times. Langone, however, offered one hundred times, possibly somewhat more. Perot hesitated for several weeks, during which he conducted a series of windy seminars within his company on the abstract moral question of whether or not a company like theirs ought to go public. Predictably, the seminars turned out to be largely a grotesque exercise in middle-management men trying to guess which way the cat would jump. But as to Perot, was all this soul-searching merely self-deception? Did his principles, like so many principles, have their price? Was his mind made up? Whatever the case, Perot said yes to Langone.

Then began Perot's education in the ways of the slickers, and he proved to be an astute pupil indeed. First of all, Langone wanted to know, who were the company's directors? His wife, his mother, and his sister, Perot reported. Langone said that wouldn't do. So Perot wrote himself a more acceptable board, consisting of Hart, Marquez, and other principal employees. Next, the company would have to be recapitalized: say, 11.5 million shares. A preposterous capitalization for a company that earned only $1.5 million a year? Necessary, Langone explained, if you wanted that high earnings multiple and also a reasonable stock price. E.D.S., then, would be the seller of 325,000 shares of stock; Perot himself would be the seller of another 325,000. The rest would be kept by Perot and the E.D.S. employees— around 1.5 million shares for the employees (he had issued it to them by way of bonuses), and not quite 9.5 million for Perot himself. Wasn't 650,000 shares for public trading a dangerously small float, likely to make for a highly volatile market in which small investors might possibly get hurt? Langone told Perot it was plenty. After all, he pointed out, R. W. Pressprich itself would make the market, and could be counted on to maintain a fair and orderly one. The offering price finally agreed upon was $16.50 a share—118 times current E.D.S. earnings, and an infinite number times current dividends, since there were none.

Through all the negotiations Perot played barefoot boy to the hilt, pretending to be baffled by Wall Street's baroque rituals while actually learning to turn them to his own advantage. Was this a way to do business, he demanded of Langone, letting natural market forces be flouted by a local social pecking order that often required higher-ranking investment bankers to abstain from participation in offerings headed by lesser ones? Langone, scarcely a lover of Morgans or Lehmans or their kind, just smiled and shrugged. Perot made outlandish suggestions such as that the original buyers of his stock be offered a ninety-day money-back guarantee—surely knowing well enough that such an arrangement would be both legally and practically impossible—and tried to write his own prospectus in Frank Merriwell language ("All alone, against overwhelming odds, with little money. . . ."), only to see it rewritten in the usual legalese. He indulged in classic frontiersmanship with the underwriters' legal counsel, the proper firm of Winthrop, Stimson, Putnam, and Roberts: in New York one of the lawyers invited Perot to lunch at a distinguished Wall Street club, and then when the lawyer came to Dallas, Perot insisted on returning the favor at a local greasy spoon. But when, on September 12, 1968, the E.D.S. stock was publicly offered and was quickly subscribed for in one of the most sensationally successful new-issue promotions of the whole headlong era, the bumpkin came out overnight with $5 million in personal cash and more than $200 million in stock equity at market value. All the tolerant Wall Street smiles faded abruptly.

Had the bumpkin, then, really been a superslicker all along, even though he pronounced head as "haid" and yes as "yais"? Perhaps; but surely not consciously. In fact, Perot could legiti-

mately claim to be by his own lights a pure-hearted moral idealist. His code embodied the early American virtues—thrift, early
rising, work, competition, individualism—and it worked for
him. He had the useful, if to many people annoying, ability of
finding a moral homily to support whatever he did. Wall Street
had made him rich, so Wall Street might not be so bad—maybe,
at bottom, a simpleminded, paper-tiger sort of villain. In the
months following the stock offering, Perot's fascination with the
place grew. He talked to Langone by telephone from Dallas
every working day, and visited in person whenever he could. On
his visits, he would frequent the Pressprich trading room where
the E.D.S. market was made. The stock took off. Institutions
began buying it. Strange orders came in from places like Geneva
and Lebanon, and this made the xenophobic Perot uneasy.
Sometimes he would protest: "Don't sell my stock to him! I
don't want him for a stockholder!" But the traders would laugh
and sell the stock anyhow at ever-rising prices. At last, early in
1970, E.D.S. sold at 160. Perot, with his 9-million-plus shares,
was now worth on paper almost $1.5 billion—which, it happens,
is about 40 percent of the whole United States federal budget for
1930, the year he was born.

The new billionaire saw himself, characteristically, not as
a grandee but as an example to the nation's youth: "Somewhere
in the United States there's a young man or woman who will
break every financial record I've set! That's the amount of opportunity that exists in this country." Again characteristically
—and in marked defiance of recent practice among other newly
rich Texans—he set about being a moral billionaire. He decided
to will only modest sums to his five children, "so they'll have the
same opportunities I've had." Substantially all of his fortune
would go, sooner or later, to "the improvement of American
life." For a starter, he gave a million dollars to the Boy Scouts
in the Dallas area. He gave over two million to the Dallas public
school system to finance a pilot elementary school in a black
ghetto area. He refused to avail himself of his legal right to take
personal income-tax deductions on his charitable contributions
on the ground that morally he owed the tax money to a country

that had done so well by him. In 1969, he became obsessed with the plight of United States prisoners of war in North Vietnam, and that December he attempted personally to intervene with the North Vietnamese authorities in their behalf. (His efforts, which included two excursions to Indochina in chartered airliners, failed, but they seem to have been not without rewards in personal satisfaction—in serving to convince people, perhaps including himself, that one man alone is *not* powerless in the modern world, and that Americans, particularly capitalist Americans, are a force for good no matter what anyone says.) By instinct he involved himself in moral confrontations in which, in his terms, he was always the winner. Once in 1969 a group of young West Coast radicals came to ask him—with tongues fairly protruding from their cheeks, it may be guessed—to finance "the revolution." Did Perot avoid them or send them away? Indeed not; rather he took the opportunity to give them an object lesson. In his most businesslike manner he asked, "How long will it take and what will it cost?" The radicals, with no ready answer, were speechless.

He made what he did a virtue, and a virtue of what he did. But was Perot a hypocrite? Hypocrisy in common morals, like fraud in common law, is an offense that requires an element of "scienter"—knowledge of the offender that he is committing the offense. Viewed in that light, Perot, without scienter, was innocent.

6

The way Perot received the news of his monumental setback on April 22 was casual to the point of comedy. All that morning he was closeted in his Dallas office with executives of a potential client company to which E.D.S. was making its sales pitch. On emerging around one o'clock, he picked up a phone and called down the hall to Tom Marquez.

"What's new?" Perot asked.

"Well," Marquez said, "the stock is down fifty or sixty points."

Later Perot was to say that he had felt nothing at all. The event, he would add, had been "purely abstract." Despite a certain liking for history, insofar as history fitted in with his preconceived ideas, Perot did not immediately put in it a historical context. As we have seen, he had philosophical inclinations of a sort, too, but these, like those of most businessmen, tended to be of the *ad hoc* rather than the *gratia artis* sort. What did occur to him was that the whole thing didn't really matter much, since the $1.5 billion he had made in eight years wasn't quite real money anyway because it was not quickly or readily convertible into cash. It also probably occurred to him that he wasn't exactly left destitute by the sudden crash, since he still had (on paper) that residual billion or so dollars. He had, he was to say later, the sense that nothing much had really happened.

Exactly what happened to the market in E.D.S. on the morning of April 22 is not known and may never be known in detail. What is certain, however, is the fact that its collapse was not based on any bad news about the company's operations. To the contrary, the news was all spectacularly good; per-share earnings for 1969 were more than double those for 1968, and even for the first quarter of 1970—a time of fast-deepening general business recession—E.D.S. showed a 70 percent profits increase over the same period for 1969. Quite evidently, there had to be some other cause.

E.D.S. was traded in the over-the-counter market. Less than a year later the operation of that long-notorious thicket of rumor, confusion, and secrecy would be revolutionized by the introduction of an electronic marvel called NASDAQ—a computer system that makes it possible for an over-the-counter trader, by merely punching some buttons and looking at a screen on his desk, to see precisely which firm is making the best current bid and the best current offer in any of several thousand stocks not listed on the stock exchanges. In effect, NASDAQ would bring the over-the-counter market up from *under* the counter, a nether region it still inhabited to a marked extent in April 1970. At that time, there was no such screen on the trader's desk; to get the best price on a thinly traded stock like E.D.S., he might have to telephone a dozen other firms to get their quotes, engage in shouted conversations with other traders in his own firm to find out what kind of bids and offers they were getting, and finally agree to a price that would never be reported to the public at all. In such a market, the opportunities for manipulation were endless. Conducted in windowless back rooms by excitable hagglers, many with a full measure of larceny in their blood, and policed only negligently by the overworked and understaffed S.E.C., the over-the-counter market in the nineteen sixties was the perfect arena for the feeding of lions and the ingestion of Christians.

What was "wrong" with E.D.S. was that the price of its stock had not dropped at all while the rest of the market had been going through a panic. By way of comparison, University Computing, a leading company in E.D.S.'s very industry, was selling on April 22 at a price 80 percent below its peak of the previous year; meanwhile, E.D.S. was selling almost *at* its peak. Good earnings record or not, E.D.S. stock at around 150 was, from a technical standpoint, in an almost freakishly exposed position. At the same time, much of the available supply of stock was in the hands of fast-performance mutual funds that, at any sign of decline, would quickly unload. This is a condition known to market players as "weakly held." Such facts do not go unnoticed, nor did they on April 22. Presumably some big punter or a group of them—perhaps in Geneva, perhaps in Lebanon, perhaps right in New York—saw a golden opportunity to recoup the drastic losses they had suffered over the previous days in other stocks. So they mounted a bear raid on E.D.S., probing its strength with testing short sales. As it gave way under the pressure and dropped a few points (it may be presumed), they increased the sales. The suddenly lower price then came to the attention of the itchy-fingered portfolio managers of the fast-performance funds that held E.D.S. With their celebrated speed and dexterity, the portfolio managers began unloading. Down and down the bid went—to 145, 135, 120—and the panic was on. The men in the back rooms decide fast and move instantly, and in their market a selling panic can blacken the sky as quickly as an August afternoon's thunderstorm.

Toward noon, with E.D.S. down in the 80-90 range, it firmed; presumably the bears who had started the slide felt that their killing was made and were beginning, leisurely, to consume their prey.

That, at least, is the scenario that may be reasonably deduced from the circumstances and events that are known. Langone of Pressprich, who was in the thick of the entire collapse, professes ignorance of what happened. He does say, cautiously, "The roof fell in. It was a terrible market, and E.D.S. at such a high price was vulnerable. No one can prove it, but it certainly appears that there was an organized raid of some kind on the stock." Certainly, no one can logically accuse Pressprich of complicity. With a substantial inventory of E.D.S. stock on hand before the selling storm struck, and thus a vested interest in keeping the price up, the brokerage firm had a bad morning that would not soon be forgotten. Some say it barely survived. But it did survive, and so, needless to say, did Ross Perot.

7

Thus the greatest one-day fall of a titan ever. But what of the investing public? The tens of thousands who, either directly or through the investments of their mutual funds, had put some of their savings into E.D.S., were far more than bemused spectators at a landmark event in financial history. In a word, they were losers, perhaps of a college fund or a vacation fund or part of a retirement nest egg. Few of them were so fortunate as to have bought their E.D.S. stock at or near its original offering price of $16.50. As is usual with hot new issues, particularly in such manic markets as that of 1968, most of the original issue had soon found its way into the hands of professional traders. Many small investors had come in later, buying from the professionals after the stock had been talked about in brokerage offices and mentioned in the market letters and pushed by the eager commission producers—and, of course, after its price had shot up almost out of sight. In the familiar pattern, the investing public, with its thousands rather than billions, had suddenly become interested in hot stocks at the very height of the boom, and had bought E.D.S. near its top. For an investor who had bought it at 150, the $15,000 he had risked had in a single day become $10,000, or the $1,500 he had risked became $1,000. To him, whatever had gone on in Lebanon or Geneva or in Wall Street or Perot's Down-to-Earth Day was emphatically not abstract. In human terms, the real and necessary hundreds or thousands that he lost were more important than the abstract millions that Perot lost.

Had the small investor, then, been gulled? The evidence is that, as such things go, he had not. E.D.S., in issuing such a small number of shares to the public, had indeed, it appears in retrospect, subjected the public to a considerable degree of risk. But the expert advice Perot had received from the seventeen investment bankers he had consulted had been that the number of shares necessary to make an orderly national market was between 300,000 and 500,000—and he had actually issued 650,000. So the error had apparently been Wall Street's rather than Perot's. Moreover, E.D.S., unlike many new companies of the era, was not known for any special tendency to mislead investors with high-pressure salesmanship of its shares or with accounting tricks to pretty up its balance sheets. It was a sound, profitable operation, and the market's madness in its shares was the market's own. And as a matter of fact, even after the big April 22 collapse investors in E.D.S. were better off than those who had plunged in many better-known issues, including most of the favorites of the boom years. As of April 22, their investment in Ling-Temco-Vought at 170 was worth 15; in Four Seasons Nursing Centers at 91 was worth 33 (and would shortly be all but worthless); in Data Processing at 92 was worth 11; in Parvin-

Dohrmann at 142 was worth 19; and in Resorts International at 62 was worth 7. And unlike Perot, those whose bad judgment, or that of their advisers, had led them to make such investments, did not still have a billion dollars left.

The very fact that E.D.S. was a relatively sound, respectable young company emphasizes the larger importance of its sudden stock collapse, so abstract to a lofty general like Perot and so concrete to the foot soldiers of finance. If E.D.S. stockholders had been gulled, so, that April, had tens of millions of other small investors.

The E.D.S crash and Perot's dizzying personal loss were symbolic, in magnitude and unreality, of the 1970 panic. They are its single event that stands out in memory, like Richard Whitney's appearance on the Exchange floor to bid 205 for Steel on behalf of the bankers' pool, at the height of the panic on October 24, 1929—Black Thursday. Nor is it without symbolic importance that the larger market calamity of which the E.D.S. crash was a part resembled in so many respects what had happened forty years before—what wise men had said, for more than a generation, over and over again as if by way of incantation, could never happen again. It *had* happened again, as history will; but (as history will) it had happened differently. The nineteen sixties in Wall Street were the nineteen twenties replayed in a new and different key—different because the nineteen sixties were more complex, more sophisticated, more democratic, perhaps at bottom more interesting.

CHAPTER II

Fair Exchange

1

On the last day of 1960 Wall Street was in a euphoric New Year's Eve mood, and volume on the New York Stock Exchange set a record for the year of 5,300,000 shares traded. It was a promising red sunset after a long stretch of leaden skies; the last Eisenhower administration was expiring amid general stagnation and a mild business recession, and the market, then as nearly always reflecting hope or fear about the future rather than current facts, was clearly reacting to the go-ahead spirit created through both instinct and intention by a young President-Elect, John F. Kennedy. People felt that now there would be action, movement, indeed forward movement; good things, never mind what, were bound to be ahead. A statistic no one in Wall Street could then imagine was that eight years later the *average* daily Stock Exchange volume would be two and a half times that 1960 *record*.

The new mood persisted and grew; very soon, in fact, it grew ominously from cheerfulness to something near mania. It was fed by the Kennedy inaugural on that well-remembered cold day in January—a speech that now appears conventional in its cold-war rhetoric and its hackneyed call for self-sacrifice to the common good, but animated by the Biblical elegance of its language and the fierce dignity with which it was delivered. By mid-February the stock averages were up some 15 percent from their October lows, and there began to be talk of a "Kennedy boom." Not even the Cuban Bay of Pigs disaster in mid-April could stem the tide; a week after Castro's men drove out the C.I.A.-backed invaders, the market was up almost 25 percent, the fastest recovery since the end of World War II. The attention of buoyant investors was turning from blue chips to more speculative issues—Brunswick, Sperry-Rand, Hupp, Ampex, Transitron—and already some of Wall Street's horizon scanners were beginning to express alarm and urge caution. On April 4, Keith Funston, president of the Stock Exchange and ordinarily, in his carefully restrained way, the nation's leading backer of common stocks, reversed his field and began emphasizing the dangers of speculation. Gerald M. Loeb, the venerable Polonius of brokers, who would live to be one of the last men on Wall Street to have vivid memories of 1929, was saying a couple of weeks later, "If you want to sleep and smile when the wonder shares return to reality, now is the time to break away from the crowd." (The wonder shares were those of new, all-but-untried companies with which investors were just then having an intense love affair. A few of them, like Polaroid, Xerox, and Litton Industries, would go on to greater things; most of them would be forgotten before the end of the decade.) In mid-May Funston was back on the same theme, this time more forcefully. "There still seems to be a preoccupation with low-priced shares because they are low-priced, and an unhealthy appetite for new issues of unseasoned companies merely because they are new. . . . Anyone who invests on a vague tip from an uncertain source is courting financial disaster."

Still seems to be? The preoccupation and the appetite, it developed, were just beginning to build up. In the second quarter there came a sharp business recovery, but that promising development was almost beside the point to avid stock purchasers. The bull market, in the classic way of bull markets, had begun to lead a happy and profitable life of its own, independent of underlying reality. The week of Funston's second warning the Welch Scientific Company of Skokie, Illinois, makers of laboratory equipment, offered the public 545,000 common shares at $28. It is pretty safe to say that of the people who bought all of the shares on opening day, and those who on the very same day bid the price for them up to $52, only a small minority were well informed about or particularly interested in Welch's profits or asset position. What they knew, and all they needed to know, was that at that particular moment in time new issues in the scientific-technical field were like found money, and the man whose broker would be so kind as to cut him in for a few hundred shares could count himself blessed.

By the end of May the blue chips were beginning to lose ground—evidently because people were digging their old certificates out of bank boxes, selling them, and putting the proceeds into the new-issues market. By autumn, when the over-the-counter averages reached an all-time high, the money-coining machine was working at full capacity. Goaded by stock underwriters eager for commissions or a piece of the action, owners of family businesses from coast to coast—laundry chains, soap-dish manufacturers, anything—would sell stock in their enterprises to the public on the strength of little but bad news and big promises. In conformity with the law, the bad news would be all spelled out in the prospectus: the company had never made any money and had no real prospects of making any; the president had a record of three business failures in succession; the competition had the market for the company's sole product all sewed up; and so on. But the effectiveness of warnings is limited by the preconceptions of those being warned, and the stock would be snapped up, leaving the under-writer with his easy commission and the owner of the company with more cash than he had ever seen before in his entire life. To top it all off, the heedless buyers of the stock would come out ahead, too; they would ride it up while waiting for the six-month tax-holding period to expire, and then they could sell, take their profits, and buy a new car—or a new issue.

When the accounts for 1961 were added up—after a final day when the Stock Exchange tape ran ten minutes late because of heavy volume, once again promising good things for the future—the accomplishments of the year, quite apart from the new-issue killings, seemed substantial indeed. Trading on the Big Board had totalled just over a billion shares, the greatest for any year since 1929. (1929? A myth of ancient horror, like the Black Death.) An analyst with a computer calculated that during 1961 all Stock-Exchange-listed issues had risen on the average 23 percent, for a dollar-value appreciation of seventy billions. Eighty-six Big Board stocks had cheered their owners by splitting two-for-one or more. Korvette had almost tripled, Certain-teed had doubled and a half, Interstate Department Stores had doubled. And in the over-the-counter market where the new issues bloomed, gains for the year of 4,000 or 5,000 percent were not unknown. No wonder John F. Kennedy was popular in Wall Street.

And yet, not quite all was euphoria and gratified greed. The year 1961 also brought a major scandal, involving not just a man or a firm but a key institution—the American Stock Exchange, Wall Street's second largest. It was, of course, the successor to the old Curb Market, roofless and raffish like the world's first stock exchange in Amsterdam in the seventeenth century; conducted outdoors, in one or another part of the Wall Street area, from long before the Civil War until 1921; a ragtaggle gang of brokers haggling daily in all weathers and wigwagging the results of their trades to office men perched in the windows of surrounding buildings. Over the loud objections of some of its members, the Curb had moved indoors in 1921, establishing itself in its present building (later modernized and enlarged) at 86 Trinity Place, behind Trinity churchyard. In 1953, under the leadership of its new, modern-minded president, Edward T. McCormick, it had renamed itself the American Stock Exchange and been quickly nicknamed the Amex. It had become a pillar of Wall Street, serving the necessary function of providing a ready market for stocks of companies too small and unseasoned to qualify for listing on the Big Board. In 1961, however, this financial pillar almost fell in disgrace, perhaps dragging a good part of Wall Street with it, but was redeemed just in time by the steadfastness and courage of a few of its members.

2

Casting a long shadow over the Amex, and indeed over all of Wall Street, during the later nineteen fifties, had been two particularly implausible swindlers, Lowell McAfee Birrell and Alexander Guterma, alias Sandy McSande. Birrell, like Richard Whitney before him, was apparently a scoundrel as much from choice as from necessity. The son of a small-town Presbyterian minister, a graduate of Syracuse University and Michigan law school, a handsome, brilliant, and charming man who began his career with the aristocratic Wall Street law firm of Cadwalader, Wickersham and Taft and soon belonged to the Union League and Metropolitan Clubs, Birrell, if he had not been Birrell, might easily have become the modern-day equivalent of a Morgan partner—above the battle and beyond reproach. He was the sort of man who has everything going for him in America—who can hardly fail to be dowered with both money and respect in return for little more than a pleasing manner and an air of probity and affable reticence. Instead, Birrell left the gilded cage of Cadwalader, Wickersham and Taft to become perhaps the leading wrecker of corporations and deluder of investors in the postwar era. Birrell's gothic deals with Serge Rubenstein, the Mephistophelian financier who was murdered in his Fifth Avenue mansion in 1955; the cool and efficient way he issued himself huge quantities of unauthorized stock in corporations he controlled, like Doeskin Products and Swan-Finch Oil, and then illegally unloaded the shares on the market; the strong-arm methods he used to keep dissident stockholders in line—such things belong in another chronicle. It is enough to say here that the S.E.C. finally caught up with Birrell in 1957, and that to escape prosecution he fled first to Havana and then to Brazil, where he served a short prison term for illegal entry but thereafter lived in splendor, beyond range of the volleys of indictments and stockholder suits that issued periodically, and harmlessly, from his native land.

Guterma was in the mold of the traditional international cheat of spy stories—an elusive man of uncertain national origin whose speech accent sometimes suggested Old Russia, sometimes the Lower East Side of New York, sometimes the American Deep South. On occasion he presented himself as a Russian from Irkutsk, at other times as an American named McSande. Whoever he was and wherever he came from, he apparently made his first fortune in the Philippines during World War II, running a gambling casino that catered to occupying Japanese servicemen. After that he married an American woman, survived a charge of having collaborated with the enemy, and in 1950 moved to the United States. During the succeeding decade he controlled, and systematically looted, more than a dozen substantial American companies, including three listed on the New York Stock Exchange and a leading radio network, the Mutual Broadcasting Company. After some sour deals in 1957 and 1958 left him short of cash, he was reduced to taking money from General Rafael Trujillo of the Dominican Republic in return for promises (never fulfilled) to boost the Trujillo regime on Mutual. The law caught up with him; in September, 1959, he was indicted for fraud, stock manipulation, violation of federal banking laws, and failure to register as the agent of a foreign government; a few months later he went to prison and vanished unmourned from the business scene.

These two rogues out of past time, both offstage—one in Brazil, one behind bars—were only catalysts in the Amex drama of 1961, but without them it would hardly have happened as it did.

It began at the end of April, with a set of sensational charges by the S.E.C. against Gerard A. (Jerry) Re and his son, Gerard F. Re, who together formed the Amex's largest firm of specialists. Stock specialists are, of course, the broker-dealers on the floor of every stock exchange who man the various posts at all times during trading hours, taking the responsibility for maintaining orderly markets in the particular stocks in which they specialize, and, when necessary, for risking their own resources in the performance of that duty. As has been widely noted, theirs is a calling with a built-in anomaly, because sometimes situations arise in which a specialist's private financial interest comes into direct conflict with his stated public responsibility. Pushed in one direction by prudent self-interest, in the other by sense of duty or fear of punishment, a specialist at such times faces a dilemma more appropriate to a hero in Corneille or Racine than to a simple businessman brought up on classic Adam Smith and the comfortable theory of the socially beneficent marketplace. Disquisitions could be written on the moral situation of the specialist, and indeed, they have been. Until recent years—when it has come to be the widely received view that eventually specialists can be replaced entirely by computers backed by a pool of money supplied by investment firms—it was generally accepted that the specialist, with all his temptations, was necessary to supply liquidity on stock exchanges. So long as most specialists were able to make a decent living (and they clearly were) while discharging their public responsibilities fairly well (as they outwardly seemed to do), it was thought best, even by the hottest-eyed reformers in the S.E.C., to leave the system basically alone and rely on strict rules and close surveillance to keep the specialists in line.

If the role of the specialist seemed to make a particular and perhaps even an unreasonable call for men of good character, this call was not always answered. According to the S.E.C. complaint, it was not in the case of the two Res, who had, it seemed, consistently yielded to the temptations while failing to meet the responsibilities. Over a period of at least six years, the S.E.C. charged, the father and son had abused their fiduciary duties in just about ever conceivable way, reaping a personal profit of something like $3 million. They had made special deals with unethical company heads—Lowell Birrell in particular—to distribute unregistered stock to the public in violation of the law. In order to manipulate the prices of those stocks for their private benefit and that of the executives they were in league with, they had bribed the press, given false tips by word of mouth, paid kickbacks to brokers, generated false public interest by arranging for fictitious trades to be recorded on the tape—the whole, infamous old panoply of sharp stock-jobbing practices. Between July 1954 and April 1957, according to the complaint, they had improperly disposed of more than half a million unregistered (and therefore legally unmarketable) shares of Birrell's Swan-Finch Oil Corporation; in 1959, their operations had been so pervasive as to account for one in every twenty-three shares traded on the Amex for the year. To cover their tracks, they had used the standard dodge of trading through dummy nominees. Two of their nominees were alleged Cubans who, in the S.E.C. men's opinion, may never have existed. A third, one Charles A. Grande, through whose account the Res had filtered several million dollars' worth of securities, did exist, though he had no money of his own to speak of; he was a retired horse trainer, and his chief asset as a dummy was his interesting home address— 10 Downing Street, which, to be sure, was not the London residence of the British prime minister but an old apartment house in the Italian section of Greenwich Village, New York. Among those the Res had managed to make victims of, the S.E.C. noted, were a number of political figures and celebrities of various kinds, including Vincent F. Albano, Jr., a New York State Republican leader; Abraham J. Gellinoff, a New York City Democratic leader; Toots Shor, the restaurant owner; Chuck Dressen, manager of the Milwaukee Braves baseball team; and —most eye-opening of all—the Amex's own president, Edward T. McCormick.

The investigation had been conducted under the leadership of the S.E.C.'s young assistant director of the Division of Trading and Exchanges, Ralph S. Saul, of whom, one way and another, the Amex would hear much more over the coming years; and when, on May 4, the charges—unrefuted by the Res—were presented to the full Commission, the upshot was the fastest punitive action in its history: permanent expulsion of the Res from the securities business, after only two hours of oral arguments.

3

Justice done, then—the bad apples had been detected and removed, if rather belatedly, from the Amex barrel. Two aspects of the affair remained disturbing. One was the ominously exact way the Res' methods of cheating had aped those of the manipulators in the bad and presumably gone old days before the New Deal had brought the S.E.C. into being. The other disquieting aspect was the presence on the S.E.C.'s list of Re associates of the name of Edward T. McCormick. If the Amex's president had been a personal participant in Re transactions, was it not implied that the Amex authorities, or at least the chief of them, may have known what was going on all along?

Before examining that question we may well take a look at those authorities. To a marked extent, they were a breed. President Ted McCormick, Arizona-born of an Irish father and a Spanish mother, a former S.E.C. commissioner who had jumped the fence from bureaucrat to businessman; Chairman Joe Reilly, slum-bred, one of nineteen children, a tough-talking self-made man who had worked his way up from floor page on the Curb to his present eminence; Vice-chairman Charley Bocklet; Jim Dyer, finance committee chairman; and Johnny Mann, chairman of the important committee on floor transactions—it was they who ran the Amex in 1961 and, with some variations, they who had run it over the preceding seven years during which the Res had romped. By and large, they had the blunt good humor and the disinclination toward fine moral distinctions of men who have bulled their way from nowhere to somewhere. Few, like McCormick, were scholars with advanced academic degrees; few had *any* degrees, and some had never finished high school. Virtually all of them were hard drinkers who brought indoors an old and honored tradition of the Curb that, in the outdoor days, had at least enjoyed the justification that alcohol helped keep out the cold and the damp.

To a man, they were of Irish extraction. The boisterous Irish like Mike Meehan and Ben Smith who had first made their mark in Wall Street thirty years earlier were now followed by a generation that had captured a key Wall Street institution, or .come near enough to capturing it so that, in the middle fifties, to speak of the Irish-American Stock Exchange was almost a definition, rather than just a joke. But they did love jokes, too, loved them as few in dour Wall Street had ever done before them, and they gave the place a kind of rough levity. Old Joe Haff, for example, an Amex man, used to like to jump off ferry-boats and race them to shore swimming, and at Christmas on the Amex floor, a clerk would dress up as Santa Claus, other clerks would mount headlights on one of the posts and pretend it was a truck, and everyone would get gloriously drunk.

The reasons this rather aberrant Establishment undertook to shelter the Res—for, in retrospect, it is fairly clear that they did in fact shelter them—can only be inferred. It was not chauvinism; the Res were of Italian extraction. Plainly, it was not a case of conspiracy for profit; there is no evidence that the Amex officials shared in the Res' boodle. On the other hand, some of them were good friends of the Res, and frequent house guests of the elder Re at his place in Florida. More important, they were by temperament boosters; they believed passionately in the Amex, wanted it to grow and to rise in public esteem; and they knew that the Res were powerful old timers who could not be eliminated without a scandal. Like politicians, they would do almost anything to avoid a scandal. As for McCormick, he may well have had only the vaguest notion of what the Res were up to. Unlike Reilly, Bocklet, Dyer, and Mann, he was seldom actually on the floor, and, as the Amex's paid administrator rather than a member, he did not know the intricacies of stock trading at first hand. He was the upstairs man, the front man, and when he wasn't upstairs he was out on the road spreading word of the expanding Amex and bringing new business to it.

During his ten-year term as Amex president, McCormick had functioned chiefly as a salesman. The holder of a B.A. from the University of Arizona (Phi Beta Kappa, at that), an M.S. from the University of California, and a Ph.D. from Duke, in

1934 he went to work for the S.E.C. in a lowly job that paid $1,900 a year. Over the subsequent years, while clambering up the bureaucratic rungs, he wrote a standard text entitled *Understanding the Securities Act and the S.E.C.*, and in 1949 was appointed a S.E.C. commissioner by President Truman. In 1951 he made the familiar switch from low-paid government work to high-paid private-industry work that has been the bane of the S.E.C. from its beginnings, constantly draining it of talent. Never before, though, had a S.E.C. man—commissioner or staffer—left to become head of a major stock exchange. McCormick's appointment to the Amex was hailed as the beginning of a new era in which government and the securities business would work in happy cooperation for the public good. As a booster for the Amex, McCormick was notably successful; by 1961, daily share volume had more than quadrupled in a decade, and the price of an Amex seat had jumped from $9,500 to $80,000. The scholar and bureaucrat had turned out to be a born salesman. But with the Amex's growth, it began to appear toward the end of the decade, a certain laxness of administration had crept in. Restless at his desk, Ted McCormick was always out selling up-and-coming companies on listing their shares on the Amex, and while he was in Florida or at the Stork Club drumming up trade, sloppy practices were flourishing back at Trinity Place.

Or so it seemed in the light of the S.E.C. report, which pointed out that as early as 1957 a federal court had enjoined the Res against further violations of the Securities Acts and further trading in the stock of Swan-Finch, and that in 1958 the elder Re had been formally accused by the Amex's Business Conduct Committee of willfully violating the rules governing specialists. Late in 1959, this matter had finally come to a vote of the Board of Governors, which had inexplicably exonerated the Res, 18 to 5. Immediately the Business Conduct Committee had held its own meeting and showed its defiance of the Board by voting to suspend Jerry Re from trading for the month of January—a painless sentence, to be sure, since January was the month Jerry Re customarily spent in Florida.

Curiously, or perhaps not so curiously, most of the Amex

members had known very little of all this. "Everybody knew
there was something smelly in Jerry Re's corner of the floor, but
only in general," one of the specialists has since said. For many
members, the S.E.C. complaint of 1961 provided their first
knowledge of the court injunction, the vote of the governors,
even the month's supension. It also provided their first knowledge of the fact that in 1954 and 1955 McCormick had been
personally involved in stock transactions with the Res. There is
some irony in the fact that he had actually lost money on the
transactions. Still, what he had done had certainly been, to say
the least, indiscreet. Leaving aside the whole matter of the Res'
later-revealed misdeeds, for the salaried administrative head of
a stock exchange to enter into deals with members of that exchange—and specialists at that—would seem to imply a perfectly clear conflict of interest. For one reason or another, only
a handful of Amex members seemed to be disturbed by the
revelation of McCormick's indiscretion, or by the implication
that the disciplinary actions against the Res had been largely
swept under the rug. The members most disturbed were another father-and-son specialist team—or more precisely, a fa-
ther-and-son-in-law specialist team. They were David S. Jackson
and Andrew Segal.

4

The big men of the Street are of two kinds: those who come to
it from outside with a driving urge to conquer, and those who
through inheritance belong to it from the start, and therefore,
because they do not need to discover it for themselves, can bring
it fresh perspectives. The first kind, obsessed with the need for
money and power, are the ones who bring innovations and
variations to the craft of money-making, and who usually become the richest. They treat Wall Street purely as an arena; they
accept its rules and customs and exploit them, often with some-

thing close to art, but they do not seek to change its ways. The second kind—who, curiously, often have a temperamental indifference to money but nonetheless stay in Wall Street, never dreaming of turning their backs on it, simply because it is their world—are the ones who most often seek to remold it nearer to their hearts' desire.

Jackson, although only a shade over five feet three inches tall, and not even a millionaire most of the time, was one of the big men of the Street in 1961, and one of the second kind. He had been born into it, though hardly in the silver-spoon tradition of, say, J.P. Morgan the Younger. His father had been a hit-or-miss trader on the outdoor Curb, in the money one day and out of it the next, and he himself had been born on Henry Street during the time that the Lower East Side was still a Jewish ghetto. Jackson had gone two years to Brown and one year to St. John's University Law School before joining his father's business. A Curb (and later Amex) specialist since 1925, he had achieved a measure of fame, and more than a measure of honor, in 1955 when a Walter Winchell radio tip had resulted in a buying panic in Pantepec Oil, one of the stocks he specialized in (and a venture, incidentally, of the notable progenitor William F. Buckley, Sr.). Jackson, at personal risk far beyond the call of duty, had saved the deluded public from the consequence of its folly by selling short a block of more than one hundred thousand shares of Pantepec, at a price more than six points lower than he might have sold it, in order to keep the market orderly. This quixotically high-minded act had made him, for a time, a sort of Exhibit "A" of the securities industry before Congressional committees (and, it appears in retrospect, an unwitting cover for the actions of other less scrupulous specialists of the era). It had also earned him—and, subsequently, his handsome young partner Segal, a graduate lawyer who joined him on the floor the following year—some surly glances from a few of their colleagues.

As a result partly of the Pantepec incident and partly of his predilection, so uncharacteristic of many Amex men, for moral issues, Jackson came to occupy a special position there, respected, somewhat feared, and by no means universally liked. This is not to say that he was generally unpopular. As an ex-governor, he was fond of boasting that he was the first Jew ever to have finished anywhere but last in an Amex election; he attributed his assimilation to the fact that he was "a pretty good golfer and a pretty good drinker." Far from being an evangelist at heart, he was a liberal by instinct, and a philosopher by choice. "Every institution needs a house philosopher," he used to say. "I'm the Amex's." During the ten years of McCormick's Amex presidency the two men had become close friends, and Jackson had practiced his philosophy on McCormick. Over those years Jackson had watched McCormick gradually changing from a quiet, reflective man into a wheeler-dealer who loved to be invited by big businessmen to White Sulphur Springs for golf, and the change had worried him. "Ted," he would say, when they were at dinner at one or the other's house, "why don't you read any more?"

"I haven't got time," McCormick would reply.

"But you'll lose your perspective," Jackson would protest, shaking his head.

During the later 1950s Jackson served two terms on the Amex Board of Governors, and, although he wasn't serving at the time of the court injunction, he learned enough about the Res' operation to argue before the Floor Transactions Committee that they ought not to be allowed to serve as specialists. His motion was defeated. Jackson, incidentally, had always liked Jerry Re, in the rough-and-ready manner of Amex friendships. Back in the forties Re had organized a softball team up at Monroe in the Catskills, where he had a summer place, and Jackson had sometimes gone up there to play on it. "Jerry *looked* like a crook, and it's my tendency to sympathize with people whose appearance is against them," Jackson said long afterward. "For example, take me. I'm not exactly prepossessing in appearance myself."

Now came the S.E.C. exposure and suspension of the Res, and—more shocking to Jackson—the peripheral revelations about McCormick. These things led Jackson and Segal, almost alone among Amex members, to be seriously concerned about whether McCormick was fit to be their president. His dealings with the Res back in 1954 and 1955; his presumed part in brushing the Re injunction under the rug in 1957; and his taking part in the exoneration, or whitewash, of the Res by the Amex board in 1959—all those actions, Jackson and Segal felt, had been a good deal less than presidential. One day in May 1961, Segal made up his mind and said to his senior partner, "I've decided to go to Ted and ask for his resignation."

Jackson nodded unhappily; his thoughts had been running in the same direction. McCormick was his friend, after all. But all through the two weeks or so that had passed since the S.E.C. complaint had become public, he had been asking himself what to do. At home, on East Sixty-eighth Street, he had agonized so constantly and obsessively that at last his wife, Fritz, had said, "You've got to do one of two things—demand Ted's resignation, or sell your seat." And he had agreed that she was right.

Now he said to his son-in-law, "Don't you do it, Andy. Let me take care of it."

So Jackson formally requested an appointment with McCormick, and it was granted. Upon arriving at the presidential office, alone and unsupported, no longer a member of the board, knowing he represented a minority view on the floor, he found McCormick flanked by the top brass of his administration, the formidable Chairman Reilly and Vice-chairman Bocklet. Whether or not they knew exactly what to expect, they clearly enough expected trouble.

Jackson said, "I don't know how to say this, Ted, but you've got to resign."

McCormick's reaction was so violent that Jackson has since said he felt physically frightened. The president picked up a batch of papers from his desk and slammed them down. Then he walked to one of the walls of his office and punched it several times, hard enough to bruise his fist. Finally he said, "I don't know what you're talking about. I've never done anything dishonest."

"No, I don't think you have," Jackson said, his voice shaking. "But you've been indiscreet."

The confrontation ended inconclusively, with Jackson repeating his demand—indeed, extending it to include the whole
top echelon of Amex officers and the Amex counsel, Michael E.
Mooney—McCormick rejecting it, and Reilly and Bocklet remaining silent. Jackson made it clear that he did not intend to
let the matter rest there. Afterward, Bocklet, clearly a McCormick supporter and therefore now Jackson's political enemy,
took him aside and said, with a kind of admiration, "Davy, you
go home and tell your Fritz that she's married to a man."

Reilly also took Jackson aside, to make another kind of
comment. "You haven't got any proof of anything against Ted,"
he said—rather irrelevantly, it would seem, since Jackson's
charge was based entirely on published material that was now
common knowledge. "The thing for you to do is to appear
before the Board of Governors, and argue your case there."

"Joe, you know perfectly well that would be like pissing up
Niagara Falls," the house philosopher replied.

Jackson and Segal—a fifty-nine-year-old maverick and a
thirty-two-year-old upstart—were now official enemies of the
Amex management. Through the summer and into the fall, they
went on arguing their case, but not before the board. Instead,
Jackson committed what in the view of the Amex management
was almost the ultimate sin—he argued it in the newspapers.
This was in defiance of explicit orders from Reilly to all Amex
members, and particularly specialists. The House Committee
on Interstate and Foreign Commerce had scheduled hearings on
the Amex for that summer, and the S.E.C. had laid similar plans
for early fall. Anticipating that many Amex members, and specialists in particular, would be called to testify at the various
hearings, Reilly began taking them aside separately and in
groups. "When you talk to the government people, don't tell
them anything you don't have to," Reilly, according to Segal,
would caution in his characteristic corner-of-the-mouth style.
He would go on to say that, in view of the delicate state of affairs
at the Amex in the wake of the Re exposure, in the Exchange's
best interest it was equally necessary to avoid talking to the
press under any circumstances. And in the case of Jackson,
Reilly added a further urgent instruction—do not, he said, press

the matter of McCormick's resignation any further, at least until the hearings are over and things have had a chance to cool down.

But Jackson had made his decision; he talked to the press— Ed Cony of the *Wall Street Journal* in particular—and he pressed his case against McCormick in conversations with other members on the floor. In early summer, Reilly took the unusual step of mounting the podium overlooking the floor and interrupting trading to make a brief speech. In it, he asked the members for loyalty in a time of crisis, emphasized that the good name of the Amex must come first in all considerations, and defended McCormick, whom he said had been publicly maligned. But he made no mention of Jackson or Segal. Then in July the House held its hearings, at which both McCormick and Reilly testified in public. McCormick listed some of the mighty American companies that in their salad days had been traded on the Amex— Armour, Swift, Cities Service, Eversharp, Alcoa, Gulf Oil, Pittsburgh Plate Glass, Quaker Oats—and said roundly, "I will stack the honesty and efficiency of our specialists against any other specialists . . . in the country." He admitted his 1954 and 1955 dealings with the Res, but pointed out that such things belonged to a closed chapter in his past: "I have not owned a single share of stock traded on the American Stock Exchange since 1957." The implication—though only an implication—was that the Congressmen were looking at a penitent who had reformed. The reason McCormick would not come out and say that he was reformed was, of course, that such a statement would be an admission that he had previously been *un*reformed.

Reilly, after telling the Congressmen about his rise from lowly beginnings in a huge, impoverished family, described in some detail the Amex's rules for specialists and its disciplinary procedures against erring members. He insisted that the only reason the stock manipulations and nominee trading of the Res had not been uncovered by the Amex authorities as early as 1957 was the fact that they, unlike the S.E.C. and the courts, lacked subpoena power over nonmembers of their institution like the useful dummy Charles A. Grande. This seemed to Jackson to be a poor excuse, and when Reilly stopped him on the floor a few days later to ask what he had thought of the testimony, Jackson replied that he had found it inadequate.

5

By this time, the floor was seething. A little cluster of a dozen or so other members, most of them under forty and soon nick-named the Young Turks, had rallied to Jackson's and Segal's standard and joined them in calling for McCormick's resignation and a complete reorganization of the Amex. But they were badly overmatched in both numbers and influence, and soon they found the power of the in-group pressing upon them most uncomfortably. According to Segal's account, the classical arm-twisting methods of ward politics were applied to the dissenters by representatives of the administration. One Young Turk, for example, was pointedly reminded of a questionable stock trans-action in which he had been involved some years earlier, and of how easily the matter could be called to the S.E.C.'s attention; to another it was suggested that certain evidence at hand, if revealed, could make a shambles of his pending suit for divorce; and so on.

So it was a hot summer on Trinity Place for the Young Turks, and when Labor Day came bringing with it the first breezes of autumn and the real beginning of a new Wall Street year, they were all but routed, leaving Jackson and Segal stand-ing almost alone. And then came the turning point. It came in a strange form—that of a savage attack, or what Jackson con-strued as such, on him by the only people he still had reason to think of as his allies in the cause of reform. On September 18, Jackson, under subpoena, appeared before representatives of the S.E.C. at their New York office on lower Broadway. The S.E.C. men present were the agency's top investigators—Ralph Saul, who had headed the Re investigation, and two other lawyers, David Silver and Edward Jaegerman. Possibly the investigators came to the hearing with the preconceived idea that Amex specialists were a bad lot and that, the Pantepec affair notwithstanding, Jackson was no better than the rest. At all events, for more than four hours they grilled him with what seemed to him to be hostility, scorn, and sarcasm. Their attention focused on a single incident several years earlier in which a former member of Jackson's firm had, by his admission, done a poor job of specializing. But the S.E.C. men were not to be put off by admissions; hour after hour they bored in until Jackson, on the verge of hysteria, found himself in tears.

He was released early in the afternoon, and when he got to his Amex post, his partner Segal was alarmed to find him completely distraught. "So that's the way they treat an honest man," Jackson was muttering. "As if he were a criminal and they needed a confession."

"But Dave, what happened?" Segal asked. "The S.E.C. is supposed to be our friend!"

"I can't talk about it now," Jackson said. He went home, and that evening, after consulting Segal by phone, dashed off in longhand a furious and agonized letter that he planned to address to various public officials, including Senator Jacob Javits of New York. "I was besieged and harassed continously," he wrote of the hearing. "The questioners were never satisfied until they got the answers they wanted. . . . I never really understood brain-washing before. We in America believe people innocent until proven guilty. When those of us with immaculate records of ethical and moral responsibility are treated with scorn and contempt, badgered to the point of emotional breakdown, then our representatives must take action. . . ." That evening, feeling like a prophet without honor not just in his country but everywhere, Jackson almost let despair persuade him to abandon the fight to reform the Amex.

What he did, instead, after finishing his letter, was to read it on the telephone to Ralph Saul of the S.E.C. before mailing it to Javits. Horrified, Saul pleaded with him not to mail it, apologized for the excessive zeal of his colleagues, and promised that some sort of amends would be made. Somewhat mollified,

Jackson did not mail the letter. (But neither did he destroy it. He still has it, the almost illegible scrawl testifying eloquently to his emotional state at the time.) A couple of days later a delegation of S.E.C. men—headed by none other than Silver, one of the inquisitors at the hearing—came to the Amex floor and spent the entire trading day watching the Jackson-Segal operation, trade by trade. It turned out to be an unusually lively day for them, because one of the stocks in which they specialized, Mead Johnson, was fluctuating wildly on conflicting rumors about a new contraceptive product, calling for particularly risky and fast-footed specializing. All day, the S.E.C. men watched without comment. After the close that afternoon, they declared themselves convinced that Jackson and Segal were honest, and flatly asked them to become allies of the S.E.C. in the reform of the Amex. With a lack of enthusiasm that in the circumstances must be considered understandable, Jackson and Segal agreed.

"Now, what do you know about what's going on upstairs?" Silver asked his new allies, when they were all gathered on the Amex floor, late that afternoon after the janitors had swept up and everyone else had gone home.

In fact, one of the things that was going on upstairs just then was the surreptitious retyping, with significant emendations and deletions, of the minutes of certain recent meetings of the Amex Board of Governors. But Jackson and Segal, of course, did not know this. Indeed, they told the S.E.C. men that they knew nothing of what the Amex administration was doing and could only promise to cooperate with the S.E.C. in its investigation in any way they could. The following week, Jackson made good this promise by going to Washington and, in a long session with the S.E.C. at its headquarters, giving his views on what reforms were needed.

So at last, painfully, the federal investigators came to believe in the existence of a minority element within the Amex that, if encouraged, might be able to bring about reform from within. Much later, S.E.C. officials would say that until the day when their delegates came to the Amex floor and reached an understanding with Jackson and Segal, the agency had been on the verge of exercising its legal prerogative to padlock the executive offices of the Amex and take over its operation *in toto*. Such a seizure, representing socialism rampant in one of the last bastions of free capital, would have been a crushing, perhaps fatal blow not just to the Amex but to all of Wall Street.

6

In October, the rest of the Street finally came to realize that it would be caught in a backlash from the Amex scandal. Wall Street at its highest level took action, forming a securities-industry committee to review the Amex's rules, policies, and procedures and make recommendations. Its membership was a cross section of top-echelon Wall Streeters, including the president of Merrill Lynch, the managing partner of Paine Webber, the senior partner of Goodbody, the president of Clark Dodge, and, as chairman, the formidable Gustave Levy, senior partner of Goldman, Sachs. The Amex, meanwhile, went on its bumbling way. A meeting of the remnants of the Young Turks, intended for regrouping and for planning a new offensive, was scheduled for the day following the announcement of the Levy committee. Reilly, getting wind of the meeting, arranged to have its location changed from someone's private office to the Amex governors' room, invited all Amex members to attend, and, as a final touch of irony, called in the press. Just as he had planned, the well-reported meeting fell flat in a morass of platitudes about unity. Even Jackson, thus mousetrapped, found himself saying, "Let us close ranks, forget personal feelings, and save our Exchange." Over the subsequent days, though, he resumed his defiant contacts with the press, giving his version of the state of affairs at the Amex in pointed detail; and at last Reilly was goaded to a reprisal that stands unique in the annals of Wall Street.

It was October 18; Reilly had just learned that Jackson had talked frankly again, this time to Robert E. Bedingfield of the

Times, and that the result would be printed within a couple of days. During that day's trading the following notice was distributed on the floor:

TO THE MEMBERS:
> The Chairman of the Board will address the membership today, October 18, 1961, at 4:00 o'clock P.M.
> In view of the importance of the subject, members are requested to remain on the trading floor for the Chairman's statement.
>
> Charles E. McGowan, Secretary

What subject? The day's trading ended as usual at 3:30; the members, or most of them, stayed on the floor instead of going to their lockers on the floor below to change their coats and shoes and exchange gossip before going home. Right on time, Reilly appeared on the podium. Whether by intention or coincidence, a brand-new hi-fi public address system had just been installed. Only one newspaper reporter was invited—a man from the old *Herald Tribune* whom the Amex administration considered to be relatively sympathetic to it. On the stroke of 4:00, Reilly's rasping, tough-guy voice, duly amplified and faithfully reproduced by the shiny new speakers, began to be heard, and spoke in part as follows:

MEMBERS:
> Although I have frequently faced troubled waters since I became Chairman in 1960, nothing has disturbed me more than the painful task I feel it is my duty to perform this afternoon.
> My heart is heavy as a result of the news articles in the *Wall Street Journal* and the subsequent coverage by other newspapers. Since I have accepted your mandate to lead our Exchange I . . . permit you to judge a man who has made our Exchange a public spectacle.
> I know Mr. Jackson, along with others, gave interviews. I also understand Mr. Jackson was asked to correct the latest story before it was printed. He refused! As long as he was so glib with his tongue he should at least have checked his handiwork since those news articles shook the very foundation of our Exchange. I hope Mr. Jackson realizes now that the caption could have read:

"Young Turks led by David Jackson publicly assassinate the American Stock Exchange."

Whether or not he or Mr. Segal was the leader is not important! Since Mr. Jackson sought the fame I will give him the title.

How he or anyone else can judge any official or the governing Board without knowing the full record and before the facts, goes beyond my comprehension. How he, through thoughtless action, can re-open the wounds caused by the Re case, goes beyond human understanding. . . .

I have been asked since the articles appeared in the newspapers to recommend that measures be taken against the members involved. I will refuse to do so unless I am commanded by the proper Standing Committee or the Board of Governors, because, in my opinion, any member or members who personally indict their own weak characteristics by causing these disturbances must be going through a greater punishment than any that could be levied by the Board of Governors.

I would like it thoroughly understood that it is my belief that members should have the right to protest any weaknesses that develop on our Exchange whether they be of an operational or administrative nature. Common sense also dictates that in order to overcome such weaknesses—if they exist—members must have the right to express their opinions and politic amongst themselves seeking stronger candidates to make the necessary changes. But while I wholeheartedly endorse such action I must remind all that you have signed our Constitution—agreed to abide by it, and all amendments thereto. Therefore, all expressions should be made to the proper Committee provided for that purpose; that is, the Nominating Committee. And, as in the past, if you are not satisfied with the candidates proposed for election, you may express your objections through petitions.

At this time your Chairman wishes to state that he is very tired and, as you know, he has had quite a rough time for the last two years. It has been difficult enough to handle the routine duties of my office and at the same time devote the time necessary to fight brush-fires created by the Re and Re case. I should not have to dissipate my strength to fight for our Exchange over arguments born of dissension by minority groups aired in the newspapers which add so greatly to my burden. . . .

I am proud to represent the American Stock Exchange. . . . I am firmly convinced your officials and our members, through self-discipline, have enforced the rules. . . .

I conclude by saying, "What has been done, let it be done!"
I must insist that no member or group of members in the
future turn this Exchange into a public battleground. I am going
on record as your Chairman that I will no longer tolerate it.

At the end of this unusual oration—the only public attack
in history by one member of a leading United States stock exchange upon another, unless one is to count the minor dust-ups
with fists that used to occur from time to time on the outdoor
Curb—there was a rousing ovation for Reilly. It is ironical,
though not entirely accidental, that neither Jackson nor Segal
was there to hear it. Segal was at home for his normal day off;
no one had notified him in advance that the chairman was to
speak on the floor that day. Jackson had indeed been on the floor
during trading hours, and had been notified of Reilly's plans
along with everyone else; but he was booked to sail for a Paris
vacation two days later, and he had decided that no matter what
Reilly had to say he would go ahead with his plans to get home
early and get packed.

So neither of the stated targets of the attack knew its contents, and neither, one way and another, would know them
precisely for more than a month to come. That evening, by
which time the Reilly speech had naturally become the talk of
Wall Street, a reporter called Ted McCormick to ask for a comment. As an example of Wall Street understatement, McCormick's answer was a classic. He described Reilly's speech as "a
routine report to the membership by the chairman of the
board."

Next day Jackson, at his Sixty-eighth Street apartment, was
asked for a comment on the speech, the contents of which he
knew only by hearsay. He said only, "Mr. Reilly must live with
his conscience and I must live with mine." Then he sailed for
Europe with his wife.

During his absence, Segal held the besieged fort at the
Amex. Long afterward he said of the subsequent weeks that
every single day had been torture for him. He was systematically ostracized; in place of the Amex floor's usual joking and

backslapping he met with cold silence almost everywhere. For a month no more than six or eight members spoke to him except in the business of making trades. He was pointedly given the maximum fine allowed under the Amex rules for a minor offense against them, and was kept under daily hostile surveillance by a staff man sent by Mann's committee on floor transactions. Finally this got to be too much for him; when Mann's representative sauntered up to the Jackson-Segal post one morning, Segal angrily asked him to leave. The representative did not reappear; instead, Mann himself came over, threw an ingratiating arm around Segal in the best Amex style, and said, "You know, Andy, we wouldn't harass you!"

But still the freeze went on. And meanwhile, Jackson and Segal were in the strange position of finding themselves unable to get a transcript of the speech in which they had been attacked. On Jackson's return from Europe late in November, he found that Segal had failed in several attempts to obtain a copy through informal requests to the Amex management. Accordingly, he and Segal wrote formally to Reilly and McCormick asking for a copy through official channels. In reply, they were informed that the Amex archives contained no record of any kind of the address that McCormick had described as a "report to the membership by the chairman." They were finally told that the only such record extant might be found in the files of the Securities and Exchange Commission in Washington.

Thus, early in December, Jackson and Segal applied to the S.E.C. and got their copy. Having read it, they showed it to their lawyer and were advised that they might have a libel and slander case against Reilly, whoever might have helped him prepare the speech, and even the Amex itself. After brooding on the matter, they decided not to sue. And so matters stood at the Amex in the second week of December; there seemed to be a winter of deadlock ahead, when a *deus ex machina* emerged to bring the little drama of Trinity Place to a swift climax.

7

The *deus* was no god, and he came not from the machine but from a federal penitentiary, furloughed from a four-year, eleven-month term to testify before the S.E.C. in its Amex investigation around the end of November. He was Alexander Guterma, alias Sandy McSande, and for one reason or another he found it appropriate to reminisce for the S.E.C. about Amex people he had known from time to time, one of whom was President Ted McCormick. Back in late 1955—Guterma said, and McCormick did not subsequently deny when given the opportunity— McCormick had been Guterma's guest in Florida and subsequently in lush, pre-Castro Havana. At that time Guterma was, so far as anyone knew, a law-abiding businessman if perhaps not quite a respectable one. He was also a businessman to be reckoned with. At only forty-one, Guterma was president and chairman of F. L. Jacobs Company, chairman of Bon Ami Company, and chairman of United Dye and Chemical Corporation. Never before had one man headed three separate New York Stock Exchange firms. That he was already engaged in Byzantine crimes involving manipulation of the stock of all of those companies would not begin to come to light until more than two years later. So on the face of the matter, in associating socially with Guterma, McCormick was not even guilty of an indiscretion.

But the face of the matter was not all. Guterma just then was attempting to attain listing on the Amex of the stock of one of his ventures, Shawano Development Corporation, and it was far from clear that Shawano could normally qualify for such listing. In Havana, McCormick took to the gambling tables, as did almost everyone who visited Havana in those days. He lost in the neighborhood of five thousand dollars, and his host Guterma obligingly offered to underwrite his losses. McCormick was a big spender, but he was not a man to whom five thousand dollars was a small matter. He accepted the offer, and his losses were paid.

It was one of those borderline transactions that quasi-public officials cannot afford to engage in—or at least to be caught engaging in. In the climate of 1961, when Guterma's name stood simply for sin in Wall Sreet, the mere linking of his name with McCormick's in a dubious context was the clincher. The Levy committee quickly heard of the new scandal, presumably from the S.E.C. Inevitably, versions of it got onto the extraordinarily active grapevine of Wall Street, where gossip is money. The issue was settled: McCormick had to go. It was only a matter of when and how.

Amex men have since said that in those last days of the old regime there was a kind of tomorrow-we-die atmosphere about the "upstairs" at 86 Trinity Place—the Old Romans knowing that the Young Turks had them beaten now, and finishing out their term refusing to compromise or retreat, with a kind of bleak and bull-headed dignity. Liquor, the Old Romans' traditional solace, seems to have flowed more and more freely, and earlier and earlier in the day, to the point where the last ukases coming down to the floor from "upstairs" were all but incoherent. Jackson and Segal stayed in the background; the spark that they had ignited was now a blaze that needed no fanning. Jackson said later that his chief emotion was not triumph but sadness. Meanwhile, the Levy committee spelled out the complaints against McCormick and Reilly. When the Amex Board of Governors met on Monday, December 11, it had no choice. Everyone understood that it was too late for further stalling. McCormick's resignation was asked for and obtained, and the reorganization of the Amex was under way at last.

It proceeded swiftly. On December 21, the Levy committee issued an interim report calling for the quick selection of a new Amex president and sweeping revisions in the Amex's administrative machinery; the most substantive changes recommended were the compulsory rotation of directors to end the self-perpetuating leadership, and the elimination of standing committees to prevent domination of operations by a clique. On December 28 Reilly, at the insistent urging of the Levy committee, withdrew as a candidate for reelection as chairman. In announcing his withdrawal to the press, Reilly explained that he was "very tired" and wanted "to devote more of my time to personal considerations."

On January 5, 1962, the S.E.C. came out with its report on its investigation, accusing a "dominant group"—specifically, Reilly, Bocklet, Dyer, and Mann—of having passed the essential power at the Amex back and forth among themselves for a decade; criticizing, in general and particular, this group's discipline over specialists and floor traders; bringing out into the open the charges against McCormick, including the Guterma episode; demanding swift action to end the "manifold and prolonged abuses" of the decade past; and threatening once again to move in and assume command if the Amex should fail to clean its own house. A week later, Bocklet, Dyer, and Mann let it be known that they would not run to succeed themselves. So in February, when a new board was elected, the rout of the Old Romans was complete. Later in the year a brilliant and spotless new president, Edwin D. Etherington, was brought in to replace McCormick, and an entire new Amex constitution was written and ratified that conformed largely to the recommendations of the S.E.C. and the Levy committee. Probably never—not even in 1938 when the New York Stock Exchange was turned upside down following exposure of Richard Whitney—has any stock exchange reformed itself so thoroughly so fast.

Jackson was a backstage Richelieu during the period of reorganization, remaining out of sight to avoid further inflaming the Amex conservatives, but scrupulously consulted on each move. He moved out to center stage to serve as chairman for three years—from 1965 to 1968—and during the latter part of that term, the Amex president with whom he worked, generally harmoniously, was Ralph Saul, the man he had first met as a harsh and hostile questioner for the S.E.C. Saul built himself a reputation as one of the soundest presidents in Amex history, and could have had the presidency of the Big Board in 1971 if he had wanted it. Over the decade as a whole, the Amex made such extraordinary strides in efficiency and public confidence that by 1971, when people were talking about a merger between the two leading exchanges, it was being seriously suggested in high places that the New York Stock Exchange ought to be merged into the American, rather than vice versa. As for Jackson—not a power-lover or a natural rebel, but a simple man of unblocked feelings, as eager as the next for acceptance by his peers—perhaps he deserves a small niche among those who, at various times and in various places, have found in themselves the stubborn courage, abetted by luck and good timing, to save what was worth saving.

And at the right moment. The Amex happened to reform itself precisely at the beginning of a notorious decade of Wall Street speculation and concomitant chicanery. As if with foreknowledge, it battened down while the hurricane lay just beyond the horizon.

CHAPTER III

The Last
Gatsby

1

The stock-market collapse of 1962—which broke the 1961 bucket shops and their eager patrons, sent the Dow industrials down more than 25 percent, and taught a whole new generation of investors and gamblers alike that it is possible to lose—looked back to the past rather than forward to the future. It was a thing not of firsts but of lasts: the last crisis in which little brokerage offices in distant towns and villages, and the amateur plungers who frequented them, were a significant factor; the last time in Wall Street that the tune was called not by the computer-assisted decisions of institutions like mutual funds and pension trusts, but by the emotions—fear and greed, chiefly—of individual men and women acting for themselves.

Diabetic coma, the preventable catastrophic crisis of a human disease, comes on slowly; the sinister lassitude it induces neutralizes the rational alarm that would otherwise lead the patient to take measures to head it off. So it is with stock-market crashes. That of 1929 had actually been going on, in important ways, for a year or so before it reached its climax, and that of

1962—a smaller model in all respects—for some five months. After the Dow had reached a high just short of 735 at the turn of the year (not quite double the high of September 1929, incidentally), a gradual, fairly consistent decline began. But experts who a year earlier had been sounding prudent warnings of the dangers of speculation were now victims of the very euphoria they had warned against; in January and February, 1962, they pointed out that business was good, spoke of a "healthy correction," and recommended the continued, if cautious, purchase of stocks. What a falling market needs to become a diving market is not a reason but an excuse, and in April it found one when President Kennedy chose to engage in a to-the-death confrontation with the steel industry and its bellwether, U.S. Steel, on the matter of a price increase. In the Kennedy grand manner, the clash became a thing of high melodrama, like the Cuban missile crisis six months later; there were closed-door White House meetings between Kennedy and Chairman Roger M. Blough of U.S. Steel, there were F.B.I. men ringing doorbells at dawn, and at last there was a clean, soul-satisfying ending—the steel industry's capitulation and price rollback.

But at what a cost! Investors, who had profited so handsomely from the "Kennedy market" of the previous year, suddenly decided that the energetic young man in the White House was an enemy of business, after all. Whether or not Kennedy, in the heat of confrontation, had actually said in private, "My father always told me that businessmen were sons of bitches," was not the point; the point was that a good proportion of the 17 million American owners of corporate shares believed he had said it. For several weeks in succession, the market slumped ominously, until the week of May 21–25 saw the worst decline for any week in more than ten years. And then, on May 28, the day that has gone down in Wall Street annals as Blue Monday, the Dow average dropped 34.95 points, a one-day collapse second in history only to that of October 28, 1929, when the loss had been 38.33. Moreover, the decline took place on the then-fantastic volume of 9,350,000 shares. Later in the decade such volume would come to constitute a slow day, and up-to-the-minute Stock Exchange machinery would make it possible to handle more than twice that volume without confusion; but the type of ticker in use in 1962—the very same type that had been doggedly and perhaps sometimes rustily ticking at 11 Wall Street since 1930—was so overwhelmed that by the close of Monday's trading it was more than an hour late in recording transactions, and it did not print the last of them for the day until two hours and twenty-eight minutes after the closing bell. Twenty billion dollars in paper values that had existed in the morning had evaporated by evening.

But it was on Tuesday that confusion was compounded. Sell orders in dozens of leading stocks, including blue chips like I.B.M., so overwhelmed buy orders that trading simply couldn't be opened; the stocks that did open were down so drastically that at the end of the first hour the Dow had fallen another 11 points. Stock Exchange and brokerage communications broke down so completely under the strain that some floor brokers found that their best hope of reporting a trade to their clerks was to shout it at the top of their lungs. Many orders were simply lost in the shuffle, and perhaps these frustrated orderers were lucky; customers who did get trades executed found later that they had paid several points more than they had bargained for on a purchase, or had received several points less on a sale. Around noon, without warning, a strong rally started, and the ticker, fifty-six minutes late, was caught telling the ultimate Wall Street lie—it was solemnly recording the prior down market rather than the current up market. When the carnage ended that afternoon, the Street, with its vaunted pretensions to being an efficient market place, was clearly in disgrace. The rally continued, and by Thursday night all of the losses of Monday and early Tuesday were recouped. But soon the decline resumed at a more leisurely pace; by mid-June the Dow had sunk to 535 and the Kennedy boom—a sort of prologue in miniature to what was to come later in the decade—was something of the past.

Who lost, or lost the most, in the 1962 "little crash?" Most obviously, the hot-issue boys, the penny-stock plungers, the bucket-shop two-week millionaires of 1961, who, operating on the thinnest of margins in the most volatile of stocks, were wiped out either before May 28 or during the first hours of that disastrous day. But what about those who dealt more conservatively, on wider margins in more respectable issues? The Stock Exchange, rueful about its technical collapse, made a study later in the year to determine who had done what in the events of late May. The results were instructive. The great rising giant of American finance, the mutual fund industry, had come out with honors. Cash-heavy, still conservatively managed in the prudent fiduciary tradition, the funds had bought on balance in the falling market of Monday and had sold on balance in the rising market of Thursday; thus, besides protecting their shareholders from excessive risk, they had perhaps actually done something to stabilize the market. The panic had been among individuals —especially people in rural areas, especially foreigners, and especially the nouveau riche of whatever sex or nationality. It was a personal crash, the effect of a mass mood that swept suddenly over Broadway and Little Falls, Zurich and Grand Junction; and if May 1962 was the last great stock-market event controlled by people rather than institutions, it is fitting that its most conspicuous victim, its symbolic loser, should have been such a past-haunted romantic as Edward M. Gilbert.

Gilbert was born in December 1922 into the curious half-world of smalltime New York City millionaires and soon-to-be millionaires. His father and his uncle were substantial owners and principal operators of Empire Millwork Company, a solid little lumber business that their father had founded, and that had first flourished on contracts generated by the mysterious and lethal bombing of Wall Sreet in September 1920. Long afterward, Eddie Gilbert's father, Harry, said of him, "As a kid he ran everywhere he went." But Budd Schulberg's Sammy Glick was only a part of Eddie Gilbert; he grew up dreaming more complex and grandiose dreams than that of becoming a ruler of Hollywood. From the first, he was a bright but lazy student with a particular aptitude for mathematics, a talented and fanatical athlete, and something of a spoiled darling. His father's indulgence, then and later, was his financial strength and his moral weakness. At Horace Mann School for Boys, among other merchant princelings, he was a formidable tennis player and a champion diver and long-distance runner. At Camp Winnebago, in Maine, he was acclaimed the best athlete in four successive summers.

Matriculating at Cornell in the early stages of World War II, he made a name for himself in tennis and boxing, won the chess championship of his dormitory, and earned a reputation as a prankster, but went on neglecting his studies. In his first or second year he left to enlist in the Army Air Force. Shipped to North Africa and later Italy, he worked there for Army newspapers, and showed a marked interest in and aptitude for acquiring foreign languages. An American with this quality is, of course, an anomaly among his tongue-tied countrymen, but by this time it was clear that Gilbert was exceptional in more ways than one. In the service he continued to make a fetish of physical fitness and became proficient in more sports—water skiing and paddle tennis among them. He went at games, as he always had, as if they were work rather than play.

Back home at the end of the war, he returned to Cornell for a spell, but did not stay long; soon he joined his father's company. During the period of his business apprenticeship he embarked on a series of personal ventures that were uniformly unsuccessful. He backed a prizefighter who turned out to be a dud. He was co-producer of a Broadway play, *How Long Till Summer?* that starred the black folksinger Josh White's son and that, as a pioneer in the equal-rights-for-all genre of entertainment, won the public approval of Mrs. Eleanor Roosevelt. But *How Long Till Summer?* was either ahead of its time or wrong for all seasons; it opened at the Playhouse Theatre on December 27, 1949, got disastrous notices, and closed a week later. Gilbert also dabbled in the stock market without any notable success. While thus conforming to the old tradition that the princeling sons of successful businessmen show scant aptitude for business, he was acquiring a deep and genuine love of music and, in particular, of opera. He seemed to be assuming the familiar shape of the ineffectual, esthetic second generation—an impression that could scarcely have been more wrong.

His career at Empire Millwork came to an early crisis. The firm, flourishing in the postwar building boom, sold stock to the public, and the sale left Harry Gilbert with a liquid and bankable fortune of around $8 million. He was ever ready to use his money to indulge his son, and over the years he would do so again and again. The arrangement came to be a kind of unspoken trade between the two. Harry Gilbert had never been the brains of Empire Millwork; he was an amiable man who had inherited a tidy concern. Never a corporate rainmaker, Harry Gilbert, humanly enough, yearned to appear vital, enterprising, and interesting to his friends and colleagues. The son's deals and the electric office atmosphere they created were made possible by the father's money. Doubtless the father on occasion did not even understand the intricate transactions his son was forever proposing—debentures and takeovers and the like. But to admit it would be to lose face; and besides, what satisfaction there was in saying over cocktails, "We've got a big one going now but I just can't talk about it yet." And so, again and again, he put up the money. Harry Gilbert bought commercial glamour from his son.

As early as 1948, Eddie Gilbert had decided that the family company was too small to hold him, and he began to dream of using it as a vehicle to construct, through mergers with other companies, an enterprise that would live up to its grandiose name—a true Empire. In 1951, when he was twenty-eight, he demanded of his father that he be given greater responsibility in the form of a directorship. When Harry Gilbert turned him down, Eddie Gilbert quit to enter the hardwood-floor business on his own.

It turned out to be a case of *reculer pour mieux sauter*. There are two versions of what happened to the younger Gilbert's independent business venture. In one—the one that was published in 1962—the venture was a success, and four years later Harry Gilbert bought it out, and thus brought his son back to Empire, in exchange for 20,000 shares of Empire stock. In another, Eddie, through his own company, made a bumbling attempt to corner the lumber market, failed, lost considerable money, and was rescued by his father, who bailed him out to bury the costly mistake. At any rate, in 1955 Eddie returned to Empire with new power and freedom to act. Ever since 1948, when he had done a stint at an Empire plant in Tennessee and had there become acquainted with E. L. Bruce and Company, the nation's leading hardwood-floor company, he had dreamed of acquiring Bruce as a gem for Empire's crown. With net sales of around $25 million a year, Bruce was considerably larger than Empire, but it was a staid firm, conservatively managed and in languid family control, of the sort that is the classic prey for an ambitious raider. In 1955, Eddie Gilbert persuaded his father to commit much of his own and the company's resources in an attempt to take over Bruce.

Now Eddie came into his own at last. He began to make important friends in Wall Street—brokers impressed with his dash and daring, and delighted to have the considerable commissions he generated. Some of the friends came from the highest and most rarefied levels of finance. He apparently won over John Loeb, Sr., of Loeb, Rhoades by pledging $100,000 to Loeb's beloved Harvard; later he could claim to be an important client of André Meyer, the shy eminence of Lazard Frères and close friend of Mrs. Jacqueline Kennedy Onassis. At the same time, Gilbert began gathering unto himself a coterie of rich social allies, people who might tap him for his stock-market tips and whom he could use in turn for the aura of social acceptance their propinquity implied.

3

The key word for these new friends is "social." Like almost all of the great American financiers of the nineteenth century—and even more, like F. Scott Fitzgerald's Jay Gatsby, the bootlegger who yearned toward the green light on the dock of Daisy Buchanan, the heiress who had money in her voice—Gilbert believed that a special quality of human possibility attached to the rich. In his case the quest took the form of striving to become a part of the uneasy American version of court life that we have always called Society. It is interesting that he apparently made little distinction between Real Society, based on inherited money and Anglo-Saxon lineage, and the newer, less exclusive, more flamboyant version associated with the entertainment world called Café Society. He sought them both impartially, although he kept them separate. By 1960 the process of democratic thought, or perhaps merely the breakup of traditional fortunes by taxes, had advanced to the point where Real Society had gone suburban or disappeared within the upper middle class, while Café Society, born of the entertainment-mad depression and war years, had lost status with the growing public realization of its loose rites of passage and easy-money-spending ways.

But if Gilbert believed that Society no longer existed in turn-of-the century form, he gave no clue. On the contrary, it seems clear he believed in its vitality, and sought to fulfill himself through it. In fact, he had much to offer his new friends. In his early thirties, a short, compact man with pale blue eyes and a sort of ferret face under thinning hair, Gilbert had a direct, personal charm that compensated for his vanity and extreme competitiveness. Sometimes his newfound friends patronized him behind his back, laughing at his social pretensions and his love of ostentation, but they continued going to his parties and, above all, following his market tips. Some accused him of being a habitual liar; they forgave him because he seemed genuinely to believe his lies, especially those about himself and his past. He was a compulsive gambler—but, endearingly, a very bad one; on lucky streaks he would double bets until he lost all his winnings, or draw to inside straights for huge sums at poker, or go for broke on losing streaks; yet at all times he seemed to take large losses in the best of humor. It was almost as if he lost just so that he could show what a sport he was, and how little money as such meant to him. He was spoken of as interesting—a natural, a source of conversation to those who followed the gossip columns and who in turn spread the gossip even wider.

At his constant urging, his newfound friends bought Bruce stock—and so did his parents, his sister, his cousins and his aunts and anyone else susceptible to his persuasion. The buying began to approach its climactic phase in March 1958, when Bruce was selling on the American Stock Exchange at around $25 a share. All that spring, the Gilberts and their relatives and Eddie's friends accumulated the stock, until in June it had reached the seventies and was bouncing up and down from day to day and hour to hour in an alarming way. What was in the process of developing in Bruce stock was the classically dangerous, sometimes disastrous market situation called a corner. As the price had risen, the Bruce family management had come, belatedly, to realize that a raid was in progress; their defensive countermeasure was to begin buying the stock themselves, thereby redoubling the upward pressure. Meanwhile, a third group, consisting of speculators, had been watching the wild and apparently illogical rise, and had seen a chance for a profit in short sales— sales of borrowed stock that could presumably be bought back and delivered at a lower price later, after the bubble had burst. Thus it came about that in May and early June, much of the stock bought by the Bruce side and the Gilbert side alike was bought from persons who did not own it at all. Borrowed from a "floating supply" that was more theoretical than actual, it was stock that really did not exist; and in June when the price reached 77, the two antagonist factions together owned, or had documents to show that they owned, more shares than were actually outstanding. The short sellers were squeezed; if called upon to deliver the stock they had borrowed and then sold, they could not do so, and those who owned it were in a position to force them to buy back what they owed at a highly inflated price.

Corners have a long and infamous history in Wall Street. Old Commodore Vanderbilt engineered three of them in the eighteen sixties, causing disaster not only to the short sellers he had trapped but to the companies whose stock he manipulated. The Northern Pacific crash of 1901 was the sequel to a corner that came about in exactly the same way as the Bruce one—through a contest for control; its result was a national panic with worldwide repercussions. The last corner on the New York Stock Exchange occurred in 1922, in the stock of Piggly Wiggly Stores. In the Bruce case, probably neither Gilbert nor the Bruce mangement had wanted a corner—it was an accidental by-product of the fight for control—and, because of the insignificance of Bruce in the larger economy, there was no danger of a national panic. There was, however, a danger that Bruce stockholders not involved in the fight would become accidental casualties, and, moreover, in Wall Street—including even the 1958 American Stock Exchange—the very word "corner" was frighteningly evocative of a disreputable past. So in mid-June the Amex acted, suspending trading in Bruce to protect the innocent bystanders. Immediately the stock began to be traded over the counter, and the short sellers, wildly buying what few shares were available in a scramble to fulfill their commitments, sent the price rocketing insanely up to 188. (The available shares came from the innocent bystanders, and perhaps a few from the faithless among Gilbert's friends, who sold their loyalty for quick profit.) The S.E.C. stepped in, there were negotiations and recriminations, moves and countermoves, and at last a compromise was reached between Gilbert and the Bruce family; when the dust settled in September, Gilbert had 50 percent of Bruce stock and was made chairman of the Bruce board. Empire took notice of its new enhanced status by changing its name to Empire National; later, in 1961, when Empire National and Bruce were formally merged, the surviving company took the name of E. L. Bruce and Company.

Eddie Gilbert, coming out of the fray in the fall of 1958, seemed to have arrived at last—apparently paper-rich from his huge holdings of high-priced Bruce stock, rich in the esteem of his society backers, nationally famous from the publicity attendant on the corner he had brought about. Because of the parallel to 1901, his name had been linked in the press with those of J. P. Morgan and E. H. Harriman—giants of the past. The goal of this new, apprentice giant was one that the old ones might have treated with Olympian scorn: to become a leader of what was essentially a parasite society, the international social and fringe-artistic group that was just about then beginning to be called the Jet Set. But Gilbert did not see it that way. The metaphor he used for Bruce during his long struggle to seize it showed the texture of his aspirations; it pleased him to call it the Tiffany of the building-materials industry. Now, as the winner, he began to spread himself. He kept a regular Monday box at the Metropolitan Opera—a lover of music, as not all of his fellow-box-holders were, but one who loved appearing among them, too. He cultivated the two leading arbiters of Café Society, Elsa Maxwell and Igor Cassini; sometimes he would self-indulgently ask Cassini if he knew anyone Gilbert's age who was richer and more important than he, and Cassini, with a smooth smile, would shake his head. He hired Cassini's firm, Martial and Company, as public-relations counsel for Bruce; it does not seem to have bothered either man that the items about Gilbert's doings that appeared in Cassini's newspaper column had been supplied by Cassini himself as Bruce's press agent, meaning that in effect Gilbert was simply buying, and Cassini selling, space in the column. He sent his wife, a beautiful Brooklyn girl named Rhoda, to a speech therapist and a posture school. Eventually his market transactions came to be handled by Francis Farr, clubman and broker, brother of a member of the aristocratic law firm of White and Case and a vestryman of St. James Episcopal Church. He installed flooring in Le Club, a raffishly élite New

York membership-by-invitation discothèque, in exchange for a charter membership. He acquired a huge Fifth Avenue apartment and, when and as he could, filled it with French antiques, a fortune in generally almost-first-rate paintings, and a staff of six. Sometimes he lived in a mansion at Palm Beach, epitome of Real Society in faded turn-of-the-century photographs. He took an immense villa at Cap Martin on the French Riviera, where he mingled when he could with Maria Callas and Aristotle Onassis and their like, and gave huge outdoor parties with an orchestra playing beside an Olympic-size swimming pool. At his parties, Eddie was always the maestro, directing, giving whimsical instructions, trading hospitality for the right to command. "Let's all go bowling!" he might shout to his assembled guests after lunch, so ingenuously that forty or fifty of the rich and chic or almost-rich and almost-chic of the world would dutifully jump into their cars, or into one of his waiting limousines, and be off to Monaco's elegant four-lane bowling alley to indulge him. He was living a dream, filling out its details as he went along, and waiting, like Gatsby, for the sound of the tuning fork struck against a star.

4

And he was not really rich, in any genuine sense. Probably he spent beyond his income every year except 1961. It was believed that at his peak he had a paper net worth of around $10 million, but in retrospect this seems unlikely. His paper profits were built on borrowing, and he was always mortgaged right up to the hilt; to be thus mortgaged, and to remain so, was all but an article of faith with him. In 1959 he borrowed money from the Empire National treasury without informing the company's board. This was clearly an improper act; but he repaid the loan with interest before it was discovered by the S.E.C., and the matter was allowed to drop. He was habitually so pressed for cash that on each January first he would draw his entire $50,000 Empire salary for the coming year in a lump sum in advance. By the summer of 1960 he was in bad financial trouble. Empire National stock was down, Gilbert's brokers were calling for additional margin, and Gilbert was already in debt all over New York. He owed large sums to dozens of art dealers. Some sources maintain that, counting his personal debts to his father, he was by then insolvent by at least $1 million. But he hung on gamely; when friends advised him at least to liquidate the art collection, he refused. To sell it, he explained, would be to lose face.

What saved him at that particular moment was the bull market of 1961, and a timely psychological boost that came about in an odd way. On the advice of a friend, he sought to hire as a consultant Jerry Finkelstein, the powerful business and political figure (later New York City Democratic chairman) who was then generally considered the top financial public-relations man in the country. Depressed as he was, Gilbert made an offer to Finkelstein expecting rejection. But to his joy and amazement Finkelstein accepted, taking on the job in exchange for a fat allotment of Bruce stock options. And then came the curious part: his self-confidence restored by the mere fact of Finkelstein's acceptance, Gilbert was transformed into a demon and proceeded to do on his own the job that he had hired the leading expert to do. The act of hiring a champion released the champion in himself, and Finkelstein had little to do but collect his profits when Bruce stock rose sharply. Now Gilbert had gained clear-cut precedence over his father; when Bruce was merged with Empire National, Eddie Gilbert became president of the combined company and Harry Gilbert "chairman of the executive committee," a title that meant—as it so often does— "kicked upstairs." And now he had also, for the first time, become respectable to important segments of the business community; as a result of his success with Bruce, investment bankers who would scarcely have let him through their doors two years earlier were knocking on his and suggesting that they be allowed to help finance his subsequent ventures. Gilbert's buying power in the market had also been vastly increased, not only by the rise in value of his own holdings but by a swift and apparently miraculous increase in the number of "friends" who would gladly put their money where he told them to. It all induced a dangerous new euphoria. By May 1961, Gilbert was feeling so flush that the urge for expansion overtook him again, and he embarked on the venture that would destroy him.

What he wanted for his empire, called Bruce but truly an empire now, was Celotex Corporation, a large and important manufacturer of building-insulation materials with headquarters in Chicago and a listing on the New York Stock Exchange. He began by buying its stock at around 30, stepped up the pace when it conveniently fell back to 24 later in 1961, and then chased it all the way up to 42 early in 1962. His acquisition work was cut out for him this time, since Celotex was bigger game than Bruce; half-again as big in sales, Celotex had more than three times as many shares outstanding. But Gilbert, convinced now of his infallibility, was confident. He held perhaps half a million Bruce shares, some in Memphis, some in Switzerland with moneylenders, some in other places; it gave him several million dollars' buying power. He began using this to buy Celotex; he put his friends (and cousins and aunts) into Celotex up to the last dollar they would allow; he borrowed still more cash from his father, and put *that* into Celotex too. Even his old enemies, the Bruce family, became so mesmerized by the man who had wrested control from them that early in 1962 they authorized his use of $400,000 of the company's money to buy Celotex shares, and later they raised the ante by a round million more. In March, Gilbert showed his cards. He held 10 percent of Celotex stock, he announced, and he wanted a place on the board of directors. Henry Collins, Celotex's president, at first refused, but did so in such a tentative way that it was clear he felt he was simply postponing the inevitable. Gilbert seemed on the verge of a stunning success.

And then two events in quick succession, one public and one private, hastened the course of his destiny. The market started to go sour with the Kennedy–steel encounter, and Gilbert, whose marriage had gone sour the November before, flew to Las Vegas to serve the six-week residency that was a prerequisite to getting a Nevada divorce. Doubtless he felt, like the gambler he was, that the Celotex campaign was so near victory that he could command its final moves by long-distance telephone. Or perhaps, in what appeared to be his moment of approaching triumph, he had forebodings of disaster and yielded to an inclination to flee in panic. In any case, at the end of April, he suddenly left the suite at the Waldorf where he had been living since he and his wife had separated some months earlier, and flew to Las Vegas to establish residence.

Gilbert took elaborate security precautions, apparently to forestall any panic in the market for Bruce and Celotex stock that his flight might cause. Only a few people at Bruce were allowed to know where he had gone, and they were sworn to secrecy. He took an assumed name—Edward Heaton. (Edward with the heat on; Gilbert's sense of humor had survived his tribulations so far.) He had a private telephone installed in his motel room and connected by tie line to the switchboard of his New York office, so that callers could be put through to him immediately, exactly as if he were in his office in Manhattan. His outgoing letters were sent first to New York or to Bruce headquarters in Memphis, and then remailed with the appropriate postmarks.

His personal predilections, and the turning of the earth, imposed a strange and exhausting schedule on Gilbert in Las Vegas. The three-hour time differential meant that the New York markets opened at 7:00 A.M. Nevada time. Every morning, therefore, Gilbert would be up at the desert dawn and on the phone getting early New York quotations from brokers. Then at the market opening the pace of his telephoning would be stepped up, and he would keep the wires humming until lunch time in Las Vegas, when the day's trading ended in the East. In the afternoon he would wander into the casinos, where he would gamble on into the evening. Did he dream of the perfect *jeux*, the magic coup that would give him the means to bring Celotex within his grasp? If so, in vain; later he admitted that his gambling losses in Las Vegas had been heavy.

Sometimes, like a wary spider, he would make a quick foray out into the real world, and then hasten back into hiding. The exigencies of Nevada divorce law made such a procedure necessary. To qualify as a resident, he had to be certifiably within state boundaries at some time each day over a six-week period. He hired a permanent Nevada resident to be his witness—and, incidentally, his bodyguard; the witness would accompany him to the airport to see him off in the afternoon, and would be there to meet him, and take formal note of his presence, on his return the following afternoon. Twice, early in May, he made such trips to New York in search of additional cash. But the stock market had begun its descent in earnest now, and with it Gilbert's claim to solvency, and the moneylenders were unwilling to accommodate him. Indeed, his Nevada-based trips were not only worthless but probably counterproductive; the word spread swiftly among lenders that Eddie Gilbert was in trouble and running hard. At the middle of the month he went to Chicago to see Collins of Celotex (arising at midnight, touching foot to Nevada soil for the new day, passing the glittering lights of the Strip en route to the airport, and then flying off at 1:30 in the morning). In Chicago, Collins now offered Gilbert a seat on the Celotex board and the right to choose one other director. But Gilbert, for the sake of his crumbling credit status, needed the board seat immediately, and Collins insisted on holding up the announcement until after the next Celotex board meeting on June 20, so the victory Gilbert brought back to his desert hideaway was a hollow one.

Gilbert's Celotex holdings now amounted to over 150,000 shares, and for each further point that the stock dropped, he had to find and deliver $150,000 in additional margin or risk being sold out by his brokers. Those of his friends holding Celotex on his advice now numbered around fifty, and they, too, since most of them held it on margin, were being squeezed as the price continued to fall. Many of them also had positions in Bruce. Their alternatives were three: to sell Celotex; to sell Bruce to cover Celotex, which would depress the price of Bruce and thus be equally disastrous for Gilbert; or to find more cash margin.

Gilbert himself had all but exhausted his borrowing power. His debts to brokers, to friends, to Swiss bankers, to New York loan sharks on the fringes of the underworld, all loomed over him, and the market betrayed him daily by dropping even more.

The third week of May became for Gilbert a nightmare of thwarted pleas by telephone—pleas to lenders for new loans, pleas to brokers to be patient and not sell him out, pleas with friends to stick with him just a little longer. But it was all in vain, and in desperation that same week Gilbert took the old, familiar, bad-gambler's last bad gamble—to avoid the certainty of bankruptcy he risked the possibility of criminal charges. Gilbert ordered an official of Bruce to make out checks drawn on the Bruce treasury to a couple of companies called Rhodes Enterprises and Empire Hardwood Flooring, which were actually dummies for Gilbert himself, and he used the proceeds to shore up his personal margin calls. The checks amounted to not quite $2 million; the act amounted to grand larceny.

It was a bold stroke, based, of course, on the faint hope that the prices of Bruce and Celotex would suddenly rise enough to reduce Gilbert's need for margin and enable him to redeem the improper checks and repay Bruce. By his own calculations—which no doubt excluded his huge debts to his father—he was solvent were Celotex above 31 and Bruce above 32. On Friday, May 25, Celotex closed at 31 and Bruce at 32 3/8, actually up a fraction for the day. Thus he still had a fingerhold on survival. But for the first time Gilbert was not optimistic. That Friday he told a part-time secretary, "The way this is going, Monday will be murder." Later he told M.J. Rossant of *The New York Times*, "I suddenly knew that I couldn't get through this without getting hurt and getting innocent people hurt." It is ironic that Gilbert's market prescience, such as it was, should have worked so well at a time when, through pyramiding of debt and then through misappropriation of funds, he had trapped himself in a net so confining that it prevented him from taking advantage of what he knew. As the reader will recall, the Monday he said would be "murder" turned out to be Blue Monday, the Stock Exchange's second worst day of the century up to then.

5

That fateful Monday morning Gilbert was closeted in his motel room, his telephones in constant use, learning minute by minute of the progress of the Wall Street collapse almost three thousand miles away. All morning long, Bruce held teeteringly at 30. The blow fell at around noon, New York time, when a broker told Gilbert that Bruce was now quoted at—23. Stunned into disbelief, he hung up and called another broker, who confirmed the devastating news. Hardly a moment later, the phones began jangling with incoming calls from his frightened creditors in New York and Switzerland.

Gilbert now admitted to himself that he was beaten. He said later that he spent the rest of Monday "like a punch-drunk fighter going through the motions." Bruce closed for the day at 23, down 9 3/8, and Celotex closed at 25, down 6. Gilbert's personal losses for that Monday came to $5 million. In addition to the creditors, he had to deal all afternoon with the friends he had tipped to buy Bruce and Celotex, who now had disastrous losses of their own. In the big turnaround on Tuesday, Bruce gained 5 3/8 points, but the recovery was too moderate and too momentary to save him; Celotex did not recover at all, and his other, unredeemable debts, including the $2 million he had taken from the unsuspecting Bruce company, remained outstanding.

Late on Tuesday, Gilbert assessed his position as coolly as he could. Clearly, the dream of capturing Celotex was ended. It was a question now not of building an empire or even protecting one, but of avoiding bankruptcy and, if possible, the penitentiary. His hope, as he saw it, lay in finding a block buyer for all or most of his Celotex holding, and using the proceeds to pay back what he had "borrowed" from Bruce. He remembered that a company in the building-materials business called Ruberoid had expressed interest in taking a position in Celotex. Whatever the chances of swinging such a deal, they depended on his availability in New York for more than one-day flying trips. So, with only a couple of weeks remaining in his Nevada residency term, he abandoned another dream, that of getting his divorce, and on Wednesday, the Memorial Day holiday, he flew to New York and moved back into his suite at the Waldorf.

Thursday the storm around him gathered new force. Gilbert found that the earliest appointment he could get with the officials of Ruberoid was the following Monday, June 4. Yet all day Thursday his Waldorf suite was besieged by creditors, some of whom had come from Switzerland for the purpose. He could give them no satisfaction, only vague hopes of a possible sale of Celotex. On Friday, friends to whom he confided his position, and the criminal action it had led him into, urged him to declare bankruptcy at once. Rueful and contrite, but still stubborn, he refused.

In fact, Gilbert still had a little time—to be precise, six business days. Tuesday, June 12 was the scheduled date of the next Bruce board of directors meeting, at which the matter of $2 million loans to Rhodes Enterprises and Empire Hardwood Flooring was almost certain to come up; so he would have to have some solution ready by then or stand exposed. The six borrowed days were the last loan he could negotiate—a loan of time rather than money. On Monday the fourth—Day One—he met with Ruberoid officials as planned, freely admitted to them that he was in a squeeze, and suggested that, since they wanted to purchase a block of Celotex shares anyway, they might take profitable advantage of his distress by assuming his Celotex holdings. The Ruberoid men seemed interested, but stopped short of giving him a firm and binding commitment. On Day Two, still desperate, he told the whole story to his lawyers at the firm of Shearman and Sterling. Understandably, they were horrified, and set about taking such defensive steps as were available. To prevent Gilbert from compounding his felony in panic, they instructed Bruce officials not under any conditions to sign any more checks on his instructions. As a first step toward redeeming the felony he admitted to having committed, they ordered him to give the company personal notes backed by his personal property.

Day Three passed without any promising developments, but on Day Four—Thursday the seventh—there suddenly appeared a ray of hope when the executive vice president of Ruberoid gave Gilbert the almost incredibly good news that he believed his firm was ready to buy 300,000 shares of Celotex at a fair price. The sale, when and as consummated, would not save him from bankruptcy, but it would enable him to save his friends and followers, and to bail himself out of his improper borrowing from Bruce.

Gilbert spent the rest of Thursday and then Friday frantically rounding up the Celotex shares from his friends, to have them ready for delivery; and on Monday the eleventh, the last day before the Bruce meeting, with the shares safely in hand, he savored for a few hours the feeling that he might still end the affair with some sort of honor, and perhaps without losing everything—his villas, his followers, his place in the great world. The Bruce meeting convened at 10:30 Tuesday morning; Gilbert was there smoking a cigar, dapper in a gray suit and black loafers. For two hours he told the other directors—some of whom already knew, or knew enough—the story of his frantic, reticulated dealings and of how they had led at last to an unauthorized withdrawal from the funds with which the men in the room were jointed entrusted. There followed a heated debate; some wanted Gilbert's immediate resignation, while others counselled caution, or at least a delay until after the day's market closing to forestall a further panic in Bruce stock. It was in the midst of this tense and gloomy discussion that word came to Gilbert from Ruberoid that the company had withdrawn its offer to buy his block of Celotex shares.

It was the coup de grace for Gilbert. The meeting broke for lunch, but he did not join his fellow directors in the meal. Instead, he went home and packed a suitcase, visited his bank vault and picked up $8,000 in cash, and made a reservation on a plane leaving that evening at 7:30 for Brazil. His last legitimate escape hatch sealed off, he had decided on literal and figurative flight. Brazil at the time had become a secular sanctuary for erring American financiers; down there already, wasting time, boasting about old triumphs, playing poker, and putting together such penny-ante local deals as they could manage, were Lowell Birrell, the well-brought-up eviscerator of companies; the giant Texan embezzler BenJack Cage; and Earle Belle, almost equally Runyonesque by baptism, a youthful jobber of watered bank stocks. Gilbert must have hated the prospect of geographical association with these grimly comic rogues; later he would maintain with indignation that he had nothing in common with any of them. But the fact was that on June 12, 1962, he had one thing in common with them all—the pressing need for a distant jurisdiction like Brazil that had no effective extradition treaty with the United States.

Gilbert appeared back at the Bruce meeting, cool and confident, when it reconvened that afternoon at 2:30. His need now was to persuade the Bruce board to postpone public announcement of his resignation and its disgraceful cause until he was out of the country. Just until 7:30! he pleaded. Why that particular hour? He explained that he needed just five hours to approach one final potential lender. After another long and heated argument, the board acceded, and Gilbert breathed again. Of course, the potential lender was mythical. He departed his Bruce office around 5:30, ostensibly to see the last-hope lender, saying he would be back around 7:00 with news of the results. While the other directors waited tensely, Gilbert hired a limousine and picked up his parents, who then accompanied him to Idlewild Airport. In the car, Harry Gilbert said later, Eddie was "frantic and hysterical." But at the airport he was calm enough to pay cash for his ticket and board his Rio-bound flight without attracting attention. The plane's departure was delayed for some reason, giving him a final fright, but shortly after 8:00 it took off.

At the Bruce offices, the directors became progressively more apprehensive. At 8:15 they called the S.E.C. and reported all that they knew. It was too late. At 8:30, as Eddie Gilbert's jet reached altitude and sped southward, Harry Gilbert called the Bruce directors to say, ruefully, that his son would not be back.

6

In Brazil he lived in relative quiet, taking an only moderately plush apartment in the Copacabana section of Rio, often going unshaven, avoiding nightclubs and casinos, writing letters, dabbling a bit in local business, exercising his language skill by studying Portuguese. (He did allow himself a chauffeur-driven Cadillac.) From time to time his ever-loyal parents sent him money. "I just can't face people," he told the *Times'* Rossant, who visited him there; but he also said more resolutely, "I will pay back everything if it takes the rest of my life." Meanwhile, he was sometimes heard to put the blame for his debacle on anybody and everybody but himself: on Lazard, on Loeb, Rhoades, on Collins of Celotex, on faithless friends, on President Kennedy. To one visitor from home he complained, "I'm just an ordinary guy. They called me a genius, but I'm not. If they hadn't blown the whistle on me, it could all have been avoided."

That was his line, and that of such of his friends as chose to remain loyal to him: Gilbert, without the undue impatience of his creditors and the bad timing of the May market crash, would have bagged Celotex, covered the Bruce borrowing before it became public knowledge, and emerged a hero. In the light of retrospect, it is a line that simply does not correspond to reality. In fact, it would later appear that his debts exceeded his assets by somewhere in the neighborhood of $14 or $15 million. It is probable that neither the most indulgent set of creditors nor the most complaisant of markets could have saved him permanently from the consequences of his overweening ambition; and almost certainly the May crash merely accelerated his demise.

At home, meanwhile, there were the predictable recriminations and unseemly squabbles, lending a sort of false dignity by contrast to the lonely exile pouring over Portuguese grammar. At the end of June, the Bruce company sought and got a court injunction to prevent Mrs. Gilbert from disposing of the couple's furniture and art collection for her own benefit: particular reference was made to Boucher's *La Toilette de Venus* and *Psyche and Cupid*, asserted in the injunction plea to be worth $95,000; Monet's *Flowers*, $75,000; and Fragonard's *Portrait of a Young Woman*, $92,000. At about the same time, the Justice Department got an indictment against Gilbert on fifteen counts of securities fraud, and the Internal Revenue Service added a touch of comedy by filing tax liens against him dating back to 1958 and amounting to over $3 million. In mid-July, he was further indicted in New York for grand larceny in connection with the Bruce misappropriation. As for his friends, a few of them loyally insisted that he was a misunderstood man who had never meant to do wrong; others, however, would no longer acknowledge that they knew him. His old pal and business associate Igor Cassini, who had lost money on Bruce and Celotex, now found it appropriate to pronounce Gilbert "a crook." And then, in November, by which time there were federal and state charges outstanding against him the penalties for which added up to 194 years in prison, Gilbert suddenly came home. He got off the plane at New York flanked by federal marshals. He was arrested, and then promptly released on bail.

He said he had returned because he was bored with inaction and the Latin American spirit of mañana, and surely this was true. (Some of his friends joked that five months is as long as a Jewish boy can stay away from home.) But it also seems clear that Arnold Bauman, the New York criminal lawyer whom Gilbert's father had hired in his absence to defend him, had told him that the coast was now as clear as it would ever be. And that, it turned out, was pretty clear. Gilbert remained free on bail for no less than four and a half years, while he and his lawyer dangled before the various prosecutors the promise that he would implicate other wrongdoers. He could implicate various people, he said; he had something on Lazard and Loeb, Rhoades. These promises were never fulfilled. In May 1963, he and Rhoda

Gilbert were finally divorced, and a week later he married a Norwegian airline stewardess named Turid. The villas, the art collection, and the poolside parties were now in the past, but Gilbert and his new bride did well enough for a time. They dressed well; they lived in a Park Avenue apartment; they had two children, and went to Puerto Rico on vacation. With help, as usual, from his father, Gilbert set himself up in a new business, the Northerlin Company, flooring brokers. He was still a good salesman. Northerlin made over $200,000 its first year, and Gilbert, besides beginning to fulfill his promise by paying off some of the smaller of his old debts—$2,300 to a painter of his old Fifth Avenue apartment, $138 to F.A.O. Schwartz—began trying to live in his old way on $100,000 a year. He began again to wheel and deal in the market—in his wife's name. Very tentatively, a few of the not-so-beau monde began to take notice of him again.

There are second acts in some American lives, but not Eddie Gilbert's. Given his temperament, his comeback attempt could not succeed, but even so, it was quite a feat. Still under multiple indictments, free on bail, bankrupt for over $10 million all the while, between 1963 and 1967 he twice "got rich," twice "went broke," once even managed to get himself investigated by the S.E.C. He cut too many corners in his operations at Northerlin; the promising young company began to lose money, and finally had to be sold for a tax loss. And time ran out on his unfulfilled bargain with the civil authorities. In 1964 he pleaded guilty to twelve counts of grand larceny and three of securities fraud; in each case a sentencing date was set, and in each case, when the date arrived, sentencing was postponed. It almost seemed as if he might escape imprisonment indefinitely. But in 1967 the authorities finally lost patience with his failure to come up with usable state's evidence. That April—with only a trivial fraction of his 1962 debts repaid, and with a flock of new ones accumulated—the federal penitentiary doors finally closed on him. He would be paroled a little over two years later, but by that time his career as Gatsby was gone for good.

7

As a financier Gilbert cannot be taken seriously; at the gambling tables and in the stock market he operated by the world's oldest and surest formula for failure—to double your winning bets until the law of averages overtakes you, and you are wiped out. As a catalyst for reform, he has little importance; neither his speculative methods nor his ultimate crime were original in conception or execution, and the exposure of them did not lead to new loophole-closing S.E.C. rules or legislation. Nor, indeed, were large numbers of innocent investors, apart from his too-trusting friends and relatives, significantly hurt by his operations. Why, then, need he detain us?

It is as a social figure, a reflection of the texture of financial life in the United States at the start of the nineteen sixties, that Gilbert's career has a kind of resonance. The style that he embodied with instinctive perfection was a once-familiar but now-fading American one: the style of romantic self-destructiveness, of seeking risk for its own sake, of wild midnight rides in fast cars or on roulette wheels that ended in disaster not by accident but because the courting of disaster was integral to the style itself. The doomed and gilded youth of America, the beautiful and damned, had gone out with the depression, or certainly with World War II. But Gilbert did not know that; he had formed his unconscious stylistic aspirations early in life, and he clung to them and projected them into an alien era. A generation too late, he set out unknowing to destroy himself in the grand manner.

And so, perhaps, though in a smaller way, did all of the people who with high hopes sank their savings into the far-out new stock issues of 1961 and got wiped out in 1962. At the end of the decade, between 1968 and 1970, there would be an even bigger speculative boom and bust. But that one would be dominated by institutions; by that time the American stock market would be so huge as to be beyond manipulation by individuals or small groups operating for themselves, and Gilbert and his little band of followers would have been ineffective in it.

Coming just before the mutual and pension funds took charge of the stock market, the 1961–1962 investment scene was perfect for Gilbert, and he remains its symbolic figure. Tinsel-mad, he burned for personal transfiguration by riches and fame. Money-seekers later in the decade would set themselves more practical goals—to revenge themselves on the Establishment by joining it, to improve the nation, to thumb one's nose at the whole world; they would know what Gilbert did not, that the possession of money cannot turn life to magic. He was the archetypal loser of 1962, a stock-market crash for romantics, and yet also a harbinger of things to come.

CHAPTER IV

Palmy Days
and
Low Rumblings

1

Usually after general disaster in Wall Street or elsewhere, one man takes charge of cleaning up and putting things back together, of dragging the bodies off stage and rearranging the set for the next performance—rearranging it neatly and primly, as if in hopes that subsequent action will turn toward drawing-room comedy rather than more bloody melodrama. There was no such one person after 1929. That Street scene was a disaster of such magnitude that the whole cast of characters was left paralyzed for years, and an entire new federal government with a mandate to do anything was needed to supply resolution and to restore a semblance of order. In 1938, after Richard Whitney's fall had disorganized the Old Guard that ran Wall Street by unmasking its impeccable leader as an embezzler, there was William McChesney Martin, Jr., a quiet, scholarly bachelor of thirty-one, who wore owlish round spectacles and never smoked, or drank anything stronger than hot chocolate. It was to this prudent and serious young man that the Stock Exchange turned in its extremity, making him acting chairman and then its first paid president, to undertake the necessary job of reform.

After the shambles in 1962, however, the man Wall Street turned to was neither on the inside like Martin, nor entirely outside like the New Deal. He was the chairman of the S.E.C., William Lucius Cary.

Cary in 1962 was a lawyer of fifty-one with the gentlemanly manner and the pixyish countenance of a New England professor. A late-starting family man, he had two children who were still tots; his wife, Katherine, was a great-great-granddaughter of America's first world-famous novelist, James Fenimore Cooper. His reputation among his colleagues of the bar was, as one of them put it, for "sweetness of temperament combined with fundamental toughness of fibre." In fact, his roots were not in New England but in Mount Vernon, Ohio, although there was some New England in his blood: a New England ancestor had fought in the battle of Lexington. The family had trekked westward to Ohio in 1814, and had stayed there. He had grown up in and around Columbus, the son of a lawyer and president of a small utility company; he had graduated from Yale and then from Yale Law, practiced law a couple of years in Cleveland, then done a long stretch in federal government—first as a young S.E.C. assistant counsel, later as an assistant attorney general in the tax division of the Justice Department, then as an Office of Strategic Services cloak-and-dagger functionary in wartime Roumania and Yugoslavia. In 1947 he had entered academic life, teaching law thereafter, first at Northwestern and later at Columbia. He was in the latter post, taking one day a week off to go downtown to the "real world" of Wall Street and practice law with the firm of Patterson, Belknap and Webb, when John F. Kennedy appointed him S.E.C. chairman soon after assuming the Presidency in January 1961.

Cary never knew how he came to be tapped; he had worked in the Stevenson campaigns of 1952 and 1956 and had become a close friend of the candidate, then had worked with Robert M. Morgenthau, a New York City neighbor, in the Kennedy campaign of 1960. Thus he had many friends in the upper echelons of the Kennedy ranks, and one or another of them must have suggested his name to the President-elect. At all events, the appointment proved to have been a brilliant one—perhaps the most brilliant to that post since Franklin D. Roosevelt, to the dismay of all good liberals, had chosen the ex-stock manipulator Joseph P. Kennedy to be the S.E.C.'s first head back in 1934. Cary brought to the organization a vigor and a drive that it had lacked for years.

"Regulatory bodies, like the people who comprise them, have a marked life cycle," John Kenneth Galbraith has written. "In youth they are vigorous, aggressive, evangelistic, and even intolerant. Later they mellow, and in old age—after a matter of ten or fifteen years—they become, with some exceptions, either an arm of the industry they are regulating or senile." The S.E.C., although widely considered to be generally the most successful of the regulatory bodies, had not been immune to the aging process. Aggressive, evangelistic, and intolerant in New Deal days, during World War II, when the securities industry itself was at a near standstill, it had fallen into virtual desuetude, lying low in temporary quarters that were not even at the seat of government in Washington but were situated in Philadelphia. And in the early postwar years the S.E.C. did not noticeably revive. This was far from entirely its own fault; Presidents Truman and Eisenhower both showed a pointed lack of interest in it; its chairmanship was often used as a political payoff (as, indeed, it technically was in Cary's case), and its appropriations were cut again and again by Congress and the Bureau of the Budget. In June 1941, the S.E.C. had a roster of 1,683 employees; in 1955, by which time the industry it was supposed to regulate had expanded vastly, the number was down to 666, and when Cary assumed office some six years later the total was around 900. The S.E.C.'s premature onslaught of senility, then, was compounded by starvation. During the latter nineteen fifties it gained considerable public acclaim for the noisy campaign of its New York office chief, Paul Windels, Jr.—"Pistol Paul" to the culprits—who took after boiler-room operators peddling worthless penny uranium stocks by telephone. But meanwhile the agency as a whole was all but moribund. While the Birrells and the Gutermas were weaving their schemes and the Amex was all but falling to pieces, the sparse staff at S.E.C. headquarters —restored to Washington now, but assigned there to an unimpressive temporary building on Second Street called the "tarpaper shack"—generally contented themselves with routine; they were never seen on the trading floors of the exchanges, they enjoyed all too amiable social relations with the authorities of those exchanges, and one S.E.C. chairman developed the comfortable habit of falling asleep during the Commission's deliberations. "Literally and figuratively, the S.E.C. slept for most of the decade," Louis M. Kohlmeier, Jr., a historian of regulatory agencies, wrote of the nineteen fifties.

A strong *Report on Regulatory Agencies to the President Elect*, commissioned by the President-elect himself and written late in 1960 by James M. Landis, who had been an S.E.C. chairman in New Deal days, showed that Kennedy was bent on bringing the S.E.C. back to life, and it set the stage for the Cary regime. Landis called for more funds as well as greater regulatory zeal, and Kennedy and Congress implemented the Landis conclusions with practical backing; between 1960 and 1964 the S.E.C.'s annual appropriation increased from $9.5 million to almost $14 million and its payroll from fewer than one thousand persons to almost fifteen hundred. But the change was not only quantitative. Cary concentrated on recruiting talented and enthusiastic lawyers, devoting perhaps a third of his time to the task. His base supply naturally enough consisted of his former students and their friends; the atmosphere at the tarpaper shack soon changed from one of bureaucratic somnolence to one of academic liberal activism.

Cary treated the securities industry warily, and generally, as he liked to put it, "with deference," but hardly with friendship. As David Jackson learned, the Cary men were sometimes overzealous about boring in with hard questions, and certainly in Jackson's case deference was severely strained. Cary had a reserved opinion of Keith Funston as New York Stock Exchange president, for reasons that were scarcely Funston's fault —because, as a former businessman and college president who had been hired to fill an essentially public-relations function, he didn't really know the securities business. But Cary and his staff did not avoid face-to-face meetings with Funston or anyone else; rather, they spent as much time in Wall Street as they could, watching and listening. Although Cary himself had a few close friends holding the levers of Wall Street power—perhaps the chief among them being Amyas Ames of Kidder, Peabody and Company—he generally avoided social contacts there, and once when he took George Woods of First Boston Corporation to lunch, he was startled to find that it was the talk of the Street.

Two actions during his first year in office gave the financial district an inkling of Cary's mettle and the S.E.C.'s new mood. One was a case called *In the Matter of Cady, Roberts and Co.*, which concerned events that had taken place two years before. In November 1959, Robert M. Gintel, a young member of the brokerage firm of Cady, Roberts and Company, had been informed one morning by one of his associates, J. Cheever Cowdin, that Curtiss-Wright Corporation was about to announce a drastic cut in its quarterly dividend. Gintel had the very best of reasons to believe that Cowdin knew what he was talking about, since Cowdin was a director of Curtiss-Wright and had presumably participated in the very decision he was reporting on. Possessing this classic piece of insider information, Gintel immediately ordered the sale of 7,000 shares of Curtiss-Wright stock on behalf of his firm's customers. The order was executed at above 40; one-half hour later the dividend cut was publicly announced, and the first trade in Curtiss-Wright thereafter was at 36 1/2— not quite 10 percent lower.

Such profitable use of privileged information was apparently illegal under Rule 10B-5 of the S.E.C., promulgated in 1942 under authority of the 1934 Securities Exchange Act, and intended to prohibit precisely this sort of thing. But so firmly entrenched was the Wall Street tradition of taking unfair advantage of the larger investing public, and so lax the S.E.C.'s administration of that particular part of the law between 1942 and 1961, that not a single stockbroker had ever been prosecuted for improper use of privileged information during those two decades. In the tarpaper shack, 10B-5 had simply been considered too hot to handle. It was the law in name only, and thus it is not surprising that prior to Cary's time the S.E.C. had taken no action in the matter of Cady, Roberts. But now, in an opinion written by the new chairman himself, the S.E.C. decided that in not waiting until the public announcement of the dividend reduction before selling Curtiss-Wright stock, Gintel had violated the antifraud provisions of the law, and accordingly it suspended him from trading in securities for twenty days.

The sentence was light, no doubt in consideration of the fact that by the Wall Street standards of the time, Gintel had done nothing seriously wrong; indeed, it was his argument that his fiduciary relationship with his clients *compelled* him to act on what he knew. But the implication was far-reaching: at last the S.E.C. had affirmed that the easygoing days were over and that Rule 10B-5 now meant precisely what it said. Presumably the agency would pursue the new policy in the future—as, in fact, it did in 1966, when it brought, and for the most part eventually won, a civil complaint against Texas Gulf Sulphur and thirteen of its directors and employees charging that they had made improper use of inside information of a Canadian ore strike, in a case that shook Wall Street to its foundations. Cady, Roberts was the little-publicized forerunner of Texas Gulf, and marked a sharp turn toward stiffer S.E.C. policy on insider trading, the most ubiquitous of stock-market frauds in all countries at all times. One who immediately recognized the importance of what had happened was Keith Funston, who telephoned Cary to complain bitterly that the S.E.C. action was unnecessary and improper in view of the fact that the Stock Exchange had already disciplined Gintel on its own. There were other grumblings from Wall Street, used as it was to Washington permissiveness.

But soon the grumbling died down, and the Stock Exchange turned around and issued a strong set of new directives to its members against the use of inside information by brokers. Thus the stock market had moved in the direction of fairness for the outsider, and no pillars of finance had fallen; that is to say, regulation had worked as it is supposed to work.

The Re case and the ensuing Amex reorganization were not Cary projects. They had been initiated by his predecessors; but the success with which they were carried forward was a second feather in his cap. Many of the people involved came to believe that the rapid self-transformation of the Amex from a sort of Tammany ward in Wall Street to a reasonable approximation of a model stock exchange simply would not have happened without such a tough and conscientious regulatory climate as the new chairman was beginning to achieve. So Cary headed into his second and most challenging period at the S.E.C., the summer of the '62 market crash, the aftermath of which would give rise to his masterwork.

3

When a market panic is in progress, the S.E.C. is as helpless as a meteorologist in a storm. No power vested in it enables it to turn markets around, or cause persons and institutions that are selling stocks to change their minds and begin buying them instead. The agency's mandate, or one of its mandates, is to promote conditions that will make panics least likely to occur. When one does occur, as one did in May of 1962—and there can be little doubt that the S.E.C.'s somnolence over most of the preceding decade was one of the contributing causes—the regulators can only watch ruefully, and prepare to get back to their regulatory drawing board as soon as possible.

So it was with Cary and his S.E.C. in 1962. What comfort they could find came from the fact that the previous year they, with help from Congress, had recognized the unhealthy state of the markets and had attempted to do something about it in advance—but not far enough in advance, as things turned out. In June 1961, when Cary had been in office three months and the speculative market was near the peak of its unhealthy flowering, he told a subcommittee of the House Committee on Interstate and Foreign Commerce that he strongly favored the immediate undertaking by the S.E.C. of a comprehensive study and investigation of the adequacy of protection to investors provided by the rules of all the major stock exchanges and the over-the-counter market. There was, of course, a price tag attached. As Cary explained to the subcommittee, the S.E.C.'s current budget and manpower supply simply wouldn't support such a study: "The constant danger in our Commission is that with market activity at an all-time high, we become so overwhelmed with immediate problems that we are virtually forced to concentrate all our funds and manpower upon them and cannot do any long-range planning." He called attention to the irony of the situation—the frantic boom itself creating so much work for the regulators that they were all but prevented from exercising their regulatory function. Recognizing the need for action, in August of 1961 the House and Senate passed a measure authorizing $750,000 to the S.E.C. for a two-year Special Study of the Securities Markets—such a study as had not been undertaken for a generation—and on September 5, President Kennedy signed it into law.

Work began almost at once; a blue-ribbon staff of sixty-five was assembled, headed by Milton H. Cohen, a Chicago lawyer whom Cary imported, with the S.E.C.'s own Ralph Saul as second in command. But when the bottom fell out of the market in the spring of 1962 the Special Study could be of no immediate use because it was less than half finished.

Through that summer and fall work went on, and late in November Cary gave an indication of what was to come. The occasion he chose was a speech he gave at the annual meeting of the Investment Bankers Association, at Hollywood, Florida. Into this sun-warmed outing of fat cats only slightly thinned and chastened by the events of the past May, Cary injected a shaft of criticism like a sharp New England icicle. He spoke of the customary bland tameness of the S.E.C., so often lately looked upon as a harmless adjunct of Wall Street, and said pointedly—in allusion to an incident well remembered by all good Wall Streeters, the famous encounter of Morgan with Miss Lya Graf in 1933—"I do not intend to be a midget on anyone's lap." He singled out the New York Stock Exchange, the National Association of Securities Dealers, and the Investment Company Institute as specific organizations that had been consistently recalcitrant about regulating themselves and correcting abuses. He zeroed in on the Big Board's president, with a touch of sarcasm: "Keith Funston has framed his attitude toward self-regulation. . . . Who, he asks, can best set operating standards and determine the most effective level of service to the public? The securities industry—or the government? He did not answer that rhetorical question, but I doubt that we need to be more explicit with this distinguished audience. I can appreciate the basis for his point of view. After all, he is the head of the New York Stock Exchange." Then Cary made the most telling jab of the icicle. "Every member of the New York Stock Exchange will concede," he said, that the Exchange, for all of its ever-more-important public function, "still seems to have certain characteristics of a private club—a very good club, I might say."

It was, like the Morgan allusion, a deliberate reference to Wall Street history. On November 23, 1937, at a time when the S.E.C. was heading into its greatest confrontation with the Stock Exchange up to then on the matter of the Exchange's internal organization, William O. Douglas, then S.E.C. chairman and later a Supreme Court justice, had inflamed the Whitney Old Guard and its allies by speaking of the leading stock exchanges as "private clubs" that in the context of public marketplaces were "archaic." Their rage at the criticism had goaded that particular regiment of Old Guardsmen into excesses of intransigence that, a few months later, would be their final undoing. Cary in 1962 was a Douglas admirer of some thirty years' standing—ever since he had been a law student of the eminent jurist at Yale. His quotation from his old master was conscious and intentional and surely intended to achieve the same effect Douglas had achieved in 1937. To some extent, he was successful. Funston, commenting on the speech that evening, said curtly that he had been quoted out of context on self-regulation, and allowed himself to add that he particularly resented the private-club remark. Other sources high in the councils of the Street commented with asperity: "Such talk does no one any good at any time."

Did it in fact do the public any good this time? One might argue that it didn't, because despite their touchiness the private-club forces in Wall Street were better armed with moderation in 1962 than in 1937; they were also more sophisticated and less given to Blimpish sputtering against the plebs, and moreover, now they had no Richard Whitney to disgrace and discredit them. But the Special Study went forward in a new climate; the staff men working on it knew that their chief meant business and feared no one. For its part, Wall Street knew that it was not to be let off with a slap on the wrist. It was the climate of serious reform.

As the work drew toward a close early in 1963, Wall Street braced itself. The S.E.C. announced that the study would be released in three sections—the first on April 3, the second and third in July and August, respectively. As the date for the first installment drew near, there was such tension as had never before attended the impending release of any document from the S.E.C., or perhaps from any regulatory agency. A sharp, reactive drop in the market was feared, and elaborate precautions were taken against premature leaks of the contents of the study. At length, just after noon on the appointed day, the first part of the Special Study was released simultaneously to Congress and to the press.

The document's tone was reasonable but stern. "Grave abuses" had been found in Wall Street's operations, Cary wrote in his letter of transmittal to Congress, but the picture was "not one of pervasive fraudulent activity." He emphasized that although many specific recommendations for improvements in rules and practices are made . . . the report demonstrates that neither the fundamental structure of the securities markets nor of the regulatory pattern of the Securities Acts requires dramatic reconstruction. The report should not impair public confidence in the securities markets, but should strengthen it as suggestions for raising standards are put into practice.

Serious shortcomings are apparent and the report, of course, has concentrated on their examination and analysis. Yet it is not a picture of pervasive fraudulent activity and in this respect contrasts markedly with the hearings and findings of the early thirties preceding the enactment of the federal securities laws.

Specifically, the first installment said that insider-trading rules should be tightened; standards of character and competence for stockbrokers should be raised; further curbs should be put on the new-issues market; and S.E.C. surveillance should be extended to the thousands of small-company stocks traded over the counter that had previously been free of federal regulation. In sum, it was a fair and moderate report that Wall Street could take more or less in stride; the expected selloff of stocks did not materialize. But, of course, there was another shoe still to drop —or rather, two more shoes.

The second part of the study, duly issued in July, concentrated on stock-exchange operations, recommending that brokers' commissions on trades be lowered, that the freedom of action of specialists be drastically curtailed, and that floor traders—those exchange members who play the market with their own money on the floor itself, deriving from their membership the unique advantages over nonmembers of being at the scene of action and of paying no commissions to brokers—be legislated right out of existence through the interdiction of their activities. The third and final part, out in August, was probably the harshest of the three—and in view of political realities the most quixotic. Turning its attention to the wildly growing mutual-fund business, the S.E.C. now recommended outlawing of the kind of contract, called "front-end load," under which mutual-fund buyers agreed (and still agree) to pay large sales commissions off the top of their investment. It also accused the New York Stock Exchange of leaning toward "tenderness rather than severity" in disciplining those of its members who have broken its rules.

If the Special Study's rigor irritated much of Wall Street, its air of elaborate fairness was equally galling to some of the younger and more hot-eyed S.E.C. staff men, one of whom wrote a parody of Cary's letter of transmittal that delighted no one more than Cary himself:

> Sir:
> I have the honor to transmit the first segment of the Old Testament. The first segment includes . . . five chapters . . . and is referred to as the Torah.
> At the outset we emphasize that, although ten specific recommendations for improvements in rules and practices are made, the Torah demonstrates that neither the fundamental structure of society nor of the tribal chiefs requires drastic reconstruction. . . . The Torah should not impair public confidence in society, but should strengthen it as suggestions for raising standards are put into practice. Serious shortcomings are apparent (see Chapter III on Sodom and Gomorrah) and the Torah, of course, has concentrated on their analysis. Yet it is not a picture of pervasive sinful activity and in this respect contrasts markedly with the reign of Genghis Khan. . . .

4

All in all, the Special Study was a blueprint for a fair and orderly securities market, certainly the most comprehensive such blueprint ever drawn up, and if all of its recommendations had been promptly put into effect, what follows in this chronicle's later chapters would be a different tale. But, of course, they were not. Once the study had been published, there began the long, tedious, and often frustrating process of fashioning the recommendations into a bill and of getting the bill passed by Congress. There were meetings of S.E.C. men with representatives of the securities business; here the chance of frayed tempers was lessened by the prominent presence among the Wall Streeters of Cary's friend Amyas Ames. (Interestingly, Wall Street mounted no campaign of diehard intransigence against *any* bill such as Whitney had generaled in 1934. Three decades had passed; Wall Street and Washington had learned to live with each other, and Keith Funston, whatever his limitations, was no Richard Whitney.) Then there were endless Congressional hearings, and almost endless Congressional and bureaucratic cross-currents. The Controller of the Currency complained that the S.E.C. was trying to usurp his power over banks, Congressman John Dingell of Colorado complained that the S.E.C. was not being tough enough, and another liberal, Senator Eugene McCarthy, made a speech attacking the bill as *too* tough, only to recant later with the admission that he had misunderstood some of its provisions. The law that was finally passed—the Securities Acts Amendments of 1964—had two main sections, one extending S.E.C. jurisdiction to include some twenty-five hundred over-the-counter stocks (about as many as were traded on the New York and American exchanges combined), and the other giving the government the authority to set standards and qualifications for securities firms and their employees.

As far as it went, it was a good law, a landmark law, a signal achievement for Cary and his egghead crew. But it fell far short of what the Special Study had asked for. Not a word, for example, about mutual-fund abuses; no new restrictions on the activities of specialists; and nothing to alter the Stock Exchange's habit of "tenderness" toward its erring members. Those items had been edited out in the course of the political compromises that had made passage of the bill possible. And for Cary the greatest disappointment must surely have been that the Act left the club about as private as it had been before. The New York Stock Exchange continued to have thirty-three governors, only three of them nonmember representatives of the public; and of those three, two continued customarily to be corporation heads hardly likely to be passionate proponents of the small-investor point of view. The Exchange continued to have rules and qualifications for election to its board that stacked the deck strongly in favor of "floor" members—those who never dealt with the public and often felt little concern for its welfare—over "upstairs" members, the commission brokers who were more inclined to consider the public because their livelihood depended on it. And—bitterest pill of all—there continued to be floor traders, those specially favored Exchange members who, to Cary, were the very crux of the private-club issue.

When Cary had come to the S.E.C. there had been more than three hundred Exchange members who sometimes availed themselves of their privilege of trading for their own accounts on the floor (and who, unlike the specialists, were not even responsible for maintaining orderly markets in the stocks in which they traded). The Special Study asked that their privilege be revoked out of hand. A fierce outcry—probably the fiercest against any of the study's recommendations—arose first from the Stock Exchange and later from business in general. The sacred freedom of the marketplace was invoked, and so, at the other extreme, was the welfare of the investing public. The Exchange commissioned the management firm of Cresap, McCormick and Paget to study the problem and come up with a conclusion as to whether floor trading served the public weal or not.

Built into this situation was one of those moral absurdities that are so dismayingly common in American business life. The Stock Exchange, largely run by floor traders and their allies, had a vested interest in finding that floor traders serve a socially useful purpose. Cresap, McCormick and Paget, being on the Exchange payroll, had a vested interest in pleasing the Exchange. If a schoolmaster were to assign one of his pupils to write an essay (to be graded by the schoolmaster himself) on whether or not he was a good schoolmaster, it might be cause for merriment all around. Similar practices cause little mirth in business life because they are done all the time.

Cresap, McCormick and Paget labored mightily. One may

imagine the Exchange's gratification when the report, finished at last, concluded that abolition of floor trading would decrease liquidity and thereby introduce a dangerous new volatility into Stock Exchange trading, doing "irreparable harm" to the free and fair operation of the auction market. But perhaps the Exchange's gratification was less than complete. The magisterial authority of the report was somewhat sullied when James Dowd, head of the Cresap team that had compiled it, stated publicly that his actual finding had been that floor trading was far from an unmixed blessing for the public, and accused the Stock Exchange of having tampered with the report before publishing it. It seemed that the schoolmaster had not entirely liked the student's report on him, and so had exercised his prerogative to improve upon it. Cary wanted to hold S.E.C. hearings on the matter, but was voted down by his fellow commissioners.

At all events, the report as finally published did not seem to be a triumph of logical thought.

Essentially, what it said was that if a few insiders with a definable advantage over everybody else were to be ruled out of the stock-market game, the interests of everybody else would be irreparably harmed. It sounded like *Alice Through the Looking Glass.* But the myth of the perfectly free market is still strong, and moreover, there was a grain of truth—just a grain—in the liquidity argument in favor of floor trading. At all events, enough of the people's tribunes in Washington accepted the Stock Exchange's point of view to keep abolition of floor trading out of the 1964 Act.

Thus frustrated, Cary's S.E.C. came to achieve through administration much of what it had failed to achieve through legislation. In August 1964, just before the bill became law, it issued stringent new rules under its pre-existing authority requiring Stock Exchange members to pass a qualifying examination before being allowed to operate as floor traders, and once qualified, to hand in after each day's trading a form detailing each of their transactions. Whether through the threat of exposure, or the extra work, or just the insult to dignity implied in the test and the daily reports, the new rules had the desired discouraging effect on floor trading. "They sat us down with a pencil and a glass of water and handed us this test, right in the Board of Governors room," a floor trader cried in outrage. "Our seats were even spaced far apart, so we couldn't crib!" Shortly after imposition of the new rules, the number of floor traders on the Stock Exchange dropped from three hundred to thirty. As an important factor in the market, floor trading was finished. Cary had won through indirection.

5

On November 22, 1963, Wall Street did itself little credit. During the twenty-seven minutes between the moment when the first garbled rumors of the President's assassination in Dallas reached the Stock Exchange floor and the emergency closing of the market at 2:07 P.M., stocks declined at their fastest rate in the Exchange's 170-year history to erase $13 billion in values. For an ordinary citizen to react to news of a President's death by thinking first of protecting, if not of enlarging, his personal treasure, is perhaps defensible behavior in a materialistic civilization, though it can hardly be called attractive behavior. But for investment professionals, whose jobs have a fiduciary aspect, to react similarly is not defensible. A certain small percentage of the $13 billion lost that day apparently went into the pockets of Stock Exchange members. A subsequent S.E.C. report maintained that a few specialists—among them, those who dealt in Korvette, International Telephone and Telegraph, American Motors, and American Photocopy—not only failed to perform the stabilizing function to which they were pledged but rather acted in such a way as to aggravate the decline. Asked to comment on these findings, Funston said, "Quite humanly, some people do not perform as well as others in a crisis"—a strangely mild reaction, some felt, to the stock-market equivalent of looting during a fire.

Did the pathetic, rootless Lee Harvey Oswald really kill for once and all the spirit of a proud nation? Or had the nation, having citizens who could act as some did in Wall Street, lost all unnoticed the spirit at some earlier time? Those are questions still unanswered a decade later. For the short term, the nation and its barometer, Wall Street, chose—quite humanly—to pretend that nothing irreparable had happened, that no national wound had been opened, that everything was somehow going to be all right. On November 26, the first day of business after the assassination, the market performed its symbolic function of eliminating—literally wiping out—the damage that had been done Friday, by producing the greatest one-day rise in its history. And the new President, wanting to thank someone for this timely miracle, grabbed his telephone and congratulated Funston.

The rise continued through December; 1963 ended with the Dow at an all-time high, and when the Stock Exchange trading volume for the year was added up, it, too, came to an all-time record, topping even 1929. Then came 1964, a market year for bulls to dream about, as everyone's taxes were cut and an American space craft took the first close-up pictures of the moon and northern children went to Mississippi to spread the gospel of equal rights (three not to return) and the United States asserted itself at Tonkin Gulf ("Don't tread on me!") and people talked about what was "In" and what was "Out" and Johnson was elected President in his own right along with the most liberal Congress ever. In Wall Street's little world, meanwhile: in February, the Dow went through 900; in April, Texas Gulf Sulphur hit the biggest mine of modern times near Timmins, Ontario, touching off a wild binge of speculation along Toronto's Bay Street, and Lowell Birrell turned up in New York to face charges; in June, Funston put down a mild rebellion of Stock Exchange members against his administration, commenting jocularly that he, like a former Yale football coach, aimed to keep his constituents "sullen but not mutinous" (Exchange members quickly got in the spirit by appearing on the floor wearing buttons reading SULLEN or MUTINOUS); in August, the Securities Acts Amendments were passed, showing that God was properly in his heaven if all was not quite right with the world; in December, the Stock Exchange finally unveiled its new 900-character-a-minute ticker that could handle 10 million shares a day without delay and thus laid the ghost of the May 1962 mess; and at the end of the year it was found that so many previous Wall Street records had fallen that it was hardly worth keeping track of them any more. No one could know, of course, that 1964 would be the last year of the decade in which the market would rise in an almost straight line.

Meanwhile, Cary's day as Wall Street's conscience came to an end. He found himself less happy under Lyndon Johnson as President than he had been under Kennedy; Johnson had a habit of telephoning him from time to time about political matters, something Kennedy had never done. Moreover, in December 1963, Johnson called the heads of all the various regulatory agencies into the Cabinet Room of the White House and said to them, in connection with the role of regulation, "we are challenged . . . to concern ourselves with new areas of cooperation before we concern ourselves with new areas of control." It was a clear enough warning to slow down and not rock the boat; and Cary, over the following months, gradually made up his mind that he had been at the S.E.C. long enough. He resigned on August 20, 1964, the day the Securities Acts Amendments became law, and was succeeded by Manuel F. Cohen, who, Johnson's warning notwithstanding, would run a reasonably tough S.E.C. regime over the next five years. As for Bill Cary, gentle strongman or strong gentleman, he went back to his favorite parlay, teaching law at Columbia and practicing it one day a week in Wall Street.

6

In mid-1965 the market underwent a substantial correction—from 940 to 840 on the Dow, or just over 10 percent. It began in late spring, and President Johnson was soon on the phone again, asking Funston to do something about it. Funston may be presumed to have explained to the President that it was neither proper nor possible for him to control the course of stock prices; shortly afterward, Johnson is known to have called Cohen at the S.E.C. and asked *him* to do something. For a change, Funston and the S.E.C. had a problem in common: a President who thought the market could be made to do what he wanted it to do when he wanted it to be done.

Then on the first day of June, William McChesney Martin, Jr., once the high-level Wall Street white wing and now the respected old warhorse who had been chairman of the Federal Reserve Board since 1951, gave the principal address at a Commencement Day luncheon of the Alumni Federation at Columbia University in New York City. As boss of the Fed, Martin had long since gained a reputation as any federal administration's dour conscience in economic matters, ever counselling unpleasant restraints on money and credit while the politicians in the White House and Congress revelled in the political hay that was to be harvested from expansionist policies that promoted stock-market booms. In particular, relations between Johnson and Martin were said to have become severely strained over this very issue. Now, at Columbia, Martin preached a rip-snorting sermon of old-time economic religion. He saw, he said, "disquieting similarities between our present prosperity and the fabulous twenties," with the concomitant unsettling implication that the present boom might end as painfully as had the earlier one. "Then as now," he pointed out,

> many government officials, scholars, and businessmen were convinced that a new economic era had opened, an era in which business fluctuations had become a thing of the past, in which poverty was about to be abolished, and in which perennial economic progress and expansion were assured.

He spoke of the resolve of "responsible leaders" (for which it took no genius to read "Lyndon Johnson and his economic advisers") to prevent a repetition of 1929—"but," he went on, "while the spirit is willing, the flesh, in the form of concrete policies, has remained weak. With the best intentions, some experts seem resolved to ignore the lessons of the past." Getting down to specifics, he ticked off the similarities he saw between the present and the period just before 1929: then as now, there had been seven years of virtually uninterrupted economic progress, in each case following a period of disruption by war; then as now, world prosperity was unequally concentrated in the developed countries and, within them, in their industrialized sectors; then as now, private domestic debt was soaring, and the supply of money and bank credit was continuously growing with no increase in gold supply; then as now, international indebtedness has risen along with domestic, and the payments position of the main reserve money center—Britain in the first instance, the United States in the second—was shaky in the extreme. In sum, Martin saw the footprints of impending disaster everywhere. Toward the end, he shaded the picture somewhat by pointing out some differences between the two situations—for example, national income was better distributed now, wholesale prices were more nearly stable, stock-market credit was under better control. But even so, the old preacher, when he sat down, had painted the fires of economic Hell in vivid colors, and had warned sinners and blameless alike that they all stood on the edge of the descent.

The Dow dropped 9.81 points that very day. In the next three weeks it dropped another 60 points, to its lowest level in nearly a year. Wall Street began talking of the "Martin market." Meanwhile, Johnson did not deign to take public notice of Martin's tongue-lashing, or to alter his expansionist policies. July arrived without any apocalypse, and then the market turned around. It kept charging upward the rest of the year, passing the old Dow record of 940 in October, a month when the Stock Exchange saw its busiest week in history up to then, with almost 45 million shares changing hands. (And when had that previous record been set? At the end of October and the start of November, 1929.) The Martin market was consigned emphatically to the past—and so, it seemed, was Martin himself as a prophet.

The talk of Wall Street that glorious autumn, the last one quite so glorious for quite so many people, was of 1,000 on the Dow—that, and of the great new force in the market, the mutual funds. The magic 1,000 had not even been dreamed of in the boom of 1929, when the peak reached by the giddy bull market was a mere 381.17. Nor, indeed, had it been dreamed of in 1961, when the peak had been 735. But now the magic figure was within easy reach, mentioned on every financial page and in every market letter: in October the Dow just missed touching 960, in November it passed 960, in December it went on to 970. Just a good week or two, and Wall Street's millenium, or the nearest thing it had to one, would be achieved. . . .

And then there was the mutual-fund industry, the force that was in the process of transforming Wall Street both economically and socially, a vast new shadow of uncertain portent looming across Wall Street's sky. As recently as the end of World War II, the funds had been a trivial element in securities trading, with just over $1 billion under their management; now the figure was $35 billion and rising fast, with new money flowing into them at net annual rate of $2.4 billion; already fund trading accounted for a quarter of the value of all Stock Exchange transactions. And with such momentum, it was clear that this was no more than the beginning.

It was said repeatedly in Wall Street that autumn that at last the funds were making "people's capitalism" a reality instead of a catch phrase; through fund investment the small investor could get the expert advice and fast action his limited resources otherwise denied him. Skeptics at the S.E.C. retorted that their contractual plans with large front-end commissions, sometimes amounting to half of the initial investment, were almost fraudulently unfair to the new investor with small resources—the very person the funds were supposed to benefit most; the Wall Street wisdom replied that such contracts were necessary incentive for the salesmen who made such growth of the fund industry possible. Skeptics feared that the funds, with their unmatched power to buy or sell huge blocks of stock, had almost precisely the same muscle and incentive to manipulate the market to their own advantage, and to the disadvantage of others, that the infamous private investment pools of the nineteen twenties had had; the Wall Street wisdom replied that the securities laws, and the integrity of mutual-fund managers, made such abuses unlikely. Skeptics worried about the "redemption nightmare"—how, in a sudden market panic, mutual-fund shareholders might redeem their shares in great quantities, forcing the funds to sell portfolio holdings, leading to further redemptions, and so on down into a 1929-type pit; the Wall Street wisdom replied—most convincingly—that the funds' ability to withstand a panic had been tested in May 1962, and they had passed the test with flying colors.

The paradoxical thing was that the funds, in making the American stock market for the first time a market primarily of institutions rather than of persons, were bringing back the power and fame of individual men. The old Wall Street star system, in its heyday before 1929 and now entirely absent from Wall Street for a generation, was returning. The new stars were the portfolio managers, the men who made the investment decisions for the mutual funds. It was coming to be more and more widely believed that these decisions could not be made by committees in the traditional way of money managers; they required the speed, dash, and intuition of one man working alone on his sole responsibility.

Dangerous power, and the potential for dangerous abuses, yes. But there was a final, crushing argument in favor of the funds in 1965. With almost $2.5 billion net in new money a year coming into the stock market through the funds, wasn't the market, over the long term, bound by the law of supply and demand to go up and up and up, to everyone's benefit? Weren't the funds, so long as they thrived, a sort of guarantee of a permanent bull market?

Poor old Bill Martin! He was still living back in the nineteen thirties (the Street wisdom went) when mutual funds had scarcely existed; he simply did not comprehend this new and decisive force. Gerry Tsai, hottest of the new fund managers, predicted that the Dow would go through 1,000 before the end of 1965. He was wrong, but not by much; it was during the morning of February 9, 1966, that it touched 1,001.11, and stayed above the magic number for a matter of minutes before falling back. As things turned out, that was the peak. The Dow would not again touch the 1,000 mark during the decade, and in the fullness of time, Bill Martin would have his day.

CHAPTER V

Northern Exposure

1

By 1965, Wall Street as a social context—a place to have one's being half of one's waking weekday hours—had changed in a generation probably more than it had ever previously changed in a lifetime; but it had not had its real revolution. Like the rest of the nation, it was poised on the verge of a strange take-off into new, totally unexpected and totally uncharted directions, new ways of looking at life and dealing with it that would seem not to have come out of evolution from the past or from reaction against it, but out of the blue, as if the past did not exist.

Wall Street as a social context? Twenty paces across from building to building, some six hundred paces end to end, a few hundred acres comprising the whole district that goes by the name—Wall Street as a social context seems at first glance not to exist, not because of its limited acreage but because of its artificiality. It is a region where no one—apart from a thousand or so seamen and artists and urban hermits—really lives; where nearly half a million people arrive in the morning and depart in the afternoon, passing the hours between, unless they are so money-obsessed as to want nothing out of life but money for its own sake, with their deeper and more pleasurable thoughts playing over other scenes, other people somewhere else; a place where, at night, a few students and late-working clerks hurry down vacant streets, wary of muggers or perhaps ghosts; where work is everything, and yet no cows are milked or potatoes dug, no lampshades or shirts or steel ingots produced; where love and desire wax as often and as strongly as anywhere else, but cannot often be consummated without a trip several miles away by subway, car, train, or boat. For most of this century, the whole area south of Fulton Street has got along without a single hotel or apartment house above the marginal-slum level, and hardly anyone has ever thought twice about this strange fact.

Wall Street, then, would seem in this sense to be what the painter Willem de Kooning used to call a no-environment.

And yet, through history it has been not only a social context but a style-setting one. In the nineteen twenties, Wall Street's last great era before the present one, it was a kind of super-university as well as a marketplace. The young Corinthian of ambition, coming there in those days to learn the bond business, could get an Athenian education in manners as well as a Spartan outlook as to life strategies while meeting the people who would help him to become first rich and later influential. Walking the storied canyons, as compact as a large campus, as ingrown as any academic community, he might brush shoulders with the newly mighty or the ancient great: with J.P. Morgan himself, Wall Street's unquestioned ruler who, though born to the purple, had overcome an armed assassin with his bare hands; with Thomas W. Lamont, the ambassador of Morgan to nations that needed loans or financial advice; with Herbert Lehman, Otto Kahn, Franklin Roosevelt, Averell Harriman, Ferdinand Eberstadt, Robert Lovett, Thomas Finletter. And—provided only that his background was proper Protestant or old-family German Jewish—he might even meet some of them. Then having profited over a period of fifteen or twenty years, he would find the grandees he had met along the way easing his path into the important clubs, committees, and even councils of state. Thus Wall Street triumphed over (or perhaps profited by) its limitations of space, function, and human situation and emerged as a kind of American Mount Olympus where the gods walked, bluffed and blustered, gossiped, made mistakes, and sometimes touched aspiring mortals with financial godhood.

2

Almost all that was gone now. The reign in Wall Street of the Old Establishment and its archetypal figure, the Protestant gentleman, had long since been ended by a whole complex of forces and events, of which the paradigmatic one was the exposure of Richard Whitney. The Wall Street of the middle nineteen sixties was a far more open society where performance (a new key word in Wall Street) counted for more than education, manners, or breeding. Within limits, that is; for in the year of the Selma march and the second Civil Rights Act, the year when the Texan President of the United States cried, "We shall overcome!," there was no black member of any stock exchange and there were no more than half a dozen blacks working above the messenger-boy or clerical level in the whole nationwide securities business.

To begin with, Wall Street in the physical sense was still the national financial center only by the grace of God—or, perhaps, by that of William Zeckendorf. In the early nineteen fifties, with the tremendous midtown office-building boom, one great corporation after another moved its headquarters northward, and the money world showed signs of following. Once upon a time the corporations, credit-starved, had come willingly to the commercial and investment banks, but now with the growing wealth and power of corporations the balance had shifted. First National City Bank moved uptown, and Manufacturers Trust, soon to become Manufacturers Hanover, followed.

Wall Street took to living with its hat on, ever ready to jump in a cab and fight traffic through the tortuous streets to midtown where the big clients held court. Not a single new office building had been started in the downtown area since before the Depression, and no one wanted to be the first to build one. There was talk of the financial district becoming a ghost town.

Then the Chase Manhattan Bank, which needed a new and larger headquarters to replace its old one at 18 Pine Street, took the plunge by deciding to stay in the area—and to stay in a big way—and suddenly the tide was turned. In Zeckendorf's account, the decision was made at a meeting he attended, and dominated, at 18 Pine Street in 1954. Present, in addition to the mercurial real-estate man, were the Chase's young suzerain David Rockefeller and several of his distinguished colleagues. After making an eloquent plea for the survival of Wall Street as a financial center, Zeckendorf pointed out the window to the old Mutual Life site at Pine and Nassau, then owned by the Guaranty Trust Company, and said that it could be bought for under $5 million, but only by instant action. When the Chase men hesitated and talked about consulting their board of directors, Zeckendorf made his strongest pitch: "Your whole future is at stake, you can't wait to go to your board with a silly thing like that." According to Zeckendorf, they didn't wait; the $5-million deal was consummated over the telephone that day; there followed a rounding up of adjacent properties and a protracted game of musical chairs among the other leading banks, which, emboldened by the Chase, decided to stay, too; and the new sixty-four-story Chase Manhattan Plaza, opened in 1960, immediately became—almost as much as the Stock Exchange itself —the vital center of a firmly reconstituted Wall Street. (Zeckendorf went broke in 1966, four years before a good part of Wall Street did. Once again, he showed it the way.)

So it was, to some extent, a rebuilt Wall Street in the nineteen sixties—an old house nearly abandoned by its tenants, who had decided at the last minute to rehabilitate it instead. The new buildings were coldly and starkly modern, in contrast to the ornate palazzos and temples put up in the nineteen twenties and earlier. But the new architecture did not immediately change the style of the place.

Lunch, for example—the only time of potential leisure in Wall Street life—was still a time of rush and push and bad temper for most people. The high and mighty—and many of the not-too-high and mighty, provided only that they were white, male, presentable, and doing well enough to pay dues—had their luncheon clubs: the Down Town Association for the remnants of the old Protestant élite; the Recess, more businesslike but quite respectable, frequented by investment bankers; the huge Bankers and Lawyers for almost anyone over thirty (banker, lawyer, whatnot) who worked in the area; the Lunch Club for young men on the way up; and so on. There were still the expensive restaurants like Whyte's on Fulton Street and Oscar's Delmonico, successor to the fabled Delmonico's where the robber barons once supped in splendor. And for just about everybody else there was a wait for a counter seat, followed by a hasty bite made more urgent by the impatient presence at one's back of someone else waiting in turn, at Chock Full o' Nuts.

Most astonishing, in view of the importance of private lunch clubs in Wall Street and their all-male character, was the fact that many of the public restaurants in the area did not take advantage of the situation by encouraging women, but rather fell in line with the clubs by banning them. Whyte's maintained male exclusivity in its taproom; some other restaurants declined to serve women anywhere on the premises. Without a reservation or a long wait, a woman could scarcely get a decent lunch anywhere in the area at any price. Professionally, prejudice against women in the financial business was wide, deep, and largely unquestioned. Although women made up slightly more than half of the total Wall Street work force, there was no woman member of the New York Stock Exchange and no woman officer of a major Wall Street bank. Of the thousands of partners in brokerage firms, some sixty were women—most of them in research, the one kind of work in which by common consent Wall Street women were allowed to rise above the secretarial level. The explanation for the exception apparently lies in the fact that a research analyst works alone; that is, the ladies doing research didn't have to deal directly with men, either colleagues or customers. They could be kept hidden in a back room.

In sum, Wall Street in 1965 was still unblushingly—one might almost say innocently—male chauvinist in precisely the ways that were to be defined so acerbically later in the decade by women writers and politicians. It stood out as a last bastion of all-but-unchallenged male supremacy. It thought working women ought to be office drudges or sex objects, or both. One summer about that time, the Street took a collective notion to make a fuss over a young stenographer of exceptional physical endowments. By word of mouth it became known that she was in the habit of emerging from the subway stop at William and Wall at a certain time each day. Huge crowds began collecting to watch her appearance with cheers and whistles. Newspapers and television joined in the sport, and one day when she surfaced, there was a real mob and a near riot, as if the girl's arrival were some sort of highly charged political event. The girl herself, understandably enough, was first flattered, then abashed, and finally horrified. In a sense, this little episode *was* a political event; Wall Street was unconsciously demonstrating exactly what it thought of women and of what they were good for.

The question of why women in the United States have always been, and to a marked extent still are, considered incompetent to manage money or deal in it with men is probably one for psychology rather than for social history. The great Wall Street chronicler Henry Clews put the matter coolly: "Wall Street is not the place for a lady to find either fortune or character." Hetty Green, the nineteenth-century shipping heiress who over some forty years ran a fortune of a few million dollars, most of it tied up in trust, to more than one hundred million—and who once threatened the notoriously ruthless Collis P. Huntington with a revolver when she thought he was cheating her in a deal—stands almost alone as an American woman of unquestioned financial genius; and she achieved this standing at the cost of being generally considered a witch. Then there was the astonishing firm of Woodhull, Claflin and Company, of 44 Broad Street, *floruit circa* 1870–1872, affectionately known as "the bewitching brokers," consisting of Victoria Claflin Woodhull, free-love advocate and later free-lance Presidential candidate, and her almost equally astonishing sister Tennessee (later Tennie C.) Claflin. The sisters made a big stir and apparently even some money in the harsh post-Civil War Wall Street, but they were scarcely financial geniuses; they and their firm were protégés of the septuagenarian financier Cornelius Vanderbilt, whose mistress Tennie had briefly been. Perhaps the key, or one key, to the genesis of the lasting prejudice is to be found in the Hetty–Huntington episode: Americans of both sexes have always tended subconsciously to equate financial deals with physical fighting—the latter a form of competition in which the hardest-shelled feminist admits that women are usually ill-equipped to compete equally with men.

At any rate, women in the middle nineteen sixties still tended to accede to the view that they could not or should not compete with men in financial affairs. Emancipated, highly competent and successful women in other fields—the arts, publishing, real estate, retail trade—still found it consistent with their self-esteem to affect a coy bewilderment when conversation turned to the stock market or the intricacies of finance. In Wall Street, women analysts accepted with little protest being excluded or jostled at lunch, and signed their research reports "Jones" or "Smith" rather than "Mary Jones" or "Susan Smith," so that their readers would not discount the reports. Wall Street feminists discussed their views only in private. "Up against the Wall Street!" a women's-lib group would snarl later in the decade, but not yet in 1965.

Blacks simply did not exist. The notion of applying for professional-level jobs in Wall Street did not even occur to them, and the concept of business firms conducting professional training programs as a social duty had not yet gained a foothold, either in Wall Street or in the nation. Even as messengers bearing securities, blacks were not much to be seen; the financial district had no "race problem" just because, like so many Northern cities a century before, it still had hardly any blacks.

3

In political ideology, by contrast, Wall Street was now somewhat more liberal—or less reactionary—than previously. The day of the Liberty League was over; there were no more J.P. Morgans requiring aides to screen from their eyes all newspapers containing photographs of Roosevelt so as to protect the master's blood pressure. Liberal Democrats, many of them Jewish, were about as common as conservative Republicans in the positions of power; now, one of them, Howard Stein of Dreyfus Corporation, would be the chief fund-raiser for Eugene McCarthy's 1968 Presidential campaign. This was not entirely a matter of high-mindedness, however. With the federal government in generally liberal Democratic hands there was little to be gained by conservative intransigence on the old issues—balancing the budget, federal meddling in business, high costs of welfare and social security. Such intransigence now led only to nasty rows with Washington officials, and those, in turn, could lead only to more regulation, bad publicity, and loss of the confidence of customers. Downtown, Colonel Blimpism no longer paid.

Many of the men putting together the stock market's new darlings, the conglomerates, were liberals—and, of course, it didn't hurt a Wall Street analyst or salesman to be on close and sympathetic terms with such men. There were even former Communists high in the financial game. Much of Wall Street had long had a surprisingly tolerant attitude toward Communism, derived from a perspective that put any alien ideology so far beyond the pale as to make it an object of exotic interest. In the early postwar years a young man out of Columbia and the Army went to work for a long-established Wall Street firm; assigned to the library, he took to browsing in the firm's extensive collection of books on Marxism and Communism; an un-scheduled conversion took place, and the young man left the library, and Wall Street, presumably intending to join the Party.

Bart Lytton, born in New Castle, Pennsylvania, in upper middle-class circumstances, came of age in the Depression, joined the W.P.A. Federal Theatre Project, and became a Communist. His proper mother wrote him, "You who were raised in country clubs, you who used to buy a dozen golf balls and two tennis racquets at a time, you who could have been governor of Pennsylvania—you want to run off and join the radicals. Well, go eat bread with your comrades then." After a time he left the Party, but without totally and violently rejecting its beliefs as so many renegades did. In 1939 he went to California to become a screenwriter and public-relations man, and in 1948 he moved into the savings-and-loan business. By 1965 his Lytton Financial Corporation had grown so fantastically that it was among the five biggest savings-and-loan companies in the country; and Bart Lytton, with hundreds of millions of his own, was describing himself without refutation as "the most successful businessman in this decade in the United States." He served for four years as finance chairman of the California Democratic Central Committee, backed John F. Kennedy with a $200,000 contribution in 1960, was a major benefactor of local art museums and a founder of one, and decorated his company's annual reports with pictures of himself with Elizabeth Taylor, Levi Eshkol, and Hubert Humphrey. He boasted that he considered a morning wasted when he didn't wake up $500,000 to $1,000,000 richer than the night before. The very next year, 1966, his headlong business style would backfire and his company collapse into reorganization; meanwhile, though, the Communist Party of the United States had apparently been for him a far more effective academy of commerce than the Harvard School of Business Administration is for most.

The sudden youth explosion that was to overtake Wall Street life, and most particularly the management of money, had not occurred yet, but its fuse was burning short. It had an easily found sociological cause. For almost a generation, from the 1929 crash to the bull market of the nineteen fifties, young men of talent and ambition grew up thinking of Wall Street as anathema and did not go to work there, leaving a vacuum when the Wall Street leaders who had started before 1929 began to retire and the positions of power and responsibility to fall open. (Between 1930 and 1951, for example, only eight persons were hired to work on the New York Stock Exchange trading floor.) The positions were being filled, *faute de mieux*, by the soon-to-be-celebrated sideburned young hotshots of the late nineteen sixties, most of whom had started working in Wall Street after 1960.

Indeed, by 1969 half of Wall Street's salesmen and analysts would be persons who had come into the business since 1962, and consequently had never seen a bad market break. Probably the prototypical portfolio hotshot of 1968 entered Wall Street precisely in 1965. Of course, he was no hotshot in 1965. He was a young man with conservative clothes and neatly trimmed hair who had a degree from a business school or perhaps only a liberal arts college, and who, assessing his chances for a quick fortune, had hit on the business of picking stocks for mutual funds as a good bet and accepted a starting salary of perhaps $7,500. Portfolio management had the appeal of sports —that one cleanly wins or loses, the results are measurable in numbers; if one's portfolio was up 30 or 50 percent for a given year one was a certified winner, so recognized and so compensated regardless of whether he was popular with his colleagues or had come from the right ancestry or the right side of the tracks. Again as in sports, the winner became an instant star, his name known and revered in Wall Street. In 1965 the gunslinger-to-be was only a brisk young man poring over reports in a bullpen or a tiny back office. In three years his salary might quintuple or he might be raking off a fat percentage of his portfolio gains; his sideburns would be longer and his shirts louder, and he would be the new characteristic figure in a new Wall Street. But not yet.

4

The loss of power and influence of the Old Establishment was partly its own fault. Morally and intellectually, it seemed to be in decline. That keen observer of Anglo-Saxon Protestant manners and morals, the writer Louis Auchincloss—who kept in touch with his fictional material by maintaining a lively Wall Street law practice—found in the nineteen sixties that the attitude of the standard bearers downtown toward ethical niceties was largely one of indifference—of "everybody else is cutting corners, why not us?" A young financial lawyer in Wall Street then was making his way rapidly upward in the hierarchy of respected firms while leaving behind him a trail of court judgments resulting from passing bad checks. Apart from the victims, nobody—including the eminent and unassailably respectable chiefs of the young man's firms—cared to blow the whistle. In the crush of business resulting from the stock-market boom, the pressure for legal manpower was such that the chiefs needed to hang onto a young man of talent, and to promote him, even though he happened to be a bit of a fraud.

Again, there is a sad and illuminating story of a Wall Streeter of those years—a man so strictly and traditionally conscientious that, after his father's death, he had paid off his father's debts even though he was not legally responsible for them and had received no inheritance out of which to pay them. This paragon of Puritan morality, having learned that another member of his firm had done something dishonest, was so disturbed by the discovery and its implications that he landed on a psychiatrist's couch. The psychiatrist's treatment consisted of pragmatic reassurance: "Don't worry," he told the troubled patient, "it doesn't matter. Nobody will say anything." And nobody did —to the painful disappointment of the patient, whose cure consisted of becoming disillusioned with his class.

It was open season now on Anglo-Saxon Protestants even when they stayed plausibly close to the straight and narrow. Their sins, or alleged sins, which had once been so sedulously covered up by press and even government, were now good politics for their opponents. They had become useful as scapegoats—as was perhaps shown in the poignant personal tragedy of Thomas S. Lamont. Son of Thomas W. Lamont, the Morgan partner who may well have been the most powerful man in the nation in the nineteen twenties, "Tommy" Lamont was an amiable, easygoing man. He was a high officer of the Morgan Guaranty Trust Company and a director of Texas Gulf Sulphur Company, and on the morning—April 16, 1964—when Texas Gulf publicly announced its great Timmins ore strike, he notified one of his banking colleagues of the good news at a moment when, although he had reason to believe that it was public knowledge, by the S.E.C.'s lights in fact it was not. The colleague acted quickly and forcefully on Lamont's tip, on behalf of some of the bank's clients; then, almost two hours later, when news of the mine was unquestionably public, Lamont bought Texas Gulf stock for himself and his family.

He thought he had done nothing wrong; indeed, inasmuch as he had known all about Timmins several days earlier and had taken no advantage of the fact by either word or deed, he had clearly resisted a powerful temptation to wrongdoing. But the S.E.C—promulgating an entirely new doctrine of insider trading to the effect that fiduciaries with inside information were required not only to wait until after public announcement before acting on it, but then to wait an additional "reasonable amount of time"—accused him of violating the securities laws. In so doing, it lumped him with flagrant violators, some Texas Gulf geologists and executives who had bought stock on the strength of their knowledge of Timmins days and months earlier, and who made up the bulk of the S.E.C.'s landmark insider case of 1966.

Could it be, then, that the S.E.C. knew well enough that it had a weak case against Lamont, and dragged him into the suit purely for the publicity value of his name? The outlandishness of the charge against him, and the frequency with which his name appeared in newspaper headlines about the case, suggest such a conclusion. At all events, the publicity and attendant opprobrium were too much for Lamont, and soon after the S.E.C. charges his health went into a decline. In the end, he, almost alone among the defendants, was vindicated through the dropping of all charges against him. Too late, however, to do him any good. The vindication came after his death, to which he was hounded, some of his friends maintained, by the ruthlessness and irresponsibility of bureaucrats who sacrificed him to get public attention to their cause—made him, because of his name and lineage, a wholly involuntary martyr to the public interest.

Even in strictly religious terms, it was hardly surprising that Protestantism had lost its dispensation as Wall Street's established church. The faith itself, in Wall Street's part of the country, had largely lost its traditional character. The Protestant church in New York City was becoming a black church. Shortly before 1960 Negroes had for the first time become a majority of the city's Protestants, and by 1965 they amounted to six out of ten. White membership was declining rapidly, and the various Protestant churches in the area, responding to their new constituency, were abandoning their old role of serving as the austere and worldly conscience of economic rulers to become agencies to fill the spiritual, and sometimes the material, needs of the culturally and economically deprived. Was this deeply integrated and sometimes activist church, then, the one for virtually all-white and surely nonactivist Wall Street? Apparently not.

The new downtown religion was liberal Judaism. German Jews had been among the founding fathers of Wall Street; the Seligmans, the Lehmans, the Goldmans and the Sachs had founded American investment banking before even Pierpont Morgan's bulky presence had arrived on the scene, and from the time at the turn of the century when Kuhn, Loeb had fought Morgan to a standoff in the Northern Pacific affair, the Jews of Wall Street had enjoyed recognition as equal to the Yankees in both prestige and power. But those Jews had tended to be sedulous apes; awed and inspired by the new nation in which they or their fathers were immigrants, inclined to put Old Europe behind them except in matters of business, they became more Yankee than the Yankees, more Protestant than the Protestants, and thus did little to change the atmosphere. Moreover, with a few exceptions (like Paul M. Warburg, the Kuhn, Loeb partner who was virtually founder of the Federal Reserve System) they were by common consent excluded from the formal and official Wall Street leadership, and it went without saying that they never assumed the leadership of any but Jewish firms. In the nineteen sixties a great change came. By that time, some of the staid old Jewish firms had literally Protestantized themselves; their Anglophilia and Yankeephilia had reached the point where many of their partners and some of their senior partners were Protestants, not by conversion but by birth. Meanwhile, a newer strain of Jews, most of them more recent immigrants than the Germans and with origins in Eastern Europe, were taking over Wall Street leadership in a way that their predecessors had never aspired to. Even at the conservative New York Stock Exchange, the power struggle had largely come down to an armed truce between Jews, Catholics, and Protestants; President Funston, a Yankee Protestant if there ever was one, was widely thought of by the membership as a compromise candidate acceptable—like a Liberal Party member—precisely because his constituency was weak.

The change brought with it a new ethical climate. The new Jewish men of power were not temperamentally religious any more than the old Protestant ones had been, but they, like the Protestants, brought with them a certain culture and set of attitudes and responses and outlook on life, which became the new climate of Wall Street. It was a style a little less dour—not less materialistic or grasping but more candid and humorous about the materialism as well as the manner; a style not less interested in the trappings and icons of culture, but undoubtedly by tradition more capable of enjoying culture; a style with more of a bent for justice and less of an acceptance of caste. It was a style neither more nor less honest than that of the Protestants, but probably less inclined to be hypocritical on the subject. And it probably was—although this would be hard to prove —a style more inclined to dash and daring as opposed to respectability, less concerned about preservation of values and appearances and more sympathetic toward speculation and outright gambling. Our story of Wall Street from 1965 to 1970 involves a number of Jewish plungers, sometimes pitted directly against Old Protestant conservators.

5

Into this fast-changing, yet still relatively complacent, Wall Street of mid-decade there came, in June, 1965, a thunderbolt from the north.

The Texas Gulf ore strike at Timmins in early 1964 had dramatically shown Canada to United States investors as the new Golconda. Here was a great, undeveloped land with rich veins of dear metals lying almost untouched under its often-frozen soil; with stocks in companies that might soon be worth millions selling for nickels or dimes on Bay Street, the Wall Street of Toronto; and with no inconvenient Securities and Exchange Commission on hand to monitor the impulsiveness of promoters or cool the enthusiasm of investors. American money flowed to Bay Street in a torrent in 1964 and early in 1965, sending trading volume there to record heights and severely overtaxing the facilities of the Toronto Stock Exchange. Copies of *The Northern Miner,* authoritative gossip sheet of the Canadian mining industry, vanished from south-of-the-border newsstands within minutes of their arrival; some Wall Street brokers, unwilling to wait for their copies, had correspondents in Toronto telephone them the *Miner*'s juicier items the moment it was off the press. And why not? Small fortunes were being made almost every week by quick-acting U.S. investors on new Canadian ore strikes, or even on rumors of strikes. It was as if the vanished western frontier, with its infinite possibilities both spiritual and material, had magically reappeared, with a new orientation ninety degrees to the right of the old one.

The Canadian economy in general was growing fast along with the exploitation of the nation's mineral resources, and among the Canadian firms that had attracted the favorable attention of U.S. investors, long before 1964, was Atlantic Acceptance Corporation, Ltd., a credit firm, specializing in real-estate and automobile loans, headed by one Campbell Powell Morgan, a former accountant with International Silver Company of Canada, with an affable manner, a vast fund of ambition, and, it would appear later, a marked weakness for shady promoters and a fatal tendency toward compulsive gambling. As early as 1955, two years after he had founded Atlantic, Morgan saw the possibilities of raising capital for expansion in Wall Street—and elements in Wall Street saw the possibilities of making profits in Toronto. Morgan was an acquaintance as well as a countryman of Alan T. Christie, a Canadian-born partner in the small but rising Wall Street concern of Lambert and Company. The founder and head of this firm—whose members liked to describe it as a *"banque d'affaires,"* and to pronounce its name the French way, "Lombaire"—was Jean Lambert, a suave gentleman in his thirties, born and educated in France, who had come to America and married Phyllis Bronfman, daughter of the president of Seagram's. A divorce had ensued, but $1 million of Bronfman money had stayed in Lambert and Company, whose founder liked to present himself as an international statesman of finance —as a delegate to the celebrated Bretton Woods monetary conference of 1944 (where he had, in fact, served, though not as a delegate but as a translator), and as the architect of a "Lambert plan" for international monetary reform. At Christie's recommendation, Lambert and Company in 1954 put $300,000 into Atlantic Acceptance, thereby becoming Atlantic's principal U.S. investor and chief booster in Wall Street and other points south.

The years passed and Atlantic seemed to do well, its annual

profits steadily mounting along with its volume of loans. Naturally, it constantly needed new money to finance its continuing expansion. Lambert and Company undertook to find the money in the coffers of U.S. investing institutions; and Jean Lambert, backed by Christie, had just the air of European elegance and respectability, spiced with a dash of mystery, to make him perfectly adapted for the task of impressing the authorities of such institutions. Characteristically, Lambert decided to start at the top. In 1959, his partner Christie called on Harvey E. Molé, Jr., head of the U.S. Steel and Carnegie Pension Fund, probably the largest institution of its kind in the world at that time, with assets of more than $1.6 billion. Christie made the pitch for the Steel fund to invest in Atlantic. Molé, born in France but out of Lawrenceville and Princeton, was no ramrod-stiff traditional trustee type; rather, he fancied himself, not without reason, as a money manager with a component of dash and daring. Atlantic Acceptance was just the kind of relatively far-out, yet apparently intrinsically sound, investment that appealed to Molé's Continental sporting blood. The Steel fund took a bundle of Atlantic securities, including subordinate notes, convertible preferred stock, and common stock, amounting to nearly $3 million. The following year, Lambert and Company—again starting at the top—approached the Ford Foundation, far and away the largest institution of *its* kind. The foundation's investment men made a check (perhaps not too careful a check) on Atlantic with the company's management, its competitors, and various Canadian banks; apparently the findings were favorable, and the Ford Foundation took a good-sized plunge in Atlantic debt securities.

After that, it was easy. With the kings of U.S. institutional investing taken into camp, the courtiers could be induced to surrender virtually without a fight. Now Lambert and Company could say to the fund managers, "If this is good enough for U.S. Steel and the Ford Foundation, how can you lose?" "We were all sheep," one of them would admit, sheepishly, years later. Before the promotion was finished, the list of U.S. investors in Atlantic had become a kind of Burke's Peerage of American investing institutions: the Morgan Guaranty and First National City Banks; the Chesapeake and Ohio Railway; the General Council of Congregational Churches; Pennsylvania and Princeton Universities (perhaps not coincidentally, the man in charge of Princeton's investment program was Harvey Molé); and Kuhn, Loeb and Company, which, to the delight of Lambert, gave the enterprise its valuable imprimatur by taking over as agent for the sale of Atlantic securities in the United States. Perhaps the final turn of the screw, as the matter appears in hindsight, is the fact that the list of Atlantic investors eventually included Moody's Investors Service, whose function is to produce statistics and reports designed specifically to help people avoid investment pitfalls of the sort of which Atlantic would turn out to be an absolutely classic case.

But nobody knew that then. Indeed, in the early nineteen sixties Atlantic seemed to exceed the wildest hopes with its almost unbelievable rate of growth. Its reported sales for 1960 were $24.6 million, for 1961 $45.6 million, for 1962 $81 million, for 1963 $176 million—a consistent improvement approaching 100 percent a year. The growth rate itself might well have been interpreted as a danger signal. In the loan business, the easiest way to expand faster than your competitors is by consistently making loans that they are unwilling to make because they consider them unsound. In fact, that was precisely what Atlantic was doing, intentionally and systematically. But the presence of the Steel fund, the Ford Foundation, and the rest on the investor list served as an effective smoke screen; any cautious critics were easily dismissed as flatulent grumps; and the bandwagon rolled on.

Late in 1964, Atlantic, hungry for capital as always, sold more stock; and early in 1965, Kuhn, Loeb helped place $8.5 million more in Atlantic long-term debt with U.S. institutional investors. By this time, Lambert and Company's stake in Atlantic amounted to $7.5 million. The firm's commitment was a do-or-die matter; it would stand or fall with Atlantic. Moreover, it is now clear that by this time Morgan and his associates were engaged in conducting a systematic fraud on a pattern not wholly dissimilar to that of Ponzi or Ivar Kreuger. Atlantic would use the new capital flowing from Wall Street to make new loans that its major officers knew to be unsound; the unsoundness would be deliberately camouflaged in the company's reports, in order to mislead investors; the spurious growth represented by the ever-increasing loans would lure in new investment money, with which further unsound loans would be made; and so on and on. Morgan had taken to intervening personally each year in the work of his firms' accountants—some of whom were willing enough to commit fraud at their client's request—to ensure that a satisfactory rise in profits was shown through overstatement of assets and understatement of allowances for bad debts. For 1964, it would come out later, Atlantic's announced $1.4 million profit, under proper accounting procedure, should have been reported as a *loss* of $16.6 million.

The game, like all such games, could not go on forever. By early 1965, suspicion of Atlantic's operations was in the wind. In April, the New York Hanseatic Corporation, a $12-million investor in Atlantic paper, asked the Toronto-Dominion Bank for a credit check on Atlantic. The response—which in retrospect appears dumbfounding—was favorable. In fact, if the bank had been able to penetrate the mystifications of Powell's accountants, it would have discovered that Atlantic was by that time actually insolvent. For several years, at the instigation of some of the various international schemers for whom Morgan had a fatal affinity, the firm had been increasingly involved in a desperate and doomed plunge in a shaky venture far from home: between 1963 and early 1965 it had committed more than $11 million to the Lucayan Beach, a hotel with a gambling casino attached, on balmy, distant Grand Bahama Island. A Royal Commission would later describe the investment as "the last throw of the dice to retrieve all the losses created by years of imprudence and impropriety." But the Lucayan Beach venture, managed incompetently and fraudulently, did not flourish, and the losses were not to be retrieved.

The ingenuity with which Atlantic's desperation was concealed from the investing public, even from its usually most knowledgeable sectors, is indicated by the fact that during the last part of May, only three weeks before the bubble finally burst, the Madison Fund, a good-sized U.S. investing institution, bought one last million dollars' worth of Atlantic paper through Kuhn, Loeb. On June 14, the Toronto-Dominion Bank abruptly refused to honor $5 million in Atlantic checks covering notes that had matured. This was technical failure; but worse was to come. That same day, it became known that forty-one Wall Street brokers had just received orders for various stocks closely connected with Atlantic, on the letterhead of "Sassoon's Far Eastern Trust, Ltd., of Nassau, Bahamas," and accompanied by ostensibly certified checks amounting to nearly $6 million, drawn on the same bank. The certification, however, was faked, and the bank on which the checks were drawn was nonexistent. Later it would emerge that this strange affair was not Morgan's doing but part of a Byzantine scheme hatched by one of his unreliable associates; but the untimely whiff of fraud did nothing to restore confidence in Atlantic in its hour of need. More notes were called, and as a result, on June 15, the firm required $25 million to cure the default. Of course, it neither had nor could raise such a sum.

So the game was up at last. Waves of shock and bewilderment ran through the U.S. investment Establishment. There were frantic thrashings for several subsequent days, including the dispatching by Kuhn, Loeb to Toronto of a member of the firm with the resounding name of Thomas E. Dewey, Jr., son of the former New York State governor and Presidential candidate. To no avail. Atlantic shortly went into formal receivership, leaving the American Burke's Peerage, which seemed to have been gulled in a way that would do discredit to a shrewd schoolboy investor, shorn of a sum that was at first estimated to be around $50 million.

The repercussions of the failure, the greatest in Canada's history, were wide, deep, and long-lasting. Shortly after Atlantic's default, a confidential report prepared for the Montreal Trust Company, Atlantic's receiver in bankruptcy, began to reveal just how unsound the whole Atlantic operation had been. "There is a paucity of credit information," the report said, "and, as far as we were able to ascertain, no real financial control. . . . There appears to have been no reporting procedure. . . . On real estate, machinery, and other types of fixed-asset loans, apparently no appraisals were obtained and there was no evidence on file of the value of loan collateral. . . . In sum, procedures considered necessary in the conduct of a financial business were missing." At the end of 1965, the Ford Foundation bit the bullet and formally wrote off $4,775,000 of its Atlantic investment as worthless; it continued to carry on its books another $2 million of Atlantic paper that showed little promise of turning out to be any better. The Steel fund revealed that it held $2.25 million in Atlantic notes, 12,000 shares of common stock, and $125,000 in convertible preferred shares. Connecticut General Life Insurance was stuck with $2 million in notes and $240,000 in convertible preferred, Massachusetts Mutual Life with $4.446 million in notes. And so it went. An officer of the First National City, still another loser on Atlantic, explained with poignant rue that the whole operation had had "an aura of respectability." Brave and candid, or simply unguarded, the comment pointed the moral. The Old Establishment of U.S. investing had fallen for its own fading mystique. Believing, with tribal faith that can only be called touching, that no member of the club could make a serious mistake, the members had followed each other blindly into the crudest of traps, and had paid the price for their folly. As for the unfortunate Lambert and Company, it simply vanished; one week its Wall Street office was present and active, the next week it was gone.

But the Atlantic collapse meant more than that. For the Canadian economy as a whole it meant the threat of a credit panic, and in the first two months after the default, the Bank of Canada was forced to increase the national money supply by a billion dollars to avert one. The northward flow of U.S. funds, already slowed by President Johnson's balance-of-payments plea in February 1965, became a trickle. In the autumn of 1965 there was a government crackdown on the casual ways of Bay Street. A Royal Commission of Ontario was formed to look into the entire Atlantic matter. In May 1966—a time when the Canadian economy was still suffering from the Atlantic shock waves—Morgan, dying of leukemia, testified dramatically to the Commission from his deathbed. The Commission reported later that his testimony had been given "under circumstances in which the physical weakness of the witness was a painful and pervasive fact," and that he had complained about colleagues of his who had their "fingers in the till," neither admitting nor denying his own complicity in fraud. He died that October, but the Commission's work went on; at last, in December 1969, it issued its final report, in four volumes comprising 2,700 pages. Among its findings and conclusions were that the misrepresentations in Atlantic's financial statements had been "deliberate, designed to encourage the purchase of shares and notes in the company"; that "the activities of C.P. Morgan, prosecuted with considerable energy and ingenuity as they were, have been shown to be dishonest"; and that the loss to Atlantic's investors in the debacle had been not $50 million as originally estimated, but in excess of $65 million. In the last analysis, much of that had come not out of the pockets of millionaire professional investors, but out of those of ordinary shareholders in mutual funds and insurance companies, donors to leading universities, pensioners of U.S. Steel, and recipients of the largesse of the Ford Foundation.

The sad affair of Atlantic, its effects spreading southward like the frigid Canadian air that often suffuses much of the United States in winter, was a foretaste of the homegrown bad weather soon to appear in Wall Street. A smooth operator with a streak of the gambler; a company more interested in attracting investors than in making real profits; the resort to tricky accounting; the eager complicity of long-established, supposedly conservative investing institutions; the desperation plunge in a gambling casino at the last minute; the need for massive central-bank action to localize the disaster; and finally, reform measures instituted too late—we will see all of these elements reproduced with uncanny faithfulness in United States financial scandals and mishaps later in the nineteen sixties. Thus the Atlantic episode neatly divides Wall Street's drama of the decade, ending the first act, and beginning the second and climactic one.

CHAPTER VI

The Birth of
Go-Go

1

When *Webster's Third New International Dictionary* was published in 1961, it defined the term "go-go" as "a vine found in the Philippines," or, alternatively, as "a Bantu people." The *Random House Dictionary of the English Language*, in 1966, ignored these arcane meanings, and under the entry "go-go" referred the reader to the phrase "à gogo," which it defined, "as much as you like; to your heart's content; galore (used esp. in the names of cabarets, discothèques, etc.)." The *American Heritage Dictionary of the English Language*, which appeared in 1969, provided the term with by far the most ancient and scholarly provenance to that date. "À go-go," it said, means "in a fast and lively manner; freely. Chiefly used as an adverb: *dancing à go-go*; also used as an adjective: an *à gogo* dance." It went on to explain that the phrase was a French one meaning, in France, "in a joyful manner," and that it was probably derived from the Old French word "gogue," merriment or hubbub, which also gave rise to the English (originally, Middle English) "agog."

Sometime in the middle nineteen sixties, probably in late

1965 or early 1966, the expression as used in the United States came to have a connotation that the dictionaries would not catch up with until after the phenomenon that it described was already over. The term "go-go" came to designate a method of operating in the stock market—a method that was, to be sure, free, fast, and lively, and certainly in some cases attended by joy, merriment, and hubbub. The method was characterized by rapid in-and-out trading of huge blocks of stock, with an eye to large profits taken very quickly, and the term was used specifically to apply to the operation of certain mutual funds, none of which had previously operated in anything like such a free, fast, or lively manner.

The mood and the method seem to have started, of all places, in Boston, the home of the Yankee trustee. The handling of other people's money in the United States began in Boston, the nation's financial center until after the Civil War. Trusteeship is by its nature conservative—its primary purpose being to conserve capital—and so indeed was the type of man it attracted in Boston. Exquisitely memorialized in the novels of John P. Marquand, for a century the Boston trustee was the very height of unassailable probity and sobriety: his white hair neatly but not too neatly combed; his blue Yankee eyes untwinkling, at least during business hours; the lines in his cheeks running from his nose to the corners of his mouth forming a reassuringly geometric isoceles triangle; his lips touching liquor only at precisely set times each day, and then in precise therapeutic dosage; his grooming impeccable (his wildest sartorial extravagance a small, neat bow tie) with a single notable exception—that he wore the same battered gray hat through his entire adult life, which, so life-preserving was his curriculum, seldom ended before he was eighty-five or ninety.

And yet, the Boston trustee was not unimaginative; he was an outward-looking Athenian, not the ingrowing Spartan he was often accused of being. As early as 1830, Justice Samuel Putnam of the Supreme Judicial Court of Massachusetts wrote in a famous opinion,

> All that can be required of a Trustee to invest is that he conduct himself faithfully and exercise a sound discretion. He is to observe how men of prudence, discretion, and intelligence manage their own affairs, not in regard to speculation, but in regard to permanent disposition of their funds, considering the probable income, as well as the probable safety of the capital to be invested.

The Boston-born "prudent man rule," as it came to be called, represented a crucial liberalization of the law governing trustees, and such a durable one that it is still their basic guide almost a century and a half later. In 1924, Boston was the site of another epoch-making innovation in American money management, the founding of the first two mutual funds, Massachusetts Investors Trust and State Street Investing Company. And then, in the years after World War II, the go-go cult quietly originated hard by Beacon Hill under the unlikely sponsorship of a Boston Yankee named Edward Crosby Johnson II.

Although never a trustee by profession, Johnson was almost the Boston-trustee type personified. In the nineteen sixties, which corresponded roughly with *his* sixties, he was a spry, smallish, clean-cut man, proud of the hole-in-one he once made at La Gorce Country Club; in orthodox trustee style, he favored a battered hat and a bow tie. He seemed much younger than he was, as if a gentle upbringing and a comfortable life had sheltered him from the whips and scorns of time. He said "annathing" and "annabody" in the charming accent of his breed, but what he said was packed with ore; his talk tumbled out enthusiastically, yet he seemed inarticulate because his mind encompassed more than his tongue could often convey.

He was born in a Boston suburb in 1898, the son of a partner in the old Boston dry-goods firm of C.F. Hubby, and a descendant of John Johnson, a Puritan freeman in seventeenth-century Massachusetts. He was named for another ancestor who had been a Union officer in the Civil War. He went to Milton Academy and then, all but inevitably, to Harvard; he married another Brahmin, his second cousin Elsie Livingston. In deference to his father's wish that he become a lawyer, he went on to Harvard Law and then joined the proper Boston law firm of

Ropes and Gray. He stayed there for fourteen years, from 1925 to 1939, specializing in corporate reorganizations and mergers. But all the while his heart belonged to the stock market.

The market bug first bit him in 1924 when he read a serialization in the old *Saturday Evening Post* of Edwin Lefèvre's "Reminiscences of a Stock Market Operator," the story of the career of the famous speculator Jesse Livermore. "I'll never forget the thrill," he told a friend almost a half century later. "Everything was there, or else implied. Here was the picture of a world in which it was every man for himself, no favors asked or given. You were what you were, not because you were a friend of somebody, but for yourself. And Livermore—what a man, always betting his whole wad! A sure system for losing, of course, but the point was how much he loved it. Operating in the market, he was like Drake sitting on the poop of his vessel in a cannonade. Glorious!" Under the influence of Lefèvre's book, this young romantic of commerce, this privileged young man in danger of becoming what he became because he had always been a friend or relative of somebody, began playing the market in his spare time between his legal chores; his colleagues teased him for keeping stock-market charts on the walls of his law office. He lost along with everyone else in the 1929 crash, but, unlike many, survived the setback and, in the following years, as the market sank into the abyss, he scored his first coup. "I'd noticed a certain group of signs that, when they came together, meant a big bust was ahead," Johnson recounted long afterward. "I saw the signs, and I anticipated the 1931–1932 drop. I sat on my little poop-deck potting away, and kept my capital intact. God, it was glorious!"

In 1935, Johnson became counsel for Incorporated Investors, a small, old-line Boston mutual-fund firm. Gradually, he was drawn by his predilection deeper into finance and further from the law. In 1939 he left Ropes and Gray to become full-time vice-president and treasurer of Incorporated Investors. Four years later, he was offered the opportunity to take over Fidelity Fund, another Boston mutual-fund operation that then managed only the unimpressive total of $3 million—and Johnson had an investment company of his very own. It is particularly significant, in the light of subsequent events, that the man who turned the Fidelity organization over to him refused to take a nickel for it, in keeping with the traditional Boston concept of a trusteeship as a sacred charge rather than a vested interest to be bought and sold.

The notion of a mutual fund as a trust was deeply ingrained in State Street at the time, and would remain so until about 1955 —this in spite of the fact that a mutual fund is actually not a trust at all. A trust is a property interest held under law by one person for the benefit of another—typically, an inheritance held by an older person for the benefit of a younger person who is the heir. The beneficiary has not chosen the trustee, or indeed the situation of trusteeship, and may have no control over either one. In the case of a mutual fund, on the other hand, the share owner, or beneficiary, has chosen the fund he wants to invest in and has thereby granted the fund's managers the right to reinvest his money, for a fee. The managers of the fund are not trustees but investment advisers, and are therefore bound not by the laws governing trustees but rather by those governing investment advisers. Nevertheless, before 1955—in Boston and elsewhere—they *felt* like trustees. Or most of them did. Edward Crosby Johnson II, for all of his trustee-like ways, clearly had a speculative background and temperament; after all, his stock-market idol was one of the master speculators. Right from the start, his approach to investing Fidelity funds was an unorthodox one that he would later describe in the following characteristically picturesque terms: "We didn't want to feel that we were married to a stock when we bought it. You might say that we preferred to think of our relationship to it as 'companionate marriage.' But that doesn't go quite far enough, either. Possibly now and again we liked to have a 'liaison'—or even, very occasionally, 'a couple of nights together.' "

His maverick operations as head of Fidelity, while they fell far short of creating a scandal on State Street, nevertheless caused a certain amount of talk there during the nineteen forties. What in Tophet had come over Edward Johnson, a good sound Boston and Harvard man if there ever was one? But what he was doing then was only the beginning, and the next stage in Fidelity's evolution began with Johnson's first encounter with Gerald Tsai, Jr.

This encounter occurred early in 1952, when Johnson received a telephone call from a friend of his at the investment counselling firm of Scudder, Stevens and Clark. "I've got a young Chinese here, a clever fellow, but we don't seem to have a place for him at the moment," the friend said. "Anything you can do for him?" Johnson asked his friend to send the young man around. When Tsai appeared, Johnson liked his looks and hired him on the spot as a junior stock analyst.

The young man, then twenty-four, had been born in Shanghai in 1928 to Westernized Chinese parents; his father had been educated at the University of Michigan and later become Shanghai district manager for the Ford Motor Company. In 1947, with the war over at last, the younger Tsai was sent to America to college. He went first to Wesleyan University; finding Middletown, Connecticut, too much of a hick community for his liking after the bright lights of Shanghai, he transferred to Boston University, where he felt right at home, and applied himself so diligently that he finished his undergraduate courses in economics six months ahead of schedule, and devoted the last term of his senior year to writing a master's thesis on "Economic Development in Shanghai." Thus, in the summer of 1949, he was able to take his B.A. and M.A. in quick succession. He worked for a year with a textile company in Providence, then for another year or so with the securities giant Bache and Company in New York, getting married along the way to a Chinese-American girl. Then he went back to Boston and, having decided once and for all that stock investment was his métier, met Johnson and Fidelity. "I liked the market," he would explain years later. "I felt that being a foreigner I didn't have a competitive disadvantage there, when I might somewhere else. If you buy GM at forty and it goes to fifty, whether you are an Oriental, a Korean, or a Buddhist doesn't make any difference." The reader's attention need hardly be called to the similarity between Tsai's reason for liking the market and that of Edward Crosby Johnson II—"you were what you were not because you were a friend of somebody, but for yourself." Boston Yankee and Asian immigrant, they were kindred souls in appreciating the market's cool objectivity, which gave both a chance to escape any feeling of prejudice. That the polarity of the prejudice differed—differed, indeed, by precisely 180 degrees—was beside the point.

2

For ways that are dark
And for tricks that are vain
The heathen Chinee is peculiar.

Gerald Tsai's Oriental appearance and background, and the aura of dark ways and vain tricks that Bret Harte in 1870 so airily associated with Orientals, were eventually to work as a powerful asset in projecting him to the public as a genius. But the bonds that drew him and Edward Johnson together in 1952 were more fundamental than a common love of the stock market.

Johnson was something of an Orientalist in two separate ways, by local tradition and by personal predilection. His ancestors, the early Yankee traders, had been Orientophiles for the most practical of reasons—that the Orient was in large part the source of their wealth. Clipper-borne around Cape Horn, Oriental culture, along with Oriental goods, influenced Boston's architecture and interior decoration and thought and even its hierarchy of social values. In the Union Club, which occupies two houses just off the Common that were once owned by the Lawrences and the Lowells, there hang among the portraits of whiskered old nineteenth-century Yankee eminences two solemn, respectful representations of Chinese traders. Again, Johnson personally had a lifelong hobby—inherited, as hobbies so seldom are, from his father—of studying Oriental religions. A sense of affinity with the Far East came almost as naturally to him as going to Harvard.

Tsai, for his part, was prepared to meet Yankee culture a good deal more than halfway. If his heart was just Oriental enough to stimulate and fulfill the fantasies of a Bostonian, his mind and manner were eminently Western. With only the faintest trace of his origin in his fluent and slangy American speech (he said "thouand" for "thousand"), he was brisk, practical, ambitious, energetic, logical, aggressive—almost a very model of a modern Yankee trader.

And one more force drew Johnson and Tsai together. The young man had always been close to his mother—a strong and remarkable woman with a trading sense of her own, whose haggling in Shanghai markets was one of her son's strongest childhood memories—but relatively remote from his father. In Edward Johnson he found, no doubt, a chance for a surrogate father, and Edward Johnson was glad and proud to assume the role. That Johnson had a son of his own, a bright and personable young man named Edward Crosby Johnson III and called Ned, who also worked at Fidelity, was a circumstance that, predictably enough, serves to thicken our plot.

At Fidelity, Tsai was not long in making his mark. Always impeccably groomed, his moon face as impassive as a Buddha, he showed himself to be a shrewd and decisive picker of stocks for short-term appreciation, and so swift and nimble in getting into and out of specific stocks that his relations with them, far from resembling a marriage or even a companionate marriage, were often more like those of a roué with a chorus line. Sometimes, to continue the analogy, the sheets were hardly cool when he was through with one and on to another. Johnson—"Mister" Johnson to Tsai, as he was to almost everyone else in his own organization and the mutual-fund business in general—was fascinated and ever so slightly scandalized. Years later Tsai said of his old boss, "Basically, Mr. Johnson was not as orthodox as other Boston investment men. He is a very flexible person, not really fond of tradition. He always wanted to give you your head, give you your chance to work on your own rather than as part of a team or committee. But when he gave you your head he was also giving you your rope—'Here's your rope,' he'd say. 'Go ahead and hang yourself with it.' That was one of his favorite expressions. Another was, 'Do it by yourself. Two men can't play a violin.' "

By 1957 Tsai felt confident enough of his position at Fidelity to write Johnson a memo asking—indeed, very nearly demanding—permission to start his own growth fund. "It took him only half an hour to decide," Tsai recalled long afterward. "He called me into his office, handed my memo back to me, and said, 'Go ahead. Here's your rope.' "

Tsai's rope was called Fidelity Capital Fund, and it was the company's first frankly speculative public growth fund. Right from the start, he operated it in a way that was at the time considered almost out-and-out gambling. He concentrated Fidelity Capital's money in a few stocks that were then thought to be outrageously speculative and unseasoned for a mutual fund (Polaroid, Xerox, and Litton Industries among them). He bought in huge blocks of ten thousand shares or more at a time, coolly notifying his brokers that if they couldn't assemble the block without pushing the price up substantially—say, more than a point or two—the deal was off. The brokers grumbled, but usually assembled the large positions; with huge commissions at stake, if one broker wouldn't deal with Tsai according to Tsai's specifications another assuredly would. His annual portfolio turnover generally exceeded 100 percent, or a share traded for every one held—a rate of trading unheard of in institutional circles at the time. He got a well-deserved reputation for catlike quickness in calling a market turn. "It was a beautiful thing to watch his reactions," Johnson says. "What grace, what timing—glorious! Why, if he had been on the Stock Exchange floor, he'd have become its number one trader in no time." As Fidelity Capital's net asset value rose and new money poured into it, Tsai came to be close to key men in corporate management: Harold Geneen of International Telephone, Nathan

Cummings of Consolidated Foods, Laurence Tisch of Loews. And, gradually—although his name was still unknown to the general public—he came to be known and feared in corporate circles. The sudden dumping of ten thousand shares of one's stock was not to be taken lightly, and the man capable of doing it on a moment's whim was worth cultivating.

All rising artists suffer setbacks, and this young Picasso of the portfolio suffered one in the bad market of 1962. His whole method of operation—emphasis on growth stocks, concentration of his purchases in a few issues in which he took huge positions—implied maximum exposure in a crash; after the carnage of May 1962, Fidelity Capital Fund suddenly looked like a punctured balloon. But Tsai was quick to recover. After the Cuban missile crisis that October he suddenly turned decisively bullish. In six weeks, he put $26 million into stocks for Fidelity Capital; the market leaped upward, and by the end of the year the fund's asset value had risen nothing less than 68 percent within three months.

Tsai had now perfected his method, and over the following three years he had the ideal market in which to project it. At the same time he began to rise within his own organization. By 1963 Tsai owned 20 percent of the Johnson management vehicle, Fidelity Management and Research—half as much as Edward Johnson—and was beginning to think of himself as Johnson's successor. Up and up went Fidelity Capital's asset value, and finally, for the vintage market year of 1965, the fund achieved a rise of not quite 50 percent on a turnover of 120 percent.

The go-go years had begun, and Gerry Tsai, more than any other one man, had brought them into being. Suddenly, he was nationally famous. Like Greta Garbo he courted publicity while quite sincerely shunning it. Fidelity never hired a public-relations firm, and when the press and electronic media began beating a path to his door, he was surprised and abashed. To a reporter from *The New Yorker* who asked to do a personality sketch of him for the magazine's "Talk of the Town" department, he had a secretary reply, "Mr. Tsai never allows anything personal to be written about him." But, of course, much was written and said anyhow, personal and otherwise, and by that manic autumn he was the stock market's certified golden boy. Once, more than a generation earlier, Johnson's hero Jesse Livermore had filled the same role, his every move and gesture studied by the hangers-on who hoped to ride to riches on his coattails. As once "Jesse Livermore is buying it!" had been the signal for a general stampede into any stock, so now it was "Gerry Tsai is buying it!" Like Livermore's, his prophecies by force of his reputation came to be to a certain extent self-fulfilling. His legend itself was self-perpetuating, and a move by him in or out of a stock could in itself add to, or subtract from, the market value of a given company by hundreds of millions of dollars in the space of a few hours. The federal securities laws, which had not been on the statute books to bother Livermore in his heyday, now categorically forbade manipulation of stocks. But what could the securities laws do about Tsai? Was it his fault that everyone else wanted to follow his bets? A law-abiding man, he was a stock manipulator in spite of himself. As the first big-name star of the new era, he created fresh problems of regulation that the regulators in Washington did not at first recognize as having arisen.

As for Edward Johnson, who dreamed of Jesse Livermore as a naval commander on deck in a cannonade, he had never become another Livermore himself—at heart he was too reticent and Bostonian for that. But now, surely without conscious intention, he had brought one up in his office.

So arises the question of to what extent, and with what moral overtones, Tsai's race and national origin contributed to the mystique of his success. Wall Street had never had a nonwhite leader—seldom enough, indeed, one who was not purest Anglo-Saxon Protestant—and now it had one. Presumably it could pat itself on the back for broad-mindedness. But could it really? The Oriental as a powerful and morally equivocal force in Western society was nothing new; he was Bret Harte's heathen Chinee in gold-rush California, or Peter Lorre in an old movie or Sessue Hayakawa in a newer one: suave, composed, his manners courtly and elegant, his intellect superior and essentially Western in character, his motives automatically suspect but subject to being used by the good guys. An un-stuffy Boston trustee had found a new, real-life Oriental genie in a bottle and loosed him on the nation. The Wall Streeters who eagerly followed Tsai into the go-go game, and the investors who flocked to get what they were beginning to call a piece of the action, were not responding to elevated social impulses. They were following a money magician whom they expected to make them rich, a winner with whom they had neither the desire nor the opportunity to engage in any human intercourse.

3

In 1965, Tsai's career with the Fidelity organization came to a fork in the road. The elder Johnson was over sixty-five now and likely to retire soon. Who was to be his successor—Tsai, or Johnson's own son Ned? The younger Johnson was a good-looking, highly competent man in his thirties, with a marked speculative flair of his own. He had a dry sense of humor. To his father he would say: "Talk all you want about your poop-decks and companionate marriages. Some people have a well-developed sense of self-preservation, and you are one of them." The elder Johnson would smile delightedly; in truth, the two men had unusual rapport for a father and son. To Gerry Tsai, Ned Johnson would say little, except when they occasionally became engaged in a heated boardroom debate about the merits of some stock—a debate in which it may have sometimes seemed that there was more at stake than was being said. Self-confident with fame and success now, a national force in the market, Tsai could no longer be expected to sit quietly in the counsels of Fidelity. Finally he put the question of succession directly to Johnson. It must have been a hard moment for both, but Johnson faced it forthrightly and without evasion; he said simply that Ned was his son and that he intended that Ned should eventually succeed him. Tsai understood; he knew that Fidelity was basically a family business. But he also knew that he could not and need not endure a future of being permanently number two man. Later that year he resigned, sold his Fidelity stock back to the company for $2.2 million, and set out to New York to organize a new mutual fund of his own.

The movement he had had such a major role in starting toward a new, exciting, and dangerous conception of how to manage other people's money was by now a national groundswell. As mutual-fund asset values went up, new money poured in. Tsai and others like him seemed to have invented a money-making machine for anyone with a few hundred or several thousand dollars to invest. There were around three million holders of shares in standard mutual funds, and at the end of 1965 their holdings in those funds amounted to $35 billion. True enough, the holders were paying through the nose for the privilege of having their money managed by Tsai or the likes of Tsai; half of their first year's investment often went for the original sales commission, and in late 1966 the S.E.C. would indignantly declare these charges to be excessive. But that was after the market had dropped; as we have seen, reform is a frail flower that languishes in the hot glare of prosperity, and at the end of 1965 the S.E.C. remained silent. So, for that matter, did the customers themselves, and no wonder. Wiesenberger Reports announced that for the year, twenty-nine leading "performance" funds had averaged a net-asset-value rise of just over 40 percent, while the laggard Dow industrial average, made up not of swingers like Polaroid and Xerox but of old-line blue chips like AT&T, General Electric, General Motors, and Texaco, had risen only 15 percent. Here, then, was a new form of investment in which it appeared that by picking your fund at random you could still make 40 percent on your money in a year's time. The trick seemed to be to pay your front-end load, relax and be happy. You got what you paid for—assuming, of course, what just about everybody did assume, that the Dow would appreciate annually around 15 percent and the performance funds 40 or 50 percent. It was the sort of assumption that is widely made only in times when people have taken leave of their senses.

A constellation of money-management stars rose swiftly around Tsai; some of the stars in that constellation will have roles, lightly or not so lightly shaded, in the rest of our chronicle. There was Fred Alger, a mere thirty years old, of Security Equity Fund in New York: a man with one foot in the Establishment and one out, his stance perfectly symbolized in the career of his father, who was on the one hand a former U.S. ambassador to Belgium and on the other a former Detroit pol; himself a graduate of Yale, yet a favorite of the scapegrace international mutual-fund operator Bernard Cornfeld; a man with tousled hair and broad suspenders and quick reflexes whose widely publicized fund set an industry performance record for 1965 by shooting up 77.8 percent. There was Fred Carr, not yet thirty-five, a veteran of the Ira Haupt-salad oil fiasco of November 1963, who had then done a stint in the Hollywood-style brokerage house of Kleiner, Bell, and who now sat in his Los Angeles office surrounded by antique furniture and op art, swinging his Enterprise Fund in and out of emerging (and, one might add, frequently merging) growth companies that nobody had previously heard of. "The Enterprise Fund," Carr professed in a pronunciamento aimed at his conservative competition, "will no longer trade an imposing building or pinstriped suit for capital gains." In Wall Street itself, there was Howard Stein, one-time violinist, eminence of the Dreyfus Fund, following in the footsteps of Jack Dreyfus, who in a decade had brought the fund's assets from $1 million to over $300 million, and showing, as Dreyfus had done, that people who stood at the dead center of the financial world—the imposing-building and pinstriped-suit set—could be light on their feet, too. These men, along with Tsai, were the early stars of the go-go years; and, at a time in the world's financial history that stock investment had become a milieu for the millions, they were becoming something like a new kind of national hero.

4

The funds had queer excrescences, exotic offshoot plants deriving from the same root, and the oddest of these was the hedge fund. The hedge fund was a private mutual fund open only to the rich, requiring a minimum investment of $100,000, or sometimes considerably more, for entry. Federal law generally forbade publicly held mutual funds to operate on margin or to make short sales; therefore their speculative leverage was limited, and although they could soar in a good market, they had little chance of doing more than hold their own in a bad one. But hedge funds are not publicly held, nor are they mutual funds. Never advertised or offered to the public, they are actually limited investment partnerships, and in the nineteen sixties were totally exempt from the federal laws governing investment companies. They could pyramid debt and sell short just as an individual investor can, playing both sides of the Street, maximizing both their risk and their opportunity for profit in good markets and bad. In certain ways, they bear comparison with the famous pools of the nineteen twenties, in which the rich and celebrated of the time—Walter P. Chrysler, Charles M. Schwab, John Raskob, Percy Rockefeller, Herbert Bayard Swope, and many others—would get together a kitty of a few millions and turn it over to a stock-market technician whom they charged, for a fee or a percentage, with turning them a profit in a few days or weeks by market manipulations at the expense of less powerful and knowledgeable investors. Market rigging became a federal crime in 1934, but the banding together of rich investors did not. Like the pools of ill repute a generation earlier, the hedge funds of the sixties were the rich man's stock-market blood sport.

Although until 1968 there were only a handful of hedge funds, their origin goes back to 1949—the very beginning of the long unparalleled postwar boom—and to a most unlikely man.

He was Alfred Winslow Jones, no sideburned gunslinger but a rather shy, scholarly journalist trained in sociology and devoted to good works. Born in Australia at the turn of the century to American parents posted there by General Electric, he graduated from Harvard in 1923, got a Ph.D. in sociology at Columbia, served in the foreign service in Berlin during the thirties, and became a writer for Time-Life in the forties. Somewhere along the line, he conceived the idea that he could make money in the stock market, and, having convinced several friends on the point, in 1949 he left Time-Life and formed A.W. Jones and Company as a private investment concern with capital of $100,-000—$40,000 of it his own, the rest from his friends. Jones' notion was to use the classic speculative means—operating on margin and balancing stock purchases with short sales—to achieve what he, at least, described as conservative ends: to increase his investors' profit while minimizing their risk. The term "hedge fund" to describe his sort of operation derives from the fact that short sales are (at least in theory) used to hedge market bets on the upside. It was characteristic of Jones the scholar that he considered the popular term for the style of investment he invented to be a grammatical barbarity. "My original expression, and the proper one, was 'hedged fund,' " he told friends in the late nineteen sixties, when the expression in its corrupt form had become fixed by common usage. "I still regard 'hedge fund,' which makes a noun serve for an adjective, with distaste."

Buying stocks, and hedging with short sales according to a complicated mathematical formula that Jones devised, the first hedge fund flourished. (Its main problem was that the market kept rising so broadly and steadily that Jones and his associates were always having trouble finding stocks to sell short.) The firm's investors—or more properly, its partners—were mainly highbrows like Jones himself, writers, teachers, scholars, social workers. An early one was Louis Fischer, prize-winning biographer; other later-comers were A. Arlie Sinaiko, a doctor turned sculptor, and Sam Stayman, bridge expert and inventor of the celebrated bridge convention "Stayman over no-trump." Jones compensated his management organization, which he personally headed, by simply taking 20 percent of profits off the top—a steep cut, but on the other hand, no profits, no compensation to management. Jones' partners had little call to complain. Year after year the fund made money on its trades, even, because of its capacity to sell short, in disastrous markets like that of 1962.

By 1965, when the name of Alfred Jones and the corrupt expression "hedge fund" were just coming into the general Wall Street lexicon after a long period of carefully preserved privacy, his fund showed a five-year gain of 325 percent and a ten-year gain of more than twice that amount. His partners for a decade had almost sextupled their money, while the Dow industrials had hardly more than doubled. The average individual investment in the Jones enterprise had swollen to almost half a million dollars. The partners, to be sure, had started out rich or near-rich; now, to a man, they were considerably richer. People pleaded to be let in. An emulative hedge-fund "industry" had begun to make its appearance, manned chiefly by alumni of A. W. Jones and Company. Jones' two principal hedge-fund competitors, City Associates and Fairfield Partners, were both run by former Jones associates who had broken away to start their own firms.

Jones neither objected to the competition nor wanted the new publicity. Exclusivity and secrecy were crucial to hedge funds from the first. As with the old pools, partnership in a hedge fund, and particularly in *the* hedge fund, was like membership in a highly desirable club. It certified one's affluence while attesting to one's astuteness. Casual mention of such membership conveyed status in circles where associations mattered. With applicants begging at his door, Jones could scarcely worry about competition. As for publicity, what could it do but harm? True enough, hedge funds were exempt from regulation—so far. But was not such a fund, potentially at least, a private concentration of capital like the old pools, free of the necessity to disclose its operations in public statements, that might (like the pools) use inside information and manipulate the market to make profits at the expense of other, smaller investors? And as such, was it not—again potentially—in violation of the Securities Exchange Act after all? At any rate, in the middle nineteen sixties representatives of the S.E.C. were beginning to pay "courtesy calls" on the offices of the various hedge funds. Nothing came of them.

The hedge funds of 1965, then—offshoots though they were of the great brawling public mutual funds that symbolized and epitomized the coming of democracy to Wall Street—were Wall Street's last bastions of secrecy, mystery, exclusivity, and privilege. They were the parlor cars of the new gravy train. It was fitting that their key figure was a man who had taken up stock investing as a sideline, an elegant amateur of the market who liked to think of himself as an intellectual, above and beyond the profit motive. Alfred Jones, in his own middle sixties, had made so much money out of A. W. Jones and Company's annual 20 percents that he could well afford to indulge his predilections. Spending less and less time at his office on Broad Street, he devoted himself more and more to a personal dream of ending all poverty. Considering material deprivation in the land of affluence to be a national disgrace, he set up a personal foundation devoted to mobilizing available social skills against it. He sometimes took season-long Peace Corps assignments in South America and Africa, leaving the management of his company to his associates. He set to work on a book (never finished) that he hoped would become a sequel to Michael Harrington's famous study of United States poverty, *The Other America*. Some in Wall Street, perhaps enviously, called him a financial hippie; the charge could not be made to stick so long as his fund was earning its few lucky partners 75 or 80 percent a year. Jones could afford to go the way of the aristocrat, treating money-making as something too simple to be taken very seriously, and putting his most profound efforts into work not in the cause of profit but in that of humanity. Rarefied and above the battle as they were, though, the hedge funds were not exempt from the common condition of Wall Street: they too were living on borrowed time, and when its time ran out, so would theirs.

5

Moving half-consciously toward apotheosis, Tsai in late 1965 cleared his desk at Fidelity, said a deeply regretful good-bye to Edward Johnson and a more coolly casual one to Ned, and moved himself to New York to establish his own Manhattan Fund. He took a suite of rooms at the Regency Hotel and a suite of offices at 680 Fifth Avenue; at the latter, he established himself in a large corner room, where the carpet was beige, the thermostat was always set at a chilly 55 degrees to keep the occupant's head clear, and the principal ornament was a large leather-covered representation of a bull. There he set about selling shares, at $10 each, to establish initial participation in his new enterprise and give him some assets upon which to work his presumed investment magic. What he was really selling, of course, was that magic and nothing else; the real initial asset of Manhattan Fund was Tsai's reputation for investment skill. In his new role as his own boss, he was cool, composed, and commanding. He had come a long way from the raw, promising youth who had walked into Johnson's office thirteen years earlier. Publicity, although he still feared it, agreed with him; he had learned well enough to live with it; in fact, he had about it the hot-stove-you-can't-help-touching ambivalence that is common among financiers. Now he sparred with the press, jocularly, easily, and with evident pleasure. Early that year someone asked him why he was always buying stocks like Polaroid, Syntex, and Fairchild Camera and never the old wheelhorses like U.S. Steel. "Well, you can't kiss all the girls," Tsai replied, extending his old boss's metaphor with an Oriental grin. Still, to preserve his and his family's privacy he kept his home telephone number a secret even from his office colleagues.

How many shares of Manhattan Fund would be sold before the official opening date, February 15, 1966? Tsai set himself on an original conservative goal of $25 million worth. But he far underestimated the extent to which he had captured the public imagination. It is possible to believe that more was at work than rational appraisal based on Tsai's record. There was in the middle sixties an underground current of thought in the country that said the West had failed, that its rational liberalism was only a hypocritical cover for privilege and violence; that salvation, if possible at all, lay in the more intuitive approach of the East. Such ideas, to be sure, did not seem to have taken firm root among the kind of people who invest in mutual funds. But perhaps many of the original investors in Manhattan Fund, contemptuously as they might reject such ideas in their conscious thought, were reacting to them unconsciously when they decided to entrust their savings and thus a part of their future to Tsai. At all events, checks poured in to Manhattan Fund in a torrent. What would the opening total finally be, then? Not twenty-five but one hundred million? Or, unbelievable as it sounded, one hundred and fifty?

Not at all. On February 15, at the staid Pine Street offices of Manhattan Fund's staid bankers, the Chemical Bank, there took place the chief event of that season in American finance. Harold L. Bache, head of the firm that managed the Manhattan Fund share offering, handed Tsai a check representing the proceeds of the sale and the original assets of his mutual fund. The sum inscribed on the check was $247 million. At the standard management fee of one-half of 1 percent per year, Tsai's new organization, called Tsai Management and Research, was starting life with an annual gross income of a million and a quarter dollars.

He was off and running on his own. As the magazine *The Institutional Investor* reported later, he

> set up Manhattan Fund just like Fidelity Capital. He loaded it with all of his big glamour favorites. To facilitate his chartist maneuverings, he built an elaborate trading room with a Trans-Jets tape, a Quotron electronic board with the prices of relevant

securities and three-foot-square, giant loose leaf notebooks filled with point-and-figure charts and other technical indicators of all his holdings. Adjoining the trading room was erected "Information Central," so aswarm with visual displays and panels that slid and rotated about that it resembled some Pentagon war room. Three men were hired to work full time maintaining literally hundreds of averages, ratios, oscillators, and indices, ranging from a "ten-day oscillator of differences in advances and declines" to charts of several Treasury issues, to 25-, 65- and 150-day moving averages for the Dow. "We keep everything," [said] Walter Deemer, a former Merrill Lynch analyst and boss of Information Central who regards his charts the way an expert horticulturalist might regard a bed of prize geraniums. "You may only want a certain graph once a year, but when you do, it's here."

All the time there were ironies abounding. The social impartiality of the stock market, and the fact that the performance record of a mutual fund was as reducible to exact figures as a ballplayer's batting average—the factors that had worked in Tsai's favor when he had been an unknown Chinese boy knocking at panelled doors in a land far from home—had now turned into factors against him. He was on the spot, watched by a nation of investors and *expected* to make 50 percent profit a year on his customers' money. Less would be failure, and the fickle public would convert its hero overnight into a bum. And the timing of the situation was inexorably bad. The market was too high. The leather idol in Tsai's office was not a bull by accident. Temperamentally he was a bull himself, and therefore he needed an up market to keep winning. But by the greatest irony of all, he happened to start his own fund only a few weeks after the bull market of the nineteen sixties, as measured by the Dow industrials, had reached a peak that it would not reach again.

So Tsai in 1966 rode unawares toward his fall, and his adoring public toward its disillusionment.

6

The epilogue is anticlimax. The first meteor of the nineteen sixties was the first to burn out. But by shrewd and nimble footwork Tsai managed to get his heart's desire nonetheless.

Through its first two years, the Manhattan Fund, as well as the other smaller funds Tsai managed from his new independent stronghold, stayed popular with investors though they were generally undeserving of popularity. Away from Johnson's benign paternal surveillance, Tsai seemed to lose his stock-picking flair. After performing creditably in 1967, his funds took a beating in the tricky market of 1968; for the first seven months of that year, Manhattan Fund's asset value per share declined 6.6 percent, leaving it 299th among the 305 leading funds whose performances were regularly analyzed and compared by the brokerage firm of Arthur Lipper. At the height of the decade, the master of go-go was going in the wrong direction. Still, in the face of such depressing performance figures, the magic of Tsai's name remained undimmed when it came to attracting new investment money; by mid-1968 the assets managed by Tsai Management and Research had grown to over $500 million, which meant that the firm had a gross annual income from fees of over $2 million. Whether, on the basis of performance, it was earning the fee was another matter. But if Tsai no longer seemed to know when to cash in the investments he made for others, he knew when to cash in his own. In August, 1968, he sold Tsai Management and Research to C.N.A. Financial Corporation, an insurance holding company, in exchange for a high executive post with C.N.A. and C.N.A. stock worth in the neighborhood of $30 million.

Thus Tsai, just in time and in one stroke, joined the nearly big rich of America. As executive vice president and the largest individual stockholder of C.N.A., he turned over the running of

Tsai Management and Research to others and devoted himself to heading C.N.A.'s acquisition program. As a fund manager, he was retired. And why not? He was now a major stockholder of a huge, long-established American corporation with a listing on the New York Stock Exchange; he had a sizable office and golf clubs and country homes; he had a trust fund that would assure his son a considerable income for life.

The immigrant from Shanghai—in his aims and aspirations the simplest and most straightforward of any of the five or six prototypical moneymen of the nineteen sixties—had, like so many Irish, Jews, Italians, and others before him, emerged from a distant foreign city in response to a glimmer on a golden shore. Yet he was already failing at his chosen calling when he got rich from it. By another strange irony, he got rich in a way that would shortly be called illegal. In June 1971, Judge Henry J. Friendly of the U.S. Court of Appeals for the Second Circuit held that any profits from sale of a mutual-fund management company belong not to the sellers of the management company but to the shareholders of the fund. The decision was a return to the traditional doctrine—from which, as we saw, Edward Johnson had benefitted in acquiring Fidelity back in 1943—that a trustee may not traffic in his trust. Had the new decision been in effect in 1968, Tsai would have been prevented from selling out.

But no matter. The Friendly decision was not retroactive; Tsai and the many other fund managers who had sold their organizations early enough were allowed to keep their gains. Tsai might now be scorned in his profession for the early loss of his investment skill, and he might even be considered in some quarters a man who had cashed in his chips just before the casino's doors were barred. But for all that, in his heyday in 1966 the young wizard from Boston had been Wall Street's first Oriental hero.

CHAPTER VII

The Conglomerateurs

1

The year 1966 found Wall Street slowly and reluctantly beginning to recognize itself as a marketplace for the millions rather than an élite gambling club with a limited membership list. Manuel Cohen, Cary's activist successor as head of the S.E.C.— a Brooklyn-born lawyer, as flamboyant in manner as Cary had been reticent, whose wife engagingly characterized her husband's job by saying, "If I were doing it, it would be called nagging"—was nagging Wall Street as vigorously as he could. That summer, his S.E.C. forced a recalcitrant New York Stock Exchange to relax slightly the ironclad monopoly implied in its cherished Rule 394, which forbade members, except in rare instances, to transact business in listed stocks off the Exchange; under the amended rule they were allowed to deal off the Exchange in cases where they could not fill an order at a fair price on it. Seeking to implement Cary's Special Study, Cohen and his men pressed for commission discounts on large-volume stock transactions, and for an end to "give-ups," the time-honored commission splits between brokers that were lately being used by mutual funds to reward brokers for pushing their shares, and that in some businesses less given to euphemism might have been called kickbacks. With enthusiastic S.E.C. support and approval, the Amex made the reform-minded S.E.C. veteran Ralph Saul its new president. In December, the S.E.C. came out at last with its long-awaited report to Congress on mutual funds. The report recommended strongly worded legislation to require that mutual-fund management fees be reduced to more reasonable levels; to prohibit contractual share-buying plans that involved "front-end commision loads"; and to sharply lower the limits on all mutual-fund sales charges to investors.

Funston, in the twilight of his day as Stock Exchange president, became a progressively more stubborn conservator of the status quo. The earlier Funston, who had been chiefly responsible for the arrangements that had saved the hapless customers after the Ira Haupt and Company disaster in November 1963, now began to look like a flaming liberal by contrast with the later Funston. When New York City, pressed for money like all large American cities, proposed to raise its relatively modest stock transfer tax by half, Funston threatened (as Richard Whitney had done in 1933) to move his Exchange to New Jersey. The new tax, raised 25 percent, went into effect in July, and the Stock Exchange stayed where it was—but with diminished credibility and diminished grace as an institutional citizen.

On the matter of Rule 394, Funston simply dug his heels in and said, "We cannot and will not budge on this issue"—and then, under S.E.C. and public pressure, he budged. In related areas, the mulishness of Funston and of others on Wall Sreet was more productive. The Exchange argued that give-ups and unreduced commissions on large transactions were necessary to the orderly and profitable functioning of the securities business; as things turned out, give-ups would not be abolished, and volume discounts instituted, until 1968. The ever-more-powerful mutual fund industry fought the S.E.C.'s proposals to Congress for dear life—and fought them so effectively that the decade would run out four years later with Congress still dithering and mutual-fund reform bills still tied up in committee.

And Funston, increasingly isolated as champion of the rear guard, announced his resignation, to take effect in September 1967.

All this happened while the market, as measured by the hoary but still standard Dow industrials, was having its worst year, in terms of net January-through-December percentage loss, since 1937. The problem was chiefly a shortage of money. Back in December 1965, in the face of mounting inflationary pressures, the Federal Reserve had applied the monetary screws in classic fashion by raising the discount rate from 4 to 4 ½ percent, and over the succeeding months it had conducted its operations in a way calculated to restrain further the expansion of credit. But the medicine failed twice, effecting no cure and causing dangerous side effects. Credit continued to expand and inflation to proceed; meanwhile, the credit-dependent home-building industry collapsed, exacerbating an already existing national housing crisis; and—more important for Wall Street—money in huge quantities deserted the stock market to take advantage of the soaring interest rates on bonds that tight money had brought about. By the end of August 1966, the paper value of all issues listed on the New York Stock Exchange had declined more than $100 billion since February, and in late December—by which time the Fed had reconsidered and then reversed its ill-fated policy—the Dow, which had started the year at near 1,000, was hovering around 790.

However, this decline was not in all stocks. Certain groups of issues not among the blue chips that made up the Dow—and one such group in particular—not only resisted the downward trend but actually bucked it. Among those in the most favored group, Ling-Temco-Vought was up almost 70 percent for the year, City Investing was up about 50 percent, Litton Industries and Textron were up between 15 and 20 percent, while International Telephone and Telegraph and Gulf and Western Industries were up by smaller percentages but were poised for huge rises early in 1967. The group, of course, was the one that comprised the new corporate wunderkinder of the stock market, the conglomerates.

2

Nobody seems to know who first applied the term "conglomerate"—which in earlier times had usually meant a kind of mineral popularly called pudding stone—to corporations given to diversifying their activities through mergers with other corporations in other lines of business. At any rate, the new usage made its popular appearance in 1964 or 1965, shortly before conglomerates became the darlings of investors. Derived from the Latin word *glomus*, meaning wax, the word suggests a sort of apotheosis of the old Madison Avenue cliché "a big ball of wax," and is no doubt apt enough; but right from the start, the heads of conglomerate companies objected to it. Each of them felt that *his* company was a mesh of corporate and managerial genius in which diverse lines of endeavor—producing, say, ice cream, cement and flagpoles—were subtly welded together by some abstruse metaphysical principle so refined as to be invisible to the vulgar eye. *Other* diversified companies, each such genius acknowledged, were conglomerates; but not his own. Roy Ash of Litton Industries thought "conglomerate" implied "a mess" and pleaded for the term "multi-company industry" to describe Litton; Rupert Thompson hoped wistfully that people would speak of his Textron as engaging in "non-related diversification"; Nicolas Salgo of Bangor Punta wanted his company known as a "*unique* conglomerate." In vain. Wide-based or narrow, stuck together by synergism or chewing gum, they were called conglomerates, and for a time, almost everybody made money on them.

The aversion of the *conglomerateurs* (as *The New York Times* social page called their leading lights) to the term is understandable. Conglomerates, like prostitutes, had from the first a sufficiently shaky moral reputation to call for the use of euphemism. During their most flourishing years (roughly 1966–1969), they were said to represent, variously, a forward-looking form of enterprise characterized by freedom from all that is hidebound in conventional corporate practice; the latest of a long series of means by which "ruthless capitalists practice the black arts of finance to their ends"; and "a kind of business that services industry the way Bonnie and Clyde serviced banks." Their increasing prevalence, for better or worse, is indicated by the simple fact that in 1968 about forty-five hundred mergers of U.S. corporations were effected—far more than in any previous year, and three times as many as in any given year early in the decade. Also in 1968, twenty-six of the nation's five hundred biggest companies disappeared, permanently, into the bellies of other corporate whales through conglomerate merger, twelve of the victims being monsters with assets in excess of $250 million, and several of these same leviathans being swallowed by predators far smaller than themselves. By that time, at least ten of the nation's two hundred biggest industrial corporations were conglomerates, and the enthusiasts were saying that this was only the beginning—eventually all but a tiny fraction of national business would be conducted by about two hundred super-conglomerates.

The movement was new and yet old. In the nineteenth century, few companies diversified their activities very widely by acquiring other companies or by any other means. There is, on the face of it, no basic reason for believing that a man who can successfully run an ice cream business should not be able to successfully run an ice-cream-and-cement business, or even an ice-cream-cement-and-flagpole business. On the other hand, there is no reason for believing that he *should* be able to do so. In the Puritan and craft ethic that for the most part ruled nineteenth-century America, one of the cardinal precepts was that the shoemaker should stick to his last. American companies were as specialized in their product lines as the vendors of dog collars and nutmeg graters in Victorian London; diversification was considered irresponsible if not a form of outright immorality, and when it occurred it usually did so inadvertently, as when the Western railroads found that the land they had acquired for settlement and track right of way made them proprietors of mines, oil wells, and forests.

Early in this century, some of the biggest companies took to diversifying from within—adding new products not closely related to their old ones simply because they had the resources and the machinery to do so. General Electric and General Motors were notable examples. The tendency of companies to purchase other companies became prevalent for the first time in the boom of the nineteen twenties when many corporate treasuries were, for the first time, full of spare money. Between 1925 and 1930 du Pont, which had previously pretty well confined itself to making explosives, ate such indigestible-sounding corporate morsels as the Viscoloid Company, National Ammonia, Krebs Pigment and Chemical, and Capes-Viscose. In a limited way, it was a pioneer conglomerate. American Home Products, incorporated in 1926, had become an *Ur*-conglomerate by 1948, its product line by that time ranging from beauty preparations through foods to ethical and proprietary drugs. It was during a new spell of general affluence in the nineteen fifties that the phenomenon of really uninhibited diversification first appeared. During that decade, National Power and Light, as a result of its purchase of another company, found itself chiefly engaged in peddling soft drinks; Borg-Warner, formerly a maker of automotive parts, got into refrigerators, other consumer products, and electrical wares; and companies like Penn-Texas and Merritt Chapman and Scott, under the leadership of corporate wild men like David Karr and Louis E. Wolfson, took to ingesting whatever companies swam within reach. The results were the first genuine late-model conglomerates—but nobody had yet wrapped up the new packages in a catchy name. Among the first companies to be called conglomerates were Litton, which in 1958 began to augment its established electronics business with office calculators and computers and later branched out into typewriters, cash registers, packaged foods, conveyor belts, oceangoing ships, solder, teaching aids, and aircraft guidance systems, and Textron, once a placid and single-minded New England textile company, and eventually a purveyor of zippers, pens, snowmobiles, eyeglass frames, silverware, golf carts, metalwork machinery, helicopters, rocket engines, ball bearings, and gas meters.

3

Corporate affluence was only one element in the complex chemistry of the conglomerate explosion. Another was a decline of the stick-to-your-last philosophy among businessmen, parallel to a decline of the stick-to-anything philosophy among almost everyone else. Another was the rise in influence of the graduate business schools, led by imperial Harvard, which in the nineteen sixties were trying to enshrine business as a profession, and often taught that management ability was an absolute quality, not limited by the type of business being managed. Still another was the federal antitrust laws, which, as traditionally interpreted over the years, forbade most mergers between large companies in the *same* line of business and thus forced companies that wanted to merge at all to be, so to speak, exogamous.

But there was one more factor, less reputable and in economic terms more ominous, behind the trend. It was the fact that merging enabled a company to capitalize on its current stock-market value. The crux of the matter was that never before had a company's reported earnings per share meant so much in terms of its stock-market price. As we have seen, the average investor of the sixties was a comparative novice, interested in just three figures concerning a company whose stock he owned or was considering buying. One was the market price of the stock. The second was the net profit per share—the famous "bottom line" of the quarterly earnings report's financial summary (which, curiously, seldom actually appears at the bottom). Let the average nineteen-sixties investor be handed the latest annual report of his favorite company; his gaze would slide rapidly over the shiny four-color cover, over the glowing (but perhaps a bit glutinous) prose of the chairman's report, over the pictures of happy employees and earnest, manly executives, and would fix raptly on that bottom line. (It may come as a surprise to some modern investors to learn that this was not always so. During the boom of the nineteen twenties, the big news for both brokers and investors was more commonly dividends than earnings. High taxes on ordinary income, and favored tax treatment of capital gains, were the principal factors in bringing about an historic postwar shift in public attention from dividends to earnings.)

The third figure that engaged our investor's interest was, of course, the relationship between the other two. Called the price-to-earnings multiple, or ratio, its function was to give the investor a yardstick with which to judge whether the stock was a bargain or not. A multiple of ten was usually considered a bargain, while a multiple of forty might be (but often wasn't) thought to be too much. In the absence of his friendly broker, the average investor had to calculate the multiple for himself, a feat he could easily accomplish provided he had the two other figures and a command of short division. Making this calculation marked the outer limit of his investment sophistication.

Unfortunately, in the case of conglomerates this degree of sophistication was inadequate. Where a series of corporate mergers is concerned, the current earnings per share of the surviving company lose much of the yardstick quality that the novice investor so trustingly assumes. The simple mathematical fact is that any time a company with a high multiple buys one with a lower multiple, a kind of magic comes into play. Earnings per share of the new, merged company in the first year of its life come out higher than those of the acquiring company in the previous year, even though neither company does any more business than before. There is an apparent growth in earnings that is entirely an optical illusion. Moreover, under accounting procedures of the late nineteen sixties, a merger could generally be recorded in either of two ways—as a purchase of one company by another, or as a simple pooling of the combined resources. In many cases, the current earnings of the combined company came out quite differently under the two methods, and it was understandable that the company's accountants were inclined to choose arbitrarily the method that gave the more cheerful result. Indeed, the accountant, through this choice and others at his disposal, was often able to write for the surviving company practically any current earnings figure he chose—a situation that impelled one leading investment-advisory service to issue a derisive bulletin entitled, "Accounting as a Creative Art." All of which is to say that, without breaking the law or the rules of his profession, the accountant could mislead the naïve investor practically at will.

The conglomerate game tended to become a form of pyramiding, comparable to the public-utility holding company game that flourished in 1928, crashed in 1929, and was belatedly outlawed in the dark hangover days of 1935. The accountant evaluating the results of a conglomerate merger would apply his creative resources by writing an earnings figure that looked good to investors; they, reacting to the artistry, would buy the company's stock, thereby forcing its market price up to a high multiple again; the company would then make the new merger, write new higher earnings, and so on. The conglomerate need neither toil nor spin—only keep buying companies and writing up earnings. It was magic, until the pyramid became top-heavy and fell.

4

Accounting was and is an honorable profession, whatever its pretensions to creativity. One of the most dismal corners of what Carlyle called the dismal science of economics, accounting is seldom scrutinized by reformers or populist legislators; like a skunk, it acquires immunity against attack from its repellency. But it is of the utmost importance in an economy of affluence, so let us try to put the profession of accountancy into current perspective.

It began long ago—with a Franciscan monk of Renaissance Italy, Fra Luca Pacioli (*c.* 1445–1523), whose invention of double-entry bookkeeping was later acclaimed by Goethe as "one of the finest discoveries of the human intellect." It did not become important to substantial numbers of people until the nineteenth century, when public ownership of private companies became common. It rose to eminence as an aristocratic occupation, calling for the qualities usually associated with judges: wisdom, learning, unassailable probity. The pioneer accountants—Turquand, Touche, Cooper, Deloitte, Waterhouse, Griffiths, Peat, Plender—were all gentlemen as well as scholars, above the battle because to the manor born. This tradition of disinterestedness and individual honor was imported, with democratic modifications, into the United States, where accounting first became important in the wave of reform that followed the chicaneries and depredations of the robber barons. Turn-of-the-century American accountants viewed themselves as crusaders and evangelists for the cause of accurate and honest business relationships. The new profession's first fall from grace came, however, during the boom of the nineteen twenties, when many accountants found devious and misleading ways of writing up companies' book value to inflate stock-market price. (Not earnings; accountants took little interest in earnings in those days, and indeed, many companies did not bother to report their earnings at all.) Then came the great crash and a new wave of high-mindedness and reform. A key section of the Securities Exchange Act of 1934 gave (and still gives) the S.E.C. all but dictatorial power over the accounting practices of companies under its jurisdiction; but, in line with the S.E.C.'s policy of encouraging Wall Street and industry to regulate themselves, those powers were never exercised. The American Institute of Certified Public Accountants became the instrument of accountancy's self-regulation. All through the thirties, forties, and fifties, the A.I.C.P.A. chipped away at the old abuses that had grown up in the twenties, and progressively tightened the lax rules that had permitted them. In 1959, it empanelled an Accounting Principles Board, consisting of eighteen members—eight from the leading accounting firms, six from smaller accounting firms, two from corporations, and two from the academy—with effective power to set standards and rules for all accountants. With that step, the reforms were largely accomplished; the accounting profession sat back to congratulate itself on its wisdom and its good works.

The trouble was that, all unknowing, the Institute had built a flimsy lean-to with which to resist a coming hurricane. In the sixties, as Wall Street moved rapidly through the revolution that made it the first genuinely public securities market in the world's history, the crucial new element in stock trading was the financial and accounting naïveté of the millions of new investors. Naïveté led to a search for simplicity, and simplicity, as we have seen, was found in focusing attention on the bottom line. And this simplified view of business performance soon led accountants, including some of the best, to descend almost unawares from their pedestals of disinterestedness and become at times the willing accomplices of ruthless corporate managements and essentially dishonest promoters. In brief: to sell their souls.

The mechanics of accounting "creativity" did not end with the pooling-versus-purchase option in recording mergers. Indeed, such matters merely began there. To suggest the possibilities, let us review briefly the typical mechanics of a takeover. A conglomerate seeking to swallow another company would make a public bid, or tender offer, for any and all of the target company's shares. The offer would be at a price above the current market, to the delight and potential profit of the target company's stockholders. (Such stockholders came to love predatory conglomerates the way old-time New York City voters loved old-time Tammany Hall.) But there was a catch: the payment for the shares was seldom in cash. Instead, it was usually in the form of debt security—debentures or bonds, the famous "funny money" of the conglomerate years, perfectly good the day one accepted it but quite possibly nearly worthless a few years later when the conglomerate house of cards had collapsed. There were endless refinements. Sometimes a conglomerate, by buying a company with debentures, could arrange things so that after the merger had been completed and the new company had settled in, it could transfer the cost of the purchase to the books of the taken-over company—that is, make it pay for its own enslavement. Sometimes, debentures alone were not thought to be sufficient inducement to the stockholders of companies being sought for acquisition, and in such cases conglomerates augmented the tender offer with a variety of extras, of which the principal ones were warrants and convertibility—what Professor Warren Law of Harvard called "the underwear of corporate securities." A warrant is an option to buy a certain amount of a company's common stock at a set price anytime within a set period, while a convertible debenture is an IOU that has embedded within it a similar privilege. In both cases, the additional tidbit, or "sweetener," is included in the tender-offer package in order to give the recipient the alluring prospect of getting his hands, presumably risklessly, on some of the conglomerate's ever-soaring common stock. The unfortunate effect of such grab-bag tender offers was to dilute the equity of the conglomerate's pre-existing stockholders—to water their wine. Another effect was to confuse everyone concerned, and it cannot be said that the confusion was always entirely accidental; often enough it was plainly intended to throw dust in the eyes of the average investor with his tunnel vision trained on the bottom line.

By following conservative practices and their consciences, accountants could have prevented most of this jiggery-pokery; they did not.

5

To what extent, then, and for what reasons, did the high and proud profession of accounting fall from grace in the matter of merger accounting? To begin with, those who set the tone were taken by surprise, so encased in the old ways that even in 1960 many accounting mentors still felt that earnings per share were scarcely their concern at all. The profession was preoccupied with the principle of disclosure; it failed to allow for the fact that in the new situation, with a vastly expanded securities market full of novices, truthful disclosure could be made to tell lies to the untutored and the unwary. As early as 1960 the A.I.C.P.A. did decide to commission a University of Illinois professor to do a research project on merger accounting; the professor made stern and stringent recommendations—and they were ignored. The years went by, and the Accounting Principles Board was silent. The great conglomerates waxed; immense sums of money and concomitant power came to be involved; accountants came to think legalistically rather than conscientiously, and to do more or less what they were told to do by corporate management. It was seldom so crass a matter as consciously "selling out" to management to keep a client's fee. Management kept pressing the accountants in sophisticated ways, mesmerizing them with new and exciting subtleties. Under such abstract and value-free pressure, accountants began to take on the corporate mentality, to think of themselves no longer as independent, critical, perhaps even judicial examiners, but as part of management, members of the corporate "team." As Lee J. Seidler has said, "it was a question of role definition." Accountancy was losing its soul, then, the way so many souls are lost—by definition and by degree.

Its backbone weakened. (The S.E.C. was a spine stiffener, but not a sufficiently strong one; its chief accountant, Andrew Barr, was an able and conscientious man but one who harbored obsolete attitudes; he was hung up, like so many of the accountants themselves, on the old notion of disclosure as panacea.) In December 1966, the Accounting Principles Board labored and finally delivered itself of a stiff opinion requiring that convertible debentures be accounted for partly as debt and partly as the equity into which they were, by definition, convertible. This overdue proviso hit directly at conglomerate bottom-line magic; the protests were so loud, so strident, and from such powerful sources that the A.P.B. felt the need to back down and suspend its ruling. Considered morally, was not this as shocking an abdication of responsibility as if a judge, say, who had sentenced a Mafia member then reversed himself after having been threatened?

Not until 1970—when the conglomerates had collapsed, and the public had been shorn—would the A.P.B. muster its courage to take, too late, a strong and responsible line on merger accounting.

This sorrowful digression may appropriately end with a contrast between the current attitudes toward accountants in Great Britain and in the United States. Accountants have long enjoyed higher standing in the British business and social hierarchy than in the American one. In the late sixties, thirteen members of the House of Lords were professionally qualified accountants, as were nine members of the House of Commons, including the Chancellor of the Exchequer himself; on this side of the Atlantic, not a single accountant was to be found among the 535 members of Congress. Moreover, every major British government investigating body customarily includes at least one chartered accountant, while their presence on comparable bodies in the United States is rare. It is lawyers in whom we Americans traditionally invest our hopes for legislative and fiscal leadership; Congress and government commissions swarm with them; the ordinary citizen, finding his aspirations to wisdom falling short in almost any discussion, will often resort to the apologetic phrase, "Well, of course, I'm not a lawyer"—as if a law degree conferred a mantle of authority and expertise over our national life. Seidler, a perceptive scholar and practitioner of accountancy, conducted an informal poll on the subject of relative social status in 1969. On a visit to London, he asked twelve nubile young women, "If you had your choice, which would you prefer to marry, a doctor, a lawyer, or an accountant?" Accountants came out on top, as it were, not only with the young ladies themselves but also as the choice for them of their fathers; lawyers were second, and doctors last. Back home, Seidler carried out a similar survey among a number of unmarried American girls, and the British results were precisely reversed.

Accountants, it is true, often make appreciable money in America; but within the democratic frame they are generally thought of, and generally think of themselves, not as hereditary leaders but as bright and ambitious new men taking advantage of a calling celebrated for permitting upward social mobility.

As to performance, or reputation for performance: All through the conglomerate era British accountants seem generally to have preserved their traditional standing as the unassailable consciences of private business management. Seidler asked a number of British stockbrokers, security analysts, and Stock Exchange officials, "Assume that at the conclusion of an audit there was a substantial disagreement between a large firm of accountants and the management of a large corporation over a point of accounting principles . . . under what circumstances, other than a demonstration of the sheer logic of its stand, might the client influence the auditor to accept its view?" The resounding and unanimous response was, "None." Asked the same question, a comparable group of American financial men almost all replied that the accountants would, in the majority of cases, yield to the client's wishes regardless of the accounting principles involved. One respondent put the matter bluntly: "Accountants are unable to bite the hand that feeds them." It need hardly be emphasized that any accountant thus morally disabled is not just worthless to the public he is supposed to protect, but worse than worthless.

Seidler concluded, "Excluding considerations of social justice, it does appear that the result of the higher social position of the British accountants has been to make them a stronger profession, both relative to other professions and in terms of their relationship with clients." A faintly snobbish view? Perhaps. Aristocrats can and sometimes do compromise with principle in any country; and, contrariwise, one of the glories of the United States has always been the stubborn conscience of many men who by birth and circumstance could not well afford it. But the conglomerate accountants of the sixties, or too many of them, were not among those men.

6

James Joseph Ling, born in 1922 in Hugo, Oklahoma, of South German ancestry, had a rootless, drifting, poverty-ridden childhood during which he showed no special talent for anything much. After his mother's death when he was twelve, he was sent to live with an aunt in Louisiana; after two years in Catholic high school there (he liked to beat the nuns at chess) he dropped out and became one more depression-years kid on the bum, wandering aimlessly under the dust-darkened skies of Oklahoma and Texas. At nineteen he arrived in Dallas and went to work as an electrician. In 1944 he joined the Navy and became an electrician's mate, stringing power lines and recovering equipment from sunken ships in the Philippines. Released from service in 1946, he went back to Dallas and, with $2,000 savings, set himself up in business as an electrical contractor.

Later he would say, in nineteen-sixties jargon, "I don't know what turned me on"—but assuredly something did. After several ups and downs, his little company grew to have an annual gross of $1.5 million. In 1955 he decided to sell stock in it to the public; when Wall Street underwriters just laughed at him, he and some associates sold the stock themselves, handing out prospectuses from a booth at the Texas State Fair. They peddled 450,000 shares at $2.25 each. The astonishing success of this venture was the turning point of Ling's life; he learned from it that pieces of paper can be exchanged for cash. Armed with the cash, he made his first corporate acquisition—LM Electronics, a West Coast firm on which his down payment was $27,500 —and changed his own company's name to Ling Electronics. Thus the once and future king of conglomerators was on his way.

His deals over the succeeding decade were so complex, innovative, and ultimately bewildering that to describe them comprehensibly at book length would be a literary tour de force, and to describe them in a few words impossible. In essence, though, they were all geared to the crucial discovery that Ling had made at the Texas fair—that people like to buy stocks and that their overpayments for stock can be capitalized by the issuer to his advantage. His basic tool was leverage—capitalizing with long-term debt to increase current earnings. In 1958 he gained entry to Wall Street when White, Weld and Company undertook a private placement of Ling Electronics convertible bonds. Then the deals came faster and more bewilderingly. In 1959 he took over Altec, University Loudspeakers, and Continental Electronics; in 1960, Temco Electronics and Missiles (government contracts, the big time now); in 1961, Chance Vought Corporation, an aviation pioneer. So overextended personally that at one point he had to sell all but eleven shares of his own company's stock, Ling nevertheless bulled ahead. By the end of 1962, he controlled an aerospace and electronics complex (by then called Ling-Temco-Vought) capable of competing for contracts with any other in the country. Then, in 1964, he suddenly launched what he whimsically called Project Redeployment, in which he began selling to the public shares in the companies he had acquired. It looked like a stunning reversal of policy, but in fact it was more of the same—all part of Ling's basic scheme to take advantage of the public's and the financial institutions' insatiable appetite for common stocks. He would sell off, say, a quarter of the shares of a Ling-Temco-Vought subsidiary; the magic of Ling's name would propel the price of the shares well up in the market, and the three-quarters that Ling had retained would be temporarily worth far more than it had been worth a few days or weeks before. A Wall Street man called Project Redeployment "getting something for nothing."

But it worked. In 1965, Ling-Temco-Vought ranked number 204 on the *Fortune* directory of the largest U.S. industrial companies; in 1967, 38; finally in 1969, 14. Net income per share —before allowing for dilution by all those convertible shares— nearly tripled in 1966 and then went up some 75 percent more in 1967. As a result, market price of the company's stock, from the beginning of 1965 to the peak in 1967, multiplied more than ten times. Could there be any wonder that the huge new investing public loved it?

Ling at his peak was a mogul in the nineteenth-century manner, as lordly as a Vanderbilt or a Yerkes. (In that respect, he represented a striking and perhaps rather engaging contrast to his fellow-Texan multimillionares of his own time, the secretive, often penny-pinching oil men.) Ling claimed the German Field Marshal Rommel as "one of my teachers," and he talked grandly to anyone who would listen in metaphors drawn from sports and physical combat—"let's three-putt it," "a karate chop to the neck." He was short, however, with those who doubted. Once when a leading Wall Street stock analyst presumed to question his free use of debt securities to make acquisitions, Ling summoned the analyst into his presence; finding him to be a man of dignified middle age, Ling dismissed him with a contemptuous "What could I expect from someone over forty?" At a reputed cost of over $3 million, he built himself an imperial mansion in Dallas, with a façade of Roman columns, a portico lined with classic statuary, bathrooms with gold faucets (an Italian marble bathtub worth $14,000 in one of them), and its own golf course. (His address, as listed in *Who's Who*—10,300 Gaywood Road—astonishingly conveyed the democratic suggestion that his pleasure dome was merely one of many.) Inside the mansion was a collection of seventeenth-century books that their owner genuinely cherished without, in many cases, having the vaguest notion what was inside them. He was not above deceiving his guests. Once he met Oskar Morgenstern, the famous Princeton econometrician, and invited him to "a small dinner—five or six people." The dinner was for thirty, and after coffee Morgenstern, unwarned, found himself asked by his host to "say a few words." One did not refuse Ling in his house—nor did one quibble about the terms under which one was inside it. Morgenstern complied.

In 1968 Ling embarked on his most ambitious venture and the one that, along with other factors, would eventually bring about his downfall. It was nothing less than the acquisition of

Jones and Laughlin Steel, an old and solid member of American big business' traditional pantheon, for a cash tender offer of $425 million, the largest ever made by one company for another. But in 1967 the high school dropout and onetime dustbowl roustabout was a Caesar not only in his own eyes but in those of a majority of his corporate peers as well.

Meshulam Riklis, born in Odessa the same year Ling was born in Hugo, Oklahoma, grew up in pre-Israel Tel Aviv in comfortable circumstances, making such frequent and intricate deals with his playmates that they took to calling him derisively the Minister of Finance. He was no ordinary Jewish boy, but, it was sometimes maintained, an eighth-generation descendant of Baal-Shem-Tov, founder in eighteenth-century Poland of the celebrated ultra-orthodox Jewish sect called Hasidism. Nonreligious like his father—a Palestine businessman who had once been an officer in the Turkish army—Meshulam Riklis showed an early bent toward scholarship, leading his mother to hope fervently that he would get a Ph.D. and become a teacher. He did, for a time, become a teacher. Having served in the British army in wartime and later having lived for a while with his bride in a kibbutz, he came to the United States in 1947, graduated from Ohio State University in 1950, and then moved to Minneapolis, where he taught Hebrew at night and spent his days as a novice stock salesman for a local brokerage firm.

At the daytime occupation he made a quick success. Soon the rich Jews of Minneapolis were willing to finance him in independent ventures, and he began buying and combining small companies on a shoestring. He would line up backers to help him get control of Company A; then he would use the assets of Company A to take over Company B; and so on. In 1955 he took over a firm called Rapid Electrotype; in 1957 he merged it into another called American Colortype; and the combination, which was to be Riklis' key corporate vehicle thereafter, he named Rapid-American Corporation—a title so inspiriting, so beautifully characteristic of the air of guileless enthusiasm seasoned with amiable larceny of the conglomerate era, that it must endear him to any student of corporate nomenclature.

Naturalized in 1955 and a millionaire before the end of that decade, Riklis *was* Rapid-American in the flesh. In 1970 he told a reporter, "I am a conglomerate. Me, personally." He had built one and seen it nearly fall before the term "conglomerate" had come into use. By 1962 his Rapid-American controlled McCrory Corporation, a combine of retail stores, and Glen Alden, a consumer-products company. After the market crash that year the empire found itself in a bad bind, and creditor banks demanded Riklis' resignation; he refused, the market recovered, the banks relented, and the crisis was weathered. And Rapid-American went on to new heights, adding companies to its holdings at a fast pace through the following years. Eventually Riklis came to control a complex with sales of $1.7 billion, including such well-known companies as International Playtex, B.V.D., Schenley Industries, Lerner Shops, and RKO-Stanley Warner Theatres. In 1966, at the height of this headlong expansion, Riklis did a characteristically unexpected thing—he went back to Ohio State for the summer and took a master's degree in Business Administration, writing his thesis on his own business career and methods. His mother in Israel, who still regretted that he had become a businessman rather than a professor, must have been somewhat comforted.

Perhaps the most striking thing about Riklis as a conglomerator is the way he exploited his Jewishness rather than suppressing or ignoring it as so many Jewish businessmen in an alien culture had done before him. Once he began a pitch to a prospective lender with the taunt, "I understand you guys are anti-Semitic"—and got the loan. He was always ready with a dialect story, and his most famous saying—that Rapid-American owed its success to "the effective non-use of cash"—is perfectly in the tradition of rueful and realistic Jewish wit. Once, after a luncheon at the Bankers Club in Wall Street with an ex-partner of White, Weld, he described the occasion to a friend by saying, "I've never seen so many *goyim* in my life," and then went on to tell with what distaste he had eaten his first raw oyster. In making corporate acquisitions, he went almost exclusively for firms that were Jewish-controlled. Other Jews he felt he could deal with; what he prudently avoided was any confrontation with the Protestants. A man making his way, Riklis believed, had enough trouble without *that* complication. Yet the Jewish-American business world had by Riklis' time become a commodious one, and his self-imposed limitation scarcely cramped his style. "I will not go into the steel business," he once pronounced. "Jimmy Ling, he's entitled. He's got the right religion."

Of course, a heavy layer of usefully insulting implication underlay such statements. Meshulam Riklis was hardly one to be popular with the stereotyped old-shoe American executive or underwriter. But, tough and appealing, with a sure instinct for timing and survival, he was the first Borscht-circuit entertainer *manqué* to rule an American business empire, and as such he has his deserved and reserved place in our current business history.

Charles Bluhdorn, also foreign-born, lacked Riklis' subtlety, wit, and streak of intellectuality; he was more nearly the traditional brash gambler who will bet with anybody on anything, and yet—like so many brash gamblers—he was a secret conservative, more cautious and calculating than he wanted to seem. Several years younger than Ling and Riklis, he was born in Vienna, the son of a Czech-born importer, and came to the United States at sixteen, a refugee from Nazi anti-Semitism, in 1942. In his middle twenties he made his first million with a series of breathtaking deals in the commodities market. Of this period in his business life he would say twenty years later, when he was the head of a vast empire, "Today I wouldn't have the nerve." But he retained plenty of nerve in the sense of *chutzpah*. In 1957, just past thirty, he bought control of an automobile parts manufacturing company called Michigan Bumper. Bumpers moved slowly, and Bluhdorn's firm attracted no special attention; it entered the nineteen sixties with sales of $8.4 million and a small annual deficit. Eight years and more than eighty corporate deals later, his enterprise—by then famous to everyone who follows the stock market as Gulf and Western Industries—would have sales of $1.3 billion and net annual income of $70 million; over the same period its stock price multiplied twenty times, and Bluhdorn became known as the *enfant terrible* of the conglomerate scene—a distinction, from the business-Establishment point of view, somewhat comparable to being called the wickedest man in Hell.

Bluhdorn and Gulf and Western came late to conglomeration. In the first part of 1965 his was still essentially a small car-parts firm; but that year he managed to borrow $84 million from the Chase Manhattan Bank with which to buy control of New Jersey Zinc Company, largest zinc producer in the country. After that, acquisitions followed at a dizzying rate: E. W. Bliss, Desilu Productions, South Puerto Rican Sugar, Consolidated Cigar, a mixed bag of others. Bluhdorn's rationale for diversifying so widely and so wildly was simple; he wanted, he explained, to be in a lot of different lines of business so that when hard times fell on one of them the others would serve as a counterbalance and pull the entire enterprise through. He was at less pains to point out that nearly all of Gulf and Western's acquisitions were made with debt and convertibles, meaning that this year's net profit was being inflated at the possible cost of next year's; or that Gulf and Western, until belatedly prodded by the S.E.C., neglected to point out to its stockholders and the public the potential dilution of their holdings that was inherent in the issuance of all that paper.

Undoubtedly Bluhdorn's acquisition masterpiece was Paramount Pictures in 1966. The company was in trouble, losing money on feature films, wary of plunging too deeply into large-scale television production, propping up its earnings by selling off its assets. With no prior experience in motion-picture production, Bluhdorn personally took over as president and appointed a new management team charged with instituting new, bolder policies. For the short term, it was a case study of the conglomerate theory triumphant. In less than three years, Paramount became the hottest studio in Hollywood.

Bluhdorn at his most flamboyant was almost a parody of the hyperthyroid business genius—fast-talking, with just enough Viennese accent to make him type-cast for his role: emotional, visionary, impatient, an artist at the work of business. He liked to speak of Gulf and Western as "a sort of youthful disease." He ran his empire with a tiny, easily manageable headquarters staff of less than one hundred, secretaries included. He hated vacations and he disdained the word "conglomerate." Doing business on the telephone or face to face, he alternated intimidating roars with conspiratorial whispers, and could modulate at will from either into eloquent or flowery speech suffused with sincerity. He was conscious of his status as an outsider, and not without rancor on the subject—"I'll show those goddam bluebloods," he once exclaimed on encountering the cool hostility of the Establishment—but unlike Riklis, he was not totally shy of direct confrontations with the Protestants. He even made takeover overtures to Armour and to Pan American Airways—only, however, to withdraw prudently in each case when the going showed signs of getting too rough.

Essentially a haggler on a grand scale, Bluhdorn gloried in his reputation as such. He was surely aware that in conservative circles such a reputation was deemed a business liability; indeed, a sympathetic investment banker once told him that his chief weakness was his inability to conduct himself according to accepted canons—his tendency to sputter, fume, and shout when only dispassionate facts were required. Another banker has since made the curious and suggestive criticism that in his corporate acquisitions for Gulf and Western, Bluhdorn frequently showed a lack of taste—not in the way he corralled them, but in his choice of companies to acquire. The concept of taste, as applied to a chief executive's choice of corporate acquisitions, may well merit some study by business students of the future.

In one important respect, Bluhdorn was constantly maligned. Almost universally considered to be among the wildest and most suspect of the conglomerators, and certainly in truth among the least restrained users of debt and convertible securities, he was guiltless of the principal offense usually alleged against his sand-castle breed, that of "buying" spurious earnings by taking over companies with price-to-earnings ratios lower than his own. The record shows that, on the contrary, Gulf and Western usually bought companies with ratios higher than its own, and thereby temporarily *reduced* its own earnings through its acquisitions. Even in the Paramount deal, Bluhdorn paid seventy times the movie company's current earnings; the multiple of Gulf and Western at the time was less than eight. As Arthur M. Louis pointed out in *Fortune*, during the decade of the sixties Gulf and Western bought high-multiple companies so often that the transactions, in themselves, actually reduced net earnings by almost $1.50 a share. Bluhdorn floated far too much corporate underwear, he often let his accountants play fast and loose, and probably he shouted too much on the telephone; but he bought companies because he believed in them, and through most of the decade Gulf and Western's "internal" growth—the old kind of growth based on doing more business—averaged almost 20 percent a year.

7

Whether immigrants like Riklis and Bluhdorn, self-made natives like Ling and Eugene Klein, or Harvard Business School products like Roy Ash and Charles (Tex) Thornton, the conglomerators were all uninhibited free enterprisers, anti-organization men, throwbacks to the nineteenth-century age of individualism in American business. The great paradox of the conglomerate era is that it brought back such rampant individualism at the very moment when the received wisdom held that government regulation, suburban living, and the rise of the computer had bred the pawky eccentricity out of American business and turned it into a vast impersonal machine to which a man learned to abase himself, or else failed. Like the old trusts that Theodore Roosevelt set out to bust, the conglomerates were essentially one-man or two-man companies. Like the robber barons, the conglomerators tended to collect art and otherwise flaunt their wealth (in contrast to the organization men of the previous decade, whose goal was not to excel or exceed but to

fit in). James Ling's Dallas palazzo was far from the only conglomerator's marble showplace. Klein, a onetime used-car salesman who built the great West Coast conglomerate, National
General Corporation, bought an old Beverly Hills mansion,
spent a million and a half decking it out with Picassos, Modigli-
anis, and choice European antiques (a Marie Antoinette foot
bath, two Lord Nelson mirrors, a desk set once owned by a
czarina of Russia), and rode around in a $3-million corporate jet
and a Rolls-Royce formerly owned by Queen Elizabeth II. Some
were not afraid of appearing to be comically self-serving; the
Wall Street Journal reported that at the height of the era the head
of a middle-sized firm with conglomerate aspirations called a
broker and asked him to find for acquisition "some kind of
company that would be located in Florida," since he liked the
climate and wanted an excuse to spend time there. In naming
their enterprises, as in decorating their houses, the conglomerators showed a penchant for instant grandeur usually at the risk
of bombast (Rapid-American, National General), but sometimes
the names went in another direction, and suggested down-home
folksiness, which investors also seemed to love. There was Min-
nie Pearl's Chicken System, Inc., later more austerely called
Performance Systems; its stock rose wildly under the first name
and dropped disastrously under the second. Sometimes it
seemed as if the company namers deliberately injected just a
hint of comic larceny, calculating, perhaps correctly, that the
investing public and the money managers had a taste for such
things. There was, for example, the Slick Corporation—named
for its founder, it is true, but straight out of a W.C. Fields movie
all the same. And there was "Automatic" Sprinkler Corporation. Its officers explained that the quotation marks were intended to distinguish its particular automatic sprinklers from
everyone else's; but to the layman the name seemed to imply, in
an almost masochistically self-deprecating way, that the company's sprinklers were not really automatic but were only alleged to be. Whatever is in a name, the suggestion did not deter
the stock market from bidding the company's stock in 1967 up
to more than fifty times earnings.

An era of showoffs and shenanigans, then, of American enterprise parodying itself on a grand scale. But the conglomerate movement also had serious and dangerous consequences within the world of corporations. With Litton openly aiming at acquiring fifty companies a year and with dozens of lesser conglomerates eager for entry into the great world of conglomerate colossi, hardly any company anywhere in the country that had its stock on the market could feel safe from a takeover attempt at any time. As a result, executives who should have been devoting themselves to running their businesses found it prudent and often necessary to neglect such duties and spend much thought and energy on the financial maneuvers and the information-gathering necessary to anticipate or repel raids by voracious conglomerates. Some companies became battle-scarred veterans of the conglomerate wars. Allis-Chalmers weathered serious takeover attempts by Ling-Temco-Vought, Gulf and Western, and White Consolidated, one right after the other. After such an experience, how, one may wonder, could a senior Allis-Chalmers seneschal carry out his farm-machinery duties when at any moment some new raider might be secretly buying stock and readying the kind of tender offer that the other equity-holders would find it hard to refuse?

What with the arithmetic of stock multiples making it possible on occasion for smaller companies to take over much larger ones, size alone offered no protection. Every now and again, in the conglomerate era, a company minnow would successfully ingest a corporate whale, and the other monsters would tremble. Not until virtually the whole business community had been aroused in 1969 by the attempts of raffish Resorts International (formerly Mary Carter Paints) to take over Olympian Pan American World Airways, and of brash Leasco Data Processing to forceably marry matronly Chemical Bank, would the temporarily chastened conglomerates lose some of their appetite for prey bigger and more prestigious than themselves.

The defender against a hostile takeover was not without resources, however. On the contrary, a whole array of chesslike countermoves was available to him, and whole subdivisions of law and public relations sprang up overnight to devote themselves entirely to planning and executing such strategy. The defender might, for example, adapt to his own purpose a conglomerate gambit and change his own accounting practices, thereby bringing about an instant and essentially spurious increase in his own reported earnings. Along the same lines, he might make his company harder to swallow by quickly doing a bit of swallowing himself—by taking over some other company. A shrewd variation of this move was to buy up a company that sold products in direct competition with some of those made by the aggressor conglomerate, in hopes of creating an antitrust obstacle to the takeover. Or he might use persuasion, issuing barrages of mailings and newspaper advertisements urging his stockholders not to traduce him by accepting the tender offer. If he had good government connections, he could go straight to Washington and get a legislator or two to introduce a bill specifically designed to forfend his engorgement (as Pan American did when it was purposefully eyed by Resorts International). Of course, his best defense of all was to persuade investors to bid up the price of his stock, thus achieving the same sort of defensive effect that a blowfish achieves in the presence of a hungry striped bass.

What came to be regarded as the classic defense was mounted in 1969 by B. F. Goodrich, the celebrated old-line rubber company, to foil a takeover attempt by Northwest Industries (clothing, pesticides, steel, and for a time the nation's only profitable commuter railroad, the Chicago and North Western). Goodrich used all of the methods just mentioned and some others besides. It changed its accounting methods so that its 1968 earnings appeared to have increased by $1.28 over 1967's, whereas under the old methods the increase would have been only forty-three cents. It achieved not one quickly planned merger of its own, but two. It bought newspaper ads to revile Northwest and its tactics. It changed its charter to provide for staggering the terms of its directors, so that regardless of who might own the stock, no aggressor could control the board for several years. Goodrich vigorously—or, in another view, ruthlessly—used its influence to get government intervention in both its home state, Ohio, and in Washington, and it did this so successfully that the Ohio attorney general issued an injunction against the merger, while the Department of Justice brought an antitrust suit to block it. The defense won; B.F. Goodrich, an unexpectedly formidable old monster when aroused, survived unconsumed.

And all the while individual people, as well as corporations, were being profoundly affected. The executives, particularly the top executives, of the captured companies were subjected at worst to summary dismissal and at best to reshuffling and serious loss of morale. Occasionally a takeover was followed swiftly and grimly by mass firings among the victim's management, but even when, as more often happened, the victim was left to operate as a more or less autonomous division of the merged company with generally the same personnel, the executives were likely to be overtaken by apprehension and anomie. Each man's place in the company hierarchy, perhaps painfully won over many years, became meaningless if his new super boss, the conglomerator, didn't see things his way. Robert Metz told in *The New York Times* about an executive of an acquired company who observed that he and his colleagues had been given what he called the "mushroom treatment": "Right after the acquisition, we were kept in the dark. Then they covered us with manure. Later they cultivated us. After that, they let us stew for a while. And, finally, they canned us."

The economy and amour propre of whole communities became disrupted. Conglomerates' headquarters were mostly on the two coasts, and often enough their corporate victims resided in the cities in between. The result was the repeated reduction of mid-American cities' oldest established industries from independent ventures to subsidiaries of conglomerate spiderwebs based in New York or Los Angeles. Pittsburgh, for one, lost about a dozen important corporations through conglomerate mergers. To Andrew Carnegie's city, cradle of the steel industry, the conglomerate phenomenon was like a tornado that left it battered and shaken; it is unlikely to think of itself in quite the old way ever again.

Finally, there is the profound question of the vast social and political power that conglomerates might derive, if they so wished, from their huge concentrations of wealth—and of how they might choose to exercise such power. For the most part, to all appearances, they chose not to try to exercise it at all. Preoccupied with further growth, internal organization, and raising profits, they stuck strictly to business and seldom sought to alter the social order or to usurp the functions of government. The looseness of their structures, just possibly the liberalism of their bosses, certainly their sheer busyness, all seemed to militate against such activity. Or so it appeared until the largest of them all, International Telephone and Telegraph, began to emerge as a monstrous exception.

Founded in 1920 as a communications service company operating outside the United States, I.T.T. in 1960 was still essentially that, its business overwhelmingly overseas, its assets just under the $1-billion mark and its net annual income around $30 million. That year its new president—Harold S. Geneen, flinty, British-born but naturalized an American in childhood, then just fifty and already spoken of as one of the most brilliant executives in the nation—began remolding it into a conglomerate giant. Nine years and more than one hundred mergers later, I.T.T. had amassed assets of $4 billion; its net income, running at an annual rate of $180 million, had gone up for forty-one consecutive quarters; and it had become the eleventh largest American corporation. Because of the breadth and importance of its acquisitions, its hand seemed to be everywhere in the American marketplace. As *Time* pointed out in 1972, a consumer who became annoyed with I.T.T. would have a hard time boycotting it: "He could not rent an Avis car, buy a Levitt house, sleep in a Sheraton hotel, park in an APCOA garage, use Scott's fertilizer or seed, eat Wonder Bread or Morton's frozen foods. . . . He could not have watched any televised reports of President Nixon's visit to China. . . . [He] would have had to refuse listing in *Who's Who*: I.T.T. owns that, too."

Through the years of its growth under Geneen, I.T.T. had been generally thought of in the conservative business community as an atypical "good" conglomerate, its emphasis on real growth, its takeovers nonhostile, its resorts to accounting tricks few. Even its stock-market performance was moderate by conglomerate standards; between the 1962 low and the 1968 high, its price hardly more than tripled. Even the style of its managers appealed to business conservatives. Taking their cue from the hard-driving and colorless Geneen, they refrained from building mansions or amassing art collections and devoted themselves with fierce dedication to unmitigated work. I.T.T. embodied the old Protestant ethic clad in new conglomerate clothes. It was the Establishment's conglomerate.

Not surprisingly, in view of these attitudes, I.T.T. was also the most Republican-oriented of conglomerates. And when, in 1969, after years of coexisting with Democratic regimes, it found itself with friends in power in Washington, I.T.T.—like so many earlier business enterprises that had found themselves in similar circumstances—seems to have lost its head and its Protestant ethic. Whether or not in 1971 it offered a contribution to the Republicans in exchange for a favorable settlement of a government antitrust suit remains in dispute (although the company's use of its now-famous paper shredder to destroy documents scarcely suggests a clear conscience). Most persuasive, however, is the clear evidence that in 1970 the company maneuvered—and offered to contribute $1 million—to block the election as president of Chile, where I.T.T. controlled the Chilean Telephone Company, of the Socialist Salvador Allende; or the evidence that, having failed to prevent Allende's election, I.T.T.'s self-designated proconsuls negotiated with the United States government at the White House level with a detailed plan, involving economic sabotage and the use of the Central Intelligence Agency, to bring about the overthrow of the Allende government.

The plan was turned down, but the damage was done. Here were shades of Manifest Destiny and gunboat diplomacy; here, naked and unashamed, was immense power without a sense of place, proportion, or responsibility, a planned attempt to enlist public officials to tamper with another nation's affairs in the cause of private profit. With the revelations, made in 1972 and

1973, I.T.T. came, with one stroke, to win the gold from General Motors as the ordinary man's prize symbol of consummate corporate arrogance and insensitivity. The sinister possibilities of conglomerates, including the multinational ones, for the first time exposed themselves to the public in a manner to cause not-soon-to-be-forgotten comment and concern.

8

Revitalizers of the moribund and modernizers of the obsolescent, or wreckers of lives, plunderers of cities, and meddlers in the affairs of nations, the conglomerates for a time made American boardrooms and executive suites into a takeover jungle where there were only the hunter and the hunted, and where fear and aggression dominated the world's greatest marketplace. But only for a time. It could not last, because—perhaps happily —the aggressors, sleek beasts of prey during the years of plenty, would in due course be revealed for the most part as stuffed and toothless tigers.

The start of the decline of conglomerates can be dated. By 1967 Litton Industries had become a gray eminence among conglomerates, its reputation impeccable, its stock soaring, its earnings rising steadily as they had been doing for a decade, its self-image so assured that it could decorate its annual report for that year with pictures of medieval stained glass "so that we may signify our respect and responsibility toward the achievements of the past." No market expert on Litton, whether in Wall Street or in the company itself, seems to have dared dream that profits might not continue to rise in 1968. But that January, when Litton's top officers met at the company's Beverly Hills headquarters, a totally unanticipated state of affairs was revealed. Several of the divisions were discovered, apparently for the first time, to be in serious trouble; as a result, profits for the quarter ending January 31 would, it now became clear, fail to rise at all, and in fact were headed substantially down. In simple words, business was decidedly off, and top management—so vast and various was the empire—hadn't seen it coming. Management control had been lost.

When the public earnings announcement was made—21 cents profit a share against 63 cents for the same quarter the previous year—in the stock market it was, as a Wall Street pundit put it, the day the cake of Ivory soap sank. Litton stock dropped 18 points in a week, and within a month or so it had lost almost half of its peak 1967 value. Gulf and Western and Ling-Temco-Vought slumped in apparent sympathy, and the first tremors of panic shook the whole conglomerate world.

It wasn't all over by any means; there would be some wild conglomerate maneuvers and some soaring conglomerate shares in the two years ahead. But the era was on its way to its end when, in January of 1968, it was shown for the first time that conglomerate management—even the best of it—could lose track entirely of the progress or regress of the far-flung enterprises it ostensibly controlled and thus fail utterly of its function. In short, the root theory of conglomeration might simply be wrong, its temporary success founded chiefly on the gullibility of the stock-buying public and its professional advisers.

CHAPTER VIII

The Enormous Back Room

1

It has become a commonplace for social commentators to say that 1968 was the year when the fabric of American life un-ravelled—when the moral ground shifted and quaked under American feet; when the political far left turned violent and took on ominous fieldmarks of the far right; when the demo-cratic idealism and optimism of the mass of Americans seemed to become a delusion. In January, the U.S.S. *Pueblo*, on a mission of espionage, was seized in the Sea of Japan with its eighty-three-man crew by North Koreans, and so the mightiest nation in the world was humiliated both morally and physically by one of the smallest and weakest. In February, the Kerner commission on civil disorders, a formally constituted government body, affirmed what many Americans had uneasily come to suspect—that the black violence and riots of the previous year had been caused chiefly by a profound racism on the part of the white majority. In March—although it was not known until much later—American soldiers murdered hundreds of unarmed women and children at My Lai. At the end of that month, the then President made a personal confession of failure by with-drawing from candidacy for re-election. In April, Martin Luther King, Jr., was murdered; in June, Senator Robert Kennedy. In May at Columbia University, students made a public mockery of parental and educational authority while parents and teachers stood by and let them. In August, there was disheartening police violence attending the national convention of the Democratic Party in Chicago. In December, when the United States astronauts Borman, Lovell, and Anders became the first men to see the far side of the moon, there were many of their countrymen too stunned by the year's events to feel properly proud.

And while this systemic eruption of sores covered the body politic, Wall Street, an organ of barometric sensitivity, had its own convulsions and its own loss of grip and tone. The loss amounted, indeed, to perhaps the single most dramatic technical failure of the free-enterprise system on record anywhere.

2

It was the year Wall Street nearly committed suicide by swallowing too much business, and by compounding its own near-fatal folly by simultaneously encouraging more of the same. The pace of trading had been picking up in the latter months of 1967 as a new speculative binge—the second in the decade—began to take shape. The average daily trading volume for 1967 on the New York Stock Exchange came to 10,080,000 shares, an all-time record by a wide margin. But not one destined to stand. Nineteen sixty-eight was to be the year when speculation spread like a prairie fire—when the nation, sick and disgusted with itself, seemed to try to drown its guilt in a frenetic quest for quick and easy money. "The great garbage market," Richard Jenrette called it—a market in which the "leaders" were neither old blue chips like General Motors and American Telephone nor newer solid stars like Polaroid and Xerox, but stocks with names like Four Seasons Nursing Centers, Kentucky Fried Chicken, United Convalescent Homes, and Applied Logic. The fad, as in 1961, was for taking short, profitable rides on hot new issues. Charles Plohn, an underwriter known as "Two-a-Week Charlie" for the number of new low-priced issues he brought out, described his philosophy by saying, "I give people the kind of merchandise they want. I sell stock cheap. I bring out risky deals that most firms wouldn't touch." The public paid the astronomical amount of $3.9 billion for new stock issues alone during the twelve-month period.

Trading volume was such as had never figured in any broker's wildest dreams of avarice. During the week after the Johnson withdrawal, which the market considered highly bullish, the Stock Exchange set new volume records almost every day. April 10, 1968, was the first day in history when Exchange trading exceeded 20 million shares; before the year was out there had been five more 20-million-share days, with a peak of 21.35 million on June 13. New investors and new money were coming into the market in torrents. During the first five months of the year, Merrill Lynch opened up over 200,000 new accounts; in other words, that winter and spring one American in every thousand—counting men, women, and children—opened a new brokerage account *with a single firm.* Brokers, of course, were reaping the harvest in commissions. Some of them had personal commission incomes for the year running to more than $1 million.

One million dollars income in a year, with no capital at risk —merely for writing orders for stock! It was enough to convince anyone that the Stock Exchange had indeed become Golconda revisited, that ancient city within whose portals all, according to legend, became rich, and so desirable was membership in the Exchange that the price of a seat rose from $450,000 in January to reach an all-time record in December of $515,000, topping even the peak prices of 1929.

As early as January, there began to be high cirrus cloud warnings that the back offices, the paper-handling departments of the brokerage firms, were in for a storm of trouble—that, as constituted, they were simply unable to process the new business, and that therefore, as Hurd Baruch of the S.E.C. would put it later, the best of times for Wall Street were in danger of becoming the worst of times. That month, January, the S.E.C. wrote to the two leading exchanges and the National Association of Securities Dealers, guardian of the over-the-counter market, expressing concern about "accounting, record-keeping and back-office problems and their effects on the prompt transfer and delivery of securities." The main barometric measuring-device for the seriousness of back-office trouble was the amount of what Wall Street calls "fails." A fail, which might more bluntly be called a default, occurs when on the normal settlement date for any stock trade—five days after the transaction itself—the seller's broker for some reason does not physically deliver the actual sold stock certificates to the buyer's broker, or the buyer's broker for some reason fails to receive it. The reasons for fails in most cases are exactly what one might expect: either the selling broker in his confusion can't find the certificates being sold on the designated date, or the buying broker receives them but in *his* confusion immediately misplaces them, or someone on one side or the other fouls up the record-keeping so that the certificates appear not to have been delivered when in fact they have been. Of course, not all fails—in 1968 or other years—are the result of innocent mistakes. In a certain number of cases, one brokerage firm or the other intentionally misappropriates the certificates to an improper purpose, or an employee of one firm or the other steals them. There is another problem related to that of the fail. Often, in times of back-office confusion, deliveries of certificates by brokers—particularly deliveries to banks—are rejected by the recipient with the notation, in effect, "I don't know anything of the transaction." This confession of nescience is officially and rather charmingly designated a "Don't Know," or "D.K." Incredible as it may seem, a subsequent RAND study indicated that in 1968 between 25 percent and 40 percent of *all* brokers' deliveries of stock to banks were thus rejected.

As to fails, which are a more important indicator than D.K.'s of the degree of paperwork chaos in the securities business, the rule of thumb in Wall Street in 1968 held that an acceptable level of fails on New York Stock Exchange transactions at any given time ("acceptable," the bemused observer must conclude, in relative terms) amounted to one billion dollars' worth. Let a mere billion dollars of the customers' money be more or less missing in Wall Street, the conventional wisdom went, and things were still within the ball park. Late in January, the fail level rose well above that figure, and the exchanges took action. Starting January 22, they and the over-the-counter market cut back daily trading hours by an hour and a half; closing time for an indefinite period became 2 P.M. instead of 3:30. The move—in retrospect an extremely timid one—was nevertheless made over loud opposition from a minority of the exchanges' governors. (The governors were brokers, and brokers, to say it right out, make money on heavy trading.)

In February, the opposition continued. And so did the rise in both trading volume and the level of fails. The early closings appeared to be having little if any effect, and in March they were quietly abandoned, and not replaced by any other restraining action. Would the problem, just possibly, go away? It would not. In April, N.Y.S.E. fails were up to a level of $2.67 billion; in May, to $3.47 billion. All over Wall Street, committees were formed and recommendations made on the back-office problem, but nothing substantive was done. By June, the old, established firm of Lehman Brothers was in such total confusion that its customers' securities were in clear jeopardy. Back in April, Lehman had converted to a fully automated accounting system, and, as is so often the case, the new system at first simply didn't work. Stock record discrepancies at the firm, by the end of May, ran into hundreds of millions of dollars. Lehman reacted by eliminating a few accounts, ceasing to make markets in over-the-counter stocks, and refusing further orders for low-priced securities; it did not augment these comparatively mild measures with drastic ones—the institution of a crash program costing half a million dollars to eliminate stock record errors—until

August, when the S.E.C. threatened to suspend Lehman's registration as a broker-dealer and thus effectively put it out of business. Lehman's reluctance to act promptly to save its customers' skins, and ultimately its own, was all too characteristic of Wall Street's attitude toward its troubles in 1968.

At last, when the fails level was up to $3.7 billion, the exchanges finally took a measure of drastic action themselves. Beginning on June 12, the securities markets were closed tight every Wednesday—a measure not used since 1929—in order to give the back offices a regular midweek breather in which to make a stab at catching up. But the order for Wednesday closings was unaccompanied by such logical, if painful, further measures as a prohibition on advertising and promotion designed to bring in still more business, or on the hiring of still more salesmen and the opening of still more branch offices. The lure of new money and additional commissions was irresistible. Brokerage ads continued to fill the financial pages and the airwaves; new salesmen were hired, new offices opened. Wall Street had become a mindless glutton methodically eating itself to paralysis and death.

3

Why? Where were the counsels of restraint, not to say common sense, in both Washington and on Wall Street? The answer seems to lie in the conclusion that in America, with its deeply imprinted business ethic, no inherent stabilizer, moral or practical, is sufficiently strong in and of itself to support the turning away of new business when competitors are taking it on. As a people, we would rather face chaos making potsfull of short-term money than maintain long-term order and sanity by profiting less. A former high S.E.C. official, talking to me in 1969 about the situation the year before, defended the S.E.C.'s relative passivity by describing its rightful function as that of being "an arbiter between powerful industry groups pulling in different directions." An arbiter, rather than a conscience? And indeed, did Wall Street that year deserve an S.E.C. that would act vigorously to save it from itself? After all, the Securities Acts, not by chance, were based on self-regulation on the part of Wall Street. Where was self-regulation in 1968?

Essentially, it was in the hands of the leaders of Wall Street's key institution, the New York Stock Exchange, whose president since the previous September had been Robert W. Haack. Haack was no Keith Funston. He lacked his predecessor's fire and flair, and also, more happily, Funston's sometimes fanatical protectiveness of Wall Street and all its self-indulgent ways. Born in 1917 and raised in Milwaukee in modest circumstances, Haack had worked his way steadily and surely to his present eminence: a B.A. from little Hope College, in Holland, Michigan (once famous as the home of Holland rusk); an M.B.A. from Harvard Business School, where he had earned part of his keep by waiting on tables; three wartime years in the Navy; a slow rise, during the nineteen forties, from research assistant to partner in a Milwaukee securities firm; a move to the East, where he joined the bureaucracy of the National Association of Securities Dealers, of which he became a governor in 1961 and full-time paid president in 1964; and then, in 1967, election to what was still the key position in Wall Street. He was the third choice, after Edwin Etherington and Donald Cook had privately made clear that they wanted no part of the job. Funston was a hard act to follow, and Haack, moreover, came to the Stock Exchange with a reputation as a technician, a plodder, a bureaucrat, what the Russians call an *apparatchik*. Still, he soon showed himself to be something more. He did not hesitate to shake up the entrenched Exchange staff to make it conform to his style rather than to Funston's; he instituted badly needed long-range planning; he gradually ended Funston's emphasis on high-pressure promotion of the concept of stock investment for every man; he generally ran a taut ship. Significantly, he kept the home he had bought in Potomac, Maryland, when he had been negotiating constantly with the S.E.C. on behalf of the over-the-counter market, and he commuted from it to Wall Street as often as circumstances allowed. His continued residence near Washington gave evidence of the way in which he conceived of his Stock Exchange role—not as an obdurate defender of Wall Street, but as a mediator between Wall Street and Washington.

An able and conscientious man, then, as even his most disillusioned former employees have conceded. But in the 1968 back-office crisis, Haack was as inadequate as everyone else. "Exchange-imposed restrictions were critical in coping with the paperwork problems of troubled firms," he observed later. Critical, indeed. Haack might better have used the subjunctive: "would have been critical" might have made more sense. All through the crisis, the Exchange trod on eggs, administering a slap on the wrist here, a pat on the backside there, "urging" and "advising" member firms to take "strong steps" to curtail business, but never itself taking the strong and clearly required step of imposing sanctions to make the members comply. Apart from the ill-fated January and February early closings, the Exchange made no strong positive move until it was confronted with general disaster. In March, for example, it sent member firms a letter pointing out the extent of the problem, and then continuing,

> Firms with serious problems may be asked to take steps to limit the growth of business or to reduce business. . . . In the absence of voluntary action, restraints may be imposed by the Exchange. . . .

Faced with such pussy-footing, it is small wonder that the member firms did little in the way of compliance. By early June, shortly before the Wednesday closings were instituted, Haack was at it again, pleading with member firms in a new cajoling letter. Now, he said, it was his belief that firms should "seriously consider" adopting "voluntary" restraints on expanding business. Specifically, he suggested that they stop soliciting over-the-counter business; that they "reduce or discontinue" trading for their own accounts; that they disallow commission credit to salesmen on trades in low-priced stocks; and that they take various other steps, including a reduction of advertising and promotion. As Baruch has pointed out, a flat ban on the opening of new offices or the hiring of new salesmen, which would have been legal and proper, was not among the "suggestions." As to the effectiveness of those that were made: for July, the month after the second Haack letter and the first full month of Wednesday closings, the fail level subsided only fractionally from June's.

Late in July, the S.E.C. finally began to crack down. It issued a warning to firms that in accepting orders they were unable to handle they were violating the antifraud provisions of the securities laws and were therefore subject to prosecution. During the same month, the S.E.C. began back-office proceedings against two Stock Exchange firms, Estabrook and Company and Schwabacher and Company; in August it took similar action against seven others. The crisis lessened. The Wednesday closings, if they did nothing else, radically upset the normal pattern of trading by introducing a sort of midweek weekend. Whether they or other forces were serving to reduce the trading volume was not clear; but in any case, something was doing so, and in September fails dropped significantly. And how did the Stock Exchange react to this sign of limited progress? Under pressure from its member firms eager to get back to profitable chaos, it announced that the time was imminent for a return to a normal five-day trading week. But by now the S.E.C.'s remarkable patience had come to an end. It forced the exchanges to continue the Wednesday closings and to put special restrictions on no fewer than forty-four firms with back-office problems, compelling them to cut back their business drastically.

The surcease was temporary. In October, the bull-market tide rose strongly again; daily volume moved back up to 15 million shares, equal to the record in June, and there were two 20-million-share days, the second and third busiest days in Exchange history. Of course, the fail level shot up once more. As the autumn continued, and the public reached maniacally for easy money while Wall Street raked in the commissions, the downtown situation took on the quality of a play by Pinter or

Beckett. One Wall Streeter told about stock certificates turning up "stuffed behind pipes in ladies' rooms, at the bottom of trash baskets, in the backs of filing cabinets with old letters." Another commentator, a Stock Exchange employee, told of a small Pennsylvania investor with an account amounting to a few thousand dollars who wrote to the Exchange explaining that his broker kept mailing him statements crediting him with bonds worth $1 million—and that, despite his repeated efforts, he could not get the statements corrected. (Nor, of course, could he collect the bonds.) Investors who bought one hundred shares of a stock might receive in the mail one share, or a thousand shares, or a hundred shares of some other stock, or, frequently, an empty envelope. Sixty-dollar-a-week backroom employees, tempted by the presence of negotiable securities piled at random on every level surface around them, stole millions of dollars' worth. In December—when the bull market proceeded majestically to its climax, oblivious of all the cautious efforts of the wise men of Wall Street and the marginally stronger efforts of the scarcely wiser, but certainly more detached, wise men of Washington— the fails level climbed to a record high of over $4 billion. As never before, not in the fabled panics of 1873 or 1907 or even 1929, the American securities industry was in a state of total disarray.

4

It is time that we looked closely at the source of the trouble, the 1968 back office.

Known informally, and suggestively, as "the cage," the back office was an unlovely and constricting place to work. In its role as the dirty and clanking machinery of Wall Street, unseen and taken for granted by stock salesmen and customers alike, it had no need, from a sales point of view, to be impressive or evenly humanly gracious in its physical appointments. Instead of the thick rugs, leather chairs, shiny desks, and old prints of the reception area and boardroom, it was often sparsely and frugally furnished with dilapidated tables in need of paint, chipped desks with drawer handles loose or missing, malfunctioning typewriters, and creaking swivel chairs with missing casters. In fulfillment of its sole purpose—to keep records and to move physically money and stock certificates in conformity with transactions made in the front office—it was subdivided into a bewildering variety of departments with such discouraging names as "receive and deliver section," "box and vault section," "box tickets," and "update stock record." Operating this complex machinery required the performance of a wide variety of small jobs, all routine. Merrill Lynch, the biggest broker and therefore the proprietor of the biggest back office, had about five hundred separate clerical titles; "input typist—stock transfer department" was a typically uninspiring job description. So compartmentalized was the responsibility that there were few back-office jobs that could not be mastered by almost any high-school graduate within a matter of days. Pay was low—much below that for unskilled blue-collar work; the back-office worker's hope for a decent year's pay lay in the possibility (never a certainty) that the firm would have a good year and hand out big bonuses in December. Opportunity for advancement was slight, and for the most part confined to a few pre-selected favorites who were assumed, under the ancient American business formula, to be serving a term at the bottom in order to "acquire experience." Everyone else was assumed to be in the back office to stay. Or to leave: annual back-office turnover ran around 50 or 60 percent.

Enter a 1968 Wall Street back office and what kind of atmosphere did a visitor find? A workaday, time-serving atmosphere, as might have been expected, the tedium of routine chores performed under close supervision relieved by a good deal of horseplay, grudgingly tolerated by the supervisors. The jokes revolved around a single theme: "Any idiot could do this job without straining himself." On a busy day the atmosphere was friendly, but on a slow one it was apt to turn mean—needling, veiled insults, not-so-veiled racial slurs. (By this time, a good number of back-office employees were black.) As a social unit, the back office was much like an army platoon, its morale high when there is a job to do and low when there is time to waste. And the supervision of the back office was often patterned closely on military command. At Merrill Lynch, in the interest of keeping good order, back-office employees were told when to take their lunch breaks, and sometimes even marched to the rest rooms under supervision. Small wonder that they complained about being treated like children.

It is fair to say, then, that Wall Street in 1968, like the sweatshop owners of an earlier time, had cut its own throat through its complacency, greed, and lack of foresight. And yet the solution was easy only in theory. Two clear-cut steps might have prevented the whole mess: automation of back-office operations, and elimination of stock certificates. As to the first, it would have required a degree of planning, and an amount of capital outlay, that Wall Street in 1966 and 1967 clearly had not been able to muster. Even if such foresight and willingness to spend had been present in 1968 all over Wall Street (as it was at Lehman Brothers), the short-term result might have been to worsen the crisis rather than to relieve it. The difficult transition from hand work to machine work might have coincided with the speculative binge and made for an even greater disaster. The second step, elimination of stock certificates, called for something more than planning or expense, and something that perhaps no amount of wisdom could have accomplished—finding a way of persuading the cautious and possession-proud American stockholder that a monthly statement from his broker showing his holdings was an adequate substitute for the embossed stock certificates that he kept locked so lovingly in his bank safe-deposit box. The certificates served no essential purpose in financial terms, and were unquestionably the chief cause of the back-office problem; there was even a precedent for certificateless investment in the mutual-fund industry, which generally did not issue certificates to shareholders except on special request. But direct stock investment was another matter. There, certificates served a symbolic cultural purpose. A century and more of tradition backed up the embossed certificate with its bombastic industrial iconography. The first possession of such a certificate, through gift, inheritance, or purchase, had come to be a milestone in American middle-class life; it marked the moment when the possessor felt himself to be a person of substance and importance—a stockholder; a true capitalist. Rites of passage and symbols of possession are not readily given up, even in times like 1968 when the rites and symbols themselves stand in danger of destroying what they symbolize. Some states made certificates mandatory by law.

So immediate elimination of certificates was, for all practical purposes, a mirage. And, of course, once the back-office crisis had fairly begun it was not even that. Who would suddenly begin to trust in a broker's records as evidence of ownership at a time when those records were in such a state that the broker could not trust them himself?

In mid-1968, the Stock Exchange made a good, but far too late, effort to ease the situation through automation. For a decade, it had been toying with the notion of establishing a Central Certificate Service, a huge stock depository, with computerized record-keeping on such a scale as most individual firms could not afford, that would make possible the electronic transfer of stock held in brokers' names, and would thus theoretically reduce the handling of certificates in brokerage-firm back offices by as much as 75 percent. Essentially, the plan was to set up a master back office for the mutual use of all member brokers and thus largely replace the individual back offices. For years the Exchange had been postponing the establishment of C.C.S. on grounds of expense. Now, in the press of crisis, it hastily activated the plan, setting up a vault and a row of computers in the sub-basement of 44 Broad Street, and pronouncing C.C.S. open for deposits. A good try—but one destined in the short run for an ironic fate. Christopher Elias, an Exchange employee at the time, has described how in the first weeks of operation the C.C.S. vault was inundated with certificates in such quantity that they could not be handled by man or machine; how, in sickening imitation of the familiar back-office scene, certificates accumulated in disorderly piles on every flat surface at 44 Broad; how C.C.S. employees, hastily recruited from the scarce labor market or drafted from other Exchange departments, were helpless to create order; how for weeks the C.C.S. computers broke down almost daily. Eventually, C.C.S. would get its bearings and become a useful service. But in the time it was needed most, its first months of operation in early 1969, the facility intended to eliminate brokerage back-office problems became, instead, one more monstrous back-office problem itself.

5

The key Wall Streeters of the 1968 crisis were the back-office employees themselves.

They were young—seventeen to twenty-five in most cases; they were high-school graduates or dropouts. Few had attended college even for a year. They were quite thoroughly mixed as to sex and race; white male supremacy in Wall Street, at the clerk level, had yielded to social change and practical necessity. A solid majority, nevertheless, were white, coming from the near suburbs or the city boroughs other than Manhattan. An important brokerage official later stated his belief that many of them were hired through Mafia-controlled employment agencies. The question of the role of organized crime in the back-office snarl and the accompanying rash of securities thefts remains unanswered. In 1969, a hooded witness created a sensation when he testified before a committee of the New York State legislature as to how easy it was to steal securities. U.S. Attorney Morgenthau, after conducting an investigation, concluded that securities thefts were running at an annual rate of nearly $50 million, but that "the penetration of organized crime in Wall Street is not significant." Whatever the case, it is hard to believe that very many back-office employees in 1968 were anything more than innocent pawns of organized crime. Most of them brought little ambition to their jobs, or even the intention to remain there for long—a year, perhaps two at the most. They thought of their jobs as something to do until something better, or better paid, presented itself.

Why, then, did they come at all? For a dream of glamour; for the chance to handle or merely to be close to great sums of money; for the chance to be "where the action was"; or simply out of curiosity and the quest for experience, to find out "what Wall Street is like." Or, indeed, even for prestige: to be able to say, in the local bar or the social club, "Don't tell me about Wall Street. I work there," and to watch the heads turn and the eyes widen and be asked for a hot tip on the market. What did they ask for? A living, a sense of doing a job, office companionship, the possibility of meeting a date or a mate—all the things youth asks of routine office jobs everywhere. An ambitious few dreamed the old Wall Street dream of rising from clerk to partner. But what most of them found was tedium, disappointment, long hours, quasimilitary discipline, occasional racial flare-ups, and finally, the nightmarish frustration of being called upon to do what simply could not be done in good order and in good time.

A brilliant and dedicated observer—John W. Faison of the Wall Street Ministry, formerly a sales executive of Allied Chemical—adopted in the latter part of 1968 a classic investigative technique to the study of the goals, problems, and aspirations of back-office people. He, and four students working with him, took clerical jobs in back offices themselves.

Faison's first conclusion, based on his firsthand back-office experience, was that "we are all playing in a new ball game: this goes for Wall Street as for the universities, the political conventions, the cities, the unions. People in all their associations are calling for new rules and the umpires cannot call 'safe' and 'out' the way they could a few years ago." For example, those familiar old forces so long so helpful to business management in getting the most possible work out of low-level employees—company

loyalty and personal competitiveness—scarcely seemed to operate on the new breed of back-office employees at all. Faison
found that their loyalty was chiefly to themselves, and that it
consisted almost entirely in a desire to do the job decently and
to appear knowing in their own eyes and in those of their colleagues. There it stopped. They were offended by the thought
that they *ought* to feel commitment of any deeper sort to a job
so routine and so intellectually unchallenging. Loyalty to the
company? Considering the way it was treating them, they felt
that such loyalty would only brand them, in the opinion of their
colleagues, as "squares." Generally, Faison found, the back-
office employee "does give a day's work and that's as far as
loyalty does or should go in his eyes."

Faison found a pervasive mood of disappointment. The
clerks would put up with unlovely and overcrowded working
quarters, and even with overwork; such things they could understand and accept. What they could not understand or accept
was the sense of not, after all, being where the important things
were happening—the sense of being segregated out of sight,
brushed under the rug; of never seeing, except indirectly
through the ever-mounting work load, the excitement of the
floor and the front office in the throes of a memorable and
historic bull market. Sometimes, after the markets had closed for
the afternoon, floor clerks would come into the back office to
help straighten out mismatches—or merely to bask in adulation.
These emissaries from the exciting world "outside" would be
hungrily greeted by the back-office gnomes as people to be envied and admired, as deities descending to mingle briefly with
the groundlings.

Meanwhile the back-office supervisors seem to have had no
idea that it was a new ball game, and went on calling "safe" and
"out" in the old way. They could not understand why their
charges did not feel company loyalty or want to compete for
advancement. Nor could they understand why the clerks felt an
absolute right to joke and talk while working, or why measured
praise for work well done was received with cynicism. Faison
told later of a teletype man who was praised by his supervisor

for his fast and efficient work on the previous day. "That and a token will get me home on the subway," the teletypist retorted and turned back to his work. When the supervisor had left, the teletypist turned to Faison, who was working next to him, and said, "Some day I'm going to give him an honest answer. The reason my figures were good was that we were talking the whole day. If you do nothing but this dum-dum job all day you make mistakes out of . . . out of . . . well, I don't know out of what, but you make mistakes."

And the reverse was true; the loafers, the inevitable gold-bricks and time-servers, played scrupulously by the old rules of the supervisors, and got much of the credit. "Don't talk," they advised each other and new recruits, "look busy, and no one will bug you." Thus back offices became at times the image of a headquarters scene in some satiric movie about the old, pre-atomic army. Again as in the army, underlings' attempts to solve problems beyond their stated responsibility were greeted with indifference or hostility. Anyone who tried to find a better way of doing things was quickly labelled a wise guy. Soon would come the warning, friendly but unmistakable, from his supervisor: "Trying to put me out of a job?" Indeed, according to Faison's report there seem at times to have been positive inducements to make mistakes, which might be a way of attracting attention—even favorable attention if one played it right. Faison remembers Jim, a clerk who made a mistake and whose supervisor later came up and said, "I caught this and it's been corrected, but for God's sake, watch it next time." Jim, following the grapevine wisdom of the back room, acted obedient and penitent; the supervisor grew expansive. It was a small thing, he allowed graciously, a mistake anyone could have made; it surely would not happen again; Jim was a good fellow. The supervisor preened, his self-esteem doubly raised—once because he had caught the error and again because now he was being so magnanimous about it. When the supervisor moved on, Jim's colleagues were quick to close ranks with him, commenting sarcastically on the supervisor and his lordly manner: "Big deal— the big noise from Nyack." And Jim, warmed by appreciation, smiled and said, "At least he knows now I'm alive." So everyone involved felt better than he had before—everyone, that is, but the all unknowing owner of the stock certificates that had nearly been lost.

In their frustration and boredom, back-office employees found satisfaction in asserting their individuality through constantly discussed outside hobbies and eccentricities, through acquiring nicknames like Damon Runyon's Broadway characters: Surfin' Sally, Harry the Handicapper, Poolroom Marty. "I have borrowed a word from the hippies, and call these interests 'things,'" Faison wrote. "When the subject came up for discussion, the final word belonged to the clerk who had this or that as his 'thing.' The 'thing' was more important than the job, the office, the company. It got the possessor status. . . . The clerk who attacked a 'thing' made an instant enemy. If he wanted to stay inside the gang, he made amends and recognized his colleague's 'thing' at the earliest possible opportunity. But what does this tell us of his job, if his major commitment is to some 'thing'?"

The back office was an old story, then, told before by Dickens and Charles Chaplin, among others; a story of "young people risking what are to them the golden years," as Faison put it, and getting their return chiefly in frustration. But the old story now had an entirely new twist. Its characters were different. The young people this time were the new breed of human beings born since World War II: born, that is, as no one had ever been born before, not knowing a world without television, or jet travel, or automation, or nuclear weaponry; and knowing only by hearsay, if at all, of a world with the shared standards, conventions, and assumptions that had been undermined and finally destroyed by too-rapid technological change. Margaret Mead suggested how profoundly different were the postwar young from anyone who had come before when she wrote, "Even very recently the elders could say, 'You know, I have been young and you never have been old.' But today's young people can reply, 'you never have been young in the world I have been young in, and you never can be.'" This special self-confidence, this belief in having an understanding of the climate of the modern world that their elders could never share, was characteristic of the back-office people. As well expect them to feel loyalty to the company, or be sincerely pious about small errors in accounts, as ask a modern scientist to devote his life to alchemy.

6

Lunch time in 1968 Wall Street: the clerks, typists, and certificate-sorters of the back office pour out for an hour into the gray, mostly sunless canyon bottoms of the area, to eat sandwiches or exchange gossip or just sit and unwind, on the Subtreasury steps or in Chase Manhattan Plaza or in Trinity churchyard.

An extraordinary picture of that summer in those streets has been given by a man who prefers to be known simply as Blackie. He is a smallish man from Staten Island, a householder with a wife and children, who wears black-rimmed spectacles and has an alert, nervous manner. In 1968 he was thirty-six years old, and was a plainclothes detective of the New York Police Department.

Since 1962 Blackie had been an undercover man for the narcotics squad. His assignment was simple and straightforward: posing as an addict, to buy narcotics from sellers on the streets of the city, under observation by fellow members of his police team; after such outlaw sellers had thus been observed in action and arrested by the members of the team, to go to the precinct station and confirm the identification of the suspects (through one-way glass, to preserve Blackie's cover); to deliver the material he had bought in the street to a police laboratory for analysis to confirm that it was in fact contraband; and, finally, to appear before a county grand jury and give evidence as witness for "the people." Between 1962 and 1968, Blackie had gone through this monotonous yet hazardous procedure hundreds of times. At different periods, he had worked in Chelsea, in Harlem, in the West Eighties, in other parts of the city. Once, in 1967, working the Lower East Side, he had been mistaken for a seller by a group of men who wanted to steal from him. Unable to convince them that he had no narcotics, he had been badly beaten—a broken nose and a concussion. Another time he had had a narrow escape from death at the hands of an armed pusher who correctly suspected him of being a policeman; only Black-ie's glib tongue had saved him that time. Early in 1968, when his superiors assigned him to work the Wall Street area, he thought he was being given a rest cure in recognition of his years of dangerous duty. He says:

"Narcotics in Wall Street? Some kind of a gag, I thought. Prior to that, they hadn't assigned a single undercover Narc Squad man to work down there. Nobody dreamed there was any action on Wall Street. Oh, once in a while there'd be a complaint from the Stock Exchange that some of the boys were blowing a little pot in the building. But it was considered an isolated thing, and it was believed that the pot had been bought outside the area.

"Well, in the summer of sixty-eight I began working there, along with an arresting team. As always, my colleagues would make themselves scarce while I worked, posing as an addict, trying to score. When we had evidence against somebody, my colleagues would make the arrest and my cover would be preserved. I was the only undercover man in the area. I thought it was a waste of time, but, what the hell, I'd enjoy myself. I used to eat lunch every day on the Subtreasury steps. It was a pleasure. I'd bring a big hero sandwich and sit there, looking around at the boys and girls. I talked to them. I got myself known—as Blackie. In this game, you wear a costume appropriate to the neighborhood. In a Puerto Rican neighborhood, Puerto Rican clothes. In Harlem, clothes appropriate to Harlem. In Wall Street I wore bellbottoms, a neat shirt, maybe even a jacket—like a securities runner, or a clerk. I'd carry a manila envelope. I'd sit down there on the steps and smoke a cigarette, and look around. It wasn't long before I realized how wrong I'd been about the area. It was wild. It was like nothing I'd ever seen. Kids were just sitting there and smoking pot openly, as if they were smoking Chesterfields. I couldn't get over it, at first. I could sit there and look around and say, he's smoking pot, and so is he, and he, and she. All around me. They were so naïve, it was as if they were living in a dream world. Well, I wasn't out to arrest pot smokers—only sellers. But that was no problem. The kids hadn't bought the stuff outside the area. There were sellers right there—plenty of them. They'd get up behind the pillars at the top of the steps, and the kids would go up there to deal.

"We busted some of the sellers. It was our job. But that was only pot. Pot you can survive; I've never in all my experience seen anybody badly hurt by pot alone. What really shocked me was the heroin sold all over the place down there. As an undercover man, I bought it that summer in Chase Manhattan Plaza, in Trinity courtyard, even right on the Subtreasury steps. The sellers were everywhere. It even got so the sellers in other areas got the word that Wall Street at noon was a hot area. So they'd come down there to do two hours' fast business. There was one very popular area for dealing pot or skag or pills. For dealing anything. It was right in Trinity churchyard. Way up in the northeast corner there's a little spire with steps leading up to its base—a memorial to the patriot prisoners in the American Revolution. It can be reached only by a narrow path bounded by heavy privet hedges. Perfect protection—a cop can't approach except along that one path. I went up there and got introduced around—as a user, naturally. I was just Blackie to them. Everybody blew smoke there. You could buy hash. A guy who hung out there sold little balls of hash for a dime—ten dollars. I bought from him, and then we busted him. He was a problem though. He knew the ropes, and we finally had to chase him all the way up to City Hall to arrest him.

"I remember some of the other Wall Street pushers from that summer. They were almost local characters. There was one real slick dude, Slick I'll call him, who always wore a porkpie hat and a trim mustache. He looked like the average office worker. He had one of the best bags in Wall Street—topnotch stuff, I mean, or at least that was his reputation. There was another guy who wore sneakers and green pants—Rudy. He stuck out like a sore thumb down there. He was easy. I bought from him twice, and we busted him. Two weeks later, he'd made bail and was out there again—'Want to score, Blackie?' He still had no idea I was a cop. Naturally, I busted him again. Then there were two guys everybody called the Gold Dust Twins, one sold pot and the other heroin. They'd roam all over the area together, up and down Wall, through William down to Hanover Square, back to Trinity, everywhere. They were very square. When I went up to them and said I wanted to score, they'd bring everything out, like it was a candy store—'Pick whatever you want, Blackie.' No experienced seller does that. We busted them. The sellers in the area weren't all addicts, like the sellers in Harlem. Some of them were just businessmen making a buck. Rudy might have been skin-popping, but nothing more. Slick definitely wasn't strung out on anything. On the other hand, some of the office workers I saw were really strung out, so bad they couldn't sit down at their adding machines without getting straight first.

"What disturbed me most was seeing young office girls on pills—Tuinal, Seconal, Blue Angels. They didn't look exactly like average office girls. Not exactly. They looked *almost* like average office girls. They were just a little more dishevelled, and they'd be scratching at themselves—using pills makes you do that. Once, I saw some of them using pills right in the foyer of Trinity Church. I went to the minister and asked for permission to stay there, with my team, during the noonday service. He said no, he threw us out. Maybe he was right.

"There was a guy on crutches selling heroin in the Street. Can you imagine it—a skag dealer on crutches? I tailed him, and lost him. I actually did. It was incredible. It was at noon and the streets were crowded, and somehow he ducked into the mass of humanity and got lost. It's been a classic joke in our office ever since, the only cop who ever lost a man on crutches in a chase. And I recall another guy I lost. He had a big black attaché case, which he'd whip out and offer huge bags of smoke. When he offered them to me I was caught short. I didn't have enough money on me to pay for one of his bags, so I lost him.

"The users, the clerks and office workers, were all naïve. I can hardly believe it, looking back. They weren't people who were conditioned to the police—they acted as if it was a carnival or something. Mostly the users, even the heroin users, weren't strung-out hardcore junkies. I'd say many of them came from middle-class families. Maybe it's different now, I don't know— I don't work there any more. One thing I do know. Your average Wall Street security guard who stands around with his finger in his ear, in 1968 he didn't believe what he saw. He shut his eyes to what was in front of him. He just didn't believe it, and neither did I, until I came and worked there and found out."

Could it be, then, that part of the truth about the great Wall Street back-office crisis of 1968 is what no one has suggested above a whisper—that a major factor in it was drugs and the blessed escape into instant euphoria that the hard stuff affords? If so—and surely Blackie's story is persuasive evidence—then the implication for day-to-day commerce in the world's greatest commercial nation is large and alarming. It is that a moment arrived in Wall Street in 1968 when the necessary minions of industrial life found their work, or their lives, or both, so un-fulfilling as to drive them to chemical escape that, in its turn, made them incapable of performing the necessary work. The life-sustaining cycle of commerce had been broken.

7

When at length the back-office crisis passed, it did so without benefit of the wisdom of either Wall Street or Washington.

During a wild December, the fails level peaked out at the all-time high—$4.12 billion. Nevertheless, beginning on January 2, 1969, the exchanges resumed a five-day trading week with 2 P.M. closings. Haack explained later that the Wednesday closings had been abandoned not because they had accomplished their purpose but because they had failed to do so; too many brokerage firms, rather than using them to catch up, had simply treated them as holidays. "Frankly, I don't see any end in sight," a leading brokerage partner said. Wall Street at the turn of the year had tried all such remedial measures as it was willing and able to make, and they had all failed; it was at the end of its rope.

It was saved, not for the first time, by a *deus ex machina*. The end of the crisis was coming, and coming in its own way in its own time. In January, prices and volume both dropped sharply on the Stock Exchange, average daily trading from 15 million shares to 12 million, the Dow industrials from the December peak of 985 to the 920–930 range. The fails level responded by dropping 20 percent to $3.3 billion. In February, volume dropped to 11 million shares a day, the Dow to below 900, fails to below $3 billion. By the end of March, fails were down below $2.5 billion; in June the Dow sank to 870, in July almost to 800. Starting early in July, the exchanges began lengthening their daily trading hours, in thirty-minute stages, until closing time was back to 3:30.

The back-office crisis was over, ended less by reason and intelligence than by the advent of a bear market destined to bring new and unforeseen crises.

CHAPTER IX

Go-Go
At High Noon

1

Not by chance, cultural and social revolution hit Wall Street, New York, at the same time that it hit Wall Street, U.S.A. It was in 1968 that New York City first came to seem ungovernable, out of hand, to large numbers of formerly optimistic citizens. Those who loved the city had clung to the belief that for all its passing anarchies—soot, noise, clogged streets, racial tension, the deadly cycle of drugs and crime, unconscionable strikes against the public, corruption in office—some deep, underlying civic principle of order and good will ruled it with an invisible hand, so that things would come out all right in the end. But in 1968—perhaps chiefly because of the infamous teachers' strike, as shocking for the shrugging public acceptance of closed schools as for the cynical political maneuvering that caused and perpetuated it—the sinking feeling overtook many citizens that the invisible hand had disappeared, if it had ever existed at all, and that there was no longer any foundation of order.

But of course, it was still a great city, and in time the sinking feeling would pass. The new stridency of minorities was a result of new freedom rather than a response to new oppression, and, as the music critic Harold C. Schonberg pointed out, "around the corner, almost anywhere, is at your disposal the best art, the best music, the best libraries, the best restaurants, the most varied entertainment, that any city in the world can offer." New York's brave, hardy flowers of art and culture went on blooming in the ruins of its social order. Breaking must come before rebuilding, and it was possible to look upon New York in 1968 as not a city dying—as so many pundits inside it and out so confidently proclaimed it to be—but as one being reborn.

Almost all of the great cultural centers of history have first been financial centers. This generalization, for which New York City provides a classic example, is one to be used for purposes of point-proving only with the greatest caution. To conclude from it that financial centers naturally engender culture would be to fall into the most celebrated of logical fallacies. It is nonetheless a suggestive fact, and particularly so in the light of 1968 Wall Street, standing as it was on the toe of the same rock that supported Broadway, off-Broadway, Lincoln Center, the Metropolitan Museum, the Museum of Modern Art, and Greenwich Village. At that moment, the revolution in Wall Street standards and mores that we saw emerge in 1965 was rampant: the physical paralysis of the back offices was paralleled by the sort of overthrow of old authority and abrupt disappearance of old norms that is characteristic of social revolution at all times and places. But Wall Street's revolution, like New York's, was not entirely bad. There were new flowers budding and even blooming in the ruins.

2

Begin with the old social edifices that survived more or less intact. In many instances they were Wall Street's worst and most dispensable; for example, its long-held prejudices, mitigated only by tokenism, against women and blacks.

Women in Wall Street (as in the nation) were fighting their

way to positions of importance, but not in numbers. By 1968 there were hundreds, perhaps a few thousands, of women brokers handling primarily the business of the rising number of women investors who trusted chiefly other women—a happy case of common interest between social reform and profit. But at the higher levels, women downtown were scarcely pushing the male chauvinist pigs up against the Wall Street. On December 28, 1967, Muriel Siebert, a tough, affable, and ambitious woman broker in her thirties, who had been a stock salesman with several different firms and then decided to go it on her own, became the first woman member of the New York Stock Exchange in modern times; on the day she first went on the floor to make a trade, the Exchange bureaucracy, never noted for its delicate sensibilities, required her to wear a trainee's badge. In July 1970, Madelon Talley, a New York housewife who had tired of full-time housewifery and taken some courses in finance at Columbia, became co-manager of the Dreyfus Leverage Fund —and Wall Street's first female fund manager. A couple of long-locked doors opened a crack, then; but only a crack.

As to black men (not to speak of black women) in positions of influence or power, Wall Street had advanced the miniscule distance from the no-tokenism of 1965 to tokenism at the end of the decade. In July 1968, Shearson Hammill and Company began working on plans to open a branch office in the heart of Harlem—the first brokerage branch ever in any black ghetto in the country. It would have been quite unrealistic to assume that the local Harlem community could afford to generate sufficient brokerage business to support a profitable office, and Shearson Hammill made no such quixotic assumption. The hard-nosed notion was that white financial institutions—major foundations, mutual and pension funds, endowments—would be willing, out of charitable or public-relations motives, to channel part of their brokerage business through a Harlem office for the deliberate purpose of feeding commission money into a poor black community, instead of handing such commissions over, routinely, to prosperous Wall Streeters. There were squabbles over terms with various Harlem groups, particuarly the local chapters of CORE. Out of them came a decision by Shearson Hammill to establish a foundation—named for Crispus Attucks, the black man believed to have been the first American killed in the American Revolution—to be "dedicated to helping foster a viable economy in the Harlem community," and to be financed by pledged contributions of 7½ percent of all gross revenues of Shearson's Harlem branch. The office opened on Harlem's main drag, 125th Street, with a largely black staff, in July 1969, under the managership of Russell Goings, Jr., a firm yet amiable black man in his thirties who had once shined shoes in a suburban office of Merrill Lynch, and had briefly been a member of the Buffalo Bills football team. Enough white institutions threw business to the office to make it modestly profitable (from the start, its dealings were over 99 percent institutional), and to bring the Crispus Attucks Foundation significant revenue. Looked at cynically, the Shearson Hammill Harlem operation could be viewed as just one more instance of guilty or frightened whites paying tribute to blacks. Still, in the context of insular Wall Street—surely in most times one of the least guilt-ridden communities on Earth—it was a substantial step forward.

Downtown at the Stock Exchange, there were signs of similar progress, not yet in 1968 but soon thereafter. In February 1970, Joseph Louis Searles III, a thirty-one-year-old black man, would become the first black member in the history of the New York Stock Exchange, as a general partner of and floor broker for Newburger, Loeb and Company. Like so many Stock Exchange members before him, Searles borrowed money to buy his seat; like Russell Goings he was a former star football player —a record of participation in America's favorite weekend sports entertainment apparently being, at this time, the *de facto* prerequisite for black men in the brokerage field. But irony intruded; Joseph Searles joined the Exchange at the worst possible moment for any man of whatever color or race. The market itself is coolly impartial and, by November of the same year, Searles had lost his entire personal stake in the general 1970 crash and would soon resign his seat and leave Wall Street for a new career elsewhere.

At the end of 1970, then, the Stock Exchange would be left with a single woman member, and with no black members at all.

3

Hardly anything else on Wall Street had remained the same since 1965. The most conspicuous change was the triumph of youth. The battle of the generations had ended in a rout; living out the Freudian fantasy, Wall Street by now had killed its father. The late sixties became, for a shockingly brief moment, the heyday of the young prodigy, the sideburned gunslinger. What manner of young man was he? He came from a prospering middle-income background and often from a good business school; he was under thirty, often well under; he wore boldly striped shirts and broad, flowing ties; he radiated a confidence, a knowingness, that verged on insolence, and he liberally tossed around the newest clichés, "performance," "concept," "innovative," and "synergy"; he talked fast and dealt hard (but unlike the back-office people he seems to have seldom used drugs, including marijuana); and, if he was lucky, he made 40 or 50 percent a year on the money he managed and was rewarded with personal earnings that often exceeded $50,000 a year.

Indeed, the gunslinger hardly needed to "perform" at all. His youth itself was his stock in trade; he was a winner on board, so to speak, by virtue of an abrupt and scarcely believable reversal in local cultural fashion. *The Institutional Investor* magazine told of an under-thirty stock analyst with three years' experience (a good average for young analysts of 1968) and a salary of $25,000, who decided to better his situation by changing jobs. Within two weeks of making known his availability he had fifteen job offers, including one of $30,000 plus bonus and equity in the firm, one of $30,000 with the virtual promise of $50,000 and a partnership in two or three years, and one of $30,000 plus bonus, profit sharing, and deferred compensation. Again, *The Institutional Investor* reported, a thirty-two-year-old already making $50,000 was approached by an executive recruiter with a package offer from a mutual fund that amounted to something in the vicinity of $150,000 a year. "And you know what this character says?" the dumfounded recruiter reported. "He says he wants to *think* about it!"

In plain numbers, youth had taken over Wall Street. An old-line Boston investment advisory firm estimated, and reported to its clients with something like horror, that 10 percent of all investment people in 1969 were forty-five or over, 25 percent were twenty-five to thirty-five, and the other 65 percent were under thirty-five. In the new climate, an under-thirty had so much going for him that he sometimes needed to pick only a single stock-market winner to become nationally famous. Martin Sass, twenty-five, of the advisory firm of Argus Research, spotted a knitwear company on the rebound called Duplan, liked its management and its key product—women's pantyhose —and recommended it in April of 1968; Duplan turned out to be the biggest percentage gainer on the Big Board that year, and when *Business Week* came around to interview Sass early in 1969, he could afford to lean back and allow that "about ninety-five per cent of the stocks I screen turn out to be pretty dull"—with the off-hand manner of an elder statesman. Then there was Bill Berkley. In 1966, when he was a portly, confident, twenty-year-old second-year student at Harvard Business School, a speaker is said to have proposed to his class that all those students who would be satisfied to make twenty thousand dollars a year stand up. A few students arose. How about fifty thousand? Some more students. Well then, one hundred—two hundred thousand? By then the whole class was standing, except Berkley. Immediately after graduation in June 1968, he and an "older" partner (aged twenty-five) formed Berkley, Dean and Company; by the following January they already managed $15 million in investment accounts and had just launched their own mutual fund.

Fred Carr of Enterprise Fund was all of thirty-seven by

1968, and the once-redoubtable Fred Alger of Security Equity was going on thirty-five—fast-fading stars. ("Which Fred do you like?" insiders had asked each other a couple of years earlier; but no longer.) Gerald Tsai, at forty, was a man of the past to be revered but no longer to be heeded. It was coming to be believed, in the absence of evidence to the contrary, that almost any man under forty could intuitively understand and foresee the growth of young, fast-moving, unconventional companies better than almost anyone over forty. In the face of this clearly prejudiced new view, age continued to fight a desperate holding action. "Competence and judgment are not the product of age alone," tradition-oriented David L. Babson and Company grimly wrote its clients, "but there is a high correlation between experience and the ability to assess the risk factor." One may imagine the chortling of the gunslingers at that.

Among the weaknesses of youth is intolerance, and the youth takeover brought with it a new intolerance toward the very qualities Wall Street had always most revered, age and experience. No imaginable social change could have rocked the traditional Wall Street order more profoundly. How, then, did this sudden reversal of values come about, and was it a good thing? As to the first question, we have already noted the effect of Wall Street's missing generation, the vacuum left by the disinclination of young men of talent and energy to go there to work between 1930 and 1950. But surely something else was involved—the confluence of great worldwide trends during the late nineteen sixties toward youth-fear and youth-worship; toward allowing and even urging students to set attitudes and fashions for their elders; toward a belief that only the young were equipped to understand and master the new world that the old had created but could not control; and, finally, toward rejection of irrelevant experience and uncritical acceptance of intuition unsullied by fact. Wall Street, which lives on dreams and fashions, was, for all of its pretensions to rational practicality, precisely the milieu within which the new gospel of youth could proliferate.

Wall Street provided a climate that permitted a trend to

feed on itself; the quite traditional levers of Wall Street success, personal contacts and the possession of privileged information, now worked in favor of the young money manager or brokerage deal-maker and against the old one. Would the thirty-year-old president of a fast-moving franchising or computer-leasing firm prefer to break bread or close deals with a Wall Streeter of sixty, or with a self-anointed swinger of thirty very much like himself? When it came to the hot stocks that were the darlings of the 1968–1969 market, the Street's elder statesmen were all out to lunch. They could still get through promptly to GM or to Telephone whenever they wanted to, but that wasn't where the action was.

And yet, did it work? Did the intuition and kindred spirit of youth, as instruments of security analysts, do well by the broad mass of investors? Not judging by results. In 1970 most of the glamour stocks would fall out of bed and many of the gunslingers who had touted them would leave, or be fired from, the securities business. As John Kenneth Galbraith remarked in the spring of 1970, "Genius is a rising market." The look of eagles became a vacant stare once the ever-rising market began to plunge. But the revolution in Wall Street faiths and values that the youth binge briefly produced was a necessary corrective to some venerable shibboleths, an antithesis that might later lead to a synthesis. It taught Wall Street that old men make mistakes, too.

4

Meanwhile, the financial community had somehow, for the first time in this century, reversed its tightly held tenet that war is bullish and that peace is for the bears. This pragmatic hawkishness had become firmly established at the time of World War I, which changed the United States from the world's leading debtor nation to the world's leading creditor nation, and gave rise to the famous munitions profits so scathingly exposed by the Nye Committee during the time of the New Deal. World War II failed to produce a major bull market in large part due to the excess-profits tax, but it certainly did not produce a bear market, either; the Dow industrials on V-J Day stood some 50 percent higher than they had stood the week before Pearl Harbor. The Korean conflict, in Dow terms, was modestly bullish. The fact is, as Eliot Janeway wrote in *The Economics of Crisis*, that "America's wars seem to have paid not only somebody but usually almost everybody." International conflict was good business-page news because war, or the threat of it, kept people and machinery busy; conversely, international reconciliation or its illusion raised specters of idleness and overcapacity. Just as the Communists were always saying, finance capitalism seemed inherently to thrive on war. Or—if the matter is regarded from a moral rather than a political stance—the reaction of the Dow to peace and war over the years provides the most dramatic possible demonstration of the fact that the market, although a product of human psychology, lacks anything resembling a human soul.

The disheartening attitudes of the late nineteen fifties—those edgy years of Cold War confrontations, competitive nuclear tests, and the stockpiling of unthinkable weapons, when it had become routine for Wall Street to treat the slightest, most transient breath of international reconciliation, not to mention international amity, as a signal for panic—carried over far into the nineteen sixties. The hair-raising Cuban missile crisis in October of 1962 passed with only a momentary stock drop, apparently because investors realized with shock that while war may be good for the market, enjoyment of a good market depends on being around to enjoy it. In 1966, when demonstrations against the Vietnam War first came to Wall Street, it reacted in general with a measure of disdain. That April 12, a group of about a dozen boys and girls calling themselves Youth Against War and Fascism briefly disrupted Stock Exchange trading by throwing antiwar leaflets onto the floor from the visitors' gallery. They were dragged from the gallery by armed guards, and Exchange officials commented, no doubt justifiably, "We don't want the gallery used as a political platform." Needless to say, the stock market averages were unaffected. Two days later there was a small, acrid pitched battle on Broad Street outside the Exchange, in which Y.A.W.F. kids traded punches and insults with members of a right-wing group, American Patriots for Freedom. Official Wall Street took no notice, but open controversy over the war had invaded its precinct at last. Then, a bit more than a year later, Abbie Hoffman and his friends threw their dollar bills on the floor and elicited the response they desired.

> At first I thought throwing out money at the Stock Exchange was just a minor bit of theatre [Hoffman wrote later]. . . . We didn't even bother to call the press. About eighteen of us showed up. When we went in the guards immediately confronted us. "You are hippies here to have a demonstration and we cannot allow that in the Stock Exchange." "Who's a hippie? I'm Jewish and besides we don't do demonstrations, see we have no picket signs," I shot back. The guards . . . agreed we could go in. We stood in line with all the other tourists, exchanging stories. When the line moved around the corner, we saw more newsmen than I've ever seen in such a small area. We started clowning. Eating money, kissing and hugging, that sort of stuff. . . . We were ushered in and immediately started throwing money over the railing. The big tickertape stopped and the brokers let out a mighty cheer. The guards started pushing us and the brokers booed. When I got out, I carried on in front of the press. . . . We danced in front of the Stock Exchange, celebrating the end of money. I burned a fiver.

The event was entirely without explicit antiwar content; but hippies were associated in Wall Street minds with the antiwar cause, and perhaps the summer day of 1967 when the ticker stopped and the brokers cheered for the hippies marked the moment when Wall Street began to reverse itself on the war. In any case, the change had been fully accomplished by the following spring. The astonishing market of the first two weeks of April 1968, when prices rose wildly on record volume to usher in the manic phase of the go-go era, was manifestly a peace market, in response to President Johnson's abdication speech of March 31 and the accompanying prospect of Vietnam peace talks in Paris. The portents of peace were to prove false. But to one who happened, as I did, to be inside the Exchange on April 3—a day of all-time record volume, and incidentally a soul-stirring spring afternoon—Wall Street response was heartfelt and very nearly inspiring. By ten minutes before closing, the day's trading volume had passed the 19-million share mark, easily breaking all previous records, and the Dow was up half a dozen points. The quotation figures were dancing a jig across the lighted screens above the floor. The brokers were giving vent at intervals to shouts and loud whistles. One of them had devised some sort of launcher from which, now and again, he sent a paper airplane rocketing almost to the room's lofty ceiling. As the last five minutes of trading ticked off, the noise grew louder and more boisterous; in the last thirty seconds all of the brokers moving around the floor speeded up to just short of a run. When the closing gong sounded, the cheering almost drowned it out, and a corona of shredded paper flew up from each trading post to produce a festive semblance of fireworks. Everyone, it seemed, was happy.

If so, it seems fair to assume that the happiness was attributable not just to the prospect of peace but rather more to the fact that everyone was making money hand over fist. To be sure, a strain of genuine pacifist idealism is discernible in Wall Street in 1968. (For one example, a young fund manager named Fred Mates—third and last of the Freds—went so far as to decline to invest in companies making armaments because he did not choose to profit from the war.) But generally speaking, the coming of doveishness to Wall Street does not appear to have been causally related to the triumph of youth. For all of their sartorial flamboyance and other field marks of superficial rebelliousness, the young swingers as a group were apolitical, unsentimental, and unself-consciously single-minded in their devotion to profit. In this sense, as opposed to their investment techniques and their personal style, they were throwbacks to earlier American generations rather than exemplars of their own. Such antiwar idealism as Wall Street mustered came largely from their elders, an idealism that reached its peak on Moratorium Day, October 15, 1969, when Wall Street leaders by turns took part in a day-long reading of the names of forty thousand American soldiers killed in Vietnam from the two stone pulpits in Trinity Church; and the readers, with a few notable exceptions, were not the young Turks but rather the old pillars of respectability like J. Sinclair Armstrong, executive vice president of the U.S. Trust Company of New York and the former chairman of the S.E.C.; Robert V. Roosa, Brown Brothers partner and former Under Secretary of the Treasury; John R. Lehman, of Lehman Brothers; Amyas Ames, of Kidder Peabody; and Roswell Gilpatric, partner in the Cravath law firm and former Deputy Secretary of Defense.

The old cold war establishment had done a flip-flop and was now leading Wall Street toward peace; and the reasons were almost certainly chiefly practical. Just as Britain, back in 1910, led by the eloquent Norman Angell, had suddenly realized that the Empire was no longer a paying proposition, so the Wall Street leadership in 1967 and 1968 suddenly realized that wars like the one in Vietnam were simply no good for business. The practical considerations had changed; mounting labor costs and federal deficits had made government contracting far less profitable than it had formerly been (if profitable at all), and the mounting drain of dollars abroad put the dollar constantly in trouble on the international markets. Foreign wars, it suddenly became clear, were now a national liability.

Hard heads and a soft currency had made Wall Street doveish. Being soulless, the market cannot be congratulated on a spiritual conversion. Still, those wild days in April 1968 were a time and place when human self-interest appeared to be more than customarily enlightened. It was a time when Wall Street accordingly took on a new and unaccustomedly attractive aspect.

5

At a more down-to-earth level, Wall Street's conscience was, however, as bad as or worse than ever. And by the way this fact was identified hangs a tale.

In 1966, a young, vigorous, handsome clergyman, Francis C. Huntington, who in appearance and manner rather strikingly resembled New York City Mayor Lindsay, was working as a curate at Wall Street's Trinity Church. He was not happy in his job; he conceived his mission there very specifically, as a means to explore the work-related moral problems of people employed at a professional level in Trinity's immediate vicinity, the financial district. To this end, he began having discussions with brokers, bankers, financial lawyers, and the like, at which he encouraged them to tell, as Huntington put it, "What was bugging them about their jobs." The program did not flourish, because Trinity at the time still adhered largely to its traditional policy of tending to its spiritual knitting and leaving the worldly marketplace outside to its own devices—of rendering unto Caesar what was Caesar's and unto God what was God's. Frustrated by lack of encouragement from his superiors, Huntington left Trinity and, in January 1967, with only himself and a secretary in a little office on Liberty Street, he set up an interdenominational organization called the Wall Street Ministry, to carry on the programs he had begun at Trinity.

Modest financing came from various financial firms and industrial corporations—and from Trinity itself, which, while unwilling to foster Huntington's project as an in-house activity, was glad enough to encourage it as an independent project. The Wall Street Ministry immediately began holding regular luncheon seminars of Wall Street professionals at which they were urged to air their problems of conscience. In 1968, having acquired the services of the dropout executive John Faison, it conducted the survey of back-office life that I have described earlier; and in 1969 and 1970 it found itself in a unique position to study the effect on financial workers' morale and morality of a full-scale market crash. As Huntington described his organization's purpose, "We are aiming at a value-structure within the securities business."

The seminars, at first, were disappointing. They did not attract the kind of people who are inclined to bring up what Huntington called the gutsy problems, and when those who came did present problems, the problems always seemed to be someone else's rather than their own. Apart from this evasiveness, Huntington found anger and disappointment, particularly among the lawyers, when he would decline to give a clearcut moral answer to their questions. Why wouldn't Huntington lay down God's law the way the Supreme Court lays down man's? Thus confronted, Huntington would smilingly deny his identity with God. But the lawyers remained unsatisfied.

It was on the conscientious problems of stockbrokers that the Ministry's seminars and interviews were most productive. Brokers, unlike lawyers, proved to be quite anxious to unburden, and the picture that emerged from their talks, in 1967 and 1968, was of a brokerage industry ridden with guilt and frustration. The Oxford Dictionary tells us that between the years 1377 and 1694 the word "broker" meant, among other things, "a procurer, pimp, bawd; a pander generally." To judge from what Huntington and his colleagues heard, many brokers in Wall Street in the late nineteen sixties felt its meaning hadn't changed very much.

How, for one thing, to answer the eternal question of where to draw the line between investment and speculation? Just when is a broker morally entitled to encourage a customer to buy a frankly risky stock, and when is he not? Is the old argument that speculation serves national goals by providing for economic growth a morally defensible one, or just a piece of hypocritical rationalization? Can the habit of speculation, like that of outright gambling, be morally corrupting for an investor who comes to make a habit of it—or for the broker who encourages him to do so in order to earn commissions? "The evidence," Huntington reported later, "is that a sensitive and thoughtful salesman will have worked out answers to these questions." But how many stock salesmen of 1967–1968 were sensitive and thoughtful, or indeed experienced enough to have had time to apply sensitivity or thought to the questions? "Many salesmen," Huntington went on, "have not given these questions as much thought as they would like to give—and perhaps need to give for their own sanity."

But the matter on which the Wall Street Ministry found the jumpiest conscience among brokers—and, concomitantly, struck the tenderest nerve among their employers—was that of the overtrading, or churning, of customers' portfolios by brokers to increase commissions. Illegal though it was under S.E.C. rules, and unethical though it almost always was in terms of service to the customer, churning had become a brokerage way of life by the second half of the sixties. Nowhere in business is the choice between God and Mammon more cruelly evident than in stock brokerage. God's broker sits at his desk, believing, after careful study, that he has invested his customers' funds as well as they can be invested for the present. Out of conscience and professional ethics, he allows good portfolios to stand pat— and he thereby earns no commissions for himself or his firm. At the next desk sits Mammon's man, perpetually on the phone persuading *his* customers, perhaps against his or their best judgment, that the time has come to switch from Zenith to Motorola, from Pan Am to Chrysler. His customers are persuaded; commissions are continuously generated. Mammon's broker finishes the year with personal earnings in the $40,000 to $50,000 range and the reputation of being a man to know and cultivate; God's broker finishes with earnings of $15,000 and the reputation of a decent man who's a loser.

Put bluntly, Huntington found that many brokers felt they were under pressure to disserve their customers in order to increase their own and their firms' profits. No amount of formal management caveats against speculation or investment without investigation could paper over the essential conflict of interest; it seemed to be built into the business as practiced. "If you really want to know what bugs me," a broker told Huntington, "it's the fact that I take a client out of General Motors and put him in Chrysler—when in my heart I feel that he probably shouldn't be in any motors at all."

Another moral, or perhaps psychological, problem of brokers—what Huntington called an occupational hazard of the business—was their susceptibility to drastic overnight changes in financial status. It was in the nature of stock brokerage as practiced in the sixties that a man, without changing either his job or his way of doing it, might earn $25,000 one year, $80,000 or $100,000 the next, and then perhaps only $15,000 the third. Practical considerations aside, these fluctuations often left him confused and unhappy. In a bonanza year he would feel grossly over-rewarded and consequently guilty. Schooled to believe in financial success as the direct and measured reward of hard work, he would find the annual fluctuations profoundly unnerving. The money and status rollercoaster was unsettling to the spiritual stomachs of many of the strongest; the ride, Huntington found, often left the riders with shattered lives and marriages.

So the Wall Street Ministry—fulfilling in its modest way a function that fell to it by default—saw the spiritual malaise behind the general euphoria of the bull market. Its work was by no means universally popular. After distribution of a report that referred to the findings about brokers' guilt, a senior partner of a firm that had previously backed the enterprise called Huntington to say, "If that's the kind of thing you're up to, you can get along without my support." There were similar complaints from similar sources. Nevertheless, the Wall Street Ministry— its name watered down in 1971 to the Wall Street Center, because the word "ministry" had been found to have too sulphurous a ring in many Wall Street ears—did continue to find enough backers to get along: a still, small voice amid the clamor of the marketplace.

6

Trinity Church itself, which in 1966 had turned its own fishy clerical eye on Huntington's efforts, was changing with the times. More, it was speeding ahead of the times by seeking to change the outward mood of Wall Street; and it was succeeding to a startling extent.

The change began with a change of administration. The rector since 1952, John Heuss, was a man cast in the old Trinity mold: a pious man by his and his church's lights, and a social and ecclesiastical conservative, inclined toward the continuance of old ways and values rather than the inauguration of new directions and programs; an Anglophile; a worldly rector out of Trollope, with his port and clubs and love of outdoor life. In his *Who's Who* entry, Heuss listed ten different clubs: British Luncheon, Century, Downtown Athletic, Down Town Association, University, Pilgrims of America, Newcomen Society, St. George's Society, Stage Harbor Yacht, Chatham Beach (Mass.). Trinity in his regime—as, generally, in those that had preceded his—often seemed an all-too-worldly church, conscious of its wealth and rank and prestige, anxious to maintain its position with the secular leaders of society, and only casually interested in the life of the masses of men and women of various faiths, or of no faith, who worked in the shadow of its spire.

Superficially, John V. Butler, the man who succeeded Heuss after his death in March 1966, was cut from the same clerical cloth. True, he was only a four-club man at the time (British Luncheon, Columbia Men's Faculty, Pilgrims of America, St. George's Society), but he was straight out of the Episcopal establishment, having graduated from General Theological Seminary and served, since 1960, as dean of the Cathedral of St. John the Divine up on 111th Street. Nor was he any wild-eyed youngster; on assuming the rectorship of Trinity he had turned sixty. He was, however, a man sensitive to social change and to the need for society's institutions to change. In 1968, he brought in Donald Woodward, the doughty vicar who would stand exposed at the church's front gate during the riot of May 8, 1970; and with Woodward came John Wallace Moody, a clergyman in his thirties who had spent fourteen years as a pastor in Columbus, Ohio, and had taken time off to get a master's degree in painting and sculpture at New York University; a man with an air of clean-cut enthusiasm, medium long hair, and an esthetic manner, who was fond of expressing his enthusiasm with the quintessentially square adjective "neat."

Moody, as Trinity's curate in charge of "special ministries," was assigned to set up lunch-hour weekday programs to serve local financial workers, especially at the lower levels, not so much to involve them in the life of the church and thereby make converts of them—that was the traditional approach—as to enrich their lives for the sake of enriching their lives. Moody took it as his premise that Wall Street, for all of its wealth, was a sort of ghetto, a place that, because it was devoted to work to the exclusion of all other aspects of life, was as much in need of cultural enrichment as any other deprived area. Given a free hand by Butler and Woodward—and provided with a liberal supply of Trinity's treasure from real-estate holdings for the signing up of talent—Moody and his mixed lay and clerical committee on the lunchtime program promptly went wild. What they set out to do was as far as possible from trying to convert the heathen. It was nothing more, and nothing less, than an attempt to change Wall Street's classic noontime scowl to a smile.

The new program burst on Wall Street at the beginning of June 1969, with the inauguration of the first Trinity summer festival. On the opening day, a rock-and-roll band called the Communication Workshop performed to a large gathering in Trinity's front yard. During the following noontimes, well-known folksingers sang, there were classical concerts and free juggling lessons, balloons flew from the old church's soot-blackened turrets, and signs on the surrounding fences proclaimed, "Trinity is alive and celebrating!"

Celebrating what? Why, life itself, the thing least often

celebrated along Wall Street. More startlingly, by traditional church standards, the celebrating went on in hardly more subdued form within the church itself. Exhibits were shown, and coffee and sandwiches served, in the clergy vesting room off the south side of the transept. Pamphlets on drug abuse began to appear on the racks at the back of the church formerly reserved for programs on church activities. One day a week, in the narthex of the chapel, there was "informal worship"—featuring someone reading poetry or playing a guitar, in what Moody described as a "prayerful" way. Some days there were distinctly unprayerful music or dance performances in the church proper, following the regular noonday service; and on one of those early days, two scantily clothed professional modern dancers named Lynn Levine and Raymond Johnson performed to an astonished congregation from the sanctuary itself, with the altar moved back from its regular place to allow more room.

The noonday programs' novelty and visibility alone were enough to attract crowds. Within a week, between four and five hundred Wall Streeters were flocking daily into the church and its graveyard. Determined that participation be active, Moody and his staff set up in the courts at the edge of the graveyard graffiti and mural boards designed to permit Wall Streeters, were the spirit to move them, to express themselves in ways less constricted than are possible through office machines or stock transfer slips.

At first, the mural and graffiti boards were used sparsely and cautiously. Seeking to help break the ice, Trinity staff members took to chalking up provocatively incomplete sentences each morning, to be completed by the noontime visitors: "What are you afraid of?——————" "Life in the city today is——
——————" It worked; the spaces were filled in at noon, and soon the visitors were going on to chalk up whole sentences of their own. The magazine writer Mary Cole Hanna copied off some of them:

> Love is the only power man hasn't pursued—and the lack of it
> may cause his downfall.

Peace is the ultimate end of love.
Wall Street, its hands run to the sound of money.
You have a fiend at Chase Manhattan.

Not masterpieces of thought or expression, but something new in tongue-tied, routinized, single-minded Wall Street. Hardly more original but equally heartfelt sentiments were expressed on the mural board through faces, flowers, trees, flags, peace symbols, and boldly painted slogans like "Just live!"

In the first flush of novelty, the program went almost uncriticized, apart from an occasional hard-faced man leaning out of an overlooking building across Broadway and shouting imprecations against the new goings-on. "God would roll over in his grave," a man told Moody in the first week, after hearing of the modern dancing in the sanctuary; but the man was smiling. By the end of the second week, though, the smiles were fading, and a serious, concerted counterattack was under way. Some noontime visitors were talking loudly about sacrilege; others were complaining quietly to the church authorities. One day, a man walked up to the mural board and, without a word, took a paintbrush from the rack and broke it; on another occasion a young Wall Streeter stood in the courtyard for a while listening to an earnest discussion between two young girls about love, peace, and involvement in human affairs, and then suddenly shouted, "You're disgusting! If you want my opinion, you should be killed!" Meanwhile, the vestrymen who determined Trinity policy were being deluged with calls from businessmen attacking the new program. Thus under pressure, they yielded somewhat. By July 1, when the program was one month old, church officials had decided that all noontime activities must be previewed before presentation. As the result of this edict, performances by the Yale Theatre Ensemble of a play called "Wall Suite" were cancelled because the dialogue was found to include a four-letter word, and this in turn led one of the leaders of the program staff to resign in protest. As for the graffiti board, it survived under a form of censorship. Hereafter, it was decreed, it would be allowed to operate only with a Trinity staff member constantly nearby, eraser in hand to expunge on the spot any outpourings of the Wall Street psyche that were thought to transcend conventionality or good taste.

In time, the counterattack ran out of steam, and the Trinity noontime program survived to take leadership in the planning of the November 1969 peace demonstrations; to flourish and expand during the next two summers; and in 1971, to add a program of drug counselling and methadone rehabilitation in cooperation with Beekman Downtown Hospital. But more and more, as time went on, it became evident that the sudden introduction in 1969 of two hours a day of joy, color, and fun into the heart of number-benumbed Wall Street had exposed the rawest of raw nerves, and attacked Wall Street's serious if not sententious way of life head-on. Two hours a day of singing, dancing, writing and drawing, touching and smiling and talking: kindergarten stuff, to be sure. "When I was a child, I liked things like that," an investment-firm vice president said of the program. "But now that I am a man," he went on, gravely paraphrasing Scripture, "I have put away childish things." Indeed he had—but to what purpose?

And so, in a fine American paradox, childlike simplicity had its hour or two a day at the bottom of the canyon of Wall Street, at the very time when in offices far above, people obsessed with adult abstractions and symbols were riding toward general disaster precisely because they had lost touch with the concrete and the simple, with joy and wonder.

CHAPTER X

Confrontation

1

Spring of 1969—a time that now seems in some ways part of another, and a more romantic, era—was in the business world a time of Davids and Goliaths: of threatened takeovers of venerable Pan American World Airways by upstart Resorts International, for example, and of venerable Goodrich Tire and Rubber by upstart Northwest Industries. As we have seen, such brazen challenges to the long-established and mighty by the newly arrived and aggressive were made possible by a vast, if temporary, popularity in the stock market of the shares of young and fast-growing companies; whether the threatened takeovers represented, on the one hand, constructive efforts to bring legitimacy to vested power, or, on the other, irresponsible acts of unprovoked assault by ravenous treasury raiders, is still being debated. Undoubtedly, though, the David-and-Goliath act of early 1969 that most caught the popular imagination was an attempt upon the century-and-a-half-old Chemical Bank New York Trust Company (assets a grand $9 billion) by the eight-year-old Leasco Data Processing Equipment Corporation of

Great Neck, Long Island (assets a mere $400 million), a company entirely unknown to almost everyone in the larger business community without a special interest in either computer leasing, Leasco's principal business until 1968, or in the securities market, in which its stock was a star performer. In that takeover contest, the roles of Goliath and David were played, with exceptional spirit, by William Shryock Renchard of the Chemical and Saul Phillip Steinberg of Leasco. It would be excessive to call their short, intense confrontation the stuff of classic tragedy. But enough of the famous Aristotelian elements of tragedy were there, along with certain elements of farce, to show that Wall Street, in what might prove to have been its last years, could still fill its old role of stage and proscenium for interesting and moving human drama: not just life, but something rather larger than life.

William Renchard, the leader of Chemical, grew up in Trenton, New Jersey, where his father served as an agency manager for the New York Life Insurance Company. Trenton in the nineteen twenties, when Renchard was in his teens, was a characteristic old city of the Eastern Seaboard, already dominated in numbers by recent immigrants and light industry, yet in power and influence still controlled by an American squirearchy looking backward with nostalgia and pride to a historic past (Washington's crossing of the Delaware; the rout of the Hessians at the Battle of Trenton; the march to Princeton). The city's backward-looking aspect manifested itself in monuments and museums and stately old brick row houses; its forward-looking aspect, in brisk new plants and skyscrapers and freeways. It was a John O'Hara town, its privileged given to the starchy celebrations of country-club life. Above all, perhaps, its quality was provinciality: Trenton was constantly derided for

the huge sign on the Delaware River bridge, TRENTON
MAKES THE WORLD TAKES—but with stubborn pride it
kept the sign in place year after year. Chief among the things
it made and the world took were fine china and rubber con-
traceptives. Even on West State Street, where stood the town
houses of the well-to-do and long-established, as well as on Gou-
verneur Avenue where the Renchards lived in more modest
respectability, milk was still delivered every morning by a
horse-drawn wagon. After graduating from Trenton High
School, Bill Renchard, like most reasonably well-off Trenton
boys, aspired to go to Princeton, the famous university lying on
the Jersey horizon twelve miles to the northeast; unlike many
high-school boys in the days when Princeton still leaned
strongly toward preparatory-school graduates, he made it. At
Princeton he shared a room on campus with his brother John,
quietly did his academic work, joined one of the many eating
clubs, and took no part in the extracurricular activities—athlet-
ics, the *Daily Princetonian*, the Triangle Club, the humor magazine *The Tiger*— that were the recognized pathways to standing
on campus. In his senior classbook it was recorded that "Renchard is undecided as to his future occupation."

Perhaps the Renchard brothers felt somewhat disadvantaged at Princeton and consequently withdrew into themselves.
Indeed, they *were* disadvantaged, in spite of being presentable
and Protestant, first by their high-school background and sec-
ondly by the fact that they came from nearby Trenton, which
in those days was generally regarded by Princeton students as
a town good chiefly for getting drunk in. At any rate, by all
accounts Renchard at Princeton was the sort of self-contained
student whose peers, if they thought about it at all, probably
considered him unlikely to amount to much, then or in the
future.

If they so thought, they were wrong. However self-contained, Renchard was a tall, alert young man with an emergent
air of command, and he was among those late bloomers who in
adult life humble the social winnowers and sorters of their undergraduate classes. After graduation in 1928, he went to New

York City and landed a job as clerk with the National Bank of Commerce. In 1930, he moved to the Chemical Bank and Trust Company, as it was then called, where he served successively as a clerk, an assistant secretary, and an assistant vice president. By 1946, when he was thirty-eight, he was a full-fledged vice president; in 1955 he became executive vice president; in 1960 he was made president, and in 1966 chairman of the board of the same institution, which was by this time called the Chemical Bank New York Trust Company. Name changes resulting from mergers did not alter the institution's prestige or venerability; founded in 1824, it had been a national banking leader by the time of the Civil War (and in the years soon after, it was Hetty Green's bank, where she had a room assigned for her private use in which she liked to sprawl on the floor surrounded by her mortgages and certificates; later she moved on after she became convinced, erroneously, that someone at the Chemical was attempting to poison her). In 1966, when Renchard became Chemical's chairman, the bank had $9 billion in assets—one of the nation's largest capital pools—and was the nation's sixth largest commercial bank.

Renchard's rise to this pinnacle of American banking had been accompanied by marriage to a pretty and sociable woman; a move to New York banking's favorite living quarters, the north shore of Long Island; directorships in half a dozen large corporations; trusteeships of various hospitals and civic groups; and membership in a substantial list of metropolitan and country clubs, including the famous Creek Club in Locust Valley, of which he became president. In 1969, at sixty-one, Renchard was a large, handsome, well-set-up man with iron-gray hair, regular features, and candid eyes that suggested both flinty authority and a certain fatherly capacity for kindness. He carried with him a whiff of the outdoors—the scrubbed outdoors of well-kept lawns and clipped privet; he laughed easily and naturally and he had a penchant for brief, rather intimidating jokes. He seemed entirely at peace with himself—not in the least apologetic about enjoying, and joshing complacently about, his wealth and success at a time of violent social change. Once, he not only appeared with his wife at an epitome of the ancien régime, the annual Diamond Ball for a well-chosen four hundred at the Plaza Hotel (a benefit, of course—for the Institute for International Education), but, according to *The New York Times*, won "the honors in the glitter competition" by wearing as shirt studs three diamond stickpins as big as quarters—all of them obviously fake. A rather heavy joke, perhaps? But if anyone could carry it off, Bill Renchard could. He seemed to have become the prototypical old-style Princetonian, radiating the essence of gentlemanly aggressiveness, of polite personal and professional leverage.

Saul Phillip Steinberg, no relation to the celebrated Roumanian-born American artist Saul Steinberg, came from a background similar to Renchard's in only one respect—the families of both were firmly entrenched members of the American petit bourgeoisie. To begin with, Steinberg was a full generation Renchard's junior. Born in Brooklyn in August 1939, the son of Julius Steinberg, proprietor of Ideal Rubber Products, a small-scale manufacturer of such objects as kitchen dishracks, Steinberg, at high school in Lawrence, Long Island, was an unexceptional boy—an average student, an enthusiastic dater of girls, a competent but less than dedicated athlete—who was set apart from his classmates chiefly by the fact that he was a precocious subscriber to and regular reader of the *Wall Street Journal.* After high school, he went to the Wharton School of Finance and Commerce at the University of Pennsylvania. At Wharton —a senior at nineteen, precocious, brash, with a round babyface —Steinberg experienced a species of commercial epiphany. One of his instructors suggested that he write his senior thesis on "The Decline and Fall of I.B.M."—about as maverick an idea as might be imagined, because, by 1959, I.B.M. had already become the corporate Apollo of the modern business pantheon, generally regarded by friend and competitor alike as an organizational masterpiece. "My instructor was sure I.B.M. was some kind of fandangle," Steinberg told the writer Chris Welles a decade and many millions of dollars later. "And he wanted me to go out and prove it. I was the kind of student who was prepared to believe anything was bad, so I accepted the assignment. After I had gotten into it and done a lot of research, I discovered that . . . I.B.M. was an incredible, fantastic, brilliantly conceived company with a very rosy future. But when I told him this, he wouldn't believe me. He wouldn't even look at my research. So I ended up having to write on another subject."

Steinberg's scorned and discarded research left him with the conviction that I.B.M.'s method of doing business allowed a shining opportunity for a bright, ambitious young man to make a lot of money, and that he was the young man. The basic question involved was the effective life of industrial computers before they became obsolete, and the opportunity lay somewhere in the fact that nobody precisely knew the answer. I.B.M., which dominated the computer-making business, took the sort of conservative view that is characteristic of giant corporations riding the crest of a wave. Assuming that any given computer would become obsolete sooner rather than later, it offered its customers short-term leases, usually cancellable on short notice, for high rental rates. Steinberg proposed to offer computer-using corporations the opportunity to save money by gambling that I.B.M.'s equipment would have a longer useful life than I.B.M. itself appeared to assume. He would borrow money and buy I.B.M.'s immensely expensive computers outright; he would then lease them out—long-term and uncancellable—at rates that would be substantially below I.B.M.'s own rental charges, but still high enough so that he would recover most or all of the cost of the computer during the longer, uncancellable term of its initial lease. Thus, in the simplest terms, Steinberg would have got his purchase money back and still have the purchased computer itself left over to sell or lease again.

As simple as that, and as ingenious. With his bright idea conceived at Wharton, Steinberg gave birth to a new industry, independent computer leasing—an industry that produced no product; one that I.B.M. could kill at its pleasure by changing its leasing policies; one that the leading investment analyst John

Westergaard would later dismiss as mostly "an accounting gim-
mick"; and one of which its founder himself, Saul Steinberg,
would later say only half-jokingly, "Computer leasing? It's just
a way of getting free computers"—yet still an industry that,
before the end of the decade, would shake American finance and
banking to its foundations.

After graduating from Wharton in 1959, Steinberg spent a
couple of years working for his father; meanwhile he put in
further study on the computer-leasing idea, and conducted a
small side business in streetcorner newsstands. Then in 1961,
with $25,000 supplied by his father, he started his computer-
leasing business in a Brooklyn loft, with his father and his uncle
as nominal partners, and his company name—Ideal Leasing
Company—cribbed from his father's rubber-goods business.
Banks, however wary of his extreme youth and his too-bright-
schoolboy manner, liked his scheme and were willing to advance him money to buy computers provided he had leasing
customers for them. Finding the customers was another matter.
It took him three months to get his first lease; he interrupted his
honeymoon to come home and sign it. Ideal Leasing was incorporated in 1962; at the end of its first corporate year it had net
income of $55,000 on revenues of $1.8 million. In 1964, when
earnings were up to $255,00 and revenues to $8 million, Steinberg decided to go public. In June 1965, the company's name
was changed to Leasco Data Processing Equipment Corporation
and a public sale of Leasco stock brought in $750,000.

The computer business was booming, I.B.M. continued
charging high rates for cancellable leases, and Leasco's assets
leaped from $8 million in 1965 to $21 million in 1966, while
profits in 1967 were more than eight times those for 1966. Meanwhile, the stock, traded first over the counter and later on the
Amex, soared upward. Leasco began to be talked about in Wall
Street as one of those interesting little situations. As might be
expected of a young company with ambition, a voracious need
for cash, and a high price-to-earnings multiple, Leasco became
acquisition-minded. In 1966, Steinberg hired Michael A. Gibbs,
a young whiz from the management-consulting firm of Booz,

Allen and Hamilton, as vice president for corporate planning, and gave him the specific assignment of hunting up candidates for merger. In 1966 and 1967, Leasco increased its corporate muscle by buying several small companies in fields more or less related to computers or to leasing: Carter Auto Transport and Service Corporation; Documentation, Inc.; and Fox Computer Services. These acquisitions left the company with $74 million in assets, more than eight hundred employees, larger new headquarters in Great Neck, Long Island, and a vast appetite for further growth through mergers.

The events leading to the merger that put Leasco firmly on the national corporate map, and that made the Goliaths of industry begin to take notice of a Brooklyn David with an air of supreme confidence, began in August 1967, when Edward Netter, of the deal-making brokerage firm of Carter, Berlind and Weill, came out with a report entitled "Financial Services Holding Company," in which he set forth the rosy possibilities available to both sides in mergers between companies engaged in financial services, such as Leasco, and fire-and-casualty insurance companies. The nub of Netter's argument was that the ultraconservative financial policies of the fire-and-casualty companies had in many cases resulted in cash-heavy reserves far in excess of those required by law to cover policy risks. To these excess reserves, Netter gave the picturesque names "redundant capital" or "surplus surplus." State regulations restricted the free use of such reserves so long as they belonged to a fire-and-casualty company; but, Netter pointed out, the regulations could be circumvented, and the redundant capital freed for other uses, if the insurance company were to merge with an unregulated holding company. By implication Netter was pointing out—in the hope of earning finder's fees and brokerage commissions for his own firm—that ambitious diversified companies were missing a chance to better their circumstances by marrying fire-and-casualty companies for their redundant capital—or, more bluntly, for their money. Many diversified companies were to acquire insurance companies over the following years, the greatest such merger (and indeed, the greatest merger in corporate history) being the celebrated and controversial wedding between International Telephone and Telegraph and Hartford Fire in 1970.

One of the numerous desks the Netter report crossed, not by chance, was in the offices of Leasco, and near the end of 1967, Netter met with Gibbs to discuss the views expressed in it. Netter evidently got an enthusiastic reception, because, early in January 1968, Gibbs sent a memo to Steinberg setting forth in detail the considerable advantages to Leasco of acquiring a fire-and-casualty company—no specific company was mentioned—and the same day Arthur Carter of Carter, Berlind and Weill wrote to Leasco setting forth the brokerage firm's terms for handling the acquisition of such a company (still not named) through a tender offer to the insurance company's stockholders. The terms stated included a finder's fee to Carter, Berlind of $750,000, making abundantly clear why Carter, Berlind was going to so much trouble to serve as marriage broker.

It subsequently became equally clear that the unnamed firm Carter, Berlind had in mind was Reliance Insurance Company, a staid old Philadelphia-based fire-and-casualty underwriter with more than five thousand employees, almost $350 million in annual revenues, and a fund of more than $100 million in redundant capital. At the time, though, there was an urgent need for secrecy, to avoid disturbing Reliance's stock price and thereby stimulating its management to take defensive measures. To preserve this secrecy—and, just possibly, to enjoy some of the fun of cloak-and-dagger proceedings—Leasco men in their interoffice correspondence began referring to Reliance under the code name "Raquel." (The code name, Steinberg later told a Congressional committee, had been borrowed from the actress Raquel Welch).

In March 1968, preserving security by trading through a numbered bank account at the First National Bank of Jersey City, Leasco began buying Reliance stock on the open market in daily quantities of anywhere from one hundred to more than seven thousand shares. By early April, Leasco held 132,600 Reliance shares, or about 3 percent of all shares outstanding, and had completed Phase One of the takeover. Phase Two consisted of preparing a tender offer to Reliance shareholders, and contriving to overcome any resistance that the Reliance management might mount. In May, Leasco prepared a registration statement for its tender offer—a move that brought matters out into the open: since the statement was necessarily a public document, the public, and Reliance management, now knew at last what Leasco had in mind. Reliance's first action was to announce that the company was engaged in merger talks with another computer-leasing firm, Data Processing Financial and General—this presumably to let Leasco know that it had competition, and thus induce it either to desist from its takeover attempt or to make a better offer. On June 13, Steinberg and A. Addison Roberts, president of Reliance, met for the first time, and Roberts stated in the clearest possible terms that Reliance would be unreceptive to a Leasco takeover attempt. Nevertheless, on June 21 Leasco went ahead with its tender offer, writing Reliance stockholders and offering them Leasco convertible debentures and warrants—a classic bundle of those often dubious securities that we have heard derogated as "corporate underwear," but still a bundle that, because of the high price of all Leasco securities, had a current market value well above the current price per share of unswinging Reliance—in exchange for their Reliance stock. Three days later, Roberts, still defiant, wrote to Reliance stockholders strongly urging them "to take no hasty action with respect to your stock," and a month later he capped that action by filing a lawsuit (later withdrawn) against Leasco and its brokers, charging them with violations of the securities laws.

On the surface, it looked to be total corporate war. In retrospect, however, it appears that Roberts, for all his crustiness toward Leasco, was never entirely averse to a merger, and that what passed for furious self-defense was really something more akin to hard bargaining. Roberts, like Netter and Leasco, seems to have fully grasped the advantages of releasing all that redundant capital from the bondage of legal restrictions through a merger. Indeed, he had met with Netter to discuss that very subject as far back as December 1967, just about the time Netter was making his first contact with Leasco. Then, Netter had informed Roberts that he believed he could get him $45 a share in securities exchange for Reliance stock, which was selling at about $30, through a merger with some other firm—with a conglomerate, perhaps, like Gulf and Western. (Leasco was not mentioned specifically at that meeting.) Despite the tempting 1967 valuation, Roberts was unenthusiastic about the prospect of seeing his solid old company engulfed by some corporate upstart. It was not, then, that he was flatly against any merger; it was just that he thought Reliance ought to be the acquirer rather than the acquired.

Now, with Leasco apparently ready to make a takeover attempt whether its intended partner was willing or not, Roberts realized that the stock market's overwhelming preference for Leasco's shares as opposed to Reliance's made his desire to be the acquirer an idle dream. As to whether or not to be hostile, all through July he wavered. Reliance stockholders who wondered whether or not to accept the Leasco offer got little enough advice from him. Then, on August 1, Roberts declared himself. Leasco, he wrote the stockholders (whose heads must have been spinning by now), had sweetened the terms of its offer greatly, and Reliance management had "agreed to discontinue taking any action to impede." It was a surrender to *force majeure*; a majority of Reliance stockholders were in the act of accepting the tender offer anyway, and Leasco was going to gain control of Reliance whatever management decided. By mid-September Leasco had over 80 percent of Reliance; by mid-November it had over 96 percent. The takeover was complete.

Truly—to change the metaphor—it was a case of the minnow swallowing the whale; Reliance was nearly ten times Leasco's size, and Leasco, as the surviving company, found itself suddenly more than 80 percent in the insurance business and less than 20 percent in the computer-leasing business. Nor did the whale seem to have been hurt by the ingestion; indeed, at first glance everyone concerned seemed to be decidedly better off. Roberts, still boss of Reliance although now under Leasco's control, came out with a fresh five-year employment contract at his old salary of $80,000 for the first four years and a raise to $100,000 in the fifth, plus a generous portion of potentially lucrative Leasco stock options. Saul Steinberg came out a multimillionaire at twenty-nine, said by *Forbes* magazine to have made more money on his own—over $50 million, on paper—than any other U.S. citizen under thirty. His father and original backer, Julius, and his uncle, Meyer, were themselves worth millions from their Leasco stockholdings, as was his twenty-six-year-old brother Robert, the company's secretary. Carter, Berlind and Weill, in addition to its $750,000 finder's fee, had brokerage fees of almost $50,000 on the purchase of Reliance shares for Leasco, and dealer's fees of $230,000 on the tender offer, for a total of more than a million dollars on the whole go-round. The Reliance stockholders had their Leasco corporate underwear, which, provided they divested themselves of it immediately, left them (however naked in a corporate-securities sense) well clothed financially. As for Leasco, as a result of its extraordinary feat it suddenly had assets of $400 million instead of $74 million, net annual income of $27 million instead of $1.4 million, and 8,500 employees doing business in fifty countries instead of 800 doing business in only one. In stock-market terms, as of December 31, 1968, the price of Leasco stock had, over the five years preceding, appreciated by 5,410 percent, making it the greatest percentage gainer of all the five hundred largest publicly owned companies during that period: in sum, the undisputed king of all the go-go stocks. But our tale of financial derring-do is not yet ended; rather, it is only begun. Adventurous Leasco was now poised for the decade's greatest, and to defenders of the status quo most disturbing, venture in corporate conquest.

3

As early as December 1967, Leasco began looking into the possibility of acquiring a large bank. The stocks of banks, like those

of insurance companies, often sold at low price-to-earnings multiples, giving a stock-market high-flyer like Leasco the leverage
it needed to take over companies larger than itself. Moreover,
Steinberg felt, as a business principle, that it would be advanta-
geous to anchor Leasco's diversified financial services to a New
York money-center bank with international connections. It appears that during 1968, at the very time when the Reliance
takeover was in process, Gibbs's corporate planning department
at Leasco was picking out a banking target as carefully as a
bomber command draws a bead on any enemy ammunition
dump. Nor was any particular diffidence being shown about the
size and strength of targets. Bankers Trust, Irving Trust, Chase
Manhattan, Manufacturers Hanover, Morgan Guaranty—the
whole array of national banking power seems to have come
under Leasco's impudent, although secret, scrutiny as possible
candidates for assimilation.

By the fall, when the Reliance acquisition was all but
wrapped up, the gaze at Great Neck had come to light on Renchard's $9-billion Chemical Bank. As with Reliance, a code
name was assigned for inter-office use—in this case, "Faye," as
in Faye Dunaway. As a first step in Leasco's campaign, an elaborate dossier on the history and operations of the prospective
target was prepared: "Faye was originally the banking arm of
New York Faye Manufacturing Company," and so on. (Any
outsider who might have seen the memo and who knew anything about banking could easily have deduced from the context
that "Faye" was Chemical—again suggesting that the code
names Leasco used in its corporate assaults were at least as much
for *brio* as for concealment.) *Who's Who* entries of "Faye" directors were reproduced for ready reference, along with annota-
tions. Among those directors were such eminences of American
business as H. I. Romnes, chairman of American Telephone and
Telegraph; Lammot du Pont Copeland, president of E.I. du
Pont de Nemours; Robert C. Tyson, finance chairman of United
States Steel; Augustus C. Long, director and member of the
executive committee of Texaco, Inc.; T. Vincent Learson, president of I.B.M.; and Keith Funston, former president of the New
York Stock Exchange. It was convenient for Leasco—and it tells

something about the two firms—that practically all of Faye's directors had long entries in *Who's Who*, while no directors of Leasco at the time were listed there at all. In a kind of unintended irony, the standard checklist of the American ruling class was proving useful as a kind of sighting device to a band of outside insurgents.

The scenario that had been so effective in the case of Reliance was followed as closely as possible. In November, Leasco began buying Chemical stock—again, through the First Jersey National. Within a few days, 50,000 shares were quietly bought at a cost of more than $3.5 million, without giving rise to untoward rumors or market disruptions. Meanwhile, Reliance, now a Leasco subsidiary, held more than 100,000 additional shares, giving Leasco control of well over 1 percent of all Chemical shares outstanding. In January 1969—still maintaining strict security, and still, of course, with no contact established between the executives of Leasco and those at Chemical—Leasco proceeded to prepare a hypothetical tender offer to Chemical stockholders. As with Reliance, it involved offering warrants and convertible debentures worth at then-current prices substantially more than the market for Chemical stock. What had worked once would, presumably, work again. Still, Leasco had not yet decided to go ahead with the offer when, on the last day of January, Chemical through its regular intelligence channels finally got firm word that Leasco was preparing a takeover attempt.

The news did not catch Renchard completely by surprise. As early as December 1967, Chemical had begun following Leasco's acquisition activities in a wary, if desultory, way, and the following autumn Renchard had begun to hear rumors that "a leasing company" was interested in acquiring the bank. Rather astonishingly, the November purchases of Chemical stock went entirely unnoticed, no one at Chemical caught so much as a whisper of the code name "Faye," and the rumors seem to have died down. However, on getting the first firm information on January 31, Renchard was in no doubt as to Chemical's response. He and his bank were going to fight Leasco with all their strength. True enough, a merger, as in the Reliance case, would result in immediate financial benefit to the stockholders of both companies. But it seemed to Renchard and his colleagues that more than immediate stockholder profit was involved. The century-and-a-half-old Chemical Bank a mere division of an unseasoned upstart called Leasco? H. I. Romnes, Lammot du Pont Copeland, Robert C. Tyson, Augustus C. Long, T. Vincent Learson, and Keith Funston as members of a board of directors headed by twenty-nine-year-old Saul P. Steinberg? In established banking circles the thought bordered on sacrilege, and Renchard, on getting the word, reacted predictably by calling a fellow banker, the one most likely to be able to enlighten him further: Thomas J. Stanton, Jr., who besides being president of the First Jersey National was a director of Leasco. What was going on? Renchard wanted to know. "I'll call you back," Stanton replied. Presumably he then cleared with Steinberg as to what he should tell Renchard. When he called back, it was to inform the Chemical's boss, not too cryptically, that one of the items Leasco had on the agenda for its next board meeting, to precede the company's annual stockholders' meeting on February 11, was discussion of the possible acquisition of "a major commercial bank."

Thus alerted, Renchard went into vigorous if belated action. He set up an eleven-man task force to devise strategy for fighting off any such takeover attempt, under the direction of the Chemical's chief loan officer, J. A. McFadden—"a bright fellow, good at figures," as Renchard described him later, "not exactly a tough guy, but no pushover, either." He assigned another bank officer, Robert I. Lipp, to prepare a memo outlining all of the possible defensive strategies available to Chemical, and on February 3 Lipp came through with a list of seven different courses of action. (Out in Great Neck, almost at the same moment, Leasco was putting the finishing touches on its proposed tender offer, and was making further extensive purchases of Chemical stock—to be precise, 19,700 more shares at a cost of $1,422,207.) Renchard said long afterward, "At that time we didn't know how much of our stock they had, or what kind of

a package of wallpaper they were going to throw at our stockholders in their tender offer. We were guessing that they would
offer stuff with a market value of around $110 for each share of
our stock, which was then selling at 72. So we knew well enough
it would be tough going persuading our stockholders not to
accept."

On February 5, Renchard made his move, and a drastic and
risky one it was. He decided to force Leasco out into the open
by leaking a story to the press. That afternoon, H. Erich Heinemann, banking specialist on *The New York Times'* financial reporting staff, telephoned him to say that he had heard rumors
of an impending takeover attempt and to inquire whether there
was anything in them. Rather than make the routine denial that
he would have made under ordinary circumstances, Renchard
replied that there was, indeed, something in the rumors. He
went on to give a few details and some pointed comments, and
the following morning the *Times* carried a piece, under the
by-line of Heinemann's colleague Robert Metz, that read in part
as follows:

> Can a Johnny-come-lately on the business scene move in on the
> Establishment and knock off one of the biggest prizes in sight?
> That, it appears, is what the Leasco Data Processing Equip-
> ment Corporation hopes to do next in its dynamic acquisition
> program. The rumored target is one of the nation's most presti-
> gious banks, the Chemical Bank New York Trust Company,
> founded in 1824. . . .
> Try and get confirmation that something is going on . . . and
> you get nothing. In fact, Leasco's public relations people called
> to get a statement from the reporter.
> Is Chemical in the bag? Hardly. William S. Renchard, chair-
> man of the Chemical Bank, sounded like a Marine Corps colonel
> in presenting his battle plan for what he believes may well de-
> velop. . . . He said, "We intend to resist this with all the means
> at our command, and these might turn out to be considerable."

Understandably, the article was the talk of the banking
world that day. Renchard went on with his planning, holding
new strategy sessions at which one of the possibilities discussed,

as phrased in a memo prepared for one of the meetings by McFadden, was the following:

> There is some question about the breadth of the market on the Leasco stock and it might be possible to attack its value if need be.

Such an "attack"—carried out by making sales or short sales of Leasco stock over an extended period—would hit Leasco where it lived, since its high stock price was the source of its power and, above all, of the possibility of its taking over a firm like Chemical that was many times Leasco's size. The difficulty lay in the fact that such an attack—a bear raid—would constitute stock manipulation and would be a violation of the securities laws punishable by fines and imprisonment. For obvious reasons, no one has ever been willing to say that at Chemical's February 6 strategy meeting that particular recommendation was adopted for action. The striking and undeniable fact is, however, that on that very day, Leasco stock, which had been hovering in the stratosphere at around 140, abruptly began to fall in price on large trading volume. By the close the following day Leasco was down almost seven points, and over the following three weeks it would drop inexorably below 100. Rumors of impending mergers, particularly between titans, customarily drive a company's stock price *up*, not down. Long afterward, Steinberg said of the curious coincidence in timing as to the proposed Chemical takeover and the beginning of the Leasco slide, "It *is* odd—so odd that Congressman Wright Patman asked me the same question. But we've never been able to pin anything down." As for Renchard, he later told a Congressional committee that he thought the stock drop was simply the result of institutional holders beginning to lose confidence in Leasco; but still later than that, he pointed out, without elaboration, that one of the defensive techniques discussed in the Chemical strategy meetings had been drawn from a *Harvard Business Review* article called "multiple flogging." "Multiple flogging," in the context, was a fancy new name for an old-fashioned bear raid. By using various concealment devices, it is theoretically possible to carry out a bear raid without detection by the authorities. The evidence suggests, at least, that on February 6 somebody, identity unknown, started lowering a very heavy boom on Leasco.

4

Steinberg reacted to the *Times* article exactly as Renchard had planned that he should. Although Steinberg was not ready to make his tender offer and, in fact, was considering waiting several months before doing so, he decided that now he had no choice but to go ahead immediately—and from his point of view, prematurely—and, as a first step, he resolved to have an exploratory talk with Renchard early the following week.

On Friday, February 7, the day after the *Times* article, Steinberg had lunch with Heinemann. By Steinberg's account the timing was pure coincidence, since the lunch had been arranged weeks before; it was, however, an obvious windfall for Heinemann as a reporter to be seeing Steinberg at the very moment when the meteorically successful boy wonder was at the center of the biggest financial story in the nation. At the lunch, Steinberg insists that it was understood by both sides that everything was off the record; then he proceeded to discuss Leasco's plans freely, not to say indiscreetly. When he had finished, he asked Heinemann, as a man knowledgeable about banking, for his impressions. According to Steinberg, Heinemann replied that in believing for a moment that he could get away with taking over Chemical Steinberg showed himself to be "an innocent." At any rate, Steinberg later decided that he had been an innocent about Heinemann. That afternoon, Heinemann called up the Chemical Bank and talked to a public-relations officer there, to whom he reported in detail what he had heard from Steinberg. That same afternoon, the public relations officer sent Renchard a memo that read, in part:

Heinemann just came back from lunch with Steinberg, and passed on the following results.

They said they are beginning to feel the pressure. They knew there would be absolute opposition, and they fully believe that when they come in with their proposal it will be rejected. . . .

Erich was told that it is a better than 50–50 chance that Leasco will announce their intentions and plan at the annual meeting next week. Steinberg took the position that their offer will be most beneficial for us. . . . Steinberg said flatly that the way we handle international business . . . is wrong and will be changed.

(Heinemann's version of the episode differs from Steinberg's in several crucial respects. In the first place, he said later that his luncheon with Steinberg had not been arranged weeks previously but only four days before—at the urgent request of Steinberg's public-relations counsellor. Moreover—and more crucially—Heinemann avows that at the luncheon he was not asked for and did not give any assurance that what was said be held confidential, and that he subsequently called Chemical, as a conscientious reporter, in an attempt to elicit additional information for a possible new story.)

Steinberg said later that the memo gave a generally accurate account of what he had said at the lunch, with the notable exception that he had said nothing about pressure—that, indeed, he had felt no pressure from banks at that time, although he was to feel plenty of it later on. The nearest thing to pressure on Leasco as of February 7 was a conversation Steinberg had that day with Donald M. Graham, chairman of Continental Illinois Bank and Trust Company, a leading Leasco creditor, in which Graham expressed the view that a Leasco attempt to take over Chemical would not be a good thing for banking—and added, most unthreateningly, that his bank highly valued its association with Leasco and expected it to continue. (Renchard, in fact, had talked to Graham and urged him to discourage Steinberg.) The memo seemed to give Chemical a momentary edge; and, seizing the initiative, the bank took the comparatively drastic step of planning a full-scale strategy meeting at 20 Pine Street the following morning, even though the day would be Saturday.

It turned out to be a wild weekend of feints and counter-feints. Steinberg was busy with a semi-annual conference of Leasco district managers, and on that account, he stayed in town at the Regency Hotel. By another coincidence, that same weekend was the occasion of the American Bankers Association's annual trust conference, and consequently New York City was swarming with hundreds of important bankers from all over the country. At the Chemical strategy meeting—which was attended, this time, not only by Chemical's in-house task force, but by invitees from other powerful Wall Street institutions sympathetic to the Chemical cause, including First Boston, Kuhn Loeb, and Hornblower Weeks—a whole array of defensive measures were taken up and thrashed out, among them the organizing of telephone teams to contact Chemical stockholders; the retaining of the leading proxy-soliciting firms solely to deny their services to Leasco; the possibility of Chemical's making a quick merger of its own with some other computer-leasing company, to raise an antitrust obstacle for Leasco; and the possibility of getting state and federal legislation introduced through the bankers' friends in Albany and Washington in order to make a Leasco takeover of Chemical illegal. Despite the availability of such weapons, the opinion of those present seemed to be that Leasco's venture had an excellent chance of success. There was a sense of backs to the wall, of the barbarians at the gates, of time running out. Reports of the meeting filtered out that evening to the bankers assembled around town at their cocktail parties, receptions, and dinners. One such report had it that a participant at the session had finally thrown up his hands and said, "Oh, let the kid have the bank. We'll start a new one!" Levity, it seemed, with an edge of hysteria.

On Sunday, New York City was hit by a fifteen-inch snowstorm, the worst in seven years, and as a result, airports were closed, roads were clogged, rail service was disrupted, and the bankers in town were trapped. There was nothing for them to do but stay and talk—largely about Leasco and Chemical. The bankers, and the subject, were caught in a kind of pressure cooker. That evening, Chemical held a large reception for the visiting bankers at the Plaza. (Steinberg, the subject of all the discussion, stayed at the Regency four blocks away; not being a banker, he wasn't invited.) At the reception Renchard took considerable kidding; the prevailing attitude among the bankers he talked to seemed to be that the whole thing was ridiculous, an attitude that Renchard felt he had little reason to share. "Don't joke," he would say. "If this is successful, the next target may be you."

On Monday, with the city still snowbound, Renchard and Steinberg, who had previously never so much as talked on the telephone, met at last. That morning Steinberg, carrying out his plan, called Renchard at his office and asked if they could get together. Renchard said, "Sure. I'll buy you lunch, but I have to go to a meeting right afterward. Do you have transportation?" Steinberg said he hadn't. "I'll send my car to get you," Renchard replied. So Renchard sent his car to the Regency, Steinberg got in and sloshed comfortably downtown, and the lunch that Renchard "bought" him took place that noon in the Chemical Bank's private dining room. One may imagine the first reactions of the antagonists to each other. One was lean, iron-gray, of distinctly military bearing; a North Shore estate owner, very conscious of the entrenched power of the nation standing behind him, very much a man of few and incisive words. The other was round-faced, easy-smiling, a man of many words who looked preposterously younger than his already preposterous twenty-nine years, and given, as he talked, to making windmill gestures with his arms and suddenly jumping galvanically up from his chair; a *South* Shore estate owner (twenty-nine rooms, tennis court, two saunas, Picassos and Kandinskys—as Steinberg himself characteristically described it, "a modern mansion just like that of any other successful kid of twenty-nine"); a young man bubbling with energy and joy in living. (Contrary to repeated press reports, he was not fat, only chunky; photographs of his jowly face deceived people.) Now he seemed to be, in the tragicomic fashion of that year, the corporate version of a campus radical informing the university president, with a mixture of amusement and pity, that the times had changed and the freshmen were taking over.

The two men's accounts of the ensuing meeting, as told to me several years later, differ to some extent as to content, but to a greater and perhaps more interesting extent as to style and emphasis.

Renchard: "Steinberg, at some length, gave his ideas on how commercial banking was going to be revolutionized over the next few years. Mostly I just listened, and so did my colleagues [President Howard] McCall and [Vice Chairman Hulbert] Aldrich, who joined us toward the end of the session. The whole industry was to benefit greatly, Steinberg said. I asked him why he had singled out Chemical. He said he liked our philosophy, that is, we were in the process of forming a one-bank holding company that would enable us to diversify, thereby showing that we believed in the principle of bank diversification. He had evidently ruled out Citibank and Chase as too big. Bankers Trust and Irving were out for technical reasons, and Morgan probably because it was strictly a wholesale business. He seemed to like us better than Manufacturers Hanover.

"I said I wasn't sure he appreciated what might happen to our business when someone with no banking experience moved in on a takeover basis. Directors and officers might leave. I made it clear that I didn't think *I'd* be around. In the trust area, for people to leave their estates with a bank you need confidence built up over many years. Will appointments would leave in droves, I said, not because of anything about him but because it was a takeover. Then there was the worry about somebody acquisition-minded having access to our stockholder lists. The confidential relationship of banker to client might be endangered.

"I think it impressed him a little bit. Steinberg said he had no intention of making an unfriendly takeover—that is, that he didn't want to, but might. There was the hint of a threat. I said, 'If you want to get into a fight, I'm a pretty good gutter fighter.' He said, 'I've already found that out.' He said he wanted to make a full presentation of Leasco's plans the next afternoon, after his company's annual meeting, in the hope that Chemical would change its mind and want to cooperate, after all. I enjoyed the luncheon. There was some kidding around, too."

Steinberg: "When I got to 20 Pine Street that morning, I got out of Renchard's car and walked into the bank. It was a day when not many people were there, because of the snowstorm. Renchard's secretary was very friendly—'Oh, hello, Mr. Steinberg, I'm so glad to see you.' Renchard came out and shook my hand and said, 'Hello, Saul. Call me Bill. Can I take you around and show you the place?' Well, I wasn't terribly interested in looking at the real estate right then. So we went and talked, first in his office and later in the bank's dining room.

"We did some kidding at first. He asked me why I wanted to become a banker and I said, 'God looks after drunks and bankers, and I don't want to be a drunk.' Then I started in giving the facts. I told him how many Chemical shares Leasco had—more than three hundred thousand. I said we weren't going to accumulate much more because it was getting too expensive. I told him frankly that the *Times* piece had disrupted Leasco's plans; we had wanted to wait until the forthcoming new law regulating bank holding companies was passed, and that might be six months or a year. Now our hand was forced, and I volunteered that for us it was premature.

"I went into my philosophy of how Chemical's management, and all commercial-bank managements, should be more responsive to stockholders and customers, and how I thought we could make it that way. I said I thought that adding a broad range of services to a bank's regular functions would add to the intrinsic value of its money, and on that he expressed absolute agreement in principle. He began to talk about the possible detriments to the bank's business from a hostile takeover. He said top management would probably resign. He mentioned losing customers, and I said they would hardly leave in a hurry at a tight-money time like that. He talked about damage to the trust business. I asked, 'Does it make money?' He laughed, and said he wasn't sure. He said if I wanted a fight he was a pretty good gutter fighter, and I said my record as a gutter fighter was considered to be pretty good, too, at least for my age. But then I said I wasn't planning a hostile takeover, although I wasn't ruling one out. I told him that in four days I was going to Puerto Rico on vacation with my wife and kids—it was the kids' winter semester break—and that I was professional enough not to be planning such a thing as that if I were thinking of attempting a hostile takeover. He looked surprised and asked, 'Are you really going to Puerto Rico?' I said yes. He was obviously relieved. Everything became very relaxed. I thought it was a rather constructive meeting. Everything was friendly and affable. The atmosphere was dampened at the end, though, when McCall and Aldrich came in—McCall for lunch with us, and Aldrich at the end of lunch. McCall just didn't seem to want to have anything to do with me one way or the other, and Aldrich seemed downright hostile. But Renchard interrupted them to say, 'Look, Saul has stated that he has no intention of a hostile takeover.' McCall's face lit up, and he said, 'Well, when can we meet again?' I suggested after my trip to Puerto Rico, and he and Renchard said, 'Oh, let's do it before that,' and we arranged for the following afternoon, after our stockholders' meeting. I came out in a positive frame of mind. The only thing was that Aldrich was still cold. But wait—come to think of it, he wasn't any too cordial to Renchard, either."

So the first meeting of the rival chieftains was a standoff. That afternoon, Renchard heard from Roberts of Reliance Insurance. The apparently satisfied subject of Leasco's previous conquest said he thought a merger of Leasco and Chemical would be a fine thing for the bank. "I told him he was off his rocker," Renchard said later. "I said computer leasing has nothing to do with banking. He said the Leasco-Reliance merger hadn't hurt Reliance. I was disappointed in him." Also that afternoon, McCall had someone at Chemical prepare for him a list of Leasco's creditor banks, and when the list later came to the attention of a Congressional committee, it was found that checkmarks had been made beside the names of certain of the banks; the purpose of the list, and the meaning of the checkmarks, is not known, but the fact is that on that very afternoon Steinberg began to feel "pressure" from the banking business in the form of calls from Leasco's two investment bankers, White, Weld and Lehman Brothers, informing him that they would refuse to participate in any Leasco tender offer for Chemical.

That evening, there was more socializing among the bankers. Renchard went to a dinner of the Reserve City Bankers Association at which, he said later, he may have spoken to three hundred bankers. "I have no recollection of anything except general conversation about this development," he recounts, denying that he used the event as an opportunity to spread anti-Leasco propaganda or solicit support for Chemical. (He had not, however, shown such restraint during working hours; the anti-Leasco announcements of White, Weld and Lehman had followed urgent appeals from Chemical.)

At Leasco's annual stockholders' meeting, held the following afternoon in the auditorium of the Chase Manhattan Bank Building, matters proceeded smoothly enough, with no mention of the subject that was in everyone's mind, until Steinberg observed that Leasco's commitment to becoming a comprehensive financial-services organization included the objective of entering the field of banking. "The realization of so large a plan," he went on, "requires the exercise of careful and deliberate judgment. At the present time, we have not made a decision as to a particular bank."

A hush filled the room; Steinberg broke it by asking for questions. A stockholder asked flatly whether Leasco was planning to acquire the Chemical Bank. Steinberg replied that Leasco had made no statement regarding that bank or any other. Then, a bit later, another stockholder asked whether Leasco had already had merger discussions with Chemical.

Steinberg was on the spot; over the weekend he had planned to announce his tender offer on this occasion, but now, with the door still open to possible agreement with Chemical officers at the meeting to be held in only a couple of hours, he had decided to hold off. For diplomatic reasons, it would be best to evade the question, but he rejected that course. "I said to myself, 'Heck, I'm not going to lie,' " he recounted later. He answered, "Yes, we have met with the Chemical"—thereby publicly confirming for the first time what up to then had been in the realm of rumor and conjecture.

5

But later that afternoon, at the private meeting between Leasco and Chemical officers, the crack in the door that Steinberg had discerned at the previous day's luncheon seems to have narrowed perceptibly. The defense was gaining confidence. This time, the rival generals were accompanied by their chief aides; Steinberg came with three, including Roberts and Counsel Robert Hodes, and Renchard with four, including McCall, Aldrich, and Task Force Generalissimo McFadden. Steinberg went over much of the ground he had covered in the previous day's luncheon with Renchard, this time putting more emphasis on his friendly intentions and his disinclination to threaten. (Aldrich's personal notes on the meeting say: "Tender route loathesome to Leasco—but might have to go it to accomplish ends.") Steinberg also made a further concession. He said he was prepared not to be chief executive officer of the merged company, and that all of his Leasco colleagues would be willing to put their jobs at risk on the basis of the merged company's profit record. When Renchard said that he was unwilling to negotiate with "a gun at my head," Steinberg insisted that no gun was intended, that this "wasn't war." Both sides later characterized the meeting as cordial, although Steinberg felt that it had been "not overly friendly." According to Aldrich's notes, it concluded with Renchard saying, in effect, "We have lots to consider. Will do so. They will hear from us—maybe end of week, maybe middle of next week."

In fact, Steinberg would hear from Renchard again that Friday, February 14, but in the meantime the Chemical defense battalion was far from idle; on the contrary, it was now trundling up its big guns, those "resources" that Renchard had described at the outset as "considerable." Chemical held another full-scale battle meeting at which the discussion centered on the possibility of changing Chemical's charter in such a way as to make a Leasco takeover legally difficult if not impossible. There was also talk about perhaps buying a fire-and-casualty company to create an antitrust conflict with Leasco's ownership of Reliance, or even, as a last resort, of arranging to have some giant insurance company take over *Chemical*—suggesting a positively Oriental preference for suicide rather than surrender.

As it happened, none of these schemes was carried out; certainly, though, the last one reflects the bankers' mood of grim intransigence. As planned, the bank retained the two leading proxy-soliciting firms, Dudley King and Georgeson, to deny their services to Leasco. Renchard called Chairman Martin of the Federal Reserve Board to apprise him of the situation and, hardly incidentally, to try to persuade him that a Leasco takeover would be bad for banking as a whole. (Martin took no action.) And also meanwhile, from whatever cause, Leasco's stock kept dropping; by Friday it was down to 123 and in full retreat. Probably the most effective of Chemical's various salvos was on the legislative front. Beginning on February 14, Richard Simmons of the Cravath law firm, on retainer from Chemical, began devoting full time to the Leasco affair, concentrating his attention on the drafting of laws specifically designed to prevent or make difficult the takeover of banks similar to Chemical by companies that resembled Leasco, and to getting these drafts introduced as bills in the State Legislature in Albany and the Congress in Washington. Does it seem odd that a proposed new law, hand-tailored by a chief party at interest, should be accepted without question by tribunes of the people in a state or federal legislative body? Whatever the answer, Governor Rockefeller chose that very week to urge the New York Legislature to enact a law enabling the state to stop any takeover of a bank by a non-bank, within its boundaries, in a case where "the exercise of control might impair the safe and sound conduct of the bank." By Friday, precisely such a proposed law, straight from Simmons' desk, had been dispatched to Albany, and a national one of similar intent to Senator John J. Sparkman, chairman of the Senate Banking and Currency Committee in Washington.

Apparently Chemical had reason to believe that in both cases the drafts would be introduced without significant alteration.

Thus it was with a sense of a turning tide of battle that Renchard telephoned Steinberg again on Friday the fourteenth, to make a new appointment. This time there was no further talk of gutter fighters and the like. Doubtless Renchard no longer felt the need for such talk. Was Steinberg still going on that vacation? Steinberg said he was—leaving the next day, and remaining in Puerto Rico until the following Wednesday, the nineteenth, when he had appointments in Washington. Renchard said amiably, "What's the use of busting up your trip?" and invited Steinberg to come in and see him again on Thursday the twentieth. And so it was agreed.

By the following Monday and Tuesday, the would-be attackers were plainly on the defensive. A *Wall Street Journal* article published on Monday raised questions as to the future earnings prospects for Leasco. Leasco stock dropped eight points that day, to 115, and two and a half points more the following day. Simmons' anti-bank-takeover bill was duly introduced in Albany on Tuesday. (It was subsequently passed, and became law in mid-May.) Leasco suffered a further setback when the company got a letter from the Department of Justice saying it had heard of Leasco's plans to merge with Chemical and commenting, "Although we do not suggest that such a transaction would violate the antitrust laws, questions under these laws are raised thereby, particularly under Section 7 of the Clayton Act." (Section 7 prohibits combinations that may restrain trade by reducing competition; its applicability to a Leasco-Chemical merger, as it was generally interpreted at that time, would appear to be highly questionable. Just how the Justice Department came to send such a letter at that particular moment has never been explained.) While these things were happening, Steinberg was with his family at the Dorado Beach in Puerto Rico, playing tennis, swimming, and, he insisted later, talking on the phone to his office in Great Neck only twice. It is hard, though, to imagine that he did not learn one way or another about the *Journal* article, the continuing Leasco stock drop, the bill intro-

duced in Albany, and the ominous letter from Justice. For all of
his impulsiveness, Steinberg is a reflective man, and it seems not
impossible that, relaxing by the pool at the Dorado Beach, he
reflected with irony that, having conducted his company's annual meeting the previous week at a (David) Rockefeller bank,
he was now paying top rates to another (Laurance) Rockefeller
hotel for a quick vacation from the battle lines while a third
(Nelson) Rockefeller was urging on the State Legislature a law
intended specifically to thwart him in what he considered to be
a legitimate and even socially beneficial enterprise.

Steinberg's day in Washington—Wednesday the nineteenth—was a depressing one. All occasions now seemed to
inform against him. For one thing, the mysterious decline in
Leasco's stock price was reducing the company's takeover
power day by day. But the situation was not yet hopeless on that
front. Steinberg calculated that he could put together a tender
offer that would be attractive to Chemical stockholders, and that
would not cut Leasco's earnings, down to a Leasco stock price
of 85. As of February 19 the price stood at around 110, so that
an interesting offer remained entirely feasible—provided some
way could be found to prevent the stock's downward toboggan
ride from continuing. The other pressing concern was the national legislative situation—the matter that had brought Steinberg to Washington—and here he found a bleak picture indeed.
The nation's legislators were in a grimly anticonglomerate,
antitakeover mood. During the day Steinberg talked to half the
members of the Senate Banking and Currency Committee and
to several members of the Federal Reserve Board; without exception, he found his interviewees adamantly opposed to a
Leasco takeover of Chemical on grounds that seemed to him to
be entirely unreasonable. Time and again, he explained that his
object was not the destruction of a bank but its revitalization,
and he argued that takeovers of one company by another, far
from being automatically bad, are a valuable and necessary part
of the free-enterprise system, and in some cases the only way by
which backward and outmoded management methods can be
replaced by aggressive, forward-looking ones. Time and again,

he found his arguments going unanswered, and himself being treated as a sort of business pirate bent on seizing and looting property that did not belong to him. The climax of these brief and sketchy dialogues was one with the key man, Senator Sparkman, part of which went, according to Steinberg's account, as follows:

> SPARKMAN. A couple of weeks ago I had a fellow in here complaining that somebody moved in and took over his bank and then fired him. Now, we can't have things like that.
>
> STEINBERG. But, Senator, the whole economy runs on profit. If a bank president isn't delivering, he should be replaced just like anyone else. Unless you want to change the whole system—
>
> SPARKMAN. No, no, I don't want to do that. By the way, have you seen the bill I'm going to introduce against bank takeovers? (Calling to his secretary) Miss———, where's that bill the lawyer for Chemical Bank sent in? I want to show it to Mr. Steinberg.

It was thus that Steinberg learned for the first time of the bill Simmons had drafted at Chemical's behest and, as Senator Sparkman so candidly put it, "sent in." As it happened, Sparkman introduced the bill in late March; unlike the New York State legislation, it was never passed; but on March 19, the knowledge that a lawyer on Chemical retainer was apparently functioning as a sort of unofficial legislative assistant to the chairman of the Senate Banking and Currency Committee served to deepen Steinberg's gathering despair. Only much later did he come to see his conversation with Sparkman as a piece of high Washington comedy.

"I came back to New York that night feeling that I had been given a very clear message," Steinberg said later. In fact, that day, with the realization that the national powers of government as well as those of business were solidly aligned against him, Steinberg decided on surrender. The following morning, he went as scheduled to his third meeting with the Chemical's top officers, at 20 Pine Street. As things turned out, it was to be his last such meeting. Again let us hear two versions:

Steinberg: "I came into the meeting with a public statement in my pocket—a surrender statement. I told them I'd been in Washington the previous day, and I told them whom I'd met. I said I'd concluded as a result of those conversations that the only way we could proceed with a tender offer was with Chemical's great enthusiasm for the merger, and I wasn't sure even that would help. I waited a few moments. To put it mildly, nobody from Chemical expressed great enthusiasm. Then I said that in half an hour I was going to release a statement of withdrawal. I pulled the statement out of my pocket and read it to the Chemical men. You could sense the relief—almost touch it. There was a kind of quiet pandemonium. Everybody shook hands. I haven't seen any of them since then."

Renchard: "Steinberg came in with a couple of henchmen. He said he'd decided it wasn't the time to pursue the matter, and he was going to make an announcement to that effect later that day. It was a very friendly and satisfactory meeting."

The announcement that Steinberg released later—which, in view of the fact that its last part largely negates a philosophy that he had expressed previously and would reaffirm later, suggests that he had been temporarily brainwashed—read as follows:

> GREAT NECK N. Y., February 20, 1969—Saul P. Steinberg, chairman of Leasco Data Processing Equipment Corporation, stated today that he has no plans to acquire control of the Chemical New York Corporation. Without the support and enthusiasm of the management, Leasco has no interest in pressing for an affiliation with Chemical.
>
> Mr. Steinberg observed that hostile takeovers of money-center banks were against the best interest of the economy because of the danger of upsetting the stability and prestige of the banking system and diminishing public confidence in it.

It was presumably with satisfaction that Romnes, Copeland, Tyson, Long, Learson, Funston, and the other Chemical directors that afternoon read the following telegram:

PLEASED TO REPORT LEASCO HAS ANNOUNCED WITHDRAWAL OF
PLANS TO PRESS FOR AFFILIATION WITH CHEMICAL

BILL RENCHARD

6

So it was over, just two weeks after it had formally begun.
"They"—the Chemical Bank, most of the banking business, the
Cravath law firm, a cross section of Wall Street power and
influence, the leading proxy solicitors, the governor and legislature of New York State, the members of the Federal Reserve
Board and the Senate Banking and Currency Committee, and
sundry more or less related forces—had combined to beat Saul
Steinberg of Leasco, and apparently to cause him to lose his
nerve at the last moment. (He and Leasco came back—gamely,
although disastrously from a financial point of view—to take
over control that summer of Pergamon Press, a British publishing giant.)

And yet it wasn't really quite over; for American business
and society alike, it had reverberations, some perhaps beneficial,
others certainly purgative and self-revelatory. Renchard said
later, "I took the whole thing very seriously, although a lot of
people I know didn't. At the bank we're more on the alert now
for that kind of thing. I took a lot of kidding about it. If Steinberg had gone ahead, it could have resulted in quite a fight. I'm
not saying we would have been defeated. I still think we could
have successfully fought them off. I'm just as glad not to have
had to go through the process, though."

What Steinberg, for his part, chiefly remembers about the
whole episode is the aura of hysteria that seemed to pervade so
many people's reactions to it. "Nobody was objective," he says.
"I wanted objective opinions, and I couldn't get them. All
through those two weeks, bankers and businessmen I'd never
met kept calling up out of the blue and attacking us for merely

thinking about taking over a big bank. Some of the attacks were pretty funny—responsible investment bankers talking as if we were using Mafia tactics. And it went on afterwards. Months after we'd abandoned our plans, executives of major corporations were still calling up and ranting, 'I feel it was so *wrong*, what you tried to do—' And yet they could never say why. We'd touched some kind of a nerve center. I still don't know exactly what it was. Once, at a party, the head of a huge corporation asked me if there had been any anti-Semitism in the campaign against us. I said, not that I knew of. There are bankers and businessmen who are anti-Semitic, but it was more than that. I think now it would have been a good thing if we'd done a hostile takeover, and then there had been Congressional hearings, to get all those rancid emotions out in the open air."

Ruefully, Steinberg summed up his emotional reaction when he said, immediately after his surrender, "I always knew there was an Establishment—I just used to think I was a part of it." As for the Establishment, perhaps *its* last word on the affair was the apothegm allegedly pronounced on it by an officer of a lordly commercial bank, who is supposed to have said, with a lordly mixture of misinformation, illogic, and sententiousness, "Never trust a fat man."

CHAPTER XI

Revelry
Before Waterloo

1

While Steinberg was finding out that he did not belong to the Establishment, and that in its old age it was neither too gentlemanly nor too toothless to fight, the investment revolution of the nineteen sixties was all but completed, and the era was having its last great speculative fling.

By 1969, institutional investors had effectively taken over the New York Stock Exchange business. At the beginning of the decade their share in it had been less than a third; now they had 54 percent of total public-share volume and 60 percent of total public-dollar volume. The mutual funds, the fastest-growing of the investing institutions, now held assets of some $50 billion, and were moving in and out of the market at a turnover rate of 50 percent, or half of their portfolios per year, as against less than 20 percent as recently at 1962.

The market was beginning to unravel in earnest. The Dow, after peaking out at 970 in May—only a few points below the all-time high of January 1966—went into a steep three-month decline that left it just above the 800 mark late in July. The

Federal Reserve, worried about accelerating inflation, kept constricting the money supply, driving interest rates through the roof without apparently accomplishing its purpose, and there came to be the specter—confounding to classical economists—of a recession accompanied by runaway inflation, the worst of two apparently opposing worlds. The failure of the blue-chip Dow to reflect the true situation was becoming more pronounced all the time; the advance guard of the former high flyers were already crashing not 20 percent like the Dow but 50 to 75 percent, and even more. Transitron, which had peaked at 60 early in the decade, could be bought below 10 by June 1969. Early in the year, National General had sunk from a high of 66 to 35, Ling-Temco-Vought from 135 to 62, Litton Industries from 100 to 50. The Stock Exchange, which for some years had used the motto "Own your share in American business," suddenly dropped it in 1969, without explanation.

A particularly ominous foreshadowing of things to come was to be found in the abrupt decline in brokerage-firm profits. Trading volume, the source of brokerage revenue, was diminishing rapidly; for 1969 it had shrunk from the 1968 figure by about 4 percent on the Big Board, almost 15 percent on the Amex, and considerably more than that in the over-the-counter market. Meanwhile the huge expansion downtown of personnel and facilities to meet the volume rise of the previous year had raised brokerage costs enormously. Unit costs of basic expenses were skyrocketing anyhow; clerical and administrative salaries on Wall Street were up about 60 percent in a decade, and the charges of auditors and lawyers up almost 80 percent. As a result of this squeeze, most Stock Exchange member firms were no longer operating in the black after the first half of 1969.

The omens were everywhere; doom hung in the air, and a tomorrow-we-die, night-before-Waterloo mood was pandemic. The national climate was just right for a binge. The country, tired of riots and crime and liberalism, and with a new conservative Republican administration in Washington, was moving politically to the right, which in economic terms meant toward the newer forms of laissez faire. Mergers went on increasing at a fantastic rate, and so, as a result, did capital concentration: billion-dollar corporations had, in only a decade, enlarged their share of total national assets from 26 to 46 percent. "Creative accounting" continued to flourish, and accounting authorities to shrug; the Accounting Principles Board, notified by the S.E.C. in February 1969 that it should promptly curb abuses of the pooling-of-interest method of merger accounting, shilly-shallied and took no action throughout the year. (Nor did the S.E.C. press the matter further.) Deal-making brokers, meanwhile, had learned how to bring together the two great new forces in the stock market—the conglomerates and the mutual funds—in a way that all but constituted a conspiracy to deceive the public. The deal-maker would propose and promote a merger, in the process salting away for himself large blocks of the stock of the merging companies. Next, he would sell the companies' stock to funds on the basis of the secret merger plans; then when the merger was announced, the accountants would work their bottom-line magic, the merger-mad, bottom-line-loving public would bid up the stock, the insiders would unload, and the public would be left holding as big and empty a bag as in the more naïve market manipulations of the nineteen twenties.

Still, the victims of such schemes were comparatively few. Tens of millions of investors who had been lucky or shrewd enough to avoid the most popular conglomerates, and the other go-go stocks of the most-actively-traded list, were sitting pretty. As late as mid-1969, you did not have to have bought the Dow blue chips to be doing well. If you had bought, say, Fairchild Camera in early 1965, you had tripled your money. If you had bought Boise Cascade at the start of 1967, you had nearly quadrupled it. Even an old warhorse like American Home Products had doubled since late 1966, and any of hundreds of other sound stocks had yielded comparable results. Most of these handsome profits would largely evaporate within the coming year, but nobody knew that, and in mid-1969 the profits were gratifyingly there, on paper, to make the small investor feel confident and rich, and to put him in a spending mood. Private schools and colleges were hand-picking their enrollments from a record flock of applicants; tables were scarce at expensive restaurants; in some areas, a Mercedes was almost as common a sight on the road as a Pontiac; and all that summer and fall, packed airliners departing for or returning from Europe were so numerous at New York City's Kennedy International that they sometimes had to wait hours for clearance to take off or land. Catching the mood of Wall Street itself, the investing public was living as if there were no tomorrow.

Where was the S.E.C.? It seemed to have caught the night-before-Waterloo spirit itself. Its accounting department, which by statute enjoyed almost dictatorial powers over corporate accounting practices, was going its plodding, old-fashioned, and now apparently inadequate way, continuing to trust to the myopic vigilance and the checkered integrity of the accounting profession itself. And the S.E.C. staff had arrived at a state of demoralization unequalled since the Eisenhower administration. For the moment—and a short moment it would prove to be—almost anything went.

2

The rise of institutional investing had brought into being a new kind of high-risk brokerage operation, the block positioner. A time had come when a large mutual or pension fund might suddenly want to buy or sell at a single stroke a block of 100,000, 500,000, or even a million shares. Traditionally, the responsibility for matching up buyers and sellers in such an order, and rounding it out by using his own capital on one side or the other when necessary, fell on the specialist on the Exchange floor; but now with such huge sums involved in mammoth transactions the specialists' capital was often ludicrously inadequate to the task. The firm that most spectacularly and successfully moved in to fill this crack in Wall Street's crumbling edifice of traditional procedure was Salomon Brothers, formerly Salomon

Brothers and Hutzler, founded in 1910, a leading institutional trader for years not in stocks but in bonds. Indeed, so great was this firm's reputation in bond trading that at one time the Wall Street definition of a marketable bond was one on which Salomon would make a bid. In the mid-sixties, when Goldman, Sachs and Bear, Stearns had the lion's share of the new and expanding business of block positioning of stocks for institutions, the partners of Salomon Brothers, headed by canny, soft-spoken William R. (Billy) Salomon, experienced a revelation. Block positioning in stocks, they mused, was not basically different from doing the same thing in bonds. In both cases, you had to know your customers, the institutional investors. Salomon Brothers knew them already from trading bonds with them for years. You had to have the resources and the nerve to assume huge capital risks. Salomon Brothers for years had been king of the plungers in the bond market; why not, then, move into the wholesale stock business?

Beginning in 1964–1965, they did, and by 1968 were the unquestioned leader in it. Their star stock trader came to be Jay Perry, a fast-talking and fiercely competitive man in his early thirties, from Hot Springs, Arkansas, who had previously been a bond trader. In Salomon Brothers' noisy trading room at 60 Wall Street, Perry would be asked by a big institution for a price on so many hundred thousand shares of a certain stock—a block worth, say, $30 or $40 million. After consulting the firm's executive committee, he would shout into the phone a bid a little under the current market, but—and here was the nub of the matter—not nearly so far under it as would be the case if the shares were thrown directly onto the mercy of a capital-weak floor specialist. Then, working at a 120-key telephone console connecting them to all the major funds in the country (an amenity denied to the floor specialist, who was forbidden to deal directly with institutions), Perry and the rest of the Salomon organization would begin trying to round up buyers for parts of the huge block available for sale. Quite often the number of shares they could find bids for would fall short of the offered block by a couple of hundred thousand shares. That was where the positioning came in. Salomon Brothers would obligingly buy those residual shares for its own account, completing the deal, and collecting commissions from both the seller and the various buyers. Then would come the hairy part: unloading the shares Salomon had taken, and didn't really want to tie up its capital with, over a period that might drag out to as much as a couple of months, with tens of millions of capital at stake. "We'll bid for almost anything," said Salomon blandly, "and we take many baths." The risks his firm took through seat-of-the-pants plunges in stocks of companies it knew little about was balanced, and more than balanced, by the enormous commissions it could count on from both sides of its executed deals. In the first three months of 1969, Salomon Brothers "crossed" almost six hundred blocks, putting its own money continually at risk to the extent of many billions of dollars worth of transactions. One day it traded 374,000 shares of Control Data for $52,360,000, the largest single Stock Exchange common-stock transaction in history.

As for Salomon Brothers' "baths," one of the wettest and most prolonged of them occurred over the first three months of 1968, in the stock of Fairchild Camera and Instrument, one of the market's most spectacular performers of 1965. On December 21, 1967, Salomon Brothers, evidently in a free-spending Yuletide mood, bought from an investing institution 52,000 shares of Fairchild at 88, for a capital commitment of about $4.5 million. Later the same day, the firm sold off 22,500 shares at 90 ⅝, thereby turning a quick profit of $58,000. That left almost 30,000 Fairchild shares in Salomon's inventory. Eight days later, on December 29, 1967, the firm bought 41,000 more Fairchild shares at 88½ from another investing institution, and on January 22, 1968—by which time the market for Fairchild had gone distinctly sour, and Salomon Brothers had decided it was a real bargain—the firm absorbed another block of 31,000 Fairchild shares at 78, thus raising its inventory to 102,000 shares at an average cost of $85, for a capital commitment of almost $9 million.

Day followed day, and Fairchild did not recover. On the

contrary, it continued dropping—quite possibly speeded on its way by hedge funds that, knowing of the huge Salomon block hanging over the market, may have made short sales to take advantage of the situation. The days stretched out to weeks, and Fairchild stock showed no signs of recovery, and at last Billy Salomon and his partners decided that they had simply been wrong. On March 1, they unloaded 2,000 Fairchild shares at 66; on March 2, 17,400 at prices down to 59 ½; on March 6 to 9, 25,500 additional shares at prices down to 55 ⅝; and finally, between March 10 and 31, the rest of the block at prices down to 52—which turned out to be just about Fairchild's low for the year. Salomon Brothers' profits on the whole series of transactions, including the December 21 capital gain and commissions, were $105,000; its losses were $2,878,000, leaving a net loss of $2,773,000.

But why worry? Next week, or next month, there would be a new block trade that would result in a *profit* of $3 million or more, as attested by Salomon Brothers' consistently gratifying annual results. Hardly a business conducive to the afternoon siesta, block trading embodied the high-rolling spirit of the time; and besides, it allowed the mutual funds and their client, the public, to lay off some of their risks onto steel-nerved professionals like Jay Perry, who always seemed to be in motion, and Billy Salomon, who never seemed to turn a hair.

3

There were other, less salutary, developments. Many of the mutual funds themselves were taking advantage of the permissive climate by indulging in a form of sleight-of-hand—perfectly legal at the time—that gave their asset value the same kind of painless, instant, and essentially bogus boost as merger accounting could give to conglomerate earnings. Asset value was to a mutual fund what earnings per share were to a conglomerate: its advertisement, its bait for new capital, the formal measure of its success or failure. The sleight-of-hand involved the use of what was called "letter stock," and was, in the later nineteen sixties, freely indulged in by many mutual-fund magicians. The one who had the bad luck to become associated with letter stock in the public mind was Frederick S. Mates.

It may or may not be considered paradoxical that Mates, in 1968, had a well-deserved reputation as one of the most high-minded and socially concerned, as well as one of the most successful, young fund managers in Wall Street. Born in Brooklyn, a graduate of Brooklyn College with the Class of 1954, he had married a Barnard College psychology teacher, been a teacher briefly himself at a Brooklyn yeshiva, and then spent several years with the brokerage firm of Spingarn, Heine before launching his own Mates Investment Fund in August 1967. The fund was an instant success—so great a success that Mates could soon afford to integrate his social ideals into his business operations. For the Mates Fund portfolio he bought no stocks of companies manufacturing armaments, cigarettes, or products that he considered to be pollutants of the environment. He announced his ambition to use his fund to help "make poor people rich," and to that end, he planned to cut the minimum investment in it down to $50 and to make a special selling effort in disadvantaged areas. As things turned out, his chief contribution to the welfare of the poor would seem to be the fact that he never got around to carrying out these plans, and thus spared the poor from becoming investors in the Mates Fund.

He called his office "the kibbutz on William Street" and his young staff "the flower children." His seemed to be an operation entirely in tune with his times. Whether despite or because of these policies, objectives, and attitudes, by the summer of 1968 the Mates Fund was the new sensation of the mutual-fund industry, its asset value up almost 100 percent in its first year, and new money coming in at such a rate—a million and a half dollars a day, far exceeding the previous record set by Fred Carr's Enterprise Fund—that, in June, Mates had to close the sales window temporarily to keep his facilities from being overwhelmed.

It was in September 1968 that Mates made the investment

that he, and eventually much of the fund industry, would have cause to regret. A tiny conglomerate called Omega Equities privately sold the Mates Fund 300,000 shares of common stock at $3.25 a share. Omega was then selling on the over-the-counter market at around 24, so the price was apparently an almost unbelievable bargain. But only apparently. The Omega shares that Mates bought were not registered with the S.E.C., and therefore could not legally be resold until they had been through such registration; for practical purposes, they were unmarketable. They had been sold to Mates—legally—through an investment letter (whence the term "letter stock") in which these terms were set forth and the buyer agreed not to resell pending registration. So now the Mates Fund had in its portfolio 300,000 shares of Omega; the question was, What value were they to be assigned in calculating the fund's assets? Under the curious rules in force at that time, Mates might technically have carried them at $24 a share, the current market price of registered Omega shares, even though they were unregistered. Or he might, more logically, have valued them at his cost—$3.25 a share. Again, an ultraconservative fund manager might have recognized the fact that they were unmarketable by valuing them at a merely nominal amount. Instead of following any of those courses, Mates did what was the common practice in accounting for letter stock: he took the market price as his base, marked it down by one-third to allow for the shares' nonregistration, and carried them at $16 a share. It will be noted that this was almost five times as much as he had just paid for them. With no change in the market price of Omega stock, then, and with no particular good news as to Omega's business prospects, the Mates Fund had made what appeared on the books it displayed proudly to the investing public to be an investment yielding an instant profit of almost 500 percent.

The layman will have no trouble recognizing this as a form of cheating. The startling thing is not that Mates did it, but that it was being done all the time in 1968, by mutual funds and hedge funds, and that not until late 1969 did the S.E.C. get around to a mild crackdown on mutual funds' letter-stock investments, and subsequent arbitrary up-valuations of them. What made Mates a scapegoat was some untimely ill fortune that shortly overtook Omega. Early in December 1968, the Mates Fund assets, partly on the basis of the Omega deal, were up an eye-popping 168 percent for the year, making Mates, by a wide margin, the nation's leading fund performer in the greatest of all fund performance years. Then, on December 20, the S.E.C. abruptly suspended trading in all Omega stock on grounds that it was being traded "on the basis of incomplete and inaccurate information." The immediate result was as disastrous for Mates as it was predictable. Many Mates Fund shareholders demanded redemption of their shares in cash, and this demand, because of the unmarketability of all Omega shares, was one that the fund could not possibly meet. Technically, it had failed. But the S.E.C. was in no mood to force it out of business and thus damage its 3,300 stockholders. Mates hastily applied to the S.E.C. for permission to suspend redemptions for an indefinite period, and the S.E.C. hastily and meekly complied.

The fund industry shuddered. This was purest heresy; the fundamental right of share redemption without question at any time was the cornerstone of the whole $50-billion business, analogous to the right of a bank depositor to draw from his checking account; now the cornerstone was cracked, the letter-stock deception stood suddenly exposed, and dozens of other funds came under suspicion of having similar concealed weakness. Mates, cornered, acted as bravely and honorably as he could. He immediately valued his Omega holding down to his cost of $3.25 per share, ruining Mates Fund's preeminent performance record for the year. He vowed to resume redemptions just as soon as possible. That was cold comfort to his shareholders; but a leading Wall Street fund man commented with sympathy and candor, "After all, Fred Mates is only one of many." In February 1969, an S.E.C. official seemed to be remarkably calm about the whole matter when he said, reflectively, "The Mates situation really puts the problem in bold relief." That July, Mates finally made good his promise to resume redemptions—

with Omega marked down to fifty cents a share. He was hoping eventually to find a way to sell his 300,000 shares for much more; early in 1972, however, the Mates Fund still had them, and was carrying them at a value of one nickel each.

The Mates case is an edifying little modern version of the Faust legend, which is strikingly close to the core of the moral climate of Wall Street in 1969. Pacts with the Devil were being struck all over the Street and its access roads that year; and the clock would strike twelve, signalling the time for fulfillment of the bargain, soon enough. Even the paradox of the original legend was reproduced in the modern version: like Faust, Mates was no conscienceless sharper but a man as good as or better than the next. Perhaps his story may even be seen as raising the arresting dilemma, Which is worse in a time of national crisis: a young swinger who speculates with his investors' money but pursues high-minded investment policies, or a more conservative codger who keeps his clients in the comfortable blue-chip stocks of corporations that fuel the wars and foul the rivers and the air?

4

And there were other shows playing to paying customers that year Off Wall Street; the further their remove from New York's financial district, the less they resembled moral drama and the more the repertoire suggested musical comedy or farce.

There was the now-famous Bernie Cornfeld, whose name was just beginning to be recognized by the American public in 1969: Bernie Cornfeld, once a Socialist at Brooklyn College (still another unsuspected hatchery of tycoons) and now king of the offshore fund operators ("offshore" meaning, of course, "beyond the reach of the S.E.C."); who, back in the late nineteen fifties, had had the inspired idea of uplifting the poor of the whole world, and perhaps getting rich himself, by selling them American mutual-fund shares through something he called the Fund of Funds; who sold so many shares—mostly not to the upliftable poor of the world, it would appear later, but to rich men in poor countries who wanted to evade local currency restrictions—that before the end of 1969 his firm, Investors Overseas Services, had twenty thousand employees and a million customers in over a hundred countries, managed assets of $2.5 billion, and had brought him a personal fortune amounting on paper to $150 million; who had his headquarters on the borderline of France and Switzerland at Ferney-Voltaire (Bernie-Voltaire, the wags called it) and who lived so close to the borderline of legality that his operation was always getting expelled from various countries; who paid large salaries to James Roosevelt and the former vice chairman of the Federal Republic of Germany as investments in respectability; who liked to test new sales applicants with the thought-provoking question, "Do you sincerely want to be rich?"; who, fourteen years after he had started with nothing, had a town house on Lac Leman that Napoleon had built for Josephine, a castle in France with a moat and drawbridge, a pack of Great Danes, a string of racehorses, and squadron of high-powered cars, a Heep of sycophants, a live-in Jewish mother, and wall-to-wall girls.

"Where are the *customers*' girls?" John Kenneth Galbraith once asked about I.O.S., during its heyday, adapting the old nineteen-twenties Wall Street joke about the visiting dignitary who, on being shown the yachts belonging to brokers, inquired, "But where are the customers' yachts?" Sad but true: there were few mini-skirted minions for the customers of I.O.S. Its investment record was mediocre, in part because of lavish overcompensation of its salesmen—at the expense, of course, of the customers. But Cornfeld was only the top of an iceberg. By early 1969, the "offshore" fund arena included about seventy firms, some of them quietly run by outwardly respectable Wall Street houses, with well over $3 billion in the American stock market, all, presumably, for the benefit of underprivileged foreign investors but more palpably for that of a ravenous ratpack of newly overprivileged American entrepreneurs. The biggest such operation, after Cornfeld's, was Great American Management and Research, or Gramco.

If some *farceur* with more imagination than restraint had written the story of Gramco as fiction, he would surely have been accused of painting with too broad a brush. Short of a corporation president conducting his enterprise from a baby's playpen, Gramco's founder and boss Keith Barish seemed to be the ultimate manifestation of the youth revolution in finance. At eighteen, while a student at the University of Miami, Barish had helped start a bank in Hialeah, of racetrack fame; because he was legally under age, his seat at directors' meetings had been regularly occupied, on his behalf, by his mother. In 1967, when he was twenty-two and had already amassed a small fortune, he founded Gramco as a mutual fund that would invest chiefly in American real estate, rather than in American stocks. Thus he would bring to his investors the benefits of the apparently endless upward trend in land and property values. The S.E.C. frowned on such funds because of real estate's inherent lack of liquidity, but no matter; Barish planned to "invent" a new thing called "liquid real estate"; and besides, he proposed to escape the disapproving surveillance of the S.E.C. entirely by setting up his fund in the Bahamas and selling its shares only outside the United States, presumably to non-Americans. And that, briefly, was what he did. Nassau became Gramco's official domicile, London its operating base, Panama, Curaçao, and the Grand Duchy of Luxembourg its tax shelters, and most of the world ex-U.S.A. its selling territory.

Barish—might not the *farceur* at least have named him "Bullish"?—took as his partner a dispossessed Cuban just over thirty named Rafael G. Navarro, who had some mutual-fund experience. He took on others, without such experience, to other purpose. One summer, during the administration of John F. Kennedy, Barish as a teen-ager had served as a "summer intern" at the White House and had evidently spent his time well among the authorities he found striding in and around its corridors. To apply the magical Kennedy aura, so powerful in so many distant lands, to the selling of Gramco shares, Barish hired as Gramco officers and directors a group of old New Frontiersmen, among them two former Kennedy ambassadors, two former Kennedy staff assistants, a former Kennedy Undersecretary of Health, Education and Welfare, a former Kennedy Assistant Secretary of Commerce, and—most visibly—the portly, amiable, highly visible former Kennedy press secretary and later U.S. Senator from California, Pierre Salinger.

"Economics have never been my strong point," Salinger once confessed disarmingly, but no matter; Salinger was made titular head of the Gramco sales organization, which came to comprise some six hundred salesmen in fifty countries, and by May 1969 had brought in investments in Gramco of more than $100 million, a figure that would be doubled before the end of that year. The money was invested in such U.S. real-estate ventures as the Americana Fairfax Apartments outside Washington, the Clermont Towers in New York City, Harbor House in Chicago, the LTV Tower in Dallas, and a shopping center in Oklahoma City. Meanwhile, those within the Gramco organization with more of a penchant for economics were ensuring that Gramco itself got its share of the proceeds. To begin with, the firm charged fund customers the usual stiff mutual-fund sales commissions and management fees; but in Gramco's case the beginning was *only* the beginning. Running a real-estate fund gave the managers a golden opportunity to do what the managers of a stock fund legally could not, that is, to serve as their own brokers in their transactions and collect commissions accordingly. Moreover, the fact that real estate could be bought largely on credit, as stocks could not, made it possible for them to take in remarkably high commissions in relation to the amount of money invested. Gramco collected—from its customers, of course—a 5 percent commission on the full price of each transaction; since it bought on mortgages that on occasion amounted to three-quarters of the purchase price, it was sometimes able to pocket for its own account $1 million for every $5 million of its customers' money that it put into real-estate ventures. In the first three and a half years of Gramco's operation, its management took out of the fund for its own profits $43 million, or 17 percent of all the money the customers had entrusted to it. The firm's accountants, meanwhile, were doing their bit to make Gramco's books look simultaneously bearish to the income-tax authorities and wildly bullish to potential investors. Taking advantage of liberal U.S. depreciation guidelines for real estate, the accountants would report on their U.S. tax returns that the properties Gramco had bought were dropping in value. At the same time, reporting to shareholders and potential shareholders abroad on the fund's asset value, they would record, on the same properties and at the same time, substantial increases in value. What was going down in Oklahoma City and Chicago, the accountants seemed to be saying, was simultaneously rising and shining in Nassau, Panama, and the Grand Duchy of Luxembourg.

In May 1969, Gramco followed the crowd and went public: a million shares were issued, priced at $10 each. Again, everybody was rich, except, by some oversight, the far-flung investors who had put their trust in the Kennedy aura and a good bit of their money, inadvertently, into the pockets of former Kennedy men. Surely the old New Frontiersmen were finding exciting new frontiers indeed, on a new trail blazed by the stripling they had first taken a liking to that summer at the White House.

Then there was the Off-Wall Street comedy-farce to end them all, the show that had everything—deal-makers, fund managers, gambling stocks, purchased respectability, chicken-wired conglomerates, offshore operations, letter stock, Bernie Cornfeld. Perhaps appropriately, its scene was laid chiefly in Los Angeles; the action took place in 1968 and 1969. The plot · may be summarized as follows:

Delbert William Coleman, born in Cleveland, a Harvard graduate whose *Who's Who* entry conscientiously stipulated that he was a member of the Harvard Alumni Association, was a playboy plunger who in 1956 had taken over the J.P. Seeburg Corporation, a Chicago jukebox manufacturing concern. Among those he counted as his friends was Sidney R. Korshak, sixty-three, a self-made Chicago millionaire lawyer with the reputation, deserved or not, of having been an adviser to members of the Capone gang; by 1968, however, Korshak had attained a kind of ornate respectability, with plush law offices and an apartment in Chicago, a high-priced spread in Bel Air, California, a suite at the Carlyle in New York, and a certain reputation as a philanthropist. Knowing Coleman as a man on the lookout for fast business action, Korshak brought him to Los Angeles and introduced him to Albert Parvin, who at the age of seventy was ready to retire as boss of Parvin-Dohrmann, the company he had founded. Parvin-Dohrmann owned hotels and gambling casinos in Las Vegas, and had some major stockholders with suspicious credentials; but anyone who on those accounts consigned it to the demimonde of American business could be reminded, and frequently was, that for a time the president of Albert Parvin's private foundation had been William O. Douglas, Associate Justice of the U.S. Supreme Court, who had accepted a salary of $12,000 a year for his efforts. Exactly how Justice Douglas had been persuaded to take the position was, and remains, unclear.

Korshak's introduction worked like a charm. Parvin-Dohrmann as a stock speculation brought an instant gleam to Coleman's eye, partly because Howard Hughes's recent investments in Nevada had given Las Vegas's name investment pizazz, partly because the investing public was clearly in a gambling mood, and what better way to gamble in stocks than by buying stocks in gambling casinos? Burt Kleiner—the mod Los Angeles stockbroker and Pop-art collector who had put together deals for just about all of the farthest-out conglomerates, and the man at whose brokerage office on Wilshire Boulevard, called "Wall Street West," customers in 1968 and 1969 often sat watching the tape and actually chanting, "Go, go, go!"—was called in to find a customer for Coleman's Seeburg stock so that he could then buy into Parvin-Dohrmann. No problem. Kleiner persuaded Commonwealth United, a small West Coast conglomerate that was an old customer of his, to take Coleman's interest in Seeburg for $9.8 million, thus giving Coleman some spending money. Coleman promptly used it to buy 300,000 shares of Parvin-Dohrmann—a controlling interest—at $35 per share. Kleiner's firm, Kleiner, Bell and Company, took a broker's fee of $768,805 for arranging the deal. Albert Parvin went to Africa on safari. And Coleman prepared triumphantly to wheel and deal with his new vehicle, Parvin-Dohrmann.

His first move was, with Korshak's help, to sell privately 143,200 of his 300,000 Parvin-Dohrmann shares—they were traded on the Amex—to a group of organizations and individuals including Burt Kleiner (5,000 shares), Cornfeld's I.O.S. (81,-000), two owners of the Atlanta Braves baseball team, and Jill St. John, the actress. He gave them a bargain price ($35 a share, his own cost) in exchange for a letter agreement not to resell their shares, and thus keep them conveniently (for Coleman) off the market. Next, he took the $5 million obtained from these sales and plowed most of it back into strategic purchases of Parvin-Dohrmann. Aimless activity for its own sake? By no means; Coleman's purpose, or so the S.E.C. would later charge, was standard old-fashioned manipulation, designed artifically to attract attention to Parvin-Dohrmann stock and thus create public buying interest. Meanwhile, Coleman wined and dined mutual-fund managers at Parvin-Dohrmann's hotels and casinos in Las Vegas; some of the managers responded to this hospitality by buying the stock for their portfolios. To further confuse the investing public, Coleman arranged to have his mother make purchases of Parvin stock *on* the Amex while he himself was selling a comparable number of shares *off* it. Parvin-Dohrmann came to look to the uninitiated like the hottest stock of the moment, as it appeared on the most-actively-traded list day after day at ever-rising prices. To focus the spotlight of glamour still more sharply on its company name, Parvin-Dohrmann contrived, through Korshak's ubiquitous contacts with West Coast characters, to buy for $15 million the Stardust Hotel-Casino on the famous Vegas Strip. (Korshak got a $500,000 fee on that one.) Dazzled, the public took the bait and gobbled up Parvin-Dohrmann stock. By January 10, 1969, the price was up to $68.50, and a few weeks later to 110.

What Coleman and his companions seem to have done was

to have pulled off, in the Wall Street era of federal regulation and presumably general enlightenment, a classic stock manipulation remarkably similar in a technical sense to those of the unenlightened nineteen twenties—and given it to an up-to-the-minute flavor by involving gambling casinos, kicky conglomerates, a Pop-art-collecting broker-dealer, and even a Hollywood star. Moreover, everyone seemed to be making money by the potful. Apparently one could now beat the games at Vegas without even going there!

But then one day a computer at the Amex started acting peculiar. The Amex computer was programmed to give off warning signals when there was unorthodox and suspicious movement in any listed stock; and in this case, it really worked. It began giving out frantic warning signals on Parvin-Dohrmann. The Amex started an investigation, and as a result, on March 26, decided to suspend trading in the stock temporarily. The next day, the company disclosed the previously secret deal with the buyers of the 143,200 shares, causing eyebrows to shoot up on Wall Street and Off Wall Street alike. On April 14, 1969, the Nevada Gaming Control delivered Parvin-Dohrmann another blow by decreeing that the company could not operate casinos in Las Vegas any longer unless Cornfeld's I.O.S. got rid of its 81,000 shares. (Coleman would complain later that I.O.S. not only got rid of the shares, but did so at a fat profit.)

In May, the S.E.C. finally stepped in. Coleman, desperate, got Korshak to assign a fixer named Nathan Voloshen to arrange him an interview with S.E.C. Chairman Hamer Budge. Voloshen came through, and the interview took place (Voloshen apparently got $50,000 for arranging it), but it was hardly a success from Coleman's point of view, since he failed to persuade Budge to call off his dogs. So Coleman and Korshak hastily began trying to find somebody on whom to unload their Parvin-Dohrmann stock at $140 or $150 a share. They finally hit upon Denny's Restaurants, a Los Angeles coffee-and-doughnuts chain with expansive notions. Denny's was eager for the deal—the very rumors of the merger sent the stock of both Parvin and Denny's skyrocketing. But Denny's didn't like the aura of shady influence that by now pervaded Parvin-Dohrmann, mainly because one of its largest stockholders was a sometime target of various Justice Department antimob investigations. On October 13, 1969, the Denny's merger fell through, and the bottom fell out of Parvin stock. On October 16, the S.E.C. filed a suit charging Coleman, Korshak, and a long list of their associates with having manipulated Parvin stock in violation of the securities laws. Most of them signed consent decrees.

By the spring of 1970, the party was over. Coleman had turned his Parvin stock over to a voting trust and resigned from the management. The stock had sunk to $12.50 a share, so he, and all of his friends and backers, had sharp losses. Korshak poignantly complained to a newspaper reporter that all he had left after taxes on the half-million fee in the Stardust deal was a mere $68,000. Commonwealth United's stock price was down 97 percent to seventy cents a share. The cry of "go, go, go" was heard no more on sunny days on Wilshire Boulevard, because Kleiner, Bell, with the S.E.C. nipping at its heels about multiple securities violations, had prudently retired from the brokerage business. All the guys and dolls, from Korshak to Jill St. John, were sadder and wiser, but warm with nostalgic memories of the thrills they had had in the days before the electronic cop at the Amex put the arm on them.

5

Finally—to round out this inventory of the various symptoms of dementia that afflicted the 1968–1969 stock market—there were the hot new issues, the "shooters," that shot up on their first day of trading from 10 to 20 or from 5 to 14, and later went to 75 or 100, oblivious of the fact that the companies they represented were often neither sound nor profitable: the garbage stocks that everyone could make money on just so long as, and no longer than, everyone could contrive to hold his nose and

avert his eyes and imagine that the garbage was actually nour-
ishing and palatable.

If one fact is glaringly clear in stock-market history, it is
that a new-issues craze is always the last stage of a dangerous
boom—a warning of impending disaster almost as infallible as
Cheyne-Stokes breathing is a warning of impending death. But
not so inexorable; if heads could be cooler and memories longer,
investors both large and small, professional and amateur, might
ward off danger by reading the signs, eschewing the new issues,
and lightening their commitments generally. But investors, like
other human beings, tragically repeat their mistakes; when the
danger signs are plain, the lure of easy money blanks their
memories and dissipates their calm. In 1929 the shooters were
jerrybuilt investment trusts like Alleghany, Shenandoah, and
United Corporation. In 1961 they were tiny scientific companies
put together by little clutches of glittery-eyed young Ph.D.'s,
their company names ending in "———onics." In 1968–1969,
what a promoter needed to launch a new stock, apart from a
persuasive tongue and a resourceful accountant, was to have a
"story"—an easily grasped concept, preferably related to some
current national fad or preoccupation, that *sounded* as if it would
lead to profits. Such stories, like most stories, were best told
quickly and concisely, and best of all within the name of the
company itself. Were the new government Medicare and Medi-
caid programs pouring millions into the care of elderly persons?
A cunning investor could presumably get a piece of that action
by buying stocks called Four Seasons Nursing Centers or
United Convalescent Homes. Were people's recreational ex-
penditures soaring? Hardly coincidentally, there turned out to
be a stock called International Leisure. Was concern about the
environment a popular passion of the moment? Why, look here
— a stock called Responsive Environments! Was weight watching in the wind? One might grow rich while growing thin,
perhaps, with Weight Watchers International. Finally, it may be
assumed that there were some investors who, so far as company
names were concerned, didn't want to be bothered with the
suggestion of any particular product or service, and just wanted

a stock whose name made it sound like a winner. For them, there was Performance Systems, Inc., not to mention Bonanza International.

And then there was National Student Marketing Corporation, whose "story" was the youth market: half of the nation's population was now under twenty-five, and that half, the experts contended, was spending $45 billion a year. Students were constantly on the front pages those days, though more often as a threat to business than as its potential customer. Yet at the very moment when the counterculture was having its brief day, while the front-paged students were seizing campus buildings and trashing deans' offices, there was a campus counter-counter-culture, as sedulously entrepreneurial as Andrew Carnegie, vigorously in pursuit of the quick buck. Students and recent graduates who burned not to right the world's wrongs, but just to get rich in a hurry, were finding that they could possibly accomplish their aim soon after graduation, or even before it, by starting campus businesses or simply by playing the stock market. Such a young man, Andrew Tobias, wrote of Princeton in 1968, "One of the guys . . . was playing 'puts and calls.' . . . Every lunch hour this fellow would walk up Nassau Street to the local office of Tout, Ticker, Dicker and Churn, I think it was, to punch out all his different holdings on the Quotron. . . . Another fellow got daily phone calls from his broker, and the news was usually good. . . . Across the hall there was a little company selling a combination life-insurance-mutual-fund package that was about to go public.* Sometimes in the evening a Blue Cross salesman would come by to trade stock tips. He had bought a thing called Omega Equities at fifty cents a share. . . ."

The young man who set out in the biggest way to exploit the youth market, or at least to convince Wall Street that he was doing so, was Cortes Wesley Randell. The son of a Washington, D.C. business consultant, a strapping six-footer with a glib tongue and an easy smile, who had attended the University of Virginia (where his thesis topic had been "How to Start a Small Business") and then done brief stints with General Electric and

*This turned out to be Equity Funding Corporation.

I.T.T., Randell was about to turn thirty when, in 1965, he founded National Student Marketing Corporation in Washington as headquarters for a string of part-time student representatives on campuses whose job it was to distribute samples and employment guides, do market research, and sell fad items like posters and paper dresses. The enterprise took off like a bird. Sales for the first fiscal year, ending in August 1966, were $160,-000, and for the following year, $723,000. By early 1968—just in time for the great national speculative fever—Randell had nearly six hundred campus reps and was ready to take N.S.M.C. public. And Wall Street was more than ready to receive it. Not Charlie Plohn, but the solid old-line brokerage house of Auchincloss, Parker and Redpath became N.S.M.C.'s underwriter for the stock issue; its lawyers were Covington and Burling, its accountants Arthur Andersen and Company. Buoyed by this parlay of glamour and apparent respectability, the stock, offered to the public on April 24, 1968, at a price of 6, went to 14 the same day and by early June was selling at 30.

Randell, who still held more than half of all the stock, along with several million dollars of cash proceeds from the sales of the other half, was now rich, and not temperamentally inclined to disguise the fact. Soon he had acquired a $600,000 castle on the Potomac, a fifty-five-foot yacht, and a $700,000 Lear jet to buzz around in. He paid himself only a modest presidential salary of $24,000, and for good reason; by denying himself and his colleagues high salaries, he could increase company profits, and that was where the *real* money was, at least for large stock and option holders. A small event that occurred shortly after the underwriting—the sudden resignation, without explanation, of both Covington and Burling and Arthur Andersen and Company—may be considered, in hindsight, to have been an evil portent for Randell and N.S.M.C. But nobody in Wall Street was looking for evil portents just then, certainly not in connection with a shooter like N.S.M.C.

And so, armed with a red-hot stock appraised by the market at a price-to-earnings multiple of 100, Randell set out to make his company a giant through acquisitions: six of them in 1968 and more in 1969, including three school-bus companies, Arthur

Frommer's low-cost-travel guides, compilers of high-school student lists, publishers of campus telephone directories, even some companies scarcely related to the youth market at all. Since the companies acquired, almost always with N.S.M.C. stock, had comparatively low multiples, N.S.M.C. earnings automatically went up with each acquisition. And Wall Street reacted as it was supposed to do in such situations; as the earnings rose, so did the bids, and before the year was out, N.S.M.C. stock had skyrocketed on the over-the-counter market from the original price of 6 to a 1968 high of 82.

Meanwhile, Randell had moved his headquarters from Washington to New York, to be where the financial action was. Significantly, the corporate style he fostered was anything but countercultural. N.S.M.C. executives, however youth-oriented or youthful themselves (and some of them were scarcely out of their teens), did not affect long hair or mustaches or love beads or jeans, nor did they smoke marijuana; rather, they wore dark suits and narrow ties, and kept their shoes shined. The chief, indeed the sole, gesture that N.S.M.C. seems to have made to the mood of campus revolt was to try to cash in on it by selling special pillows for the use of sit-in demonstrators. In simple truth, N.S.M.C. was not primarily selling goods and services to youth at all—it was primarily selling stock to Wall Street.

Its astonishing success in that particular enterprise is a crucial sign of the times in Wall Street. Randell would impress and flatter security analysts and fund managers by taking them on tours of his castle or calling them on the skyphone from his Lear. It became his standard procedure to predict tripled earnings for each coming year over the previous one, and he was a persuasive young man—particularly when his hearers were people who wanted to believe. Indeed, even if he were not entirely to be believed, did it matter, for the short run? In the market of 1968 and 1969, wasn't an illusion, so long as it was universally shared, just as good a money maker as a reality? Bankers Trust, Morgan Guaranty, the Continental Illinois of Chicago, and the State Street Fund of Boston bought N.S.M.C. stock; so did the Harvard and Cornell endowment funds, the General Electric pension fund, and the University of Chicago. There seemed to be scarcely any investment citadels left for Randell to conquer.

And the stockbrokers—did they doubt Randell's glowing accounts of N.S.M.C.'s present and future? He was able to arrange things so that they could hardly afford to; before long a number of them were working for him, beating the bushes to find companies for N.S.M.C. to acquire so that it could keep increasing its earnings, and being paid off handsomely for their efforts with batches of N.S.M.C. stock. Finder's fees in the form of stock were paid to W.E. Hutton, Halsey, Stuart, and Smith, Barney, among others. Sometimes the brokerage firms apparently found it possible to sweeten up the deal with a recommendation of N.S.M.C. stock to their customers; thus, in 1969, Kidder Peabody gave it a rave review in a seventeen-page report, and hardly more than a week later, Kidder received 4,000 shares of N.S.M.C., then selling above 120, solely for its imagination and resourcefulness in proposing to N.S.M.C. that it acquire a company called Stuckey and Spear that manufactured college rings.

So the money factory was a closed chain, infallible so long, and just so long, as the chain remained unbroken. The weak link was, of course, the disparity between Cort Randell's promises and his company's real results, which, closely scrutinized, were unspectacular. After having predicted tripled earnings for a given year, Randell found himself forced to resort to creative accounting to make the prediction come true; then, having written artificially high earnings for that year, he was compelled by his game's inner dynamics to predict that those earnings would be tripled again in the following year—and then, somehow, goad his accountants to Parnassian heights of accounting genius to fulfill the new promise. The first serious test of his credibility in Wall Street came late in 1969. N.S.M.C.'s report for the fiscal year ended that summer showed net profit of around $3.5 million, duly fulfilling Randell's projections. But to achieve the figure, the company's accountants had been obliged, among other strokes of creativity, to defer until a future year product development and start-up costs of $533,000, even though the

money had already been spent; to include as income $2.8 million
of "unbilled receivables," which was to say, money that had not
been received because it had not even been asked for; and—
perhaps most egregiously—to include as net income more than
$3 million attributable to the profits of N.S.M.C. subsidiaries
that N.S.M.C. had not yet acquired at the close of the year being
reported on. With the elimination of that single item, which was
explained to investors in a small, mumbled footnote, N.S.M.C.'s
1969 profit would have been all but wiped out.

N.S.M.C. stock dropped briefly after the report appeared—
only to rise again to the 100-times-earnings range. But a few
Wall Streeters seem to have read the footnotes; stock analysts
and investing institutions began asking N.S.M.C. executives
pointed questions for the first time late in 1969. Simultaneously,
Randell began to be pressed by his colleagues within the company; some of them came to wince whenever he made a public
statement, and a few of the more conservative of them went so
far as to demand that he resign as president. He can hardly have
failed to realize that the game was nearly up—that he had not
succeeded in exploiting the youth market, assuming there was
one, if only because he had never seriously tried to exploit it in
his preoccupation with exploiting the stock market; and that
now, at last, investors were catching on. Nevertheless, he bulled
ahead until the last. On November 5, 1969, speaking to the New
York Society of Security Analysts, he predicted, true to form,
that earnings for fiscal 1970 would be almost triple those for
1969. The stock jumped 20 points, causing Randell's personal
worth to rise $6.5 million. That he and his colleagues had some-
what different private notions is suggested by the fact that in
December the company and its principal officers suddenly unloaded more than 325,000 shares. In January 1970, Randell—
over the frantic objections of his colleagues, some of whom by
this time would have liked nothing better than to silence their
president with a gag and adhesive tape—made a nationwide
speech tour during which he constantly reiterated his 1970 earnings projection.

In early February, N.S.M.C.'s financial vice president gave a dumbstruck group of company executives the jolting news that the actual result for the quarter just ended would be a loss. By February 17, Randell's ebullience had been dampened at last, at least to the extent that, in a speech to the St. Louis security analysts that day, he said merely that N.S.M.C.'s first 1970 quarter would be "profitable." His partial concession to reality was too little and too late. The following day, amid panic in the councils of N.S.M.C., Randell resigned as president; a week later, a first-quarter loss of $1.2 million was announced, and two days after that, the company shamefacedly admitted that there had been a "mechanical error in transferring figures from one set of books to another," and that the actual loss was more like $1.5 million. By this time the market for the stock had understandably caved in; having sold at 140 as recently as late December, it was down to 50 and sinking fast; by July it would stand at 3 1/2, a loss of more than 97 percent from its peak seven months before. By then, it may be assumed, the investing public, including many of its firmly established corporate citizens, would be sadder if not wiser about fast-talking young entrepreneurs selling companies with faddish stories. As for Cort Randell, he would by then have vanished into the obscurity of his Potomac palace, with a few million dollars intact from stock sales made in time—one more stock-market rocket of youth's short era, rich and burned out at thirty-five.

Well and good. But the question remains, How could he have fooled the Morgan Guaranty, the Bankers Trust, Harvard and Cornell, the whole brains trust of institutional investing, for as long as he did—and, of course, taken the innocent investing public along with them? The answer appears to be painfully simple: that he was plausible and they were gullible as well as greedy; that, in times of speculative madness, the wisdom and experience of the soundest and soberest may yield to a hysteria induced by the glimpse of fool's gold dished by a young man with a smile on his lips and a gleam in his eye.

6

Late in September 1968, at the height of the Presidential election campaign, the Republican candidate Richard M. Nixon sent a letter to a group of top Wall Street executives in which he attacked the S.E.C. under Democratic leadership for its "heavy-handed bureaucratic regulatory schemes," expressed the fear that a continuation of such policies "might seriously impair the nation's ability to continue to raise the capital needed for its future economic growth," and went on to promise, in effect, that regulation of the securities business under his administration would be relatively passive and permissive.

> The free and healthy operation of the market [Nixon wrote] is of utmost importance to the investor. . . . Our securities laws were designed to protect the investor by insisting on full and complete disclosure. . . . I believe in the full enforcement of the securities laws to assure absolute protection for the investor. . . . The philosophy of this [Democratic] administration, however, has been that disclosure alone is not enough and that the Government can make decisions for the investor better than he can make them for himself. This philosophy I reject.

Wall Street was electrified. What the Republican candidate was rejecting, of course, was the now generally accepted view that in an age of stock-market participation by the millions, full disclosure alone is by no means sufficient to protect the general investor; and he was clearly and categorically announcing his intention to undo the activist work at the S.E.C. of Cary and Cohen, and turn the clock back to the old Wall Street era of "Eisenhower prosperity." Could this really be happening, the thoughtful minds on Wall Street wondered, at the very moment when a new speculative binge was clearly building to its climax, when portfolio-churning brokers, letter-stock-buying mutual funds and law-avoiding offshore trusts were clearly making a mockery of "full disclosure" and taking renewed advantage of unsophisticated investors?

Some in Wall Street could hardly believe their luck—apparently the cookie closet was to be no longer watched or locked. Others were dismayed. "I'm bewildered by it all," said a senior partner of an investment banking firm. "The S.E.C. has been in the picture now for more than thirty years and it's doing its job. Regulation is here to stay." Indeed, many practical Wall Streeters believed that the public confidence in securities promoted by the presence of a vigorous S.E.C. was a positive factor for business, and that any weakening of the S.E.C. or its authority would be concomitantly bad. Such dismay was mitigated in a somewhat equivocal way by a large measure of skepticism as to whether the Republican candidate really meant what he said. It was widely known that much of Nixon's fund-raising base was in Wall Street—that Bernard J. Lasker, then vice chairman of the New York Stock Exchange, was a leading Nixon fund-raiser as well as a close Nixon friend, and that Peter M. Flanigan of Dillon Read (later a high and controversial White House aide) was a key man in the campaign. Perhaps, it was reasoned, Nixon was just trying to tell Wall Street what he thought it wanted to hear, in the familiar spirit of campaign rhetoric. There were even rumors—given wide currency by disconcerted Nixon supporters—that the letter had been sent out without its having been read by the candidate.

Such speculation was cold comfort to the more dedicated and able members of the S.E.C. and its staff. The prospect they faced, should Nixon win, was apparently that of working under a President who either opposed everything they were trying to do, or who wished to give the appearance that he did. It was scarcely a morale-building pair of alternatives. Cohen's four-year regime as chairman had been strong on enforcement and somewhat less so on policy innovation, but it had been imaginative and aggressive enough to keep most of the best S.E.C. staff men active and happy. It is axiomatic in the S.E.C. that the star performers who stay there for any length of time do so on principle and at personal sacrifice, since much higher-paying jobs on Wall Street or in the law firms are almost always available to them. Now, with Nixon's letter, the occasion for worthwhile sacrifice seemed to have been removed. Within weeks after publication of the letter, a small ebb tide of talent began to flow out of the S.E.C.; in November, after Nixon's election, the tide became a torrent.

A hard core of skilled, experienced, and well-motivated staff men hung on into the new year and new administration, doing the day-to-day job of processing new stock registrations, and waiting to see whom Nixon would appoint as Cohen's successor. The man he appointed in February was hardly one to please a dedicated S.E.C. activist. Hamer H. Budge was a short, bald former Congressman from Idaho and political protégé of Senator Everett Dirksen, who had become an S.E.C. commissioner in 1964 as a Republican appointee of President Johnson. At Commission meetings, Judge Budge—so called in recognition of a brief term he had served as a federal judge back in Idaho, and maybe just because it sounded good, too—had happened to sit on the left of Manny Cohen, and Cohen had had many a good laugh about that. Politically, Judge Budge was by no means to the left of Cohen; rather, he was an amiable Republican with middle-of-Main-Street Republican ideas and, as to the S.E.C.'s role and function, a holder of the philosophy that the best regulation is generally the least regulation.

On his first day in office as S.E.C. chairman, Budge made a surprisingly strong public attack on conglomerates and their involvement with mutual funds in the stock market, signalling the start of a Nixon administration campaign that would eventually have its focus in the office of Richard W. McLaren, Assistant Attorney General. But Judge Budge's initial burst of activism was short-lived. The S.E.C., unlike the Justice Department, actually did little to curb conglomerate power, and as the summer of 1969 came and the Wall Street bubble of widespread speculation swelled nearer the breaking point, the S.E.C.'s complacency showed signs of becoming somnolence. As promised, "heavy-handed regulatory schemes" were conspicuous by their absence; there was little evidence at the S.E.C. of plans for regulatory schemes of any sort; there were rumors (later confirmed) that the S.E.C.'s great work in progress since 1968, a huge study of the effect of institutional investors on the stock market, was losing steam; and there was some evidence that even basic enforcement activities against stock-market fraud were being relaxed. To top it all off, in July it inconveniently became public knowledge that Judge Budge, while holding office as S.E.C. chairman, had felt free to entertain an $80,000-a-year job offer from Investors Diversified Services, a giant mutual-fund complex emphatically under the regulatory jurisdiction of the S.E.C.

In view of the fact that at about the same time the S.E.C. was actively engaged in negotiations with Investors Diversified Services about its methods of operation, this bordered on scandal, at least to Congressional Democrats. Judge Budge explained himself to a Senate subcommittee to its apparent satisfaction. But even by the most charitable possible interpretation, Budge's flirtation with a high-paying industry job while he was serving at the S.E.C.—indeed, during his first six months in office—set the worst and most demoralizing possible example for the staff men working under him. Predictably, they followed that example. As early as May, Judge Budge was expressing dismay and apparent bewilderment that so many good S.E.C. men were quitting their jobs.

By the fall of 1969, talent and morale at the S.E.C. had reached rock bottom. Two new Nixon-appointed commissioners, an upstate New York accountant and a conservative Florida Democrat with no background in securities, had consolidated the Commission's new conservative, hands-off majority. Hearings on stock-brokerage rates that had begun more than a year earlier were still dragging on without results. Judge Budge was cheerfully assuring Wall Street that it could look forward, as promised, to a spell of "self-regulation" with little interference from his office. A disillusioned S.E.C. staff man observed with resigned understatement that "things are slowing down."

In one sense, they weren't. In terms of paper-pushing as opposed to enforcement of existing rules and promulgation of new ones, the S.E.C. was busier than ever before, processing the new stock-and-bond registrations that were flowing in so fast—between July 1 and September 30, a thousand of them amounting to about $12 billion—that businessmen bringing their applications to the S.E.C. building were being issued numbers to designate their turns, like customers at a crowded meat counter. And there was a final irony. Like other paper-pushing agencies, the S.E.C. charged fees to the companies whose new securities issues it processed for registration; such fees were intended to cover the costs of the staff and to finance the agency's other activities in enforcement, surveillance, and planning. In 1969, fee receipts were high and expenses were low. So it came to pass that the S.E.C., which was supposed to be paid for by taxpayers in exchange for its surveillance of profit-making Wall Street, ended the year with its own bottom line showing—a net profit.

CHAPTER XII

The 1970
Crash

1

In terms of the analogy between the nineteen twenties and the nineteen sixties with which this chronicle began, the beginning of the year 1970 corresponds roughly to the late spring of 1929. In each case, there were warning signals across the land of a coming economic recession, possibly a full-scale depression, and an uneasy Republican administration, only a year or so in office, was wondering what to do for its best friend and principal political client, the business community. In each case a steep decline in second-rank stock issues—a sort of hidden crash, since it didn't show up in the popular averages—was already under way. In each case speculation continued to flourish, and money was historically tight; and in each case the Federal Reserve, torn between trying to dampen speculation and inflation on the one hand and trying to head off recession on the other, was frantically pressing its various monetary levers to little effect.

But there was at least one big difference. Where in 1929 the stock market became the national craze as it had never been before, and in some senses had never quite been since, and interest in it was actually increased by its disintegration, in 1970 the investor mood was one of fatalism, and the decline in trading volume would become as great a problem for Wall Street as the decline in stock prices.

The Dow started the year at around 800, down about 15 percent from the start of 1969, the year before. During all of January, the market fell slowly but inexorably and, by the twenty-ninth, the Dow was at 768, its lowest point in more than three years. February and March were months of moderate recovery, still, however, on low volume; on the Amex in particular, volume set record lows for the year, day after day, particularly during a postal delivery strike in the New York City area in March. Brokerage firms, finally geared up for multimillion-share trading days that had become common in 1968 and 1969, and running such high expenses that some of them now needed 12-million-share Stock Exchange days to break even on commissions, were losing money so fast that in the first week of April the S.E.C. consented to the imposition of a $15 commission surcharge on all transactions of 1,000 shares or less. Some—like Hans Reinisch, a young man who had set himself up as the Ralph Nader of the securities business—felt that thus punishing the small investor for the unprofitability of brokerage firms, at a time when large institutional investors had recently been granted *lower* commissions, was both absurd and unfair. But something had to be done quickly, and that was what the Wall Street leadership and the Nixon S.E.C. thought ought to be done.

At about the same time, the pace of the price decline suddenly stepped up. On April 22 came the abrupt and mysterious E.D.S. collapse in which Ross Perot sustained his historic loss. Two days later, the Dow had receded to 750, and about a quarter of all issues traded on the Stock Exchange were at their lows for the year. By April 27, the Dow was at 735, and the economic analyst Eliot Janeway—"Calamity Janeway," as some had come to call him, in recognition of his reputation as Wall Street's most assiduous prophet of doom—was saying that it would certainly go below 700, and probably much lower than that. On the twenty-eighth, with the Dow at 724, President Nixon tried to stem the tide by saying for quotation that if he had the spare cash, he would be buying stocks right now.

(Pause to note: on October 25, 1929, the day after the one remembered as Black Thursday, President Hoover said, "The fundamental business of the country . . . is on a sound and prosperous basis." Hoover stopped short of saying he wished he had some money to invest in stocks, but five days later, after a further disastrous decline, John D. Rockefeller, Sr., said, "My son and I have for some days been purchasing sound common stocks.")

2

The chairman of the New York Stock Exchange in 1970, who was fated to be the key man in Wall Street's near-fatal convulsions that year, was Bernard J. Lasker, always called Bunny, a tall, athletic-looking man of fifty-nine with the semi-distant yet curiously vulnerable air of command of a tough regular-army top sergeant. In character and background, he presents a striking—and, as a reflection of social change, highly interesting—contrast to his 1929 counterpart, the ineffable Richard Whitney. Where Whitney had belonged beyond cavil to such an aristocracy as his country could muster—descendant of seventeenth-century settlers in Massachusetts, son of a Boston bank president, nephew of a former Morgan partner, graduate of Groton and Harvard, son-in-law of a president of the Union League Club—Lasker was the son of a Jewish sponge-and-chamois importer on Beaver Street, a rundown commercial area of ancient redbricks standing in the shadow of imperial Wall Street. Where Whitney's undoubted ability to lead other men had been rooted in an intimidating aloofness composed of snobbery and disdain for those he considered his terrestrial inferiors, Lasker, an eminently approachable man, derived his comparable ability from the overpowering singlemindedness—surely Whitney would have called it "pushiness"—of an aggressive yet accommodating businessman. Finally, where Whitney with all his physical impressiveness and air of Episcopalian propriety had eventually been exposed as a habitual embezzler, Lasker with his direct manner was by all accounts and evidences a man of iron sense of duty and scrupulous professional rectitude.

Born in New York City in 1910, Lasker grew up on West End Avenue in middle-class circumstances and went to a private day school. But the senior Lasker died when his son was fourteen—the sponge business was in any case to be ruined a few years later by du Pont's introduction of artificial sponges—and there was not enough money to send the boy to college. So, at seventeen, he went to work as a runner on Wall Street for the firm of Hirsch, Lilienthal and Company. There he made his way upward by the classical steps—the purchase-and-sales department, the order room, customer's man, assistant manager of a branch office—and in 1939 became a Stock Exchange member himself. Eventually, he settled in as a partner, and eventually senior partner, of Lasker, Stone and Stern, a professional firm —doing arbitrage, specializing, and floor trading, never dealing directly with the public—of the sort whose members have traditionally run the affairs of the New York Stock Exchange. In the natural course of events, Lasker gravitated into Stock Exchange management: membership on the Board of Governors in 1965, the vice chairmanship in 1967, and, in the spring of 1969, election to succeed Gustave Levy as chairman. Unabashedly loving the Exchange and his role within its canonical observances, Lasker considered it to be to all intents and purposes the center of his life, and he immediately threw himself into the unpaid job of chairman with a will, almost totally neglecting his own business affairs (as, indeed, Whitney had done) in the performance of his volunteer duties. But at the time he assumed office, he could hardly know just how onerous those duties would become, or that they would draw on energies and abilities that he may not have known he had—and draw, among other things, on his long-standing personal friendship with Richard M. Nixon.

Like so many self-made men in America, big, bluff Bunny Lasker was a bellicose conservative, ever eager to praise the free-enterprise environment that nourished him so bountifully, and quick to leap to attack or to patient explanation whenever anyone criticized it. Indeed, one is tempted to describe him as a Republican by instinct or even by religion. If someone he met turned out to be a Republican, Lasker tended automatically to think of the man as a friend; if, on the other hand, someone he instinctively liked turned out *not* to be a Republican, he was genuinely puzzled by the anomaly. Sometimes this rather elementary form of faith led to disillusionment; for example, in 1965, Lasker (albeit with some misgivings) served as finance chairman for the Republican New York City mayoral candidate John Lindsay, but a couple of months after that campaign's triumphant conclusion, when Mayor Lindsay decided to impose an increased stock transfer tax on Wall Street, Lasker's regard for Lindsay vanished rather abruptly. On the whole, though, his faith in the Grand Old Party and its members seemed to stand him in good stead. It certainly did in his relations with Nixon, with whom he first became associated as a fund-raiser in the 1960 Presidential campaign. The following year, when the defeated candidate was visiting New York, he called up Lasker to thank him for his efforts in the campaign and to suggest that, since they had never met, they do so now. The two men met at the Plaza and hit it off immediately. Nixon had never seen the Stock Exchange, so Lasker took him there; the ex-candidate was so beguiled by what he saw that he stayed for a long lunch. Then, after Nixon had hit political bottom with his 1962 defeat in the California gubernatorial election and had temporarily abandoned politics to come to New York to practice law, Lasker and his wife more or less took their friends, the tyro New Yorkers, in hand: Lasker helped the Nixons find an apartment, and Mrs. Lasker helped Mrs. Nixon find a dressmaker, and the two couples frequently dined together. It was in 1964, though, that Lasker without conscious intention put the future President most deeply in his debt. Nixon would say later that Lasker, in helping to talk him out of making the Presidential race again in that overwhelmingly Democratic year, had had a large hand in saving his political career.

So when Lasker came to the Stock Exchange chairmanship in 1969, the Stock Exchange had a friend at court, as duly attested by a telegram from the President, on the occasion of Lasker's election, that Lasker subsequently had framed and mounted on the wall of his office: "Dear Bunny: As I mentioned yesterday, I am highly pleased that you have been chosen as head of the New York Stock Exchange. Your abilities and qualities of leadership make you exactly the right man taking the job at the right time. Pat joins me in sending our congratulations and affectionate regards. Richard Nixon." Meanwhile, his religious Republicanism began creating new anomalies. Robert Haack, the Exchange's paid president and therefore the man Lasker had to work with most closely in its management, was a liberal Democrat as well as a man whose personal chemistry often conflicted with Lasker's. On the other hand, the amiable Judge Budge, Nixon's S.E.C. chairman, was a Republican and as such a man for whom Lasker felt a great affinity—an affinity that is said to have had a lot to do with the S.E.C.'s granting of the $15 brokerage commission surcharge in April 1970. So the chairman of the Stock Exchange didn't get along very well with his logical friend, his own organization's administrative head, but got along beautifully with his logical enemy, the head of the regulating body that was supposed to ride herd on Wall Street. To further complicate things—and complete the irony—Haack and Budge didn't hit it off, for the curious reason, among others, that the Wall Streeter considered the S.E.C. head too far to the right and the S.E.C. head considered the Wall Streeter too far to the left.

One hesitates to imagine what Stock Exchange-government relations in the great crisis of 1970 would have been had Lasker been Stock Exchange chairman and had the Washington administration been Democratic. As things stood, Nixon had been right: Lasker was indeed the right man at the right time, from a Wall Street point of view—for the very reason that he had the ear and the confidence of the President, whose telegraphed assurance to the Stock Exchange chairman would turn out to be its own proof. Lasker began drawing on his Washington connections on April 29—the day of the Cambodia invasion, and another day of steadily declining stock prices—when, at Lasker's suggestion and with Nixon's approval, he and a group of other Wall Street leaders met at the White House with a group of top government officials including Economic Advisers Council Chairman Paul McCracken. Each side reassured the other that everything was under control; but nevertheless, as Donald Regan, chairman of Merrill Lynch, reported later, "the tone of the meeting was dejected." Still, it served to open a wire between Wall Street and Washington that would be crucially useful in the weeks to come.

In early May, matters on Wall Street went from bad to worse. On the third, Galbraith, one of whose well-known books is a study of the 1929 crash, came out with a newspaper article drawing a series of striking parallels between the current situation and that of 1929: excessive speculation, overly leveraged holding companies, inflated investment funds, funds that invested solely in other funds, and so on. On the fourth, the Dow suffered its greatest one-day drop in seven years and finished at 714. The following day, government took its first positive action when the Federal Reserve reduced the margin requirement on stock purchases from 80 percent cash down to 65 percent cash; but the tide was running too strongly now to be stemmed by a moderate relaxation of credit requirements, and on May 13 the Dow broke through 700, closing at 694. Trading volume was still relatively low. It was not a panic but a funk—"a kind of neurosis," as George Shultz, then Nixon's Bureau of Management and Budget chief, said. Shultz did not add that the funk, or neurosis, seemed to have been brought about in good part by the actions of the Nixon administration in noneconomic fields. Cambodia and Kent State, on top of everything else, had stunned the nation. Nothing could be discerned ahead but more futile overseas war and domestic violence. The last thing people felt like doing was buying stocks.

The vast securities ant hills, and the immense credit spider-

webs, were crumbling now, and with them the network build-
ers themselves. The stock of Cornfeld's fast-collapsing I.O.S.,
which had managed in six months to send some $75 million
down the drain with bad investments and ill-considered loans,
had sold in the 20s late in 1969 and was now selling at 2; on May
8, in an acrimonious board meeting at Geneva, Cornfeld's fellow
directors forced him to step down as their head. And on May 17,
in Dallas, James Ling—whose Ling-Temco-Vought was suffering from a government antitrust suit and from debts so large
that it could not even keep up the interest payments, as well as
a stock price that had plummeted from a peak of 170 to around
16—quietly resigned as chairman and chief executive, under
pressure from the company's creditors. Thus, in hardly more
than a week, the king of the conglomerators and the king of the
mutual-fund operators were both forced from their thrones.

3

Lasker, having decided that the time had come to play his ace,
now sought a personal interview with Nixon, who, he felt, was
simply neglecting the stock market and its consequences in his
preoccupation with foreign affairs and inflation. On the afternoon of May 20, he was notified that the President would see
him the following morning at eleven o'clock. Lasker stayed up
most of the night making notes on what he would say, and made
further notes en route to Washington on an early-morning
plane. Arriving at the White House at eight-fifteen, he went to
the office of the President's secretary, Rose Woods, where he
spent more than an hour putting the finishing touches on his
notes; then he crossed the street to the Executive Office Building, where he dropped in on his friend Vice President Agnew.
In the course of this visit, he found himself listening to an
urgent appeal for help from the Vice President's secretary, Mrs.
Alice Fringer, who told him that she had tied up most of her

savings in a mutual fund only to see its price fall far below what she had paid. "Tell me what to do," she pleaded. "I can't afford to lose the money." Taken aback, Lasker gave no immediate answer.

"Soft like with Budge!" was Lasker's admonition to himself at the top of the first page of the five-page sheaf of notes that he carried with him into his meeting with Nixon. "Market break worst since 1929—no present sign of abating. Confidence is the big problem." What followed in Lasker's notes was mostly economic analysis and specific suggestions for the President about wage and price controls, government borrowing policies, and the impact that another 1929-style crash would have on the whole economy. Upon at last being ushered into the President's office, Lasker, after greetings and family inquiries, opened his briefcase and brought out his sheaf of notes. "What have you got there?" Nixon asked. Lasker replied with Stock Exchange-style humor that he had brought his lunch, since he could no longer afford to eat in restaurants. He was rewarded with a broad Presidential smile. He went on to say that the country was "five minutes till midnight of another 1929," and that Presidential action was urgently needed to avert such a catastrophe. Then it suddenly occurred to Lasker that he could best dramatize the seriousness of the situation by forgetting most of the facts and figures he had prepared and bringing things down to personalities. Accordingly, he threw aside his elaborate notes and repeated, with dramatic emphasis, what had passed between him and Agnew's secretary, concerning her worry about her mutual-fund investment.

"Tell her not to sell her shares," Nixon said immediately.

"*You* tell her, Mr. President," Lasker shot back in his best top-sergeant tones.

Nixon seems to have got the message. What the two men decided on, as an immediate step, was the scheduling, with due fanfare, of a large White House dinner for top officials of government, Wall Street, and business, to be tailored specifically to show the nation that the government was indeed concerned about the stock-market situation and was prepared to do what could be done to remedy it. (In March 1929, at the leading edge of that year's crash, Richard Whitney went to the White House to confer with President Hoover about the stock-market situation. A temporary improvement in investor confidence followed.)

Lasker went back to Wall Street the same day, well satisfied with his White House audience. That afternoon he talked with Billy Salomon, who, with his finger on the pulse of the bond market, reported that the Federal Reserve had that day abruptly started pumping money into the economy through purchases of government paper—the first fruit, Lasker was entitled to suppose, of the alarm that he had succeeded in implanting in Nixon. Plans for the White House dinner—still unannounced to the public—went forward. The stock market went on dropping; the clock was still ticking out on Lasker's five minutes. On May 22, the averages hit a new low since early 1963, and Merrill Lynch had to call for $11.5 million in new margin money from its customers who had bought stock partially on credit. The weekend break brought no surcease, and on Monday, May 25, the Dow dropped 20.81 points—the biggest one-day drop since the Kennedy assassination in 1963—to finish just above 640. Janeway had begun talking about a bottom of 500.

Midnight seemed to be at hand. Panic lurked in the wings. On Monday afternoon, after the market close, the brokerage and investment community learned of the planned White House dinner from an announcement carried on the Dow news tape. The dinner was to be held that Wednesday the twenty-seventh and was to be attended by sixty or more leading figures from business and finance. But the studied implication of Presidential concern for the fortunes of Wall Street had disappointingly little immediate effect. The next day, Tuesday, the Dow dropped nine more points, to 631. Then on Tuesday evening through television news reports, and on Wednesday morning through newspaper coverage and comment, the significance of the coming event seemed to sink in. In one of the great preprandial celebrations of American history, a cocktail hour of staggering economic importance, the Dow on Wednesday the twenty-seventh leaped upward 32.04 points for the biggest one-day gain in Stock Exchange history.

The dinner itself, taking place when the announcement of it had already largely fulfilled its purpose, was something of an anticlimax, with certain overtones of farce. (No reporters were present, and no official report of the proceedings was ever issued; but we have, as evidence of what happened, the accounts of various participants, and in particular that of Donald Regan of Merrill Lynch, who took careful notes.) In the White House's State Dining Room the full panoply of government, business, and financial power was duly arrayed. From the government, besides the President, there were Arthur Burns, chairman of the Fed; Chairman McCracken of the Council of Economic Advisers; Secretary of the Treasury David Kennedy; Secretary of Commerce Maurice Stans; Attorney General John Mitchell; and such special Presidential aides as Peter Flanigan, Charles Colson, and William Safire. From business there were, among others, Chairmen James Roche of General Motors, H. I. Romnes of American Telephone, Harold Geneen of I.T.T., Donald Mac-Naughton of Prudential Insurance, and Robert Anderson of Atlantic Richfield. The Wall Street contingent included, besides Regan and Lasker, President Haack of the New York Stock Exchange and President Saul of the Amex, as well as the top bosses of a half-dozen of the leading brokerage firms.

Lobster cocktails, beef Wellington, Chateau Lafite-Rothschild 1962—what but a Rothschild wine on stock-market night at the White House? The proceedings that followed seem to have been solemn, portentous, and in some ways rather horrifying. The President spoke first. Referring to a huge map of Southeast Asia that had been set up behind him, he characterized the three-weeks-old Cambodian invasion as the best-executed American military coup since MacArthur's landings at Inchon in Korea in 1950. Why, the President wanted to know, did Wall Street look upon such a national triumph as an occasion for selling stocks? On the contrary, he said, it ought to be considered highly bullish. On the domestic front, he predicted resumed economic growth and a cooling of inflation in the second half of the year. Lasker, speaking next, urgently insisted that a substantial stock recovery was dependent on three government actions: strict adherence to the announced plans for withdrawal of American troops from Cambodia, clear evidence that the Fed would support the price of government bonds, and further steps by the Fed to increase the money supply. Chairman Burns of the Fed, arising next, assured those present that his institution was fully aware of the magnitude and significance of the Wall Street crisis, and declared flatly, and most satisfactorily, that the Fed was prepared to fulfill its responsibilities as a lender of last resort. This, as it happened, was the only concrete reassurance of constructive economic action to be uttered by a government official all evening.

Following Burns's remarks, Nixon called for questions. There was a question as to how the President proposed to deal with the nation's young people and their campus revolts, to which the President replied, apparently to everyone's satisfaction, that junior faculty members at universities ought to show "more guts" in dealing with student protesters. According to Regan's account, "he added that he had not become President of the United States to witness the liquidation of all of our alliances and to see us lose our place of primacy in the hierarchy of nations."

The dinner, to judge from the available accounts, was getting to be a kind of Mad Tea Party, various participants giving voice to their own preoccupations without regard to anyone else's, and none of those present touching more than remotely on reality as it was perceived by most of their fellow citizens outside the State Dining Room. And then came the bombshell. A guest named Isidore Cohen, who was entirely unknown to almost everybody present, arose with a "question" that swiftly evolved into a slashing ten-minute attack on the administration's policies—its vacillation on economic matters, the badness (as the speaker thought) of Dr. Burns's economic advice to the President, and, in Regan's words, "a large helping of recommendations in a wide range of fields." As Cohen went on, heatedly and implacably, and it became clear that there was a cuckoo in this nest of the business-financial-government complex, there was general consternation and dismay. Regan, who happened to be seated next to Cohen, kept trying to pull him from his feet by yanking at the tail of his coat, but in vain; Cohen remained stubbornly standing, and talking. When at last Cohen had finished his tirade and resumed his seat, the President coolly picked up where he had left off, almost as if nothing had happened; and a few minutes later the meeting broke up to general applause.

What had happened? Who was Izzy Cohen and what was he doing there? "What was he doing there?" Bunny Lasker asked later, with rhetorical indignation. "Why, he's a Democrat!" At least as much to the point, Cohen was by no means a businessman of comparable stature to the others present. In fact, he was a principal of Joseph Cohen and Sons, a men's clothing manufacturer based in New York and Philadelphia that had recently merged with Rapid-American, which the reader will recall as the conglomerate headed by the one-time Israeli Meshulam Riklis—who had not been favored by a Presidential invitation. Cohen was there, in a word, because someone involved in the planning of the dinner had blundered. We may be grateful to the anonymous blunderer, and to Cohen himself, for making the President's dinner into something both more human and more representative of the nation than anyone had intended.

History is full of ironies, and it is just barely possible that the United States was saved from "another 1929" by this White House non-event, which is comparable in many respects to Richard Whitney's celebrated staged bid for Steel at 205 at the height of the panic on Black Thursday. ("If that market had gone through 600, it might have gone through 400," Lasker would insist later.) The reports of the dinner that circulated in Wall Street the next day emphasized Burns's reassurances rather than Cohen's contrariety, and the market rose. It bounded up 21 more points that day, and on the following day, a Friday, it climbed above 700. Early in June a fresh decline began, and threatened to turn into a rout when, on the twenty-first, the supposedly unshakable Penn Central Railroad Company, suffering from management that in retrospect would appear to have been inept beyond belief, suddenly collapsed into bankruptcy. This time, something more economically palpable was at stake than general loss of confidence in the nation's policies. What was at stake was the survival of the "commercial paper market," a revolving credit system among corporations in which they borrow money short-term and unsecured, usually from each other, and in which in June 1970 there was involved the vast sum of $40 billion. With the Penn Central's paper in default, the danger was that the unfortunate companies that had lent tens of millions to the Penn Central might themselves be unable to meet their obligations, and that other commercial-paper lenders might suddenly refuse to renew their loans, leading to a chain reaction ending in a classic national money panic and, of course, a stock-market collapse. But the Federal Reserve, this time, was on its toes; warned in advance of impending danger, it applied the classic remedy to the classic dilemma, opening wide its usually carefully restricted loan window and suspending the banks' usual interest-rate ceilings, thereby releasing a flood of money into the market and preventing the chain reaction from starting. Fast footwork by the often heavy-footed Fed kept the Penn Central failure an isolated tragedy instead of a national disaster; early in July, the Dow began a long, fairly steady rise that would carry it by the end of the year to above 840.

4

Having compared 1929 and 1970 as to sequence of events and attitudes toward events and found the similarities at least as striking as the differences, we will do well to compare the hard figures. From the September 1929 peak to the nadir of the Great Depression in the summer of 1932, the Dow industrial average dropped from 381 to 36, or just over 90 percent. From the December 1968 peak to the May 1970 bottom, the same index dropped from 985 to 631, or about 36 percent. By that standard, a pistol shot as against a mortar barrage. But, as we have had occasion to note before, that standard really will not do; the Dow accurately reflected the 1929–1932 market when house painters and office girls were making their plunges in Dow stocks like General Motors and Standard Oil of New Jersey, and woefully failed to reflect the 1969–1970 market when similar plunges were far more likely to be made in Control Data or Ling-Temco-Vought. A financial consultant named Max Shapiro, writing in the January 1971 issue of *Dun's Review*, tried to construct a new yardstick more appropriate to the new situation. As a rough modern counterpart to what the Dow represented in the old days, Shapiro made a list of thirty leading glamour stocks of the nineteen sixties—ten leading conglomerates including Litton, Gulf and Western, and Ling-Temco-Vought, ten computer stocks including I.B.M., Leasco, and Sperry Rand, and ten technology stocks including Polaroid, Xerox, and Fairchild Camera. The average 1969–1970 decline of the ten conglomerates, Shapiro found, had been 86 percent; of the computer stocks, 80 percent; of the technology stocks, 77 percent. The average decline of all thirty stocks in this handmade neo-Dow had been 81 percent. Even allowing for the fact that the advantage of hindsight gave Shapiro the opportunity to choose for inclusion in his list particular stocks that would help prove his point, his analysis strongly suggests that, as measured by the performance of the stocks in which the novice investor was most likely to make his first plunges, the 1969–1970 crash was fully comparable to that of 1929.

And again, measured by the number of people affected and the gross sums of money they lost, 1969–1970 was strikingly *worse* than 1929–1932. In 1929 there were, at the most, four or five million Americans who owned stock; in 1970, by the New York Stock Exchange's own proud count, there were about 31 million. As to the sums of money lost, between September and November 1929 around $30 billion eroded from the paper value of stocks listed on the New York Stock Exchange, and a few billion more from that of stocks traded elsewhere; the 1969–1970 loss, including issues listed on the two leading exchanges and those traded over-the-counter, totalled in excess of $300 billion, ten times the former amount.

Losses, then, of $300 billion in a year and a half, spread over more than 30 million investors—such were the bitter fruits of the go-go years: of the conglomerates and their promoters' talk of synergism and of two and two making five; of the portfolio wizards who wheeled and dealt with their customers' money; of the works of bottom-line fiction written by the creative accountants; of the garbage stock dumped on the market by two-a-week underwriters; of the stock salesmen who acted as go-betweens for quick commissions; of the mutual funds that got instant performance by writing up the indeterminate value of unregistered letter stock. But the fact remains that the human and social damage that resulted from the more recent crash was immeasurably less. In a nation far richer in real terms than it had been in 1929, the market losers of 1969–1970 could better absorb their losses, and moreover, more intelligent and conscientious federal regulation in the later era shielded the losers from the worst consequences of their gullibility and greed. With no government restrictions at all on borrowing for the purpose of buying stock in 1929, people had been free to invest their savings in stocks on 10 percent or 20 percent margin, thus assuming the suicidal risk of being wiped out on a 10 percent or 20 percent market decline. The Federal Reserve margin requirement—amounting to 80 percent through most of the 1969–1970 crisis—made it necessary for investors, except for a few who found highly sophisticated ways of circumventing the rules, to put up far more cash in relation to their risk exposure, and thereby became the key factor in preventing a repetition of the wholesale personal tragedies of 1929. Indeed, the margin requirement made it quite difficult in 1969–1970 for a stock investor to be wiped out entirely. What resulted, in fact, was a middle-class crash, productive of severe discomfort rather than disaster. If one heard of investor hardship in 1970, but not of lost homes, shattered lives, and suicides, much of the credit must go to that key piece of New Deal reform legislation, the Securities Exchange Act of 1934, which (among many other things) gave the Federal Reserve its power to regulate stock-market credit. At the very time when old-style liberalism was being widely reviled and ridiculed, a key measure of old-style liberalism, little noticed or honored, was serving as a small but significant piece of evidence that in forty years the country had learned something, after all.

And of course—not so much because of more enlightened government policies as because of the enormous industrial strength of the nation—the 1970 crash, unlike that of 1929, was not followed by a catastrophic depression. It was, however, followed by a serious one. Unemployment, which had amounted to about a quarter of the civilian labor force in 1932, never got more than slightly above 6 percent in the worst days of 1971, but that was bad enough, especially since (unlike 1932) it was concentrated in the black-minority areas of large cities—and in some of those areas, indeed, it did reach or exceed 25 percent. The Economic Report of the President for 1970 equivocated: it spoke of "slowdown," of "decline of output," of economic performance that "disappointed many expectations," but never of "recession," far less of "depression." One prominent economist went so far in his efforts to put matters in a cheerful light that he came up with the apparently self-cancelling phrase "growth recession."

But to the layman, the signs of recession late in 1970 were everywhere plain to see. In October, the Bureau of Labor Statistics reported that, with national unemployment at 5.2 percent of the work force, the figure for male black teen-agers in urban areas stood at 34.9 percent. At about the same time the tide of recession began spreading upward in the economic spectrum. It never did soak, or even dampen, the rich—corporate chieftains went right on drawing astronomical salaries, and banks in particular actually flourished because of continuing tight money—but in the autumn of 1970 the recession wave swamped the middle class. An organizer of the United Steelworkers told

Studs Terkel, chronicler of the Great Depression of the nineteen thirties, "When a guy is cashing his biweekly check at the neighborhood bar, every check for the last few years has been $300, $400. Now he brings home $150 to $170." A twenty-two-year-old described the effect of recession on the youth counterculture: "Most people with long hair have to work for dog wages. There aren't many places that hire them, so they work at rip-off joints. You know, $1.75 an hour. It's like being black."

In October, the airlines, anticipating collective losses of at least $100 million on the year's operations, were cutting back luxury services: sandwich meals now instead of steaks, fewer in-flight movies, paper towels instead of cloth ones, no more snacks of expensive macadamia nuts. The same month, the Department of Labor identified thirty-five separate major labor areas with "substantial or persistent" unemployment; the Council of Better Business Bureaus estimated that there were 400,000 currently unemployed executives; and large companies began making across-the-board cuts of executive and white-collar paychecks. The Norton Company of Massachusetts, to name one, shaved 15 percent from the salaries of 5,000 managers and white-collar workers, which for a person earning $25,000 meant a cut of about $72 a week. By November, in New York City, it was clear that the welfare rolls were being swelled faster by new applications from non-Puerto Rican whites than by those from blacks and Puerto Ricans. At the Professional Placement Center of the New York State Employment Service, the number of professional and managerial claimants for unemployment benefits had risen by more than 100 percent in a year, and there was talk of stockbrokers working as cab drivers, art directors taking jobs as layout artists, and accountants accepting sharp salary cuts and for the first time in their lives paying agency fees. That winter in Manhattan, for-hire limousines were in supply rather than in demand; for the first time in the memory of many opera patrons, there were empty seats at almost every Metropolitan Opera performance; many former Saks Fifth Avenue customers were patronizing Klein's or Alexander's, and many former taxi riders were riding buses and subways. In December, placement

counsellors at colleges began telling seniors of a sharp drop in
job offers, and warning them that the days when they could take
their pick of starting jobs were over. Most large industrial companies began cutting their campus recruiting visits sharply,
some cutting them in half. The advanced-degree job market
became a small disaster area, with new Ph.D. holders taking
jobs, when they could find them, at half the going rates of the
year before. Urban private schools, used to watching affluent
parents agonize over berths for their offspring, suddenly were
competing among themselves for scarce applicants.

And so it went. There were no breadlines or applesellers,
but bread was being eaten instead of cake, apples instead of
baked Alaska. And the reaction of worried politicians to the
deteriorating situation called forth more sardonic echoes of the
past. As the year 1970 ran out with the gross national product
down for the first time since 1958, and with industry limping
along at three-quarters of capacity, the President, with the con-
currence of Congress, began applying that old Herbert Hoover
standby, the trickle-down theory of trying to save old jobs and
create new ones through federal handouts to business. By the
end of the year, Congress had voted the Lockheed Aircraft Corporation a $250-million loan guarantee in a financial rescue op-
eration intended principally to save the jobs of 60,000 employees
by saving the company from bankruptcy; the bankrupt Penn
Central was on the way to a $125-million federal loan guarantee
to keep its passenger trains running, and their employees working; a new governmental corporation, Amtrak, was being established to operate all of the nation's intercity trains; and government shipbuilding subsidies were in the process of being greatly
increased. It all looked like Hoover's famous breadline for business, the Reconstruction Finance Corporation, all over again,
with the difference that the R.F.C. had usually driven a harder
bargain with its petitioners than the Nixon administration did
now.

Week by week and month by month, new parallels kept
appearing. In 1971, Nixon repeatedly rejected the idea of direct
federally sponsored job programs, just as Hoover had done in

1930 and 1931. Week by week and month by month, the dollar grew weaker in the international markets. When the United States had finally been forced to abandon its pledge to redeem dollars with gold on April 18, 1933, it had been three and a half years after the beginning of the 1929 stock-market crash. This time, the triumph of political necessity over national honor came sooner. When the gold default of 1933 was repeated down to all but the smallest details in August 1971, it was hardly more than a year after the height of the 1970 crash.

History, in its economic aspect, seemed to have become a recurring nightmare from which the United States could not awake. But for Wall Street, the nightmare this time had a new dimension. In the second half of 1970, Wall Street itself, as distinguished from its hapless customers, came within a hair of plunging into irretrievable bankruptcy, and the American securities market into full-fledged socialism.

CHAPTER XIII

Saving Graces

1

If Wall Street can lay claim to special expertise in any particular field, that field is the raising and management of capital. Bringing together, presumably in an orderly and mutually beneficial way, companies that need new money to run their businesses and investors who wish to hire out some of their money at reasonable risk, is Wall Street's work—the social justification of its existence. By and large, over the years, it has performed this function well. Yet in the latter nineteen sixties the capital structure of Wall Street itself became unsafe and unsound to a degree that, when hard times struck, was revealed as nothing less than a scandal. It was more than a case of a physician being unable to heal himself; it was a case of a physician habitually and systematically flouting everything he had learned at medical school, including the simplest rules of personal daily hygiene.

Matters had not always been thus. The celebrated post-1929 suicide victims had been for the most part customers rather than brokers. The brokers' yachts were scarce by 1932, but their firms had come through that crisis still solvent, partly because most of them had been conservatively financed with the personal resources of careful Puritanical partners, partly because the brokerage business in those days had been of manageable size, and not least because the terrible drop in stock prices had occurred on such unprecedentedly high trading volume as to enable brokers to recoup on commissions much of their losses on stocks they owned. When brokerage failures did occur back in those days, it was usually a matter of outright fraud, as in the famous case of Richard Whitney and Company. But in the nineteen sixties, when the securities business had broadened to become mass business for the first time, brokerage houses financed themselves not by adopting the mass-business methods they understood so well and so often urged on others, but by merely adding new and dubious twists to the traditional methods of what had been, by the standards of American Telephone or General Motors, a cottage industry. Not until 1970, for example, did the first Wall Street firm raise money for its operations from outside by selling its own stock to the public, and it took a change in the New York Stock Exchange's constitution to make such a sale possible. Like most bad business practices, Wall Street's obsolete and unsound capital-raising methods worked well enough in good times; it required only a little misfortune to expose them as the jerrybuilt mechanisms they were.

That misfortune, utterly unanticipated, consisted of the simultaneous drop in stock prices and trading volume in 1969 and the first half of 1970.

Let us look, in brief and simplified form, at a brokerage firm's typical capital structure in 1969–1970, as administered by the New York Stock Exchange and grudgingly but nonetheless leniently approved by the S.E.C.

The Stock Exchange rules imposed on such firms the requirement that the ratio between their aggregate indebtedness and their "net capital" be at no time higher than twenty to one, and the Stock Exchange through a system of surprise audits undertook to see that its members complied with this rule. And what was the nature and source of the "net capital" required under the rules? Its basic and soundest forms were the traditional ones—the cash investments of general partners, entitling them to stated shares in the profits, and the cash loans of other backers, entitling them to interest. But that was only the beginning, and, by the end of the nineteen sixties, only a small percentage of the capital of many firms consisted of such unassailable assets. There were other less substantial but still permissible forms of "capital" that, after the great expansion of 1967–1968, came to predominate over the traditional ones. One of these consisted of the loan of securities by an investor to a broker—a fair enough form of capital except that, unlike cash, the securities might abruptly decline in dollar value, thus abruptly reducing the amount of capital that they represented. Also qualified for inclusion as capital were a firm's accounts receivable, which sometimes consisted of such birds-in-the-bush as anticipated tax refunds and possibly uncollectable cash debts from customers. Then there were secured demand notes. Anyone owning a batch of securities—no matter how volatile and speculative—could pledge them as backing for a paper loan to a brokerage firm and thus technically contribute to the firm's capital. No money would actually change hands, nor would the investor actually give up the benefits of his loaned securities; there would merely be, for the firm, a cheering new capital entry on its balance sheet, and for the lender, the pleasure of regularly collecting interest on money he had never parted with and at the same time collecting dividends, were any paid, on his stocks. As if this were not a pleasant enough arrangement, under the terms of some such notes it was explicitly agreed that the lender would not have to part with any money or any securities, except in the all but unthinkable event that the brokerage firm should become insolvent, unable to meet its day-to-day obligations, or not in compliance with the net capital rule.

Shakiest of all, there were subordinated loans. Any securities-holding customer of a brokerage firm in need of additional capital could simply sign a paper headed "Event of Subordination Agreement." In this magic instrument, the customer did no more than agree, in the event of the firm's liquidation, to subordinate his claims to those of other customers and creditors; in exchange, he was allowed to go on collecting dividends on his stocks and simultaneously collecting interest on his "loan"—which, of course, had involved no actual money—while the brokerage firm was allowed to enter on its books the market value of the securities, less a reasonable discount, as new capital. Here, then, was "capital" that the beneficiary could *never* lay his hands on—unless he went broke, and even in that case the hands laid on it would be not his but those of his creditors.

The net of these perhaps rather abstruse ground rules is that the S.E.C. and the Stock Exchange allowed Wall Street firms to comply with the net capital rule—imposed for the protection of the firms themselves as well as that of their customers —with capital that was essentially a mirage. It was money that could not be seen, or rubbed together, or jangled in the hand, or, more to the point, used in the operation of a brokerage business; essentially, it was money that would become available, if at all, too late to do any good. Finally, contributors of the palpable and useful forms of brokerage capital, equity cash and debt cash, were entitled to withdraw any and all of their money at any time on only ninety days' notice, whenever for some reason they didn't like the way things were going. In 1969 and 1970 few investors in brokerage houses liked the way things were going, with the quite logical and rational consequence that there was an enormous and nearly catastrophic outflow of working capital from the nerve center of world capitalism.

Madness! the reader might understandably exclaim. And yet the reasons for such dangerous official permissiveness are not hard to find, and follow a certain logic of their own. As we have seen, the S.E.C. in 1969 wished chiefly to serve Wall Street —to avoid rocking the boat at a moment when almost everyone was happily making money. As to the Stock Exchange, it had logical reasons to treat its Rule 325, the one requiring a 1:20 ratio of capital to indebtedness, as a rule that was in effect at all times except when someone violated it. For the Exchange to stiffen the enforcement in 1967 and 1968 when things were going well, and brokerage capital was seldom a problem, would have been to play the role of spoilsport. Who, after all, *was* the Stock Exchange? The governors who made its key decisions were brokers. Conversely, when things began to go badly, a different reason, or excuse, for inaction came into play. If a member firm were found to be in violation of the capital rules and accordingly suspended from the privilege of doing business, the money and securities of the firm's customers would automatically become frozen and unavailable until such time as the firm was restored to capital compliance. Widows and orphans by the thousands or tens of thousands would suddenly be separated, temporarily but firmly, from their stocks or cash—hardly an eventuality calculated to enhance Wall Street's public popularity or leverage in Washington. So, when a member firm was found to be in capital violation, the Exchange was inclined to turn its back on its own rules, wink at the violation, and allow the firm to continue doing business while frantic efforts were made to find it more capital. Save the broker in order to save the customer: it was Wall Street's version of the trickle-down theory. (Where were the customer's yachts? Where, indeed, were the customers' subordinated lenders?) And whether the real objective was in fact to save the customers or, as some suspected, to protect members of the club from embarrassment and loss, the situation illustrates very vividly what is wrong with the principle of self-regulation in a business that serves the public.

Capital troubles began to crop up in the backlash of the 1968 paperwork crisis, and one small firm, Pickard and Company, actually failed that year as a result of too much business too inefficiently handled. The Exchange, to its credit, was ready to deal with the plight of Pickard's customers. In 1964, following the collapse of Ira Haupt and Company resulting from the infamous salad-oil swindle, it had set up a $25 million Special Trust Fund, paid for by subscription of Stock Exchange member firms, and reserved specifically for restoring the lost holdings of the unlucky customers of any member firm that should go broke. Pickard's being the first member-firm failure since Haupt, the trust fund had never been drawn upon; now it was tapped for some $400,000, and Pickard's 3,500 customers were reimbursed—or, in the rather attractive legal expression, "made whole."

Well and good: an isolated case, everyone supposed, in which the machinery had worked exactly as planned. But in the late spring of 1969, when stock prices and trading volume began to sink in unison, the squeeze on brokerage profits was on in earnest, leaving the firms' rickety capital structures increasingly exposed. Partners and backers, reacting to the bleak prospects, made things worse by availing themselves of the convenient ninety-day rule to pull out their money while the pulling was still good. (It may be noted that for a firm operating on the borderline of capital compliance, every dollar thus withdrawn meant that a debt reduction of twenty dollars was required.) In September, W. H. Donaldson—a principal in the powerful maverick firm of Donaldson, Lufkin and Jenrette that was about to force the change in time-honored Exchange rules that would enable it to raise money from outside Wall Street by selling its stock to the public—made some prophetic comments on the impermanence of Wall Street capital, and mentioned the arresting fact that probably more than 90 percent of all such capital was owned by men over sixty. In mid-October 1969, a certain Gregory and Sons went under. The Exchange promptly authorized the use of $5 million more from its Special Trust Fund to save the Gregory customers. At almost the same time, another firm—middle-sized Dempsey-Tegeler, which back in April had been fined $150,000 for record-keeping shortcomings—was forced by the Exchange to restrict its operations; it appears in retrospect that the Exchange knew the firm was not financially sound and was engaged in a furious effort to find it new capital to save it from bankruptcy—which is the terminus Dempsey-Tegeler would arrive at, in any event, the following August.

The trickle-down theory, then, was now in operation. But

it was not working. That December, most brokerage firms omitted their often-lavish Christmas bonuses. Depression had come to Wall Street. A cheerless pall of nameless doom hung over the financial district through the 1969 holiday season; secretaries and clerks who knew nothing of subordinated lenders or secured demand notes were being affected along with officers and partners.

Early in 1970, as the continuing decline in prices and volume made the situation for brokers progressively worse, a wave of brokerage mergers arose—frantic, hastily arranged shotgun marriages dictated not by love but by the need for survival. During a dreadful March, there were two more member-firm failures and a quasi-failure: McDonnell and Company, in spite of high social prestige and close ties with the Ford family of Detroit, closed its doors (cost to the Special Trust Fund: $8.4 million); Baerwald and DeBoer went into liquidation (cost to the fund: about $1 million); and out in Los Angeles, the former hottest deal-maker of them all, Kleiner, Bell, where customers had chanted "Go, go, go!" as they watched the ticker, found the going so rocky that it simply withdrew from the brokerage business. And now for the first time it began to be evident that not just marginal firms but some of the conservative, well-established giants of brokerage were in bad trouble as well. On March 16, Bache and Company reported that for fiscal 1969 it had incurred the largest annual operating loss in the annals of American brokerage, $8,741,000. Shock waves followed the announcement; investors began to experience the chills of panic, and on March 23, Haack felt called upon to refute wayward rumors by stating that all of the twenty-five largest Stock Exchange firms were in compliance with the capital rules.

Whether or not Haack knew it at the time, this was quite wide of the truth, as subsequent events would more than demonstrate. Facts were only spottily available; Wall Street was swept by confused alarms, and many firms in trouble were bald-facedly concealing the truth from the Stock Exchange. Perhaps Haack's statement should be taken as an expression of hope. His job, he clearly felt, was to spread reassurance and to ward off panic reactions. Again, in mid-April 1970, answering an urgent query from Senator Edmund Muskie, Haack wired from Wall Street: "THE EXCHANGE'S SPECIAL TRUST FUND IS NOT NEAR DEPLETION. . . SITUATION WITH RESPECT TO OPERATIONAL AND FINANCIAL PROBLEMS OF NYSE MEMBER FIRMS HAS VASTLY IMPROVED." In fact, five Stock Exchange firms were at that moment in liquidations that would end up costing the Special Trust Fund $17 million of its $25 million total; another member firm, Dempsey-Tegeler, was in its death throes, and its liquidation would eventually cost the trust fund over $20 million; and, worst of all, Hayden, Stone and Company, an eighty-four-year-old giant not far from the core of the Wall Street Establishment, with some 90,000 brokerage customers and a major share of the underwriting business, had lost nearly $11 million the previous year and was now losing money at a rate in excess of a million dollars a month. Hayden, Stone's affairs were shortly to erupt into the first phase of the crisis that almost brought Wall Street low for good.

3

At the end of May—at just about the time of the White House dinner that got credit for turning the market around—Lasker and some of his fellow governors of the Stock Exchange decided that the time had come to form a special committee to maintain surveillance over member firms' financial affairs. This was normally the work of the Exchange staff, and in particular of the Member Firms Department; but the governors were dissatisfied with the way that work was being done. The situation had become chaotic. It was increasingly evident that some firms were exaggerating, if not actually falsifying, their capital figures in their reports to the Exchange; at governors' meetings there would be talk of $40 or $45 million being required from the trust fund in liquidations already under way, but nobody was sure. The figures were guesses. It was Robert L. Stott, Jr., a well-known floor specialist, who came to Lasker and suggested that a committee of governors be formed forthwith. Responding enthusiastically, Lasker appointed to the new committee—formally named the Surveillance Committee, but usually thereafter called the Crisis Committee—himself; Ralph DeNunzio, executive vice president of Kidder, Peabody and vice chairman of the Exchange; Stott; Stephen M. Peck, senior partner in Weiss, Peck and Greer; Solomon Litt, senior partner in Asiel and Company; and Felix George Rohatyn, a partner in Lazard Frères and Company.

The chairman of the committee was Rohatyn, and it was he and Lasker, working in tandem, who would bear the brunt of its work over the months ahead. Rohatyn had been born in Vienna in 1928, and he and his Polish-Jewish parents had arrived in the United States as refugees from Hitler in 1942, after an interim stay in France. He had graduated in 1948 from Middlebury College, in Vermont, with a B.A. in physics, gone directly to Lazard, and never left again except for a spell of military service during the Korean war. As a young acolyte making the transition from natural science to the intricate and unnatural science of corporate finance, Rohatyn at Lazard had had the good luck to become a protégé of one of the leading masters of corporate deal-making, the French-born, publicity-shy, tough old wizard of Wall Street, André Meyer. Under such Cordon Bleu tutelage, sous-chef Rohatyn flourished. A compactly built man with a pug nose, heavy brows, full lips, and a slightly receding chin, he had an eager face and easy smile that made him at forty-two seem more like a student. But his appearance was deceptive. "Nobody has a record quite as spectacular as Felix's," a partner in a rival investment-banking house said of him in 1970. The record consisted of having become one of Wall Street's most ingenious experts in corporate acquisition and reorganization. That is to say, Rohatyn had become, like his mentor, a master merger-maker, and one of the firms for which he arranged intricate, multimillion-dollar acquisitions was the

Lazard client International Telephone and Telegraph, on whose board of directors he sat.

In 1972, Rohatyn would come to national prominence, of a sort, as the banker for I.T.T. who the previous year had had a series of private meetings with then Acting Attorney General Richard G. Kleindienst to argue, on public-policy grounds, for a favorable settlement of the Justice Department's antitrust suit against I.T.T. Disclosure of those meetings involved Rohatyn in considerable controversy, since Kleindienst would later deny, for a time, that he had had anything to do with the settlement. (It was never alleged that Rohatyn had any knowledge of or involvement in the famous I.T.T. financial commitment to the Republicans for their 1972 national convention.) Whatever the facts of that matter, Rohatyn in 1970 was quite possibly the most brilliant, and certainly among the most dedicated and energetic, men in Wall Street at a time when Wall Street badly needed brains, talent, and energy to save it from its own folly. Rich enough at forty-two, married to a daughter of the well-known author and Union-with-Britain advocate Clarence Streit, beginning to be spoken of as heir apparent to Meyer as boss of Lazard Frères, Felix Rohatyn in 1970 was riding the crest.

The Surveillance Committee started out by meeting once a week, for lunch on Thursdays, in a committee room on the sixth floor of the Stock Exchange building. Always present, besides Rohatyn, Lasker, and their committee colleagues, were two representatives of the Exchange staff, President Haack and Executive Vice President John Cunningham. According to Rohatyn and Lasker—both of whom later talked to me at length about the committee and its work—its first job consisted chiefly of trying to exercise due diligence as to use of the trust fund in current liquidations, and of trying to set up an early warning system as to other firms that were heading for trouble. It quickly became clear that the Exchange staff men really knew remarkably little about those other firms' financial condition. To their horror, the committee members began to see that weakness was the rule rather than the exception. Brokerage firms that the Exchange had supposed to be above reproach were revealed, under even superficial investigation, to be walking zombies, carrying assets on their books that did not exist and never had existed. "It was like a nightmare," Rohatyn said later. "You pushed here, you pushed there, at random, and wherever you pushed, you found softness."

The committee revised its schedule, and began meeting formally twice a week—Tuesdays and Thursdays at eight-thirty in the morning—and putting in so many additional hours that some of its members were soon devoting most of their time to its work rather than to the affairs of their own companies. Early in June, when the committee had been in existence for only a few weeks, it faced the first of three heroic challenges: the impending collapse of Hayden, Stone and Company.

That venerable firm had been in serious trouble since 1968, as the Exchange had ample occasion to know; in that year—a banner business year in which Hayden, Stone's gross income was at an all-time high of $113 million—its record-keeping situation had become so bad that it had literally called on the Coast Guard for help, hiring members of that service to moonlight in the back office. As early as the spring of 1969, investors in Hayden, Stone were getting the message that the good days were gone, and accordingly they began withdrawing their capital in huge amounts. The firm's attitude toward its problems at that time was vividly shown in its treatment of its treasurer, Walter Isaacson, who in the summer of 1969 began protesting that, with revenues going down, costs going up, and the capital base eroding, operations ought to be cut back drastically. Isaacson's unpleasant warnings ceased when he was summarily fired.

In September 1969, matters were hardly improved when the Stock Exchange backed restrictions on Hayden, Stone's operations by fining the firm $150,000 for rule infractions during the previous year. But, shortly thereafter, the Exchange suddenly turned soft on its erring member. In October, it removed all restrictions on Hayden, Stone's operations, and in November it made no objections to an offering circular to prospective investors in which Hayden, Stone made some extravagant and dubious claims as to its future. While no explanation was offered, it may logically be assumed that the Exchange's sudden blandness was motivated by fear that Hayden, Stone's capital situation had become so precarious that those 90,000 customer accounts were imminently threatened. At all events, the firm started out 1970 in technical capital compliance only on the basis of such gossamer assets as a tax refund claim that, far from having been approved by the Internal Revenue Service, had not yet even been filed.

By late May, when the Crisis Committee came into existence, Hayden, Stone was a huge black cloud on Wall Street's horizon, a storm latent but brewing. Its roster of branch offices had shrunk from eighty at the beginning of the year to sixty-two, and its back-office expenses had been drastically curtailed through mass firings, but, even so, it continued to lose approximately $1 million a month on current operations. Meanwhile, though, its capital problems had apparently been solved, at least temporarily and technically, at a single stroke. On Friday, March 13—of all dates—a group of Oklahoma businessmen signed demand notes lending Hayden, Stone $12.4 million, pledging stock in their own companies as collateral. They included Bill Swisher of CMI corporation, who pledged 165,000 shares then worth $4,372,500; Jack E. Golsen of LSB Industries, who pledged 200,000 of his firm's shares worth $1.2 million; and —most unfortunately, as it turned out—Jack L. Clark of Four Seasons Nursing Centers, who pledged 120,000 shares of *his* firm's high-flying stock with a March market value just short of $5 million. All told, the collateral added up to $17.5 million, apparently an ample sum to cover the $12.4 million demand note and give Hayden, Stone a rosy capital future. A rosy present income for the Oklahomans was assured by an interest rate on their "money" of around 7 percent.

However, as the reader will have no trouble discerning, something was wrong here. For one thing, Wall Street was not supposed to go knocking on the doors of little-known, unseasoned firms in Oklahoma for capital; it was supposed to be the other way around. More to the immediate point, the demand-note capital was insubstantial; the terms of the notes were such that Hayden, Stone, which so desperately needed capital to cover current operating losses, could not get its hands on a cent, unless the firm were either insolvent or in violation of Rule 325. Finally, were market fluctuations to cause the value of the loaned stock to drop below $12.4 million, the amount of Hayden, Stone's available credit would diminish accordingly. In sum, it was a classic case of phantom capital, created by a shuffle of papers and used to maintain formal compliance with a rule of the Stock Exchange's that the Exchange had no stomach for enforcing.

Then the shaky structure cracked. In mid-May, the S.E.C. suddenly suspended trading in Four Seasons Nursing Centers, which shortly thereafter expired in bankruptcy. Down the drain went $5 million in Oklahoma stock value on $3.3 million of Hayden, Stone capital. And the prices of the other Oklahoma stocks were dropping—20, 30, 40 percent—along with the rest of the market. By the beginning of June, when the Crisis Committee was hardly a week old, the market value of the Oklahoma stock had declined from $17.5 million to around $9 million, and as a result Hayden, Stone was plainly in violation of the capital rule, as a routine surprise audit would confirm a few days later. Things were in a worsening mess now; but what, the committee members asked themselves, could the Stock Exchange do? Blow the whistle on Hayden, Stone and let its customers fend for themselves? The Special Trust Fund, almost gone anyway, was ludicrously inadequate to handle such a giant liquidation. On the other hand, if the Exchange looked the other way and did nothing, apparently Hayden, Stone would be unable to meet its obligations and would sooner or later be forced into bankruptcy by its creditors. As Lasker and Rohatyn saw the matter, the Exchange had only one course—to find new capital to save Hayden, Stone, or to admit to the public that Wall Street could no longer be relied upon.

As a first step, the Exchange found some capital in a curious place. The Special Trust Fund was more than doubled by transferring into it $30 million that the Exchange had squirreled away as a building fund. No time to be thinking about new buildings now! The fund, as we have seen, was clearly intended for the single purpose of rescuing the customers of bankrupt member firms. But these were parlous times, and the language of the Special Trust Fund provisions was conveniently vague. So the Exchange's governors, on recommendation of the Crisis Committee, now voted to lend $5 million of their constitutents' money, entrusted to them specifically to save the customers of failed firms, to Hayden, Stone to keep it in business. It was just a matter of saving the broker in order to save the customers, they rationalized. More fancifully described, it was a matter of strapped parents tapping the children's piggy bank to prevent foreclosure of the mortgage on the homestead. Thus, on July 2, Hayden, Stone was restored to capital compliance—this time with real money, albeit money obtained in a most peculiar way.

But the reprieve was short-lived. By now, houses were crumbling from one end of Wall Street to the other. Day after day, time and again, the Exchange's staff would bring the Crisis Committee news of more firms that were on the brink of capital violation because of diminished business and consequent capital withdrawals. Time and again the committee would begin to probe in a new place, and find the same softness, the same imaginary assets shoring up a top-heavy façade. Several more firms, the largest of them Blair and Company, went under in June and July. In mid-August, the Exchange, through President Haack, announced for the first time the names of ten brokerage firms that were in bankruptcy or liquidation, and gave soothing reassurances that the augmented trust fund, now theoretically amounting to $55 million, was adequate to make their customers whole. Nevertheless, by the last week of August it was generally known in the Street that the fund was again depleted. And, at about the same time, there was an ominous new turn. Three more firms with in excess of ten thousand accounts among them —Robinson and Company, First Devonshire Corporation, and Charles Plohn and Company, the vehicle of our old acquaintance Two-a-Week Charlie, the garbage-stock king—were suspended for capital deficiencies and went into liquidation. For the first time, the Exchange pointedly did not commit the trust fund to the help of the customers—in the case of Robinson, on the technicality that the firm had resigned its Exchange membership back in July and was therefore not eligible for help; in the case of Plohn, because it did not believe that such help was needed; and in the case of First Devonshire, without any clear explanation. In retrospect the explanation is clear. The trust fund had been spent.

Meanwhile, Hayden, Stone went on losing money. The Oklahomans were screaming bloody murder at what was happening to their investment, and the loudest screamer was Jack Golsen. He, like the others, had little practical reason to raise a fuss; he believed now that, because of his subordination agreement, most or all of his investment was gone whether Hayden, Stone was rescued or not. He was screaming to relieve his outraged feelings—and, moreover, on principle. The conduct of Hayden, Stone's affairs, as it was now being gradually revealed, seemed to Golsen to be a public scandal. "In my business, if we are missing inventory, we stop everything and look for it," he complained. "In Wall Street, if they're missing seven million dollars, they just accept it as part of the game." This was a double standard, he insisted: Hayden, Stone would never dream of underwriting the stock of another company that operated as it did itself. The representations that the officers of the firm had made to him, in asking for the loan, now appeared to him to have been false; it seemed to him that Hayden, Stone's talk about its capital assets represented "dealings not in realities but in the abstract."

Early in August there was an attempt, prompted by the Exchange, to save Hayden, Stone through a merger with Walston and Company; but the deal fell through. The next merger candidate was Cogan, Berlind, Weill and Levitt (the same firm, with a name change, that had so profitably brokered the Leasco-Reliance merger in 1968). C.B.W.L., still doing well, was a small firm eager to expand, and the merger with Hayden, Stone would be a quick path to expansion. Unfortunately, it might also be a quick path to financial and operational chaos. Even apart from the difficulty attendant upon taking on a virtually bankrupt partner, one problem was that a merger would mean *too much* expansion; Hayden, Stone still had forty-five operating branch offices, and C.B.W.L. wanted no more than twenty of them. Knowing full well that it would have to sweeten the deal, the Stock Exchange offered $7.6 million to C.B.W.L. in exchange for its assuming the Hayden, Stone mess—a $7.6 million that the Exchange didn't have just then, in its trust fund or anywhere else, but that it believed it could raise from its membership. And that did it. At last agreement was reached that the Hayden, Stone offices would be divided between C.B.W.L. and Walston. The surviving firm was to be named CBWL-Hayden, Stone, Inc.

The whole thing almost fell through in what for the Crisis Committee was a hair-raising sequence of events on September 2 and 3. On the afternoon of the second, the Chicago Board of Trade, the nation's largest commodity exchange, suddenly announced that it planned to suspend Hayden, Stone for insolvency. Such a suspension would force the New York Stock Exchange to take similar action the next day, and that would be the ball game. Haack, Rohatyn, and Lasker pleaded with the Chicago authorities by telephone late into the night, and again early in the morning; at the last minute, the suspension order was revoked in consideration of Hayden, Stone's putting up a half a million dollars in escrow. And *that* crisis was surmounted. But there remained a single crucial detail to be carried out—that of getting approval of the merger from every last one of Hayden, Stone's 108 subordinated lenders. It was, indeed, a delicate situation. Since they all apparently stood to lose most of their money anyway, their egos could have free play, unfettered by financial considerations. Meanwhile, they found themselves in the satisfying position of being able to hold up the Wall Street Establishment—for revenge, for publicity, or for principle—by simply refusing to sign and thus forcing Hayden, Stone out of business.

All the persuasive powers of the Stock Exchange authorities were brought to bear. Haack flew to London to get one lender's signature, and got it. Others at first refused to sign, then allowed themselves to be persuaded. But time was running out; the Exchange could not go on ignoring its capital rule forever, and at last, under S.E.C. pressure, a deadline had to be set: the deal would be consummated by 10:00 A.M. on Friday, September 11 or Hayden, Stone would go into suspension, its 90,000 customers would be left out in the cold, and public confidence in Wall Street would end, possibly forever. By the morning of September 10, all of the subordinated lenders had signed except Golsen.

He stood firmly on principle. Why, he wanted to know, should he sign and thus help preserve the hopelessly and shamefully inefficient and slipshod business methods of the city slickers in Wall Street? "I'm interested in justice being done," he said. "I want an example made. The only way to make it is to go to a liquidation and let the Exchange lose twenty-five million or so. I want this crime to be brought to the attention of the public."

So for a day Golsen, in Oklahoma, held Hayden, Stone's and perhaps Wall Street's fate in his hand, while Lasker, from his office at the Exchange and his suite uptown at the Carlyle, pleaded repeatedly by phone. Lasker finally, at almost literally the last minute, won. It has been said that his clincher, delivered in the middle of the night of September 10, was a suggestion—or a threat—to have Richard Nixon himself call Golsen. Lasker vehemently denies that he went any further than to tell Golsen in general terms that he knew the President was very much concerned about the Wall Street situation and its effect on the national economy. Rather, Lasker attributes his success with Golsen to a homely coincidence. On the evening of September 10, Lasker says, an old friend and Wall Street colleague of his —Alan C. Greenberg, of Bear, Stearns and Company—called him unexpectedly and said, "Bunny, I hear you want a favor from Jack Golsen. I've known Golsen all my life. We were kids together in Oklahoma and, before we were both married, I used to date his wife and he used to date mine. You want me to call him?"

Reflecting that God must be on the side of the Stock Exchange, Lasker said yes. Greenberg called Golsen and said, "Bunny Lasker is an honest man and a good friend of mine, and I want you to do what he wants because I ask you."

Not to save Wall Street or the economy, then, or to obey the President of the United States, but for the sake of friendship. Whatever the case, something prevailed on Golsen, the Oklahoma outsider with a loaded gun pointed directly at Wall Street's head. After waiting melodramatically until ten minutes before deadline time on Friday the eleventh, Golsen signed; at ten o'clock sharp the CBWL-Hayden, Stone merger was announced, and the Hayden, Stone crisis was over. Golsen telegraphed his friend Greenberg that afternoon,

YOUR TELEPHONE CALL WAS INSTRUMENTAL IN MY AGREEING TO GO ALONG WITH BUNNY LASKER'S REQUEST THIS MORNING YOU MAY AS WELL GET ALL THE BROWNIE POINTS YOU CAN BECAUSE THAT'S ALL THAT WILL EVER COME OUT OF THIS DEAL. . . .

4

"Hayden, Stone blooded us," Rohatyn says. "After that, the Crisis Committee had some idea what it was up against." The case accomplished something else, perhaps more important: it welded Rohatyn and Lasker, both of whom would spend the rest of 1970 devoting themselves virtually full-time to Crisis Committee work, into a team. An odd team, to be sure. The two men, who had had no more than a nodding boardroom acquaintance before the formation of the committee, were a study in contrasts. Where Lasker was tall, tough, aggressive of manner, Rohatyn was small, wiry, and soft-spoken. Where Lasker was a bluff man of action if there ever was one, Rohatyn had the style of an intellectual. Where Lasker was, as we have seen, a fanatical Republican, Rohatyn was a middle-of-the-road or even slightly-left-of-center Democrat, an active supporter of the Presidential candidacy of Senator Muskie. Yet, on the Wall Street crisis, they closed ranks. Not without occasional difficulties. "But he's a Democrat!" Lasker would sometimes howl, when Rohatyn mentioned the name of someone he thought might be helpful in one crisis or another. "Well, so am I!" Rohatyn would shout back. Lasker would simply pretend not to hear, and the dialogue about the matter at hand would resume. In fact, Rohatyn's professional background in corporate reorganization made him far better qualified than Lasker to deal with the specifics of the situation. Nothing about Lasker's lifelong work—as an arbitrageur, making a living out of trading stocks with other professionals—prepared him for dealing with the gigantic problems of brokerage firms collapsing en masse as if struck down by a plague. So all through the crisis, Lasker was traveling a good deal on Rohatyn's professional judgment; and Rohatyn, for his part, on Lasker's brash leadership and government contacts. Sometimes, between them, they made two hundred telephone calls a day. It is easy to imagine that, if they had been lesser or less dedicated men, the collaboration might have foundered on political ideology alone. But Lasker, for all his Republican solemnity, possessed a quality on which liberals often think they have a patent, that is, the willingness to throw oneself into causes larger than and not necessarily consistent with one's own material benefit; as such, he was a living reproach to those who see all conservatives as one-dimensional monsters or single-minded clowns. And Rohatyn, happily for Wall Street, was not that kind of liberal.

Thus these two highly diverse, imperfect men made common cause. They were together, for example, in being highly dissatisfied with the Exchange's staff work on member-firm finances. Right after the resolution of the Hayden, Stone crisis, Cunningham, as the Exchange's executive vice president, assured a meeting of the board of governors that this was the end —no more such problems with member firms' finances could be expected. Rohatyn, appalled, jumped up to say that Cunningham was crazy—it was nowhere near the end. And in fact, only about a week later the next problem, long smoldering, burst into flame.

The new crisis involved Goodbody and Company, for decades a pillar of the brokerage community—its co-founder in 1891 had been the legendary Charles H. Dow himself—far larger than Hayden, Stone with 225,000 customer accounts, and ranking as the nation's fifth largest investment enterprise. Like almost all of the firms that were now falling apart, Goodbody had been in capital trouble for more than a year. A September 1969 audit on behalf of the Stock Exchange had revealed the frightening facts that the company had (presumably by accident) pledged $34 million of its customers' fully owned securities, which were legally required to be carefully segregated, as collateral for loans, and had simply lost track of not less than $18 million worth of other securities. Nevertheless, Goodbody at that time had apparently been in technical capital compliance, it was said to be operating profitably, and 225,000 customers reposed their financial hopes in it; as of September 1969, both the Stock Exchange and the S.E.C. had apparently chosen to look the other way and hope for the best.

The best was not to be. In July and August 1970, the Crisis Committee was getting what Rohatyn called "the numbers" on the affairs of Goodbody. These "numbers"—unaudited and uncheckable figures emanating from within Goodbody itself— were, in Rohatyn's later judgment, "worthless." With hindsight it can be seen that the firm, by August, was suffering from a monumental snarl in its extensive commodity accounts, and that, moreover, so many of its investors had prudently withdrawn their money that the company was in flagrant violation of the 1:20 net capital rule. However, this information could not be known for certain at the time, since Goodbody's routine annual audit would not begin until the end of that month. In mid-September, when the audit was in progress, the accountants' preliminary report showed conclusively that the firm was in violation and had been for many months. The Crisis Committee had its work cut out for it once again.

What to do? It was a dilemma, of a sort now becoming familiar, for both the Exchange and the S.E.C. Where did the public interest lie—in imposing justice on a firm that clearly deserved liquidation, or in letting such a firm get away with managerial murder in order to preserve justice for its innocent and unwary customers? After shilly-shallying for weeks, the

S.E.C. finally took action. On October 26, it ruled that Good-body must come up with substantial new capital by November 5 or be suspended. The Crisis Committee, which for a month had been devoting itself chiefly to a frantic search for new capital for Goodbody, now intensified its efforts. But exactly how much outside capital was needed? Despite the audit, some of the figures were still what Rohatyn euphemistically called "soft."

The Crisis Committee called Goodbody's partners on the carpet, one by one. The climax of this interrogation came in a dramatic confrontation between Rohatyn and James Hogle, a Salt Lake City investment banker who was Goodbody's largest investor. Hogle was a Goodbody man in the classic mold: dignified and respected at sixty; adorned with honorary degrees and directorships, trusteeships of private schools and chairman-ships of charity fund drives—clearly a man, as Americans judge these things, of character and probity. But he was also a man, like others of character and probity before him, exposed by a market crash as a full participant in greedy and slipshod practices; a man caught, presumably as a result of negligence, in a web of self-serving deceptions.

Rohatyn said to Hogle, "We understand that your own auditors have given a preliminary estimate of the amount of your capital shortage. We'd like to know that number."

Hogle hesitated. Rohatyn was right about the auditors, and Hogle knew the figure. However, he evidently believed that if he were to give it over, the Stock Exchange would shut down Goodbody on the spot. In desperation, he stalled for time "Give me twenty-four hours," he pleaded.

Rohatyn did not feel that he could comply. "We're not trying to crucify you, but I have a fiduciary responsibility in this matter," he said. "I can't let you leave the room until you've given me the number."

After a brief pause, Hogle replied, "Eighteen million dollars"—and tears rolled down his cheeks.

"I felt great sympathy for him," Rohatyn said later; presumably his sympathy lessened after Hogle mounted a huge lawsuit against the Stock Exchange in 1972. In any case, the

Exchange did not shut down Goodbody. With the key figure in hand, the committee moved forward; a tentative arrangement was soon made whereby the necessary capital would be put up by a group of investors headed by Utilities and Industries Corporation, a financial holding company. The deal was ready to be closed on an evening the week before the S.E.C.'s deadline. On that evening, Lasker called the offices of Utilities and Industries to get reaffirmation that all was ready for the signing. Instead, he got a rude shock. Not only had Utilities and Industries decided to walk away from the transaction, but its executives had walked away from their offices. They were, Lasker was informed, at the fights at Madison Square Garden.

Back to the drawing board again. The next day, Lasker called an emergency meeting of the top officials of the thirty leading Exchange member firms. There was a single-item agenda: how to bail out Goodbody? It was a tense and depressing session at which everyone agreed to what they might have been expected to agree to—that Goodbody had to be rescued, and that someone else had to do it. After much haggling, a generally satisfactory understanding was reached: the biggest brokerage firm was Merrill Lynch, so Merrill Lynch ought to take on Goodbody. Lasker was authorized to approach Merrill Lynch privately to ask how they felt about it, and everyone left the meeting satisfied. The only trouble was, Merrill Lynch might say no.

It was Lasker's job to see that Merrill Lynch didn't. "I walked across the street and saw Don Regan," he says. With extreme reluctance, the Merrill Lynch chairman told Lasker that he agreed the rescue of Goodbody was necessary, and that he would discuss the matter with his board of directors. Subsequently, Regan reported that his directors were amenable—provided the terms were right. Merrill Lynch, after all, held most of the cards. The Stock Exchange was going to have to buy itself another accommodation. Two days of virtually round-the-clock negotiations followed, and finally—on Thursday, October 29, with the S.E.C. deadline seven days off—Regan called Lasker to say that Merrill Lynch was satisfied and ready to proceed. A look at the terms suggests why. Merrill Lynch would supply $15 million to Goodbody, in exchange for which it would subsequently acquire all Goodbody assets and would be indemnified by the Stock Exchange to the extent of $20 million on possible securities losses and another $10 million to cover possible litigation coming out of the arrangement. Of course, the Exchange didn't have the $30 million. So that very afternoon the board of governors met and, with as much gravity as haste permitted, voted an amendment to the Exchange constitution authorizing the board to impose charges on the membership, as necessary, for special assessments—that is, to make the Special Trust Fund open-ended with the sky the limit. The money to save Goodbody, then, would probably end up coming from not just Merrill Lynch but the member firms as a group, after all.

One more detail had to be wrapped up. Lasker got on the phone to Washington to seek assurance from the Justice Department, headed by his friend John Mitchell, that it did not plan to throw a wrench in the machinery by taking the view that a merger of the largest brokerage firm with the fifth-largest would constitute a violation of the antitrust laws. The Justice Department obligingly indicated that, in consideration of the failing-firm doctrine that permits antitrust leniency in cases where one firm's survival is at stake, it did not expect to take such a view.

5

When would it end? Was it, possibly, over now? Lasker and Rohatyn were pushed to the edge of their physical and mental endurance. Later, Rohatyn would say that he felt that autumn as if he and Lasker had lived in a foxhole together, and that, different as the two were in so many ways, he had come out of the experience thinking of Lasker as "a true friend, a man who reached beyond himself when he was under pressure." Emphatically, it was not over; and the last and in some respects most harrowing phase of the crisis was to be complicated by an acrimonious controversy within the ranks of the Stock Exchange itself.

The last act concerned the Wall Street investment firm of Francis I. du Pont and Company, and it marked the point when the crisis involved not just the New York financial Establishment but the national one. F. I. du Pont was a part of the fief of America's oldest and perhaps most powerful business barony. More than a century and a half had passed since Eleuthère Irénée du Pont had come with his family to America from France on an erratically wandering clipper ship and had begun setting up a gunpowder works on the Brandywine near Wilmington, Delaware. In the early years of the twentieth century, Eleuthère du Pont's great grandson, Francis I. du Pont, had been a brilliant maverick within the family, generally regarded as the most talented chemist the company had ever had, and, more surprisingly, also well known at one time as a single-tax radical. But Francis I. was restless in Wilmington and environs. Fascinated by the gyrations of the stock market during and after the 1929 crash, he embarked in middle life on a whole new career. In 1931, at the age of fifty-eight, he started his own Stock Exchange firm, first handling the investments of a few relatives, and then branching out to deal with the public as well. By the early nineteen sixties—by which time Francis I. du Pont was dead, but his firm was still solidly controlled by members of his family and was managed by his son, Edmond—F. I. du Pont and Company was, as to retail business, the second-largest brokerage house in the country.

By 1969 it had dropped to third, after Merrill Lynch and Bache; it operated ninety-five branch offices. Like other such ventures, it had fallen upon a time of trouble. Its 1968 audit had shown that its capital-to-debt ratio was somewhere between 1:15 and 1:24, depending on how you calculated (and, incidentally, showing very graphically the imprecise nature of such calculations). The Stock Exchange had chosen 1:19 as the approved figure, thereby conveniently keeping F.I. du Pont within the bounds of Rule 325. The 1969 audit, completed in September of that year, disclosed an undeniably impermissible ratio of 1:32, representing a capital shortage of some $6.8 million. But the Exchange was prevailed upon by the du Pont partners to take no precipitate action and, by the time the report reached the S.E.C. in December, the partners had found enough new capital to restore the firm to compliance. So F. I. du Pont staggered through the year 1969, but not without incurring an operating deficit, before tax recoveries, of $7.7 million.

Knowing that the firm was sick and probably getting sicker, the Stock Exchange early in 1970 urged it to strengthen itself through a merger. It did, at least, make a merger. On July 1, it joined forces with two other brokerage houses, Glore, Forgan and Staats and Hirsch and Company, to form a new organization to be called F. I. du Pont-Glore, Forgan and Company. Making the announcement, Edmond du Pont commented ebulliently, "This is what I would call a true case of synergism in which the resulting entity should add up to a lot more than the sum of the parts." Or so he hoped. In truth, it was a case of the drowning trying to rescue the drowning, since at the time of the merger Glore, Forgan and Staats was itself out of control. Some members of the Crisis Committee, Rohatyn among them, were appalled that the merger was effected without an accompanying audit. By mid-summer, Haack went to Wilmington to plead with various members of the du Pont clan— among them Lammot du Pont Copeland, then chairman of the board of E. I. du Pont de Nemours, but soon to resign in the aftermath of his son's spectacular personal bankruptcy—that they buttress their floundering brokerage firm with an infusion of $15 million in new capital. Haack's request was refused; moreover, by some later accounts, the du Ponts seemed to be affronted that the request had even been made.

Through the Hayden, Stone and Goodbody crises, the du Pont situation simmered. It could not simmer forever, and it began to boil, by coincidence, at the start of November. Lasker would say later that the Crisis Committee did not have a single day to breathe between the resolution of the Goodbody mess and the full-scale appearance of this new and even larger one.

Early in November, the du Ponts realized not only that a time had come when their brokerage firm definitely needed new capital to stay in business, but that they were no longer able to raise that capital within the family. They further realized that they had on their payroll a man with both the motive and the ready cash to be the new investor they so desperately needed. In July, in a resolute attempt to straighten out their tangled back office, they had commissioned Electronic Data Systems, of Dallas, to handle all of their electronic data processing requirements at a cost that was expected to average around $8 million a year. The head of E.D.S., as the reader will recall, was the quixotic Texan, Henry Ross Perot, whose well-publicized financial situation was such that a few million dollars would apparently be hardly more than a drop in the bucket.

By taking on the du Pont computer contract, Perot had put E.D.S. into the Wall Street crisis perhaps more deeply than he realized or intended. The contract made du Pont one of E.D.S.'s largest customers; a du Pont failure now would mean not only lost revenue to E.D.S. but a severe blow to its reputation, and possibly a severe drop in the price of its stock, the source of Perot's immense wealth. So to some extent the du Ponts had already tangled Perot in their web; it might be cheaper for him to lend them a few millions than for him not to do so. Realizing the leverage that this handed them, the du Ponts went to Perot in early November and asked him for a $5 million loan to keep F. I. du Pont-Glore, Forgan and Company afloat.

Broadly speaking, it was Hayden, Stone all over again: another faltering old-line Wall Street firm going to the back country to find a rough and ready rescuer, with the Stock Exchange doing what it could to make the rescue possible in the interest of the innocent investors and, ultimately, of its own skin. But this time, there was a new element that changed the human equation. That factor was the du Ponts, and the fact that they *were* du Ponts: no parochial Wall Street bigwigs like the partners of Hayden, Stone and Goodbody, but—du Ponts! Why, after all, should they, wearers of the Wilmington purple, give quarter to a moralizing Texan or to the minions of the Stock Exchange?

Used to getting their way, accustomed to living and having their business in a state that they ruled like a barony, these worthies seemed on occasion to the Stock Exchange representatives during the negotiations to treat the securities industry itself as a far-flung part of their personal preserve.

Dozens of du Ponts were investors in F.I. du Pont—some of them female relatives who had never seen Wall Street and never would see it—but two of the most august and imperturbable conducted most of the negotiations with Perot's group and with the Stock Exchange. The chief representative in the early stages was Edmond du Pont. In his middle sixties, a Princeton and Oxford man, a yachtsman and leading Episcopal layman, he was of commanding bearing, often spoken of as the handsome du Pont, just as his cousin Henry Francis, founder of the Winterthur Museum, was spoken of as the artistic one. Later on, Edmond would fade out entirely, and actually disappear quite mysteriously for several months, to be supplanted in the negotiations by his son Anthony, thirty years younger but no more compromising when it came to making terms with Perot. Time after time over the months ahead, the du Ponts would meet with Rohatyn, Lasker, and DeNunzio of the Crisis Committee, along with Perot and his group of Texas associates. Sometimes the meetings would be at the Stock Exchange; sometimes in Lasker's fifth-floor suite at the Carlyle, overlooking Madison Avenue and Parke-Bernet, where Anthony du Pont and his lawyer would invariably plant themselves in the same corner, opposite a chair that contained a pillow decorated with a picture of a rabbit and bearing the legend "Bunny"; and, on one occasion, at Rohatyn's country place in Mount Kisco. Whatever the venue, Rohatyn and Lasker would say later, they generally found the du Pont family representatives inclined to be hard to deal with. Perot, horse trader that he was by training and instinct, strove to drive a hard bargain for his money; in exchange for a loan to F. I. du Pont he wanted the guarantee of as large an equity in the brokerage firm as he could obtain. The du Ponts, in turn, seemed to regard Perot as a hip-shooting high-binder with his eye on the main chance, attempting to get the best of them by threatening to let their firm fail and its customers lose their money—using Wall Street itself as a hostage. Seeing Perot as the prototypical *nouveau riche*—and accurately, since he was certainly one of the newest-richest persons in all history—the du Ponts *père et fils* bitterly resented the necessity of being rescued by him at all. But there it was; perhaps they could hold their noses and take his money. Perot, for his part, regarded the du Ponts as pompous ingrates. The Stock Exchange men were in the middle. When they would point out to the du Ponts that their firm was all but insolvent, they would talk about its "going concern value" and yield little or nothing to Perot. To hear Rohatyn tell it, all through the negotiations the du Pont representatives were inclined to be cocky and intransigent, apparently unwilling to acknowledge any responsibility for the welfare of Wall Street, the national economy, or even the customers of their firm. He said later, "The du Ponts are a great and public-minded family, but most of them seem to have been essentially in the dark as to what was at stake in the troubles of their brokerage firm. We had to sort of rap their representatives' knuckles all the time. The representatives seemed to be arrogant without having much to be arrogant about. There was an air of sullen defiance, in marked contrast to the Goodbody people, who had obviously had a genuine feeling of letting down the Stock Exchange and their own customers. I never felt that with the du Pont representatives. They seemed to have no conception of what it meant, in terms of responsibility, to have over three hundred thousand customers' money in your hands. As a result, some of the meetings were nightmarish. Of course, Tony du Pont had a hard problem—he had been the firm's chief capital-raiser for the past couple of years, scraping up additional funds from the various relatives. And now he was faced with the distasteful prospect of having to tell his relatives that the money he had wheedled out of them was down the drain."

6

Three highly diverse factions, then: a hard-trading Texan moti-
vated by goodwill, or the hope of profit, or perhaps something
of each; bred-in-the-bone Wall Streeters struggling to save the
club; and a group of Delaware aristocrats whose *noblesse* seemed
unwilling to *oblige*. And while they thrashed things out and
Wall Street's fate hung, once again, in the balance, Robert
Haack very nearly blew everything apart.

Later he would say that his timing had been bad; there is
little question that his motives were good. At all events, he chose
November 17, at the height of the du Pont crisis, to make a
speech at a dinner of the Economic Club of New York in which
he called for prompt abolition of the Stock Exchange's age-old
system of fixed commissions on brokerage transactions and its
replacement with a system of freely negotiated rates. He added,
as if to be certain to enrage all Stock Exchange conservatives,
"Whatever vestiges of a private-club atmosphere remain at the
New York Stock Exchange must be discarded." "Private club":
the classic red cape to the old bulls (and for that matter the old
bears) of Wall Street, the expression used previously to goad
them by William Douglas in 1937 and William Cary in 1962. But
this time there was a crucial difference; while Douglas and Cary
had been chairmen of Wall Street's official antagonist, the
S.E.C., the speaker now was president of the New York Stock
Exchange itself. Most unforgivable, in the view of traditional-
ists, Haack made his remarks without first clearing them with
any member of the board of governors whose paid employee he
was. If rage was what Haack had wanted, he got it. A few key
Wall Streeters like Regan and Salomon appeared to take his side,
but the overwhelming reaction was one of shock and outrage.
"I'm for fixed commissions," said Gustave Levy, speaking as a
former Exchange chairman and a present governor. "Bob is a

close friend of mine. He's entitled to his opinion, but I happen to disagree with him," he went on, in the gentle and measured tones of the irritated if not outraged Olympian. Lasker issued a tight-lipped public statement: "Under the constitution of the New York Stock Exchange, policy is made by the board of governors and not by the president, who is responsible for the administration." Rohatyn pointedly criticized Haack for speaking without first consulting the governors.

The long-simmering differences between Lasker and Haack were now out in the open. Lasker has since said that Haack might have been summarily dismissed as president but for the fact that such an action, at a time when the Exchange badly needed public and government support, would surely have been interpreted as meaning that the governors were against reform. Much later, in 1972, Lasker and Haack would shake hands and make their peace. "I'll say this for Bob Haack," Lasker would comment, in retrospect. "He wasn't trying to sell us down the river. In his own way, he was fighting for the Stock Exchange." But in the dark days of November 1970, what Haack's speech and the reactions to it meant was that in the midst of storm the Exchange's captain and its first mate were all but sworn enemies.

It also meant that the du Pont-Perot accommodation was in trouble. Freely negotiated commissions, if they meant anything, meant lower commissions and thus meant that investment in brokerage firms would be less attractive; so Haack seemed to be attacking Wall Street's profitability at the very moment when it was dying for lack of profits. The Crisis Committee was terrified that Perot would be so upset by the reduced prospects for brokerage profits, and disgusted by this unseemly squabbling within Wall Street, that he would simply pull out and leave F.I. du Pont to fail.

Then, on November 23, came further reason for Perot to be upset. Distressing new information was forthcoming as to the state of F. I. du Pont's finances. The figures on the annual outside audit were coming through, and what they showed was that the sum needed to keep the firm operating was apparently

$10 million—double the $5 million over which the dickering had
been conducted. Perot was furious, and understandably so. Having been asked for one sum with protestations that it was
needed, in effect, to save Wall Street and the national economy
from disaster, he was now being told that there had been a small,
regrettable error in the figures and that, ah, twice as much was,
you might say, required. For many men it would have been the
last straw. But not Perot. Patriot that he was, he saw that development as a new call to arms; horse-trader that he was, he saw
the greater weakness on the other side as a chance to strike a
better bargain. As he put the matter in his best country-boy
manner, "My father always used to say, 'If you can't give me
cash, give me chickens.' " And so, after recovering from his
initial fit of anger at the apparently casual treatment Wall Street
was giving him, he coolly set about seeing how many chickens
he could get out of F.I. du Pont and the Stock Exchange for $10
million.

It was in this particular endeavor that he fell afoul not only
of the du Ponts but of much of Wall Street as well. By the end
of November, when news of the du Pont negotiations had begun
leaking out in Wall Street, Perot had replaced Haack as the chief
center of controversy. What was the true character of the
Texan? Was he a ruthless bounty hunter and scalper taking
advantage of well-mannered gentlefolk in temporary distress, as
he was now regarded by the du Ponts, many of the Stock Exchange staff, and perhaps a majority of the investment community at large? Or was he an almost unbelievably long-suffering
and public-spirited citizen willing to endure appalling financial
sloppiness, and to put huge sums of his own money at risk for
the good of the country? In truth, it was a perfect Perot moral
situation, of precisely the sort he had been drawn into, or perhaps created for himself, for years, in which he could make what
he did a virtue and a virtue of what he did. He was characteristically outraged when people suggested that he was interested in
the du Pont deal chiefly for what it might bring him. "From a
businessman's point of view, I just don't want to invest!" he
raged, complaining bitterly that the ungrateful du Ponts, facing

the prospect of annihilation, were accusing him of trying to "steal" their firm. "I'm being treated like a raider when I'm trying to help!"

Raider and helper both, perhaps; in Wall Street, as elsewhere, Perot—true to the utilitarian philosophers who conceived the nation he loved so much and identified with so closely—most likely wanted to have it both ways, to be rich and right at the same time, with a little extra thrown in: to become, in the bargain, the proprietor of a key piece of Wall Street formerly occupied by, and still named after, the most celebrated commercial family in the land.

7

At the start of December, Wall Street hung by its fingertips. Roughly one hundred Stock Exchange firms had vanished over the past two years through merger or liquidation. Forty thousand customer accounts were involved in the thirteen cases of liquidation, and most of them were still tied up, the customers unable to get their cash or securities. Commitments to the Stock Exchange's trust fund from its member firms were approaching the $100-million mark, and some member firms had had about enough; a *sauve qui peut* sentiment was beginning to spread. Legislation to create a federal Securities Investor Protection Corporation, on the model of the Federal Deposit Insurance Corporation to protect bank depositors, was before Congress; it had no chance of passage until the present mess in Wall Street was cleared up, and thus, while it might help in future crises, it was powerless in this one. Worst of all, the Goodbody and du Pont deals were interrelated. In its contract to take over Goodbody, Merrill Lynch had insisted on a provision to the effect that, should any other major firm fail before the Merrill Lynch–Goodbody merger became final several months later, then the Merrill Lynch–Goodbody merger would automatically be cancelled.

So a du Pont failure would mean a Goodbody failure; the arch deprived of its keystone would fall, more than half a million customer accounts would be tied up, many perhaps never to be redeemed, and public confidence in Wall Street would end for years to come, if not forever. In the retrospective opinion of those best situated to know, the fall of the arch would have meant much more than that. Haack said at the time that the consequence of Goodbody's failure alone would be "a panic the likes of which we have never seen." Lasker said later: "If du Pont and Goodbody had gone down, a market crash would have occurred, but that would have been only the beginning. There would have been a run on the resources of brokerage firms—partners wanting their capital, customers wanting their cash and securities—causing many new failures. There would have been no federal investor-protection legislation. Mutual fund redemptions would have been suspended, putting fund investors in the same situation as customers of bankrupt brokerage houses. Undoubtedly the Stock Exchange would have been forced to close. All in all, millions of investors would have been wiped out, and as for Wall Street, it would have marked the end of self-regulation. The government would have moved in and taken over."

It did not happen. Three times round—Hayden, Stone; Goodbody; du Pont—went the more or less gallant, more or less decrepit ship of Wall Street, and it did not sink to the bottom of the sea. Through the early days of December the negotiations continued, and at last, on December 16, a deal was announced. Two of Perot's associates hand-carried to Lasker a certified check for $10 million, payable to F.I. du Pont and Company; in exchange, the Perot group would get the right to convert part of their loan into 51 percent of du Pont stock, thus taking control out of du Pont hands for the first time in the company's history. Edmond du Pont would resign as managing partner, and the firm's remaining partners would undertake to raise promptly an additional $15 million in capital.

Wall Street seemed to be saved. It wasn't, really, because the arrangement soon came apart, and the last phase of the rescue stands as a kind of gigantic, grotesque footnote. Far from putting up or raising more capital, in the early months of 1971 the F.I. du Pont partners and investors took millions more of their previously committed capital *out*. A group of the firm's investors, led by Anthony du Pont, showed that they had no taste for the original accommodation in any case, and set about trying to salvage what they could for themselves, whether at the cost of the firm's liquidation or not. Meanwhile, further errors in the du Pont books were found. By February 1, 1971, it appeared that the amount needed from the Perot group was not $5 million, or $10 million, but considerably more. At last, on April 23, the appalling fact came to light: the rescue would require somewhat in excess of $50 million.

"I want out!" Perot shouted over the telephone from Dallas; now he had been pushed too far. But the Crisis Committee would not let him out; all through the two previous months, with Rohatyn placating the Perot group, Ralph DeNunzio hand-holding the du Ponts, and Lasker serving as go-between, the negotiations had somehow been kept alive. Rohatyn would later call it a game of chicken, with each side, the du Ponts and the Perot group, using the threat of the firm's failure and the terrible social and economic consequences as a lever to improve its bargaining position. Through it all, despite the gravity of the matter, humor of a sort, in the form of the slicker-and-bumpkin joke, seems to have survived. Once, after many hours of hot-and-heavy negotiations, Lasker took Perot to dinner at the posh Côte Basque restaurant.

"I'll bet you want a big drink, after all that," Lasker said to the Texan.

"You bet I do!" Perot replied, in heartfelt tones; and commanded the hovering proprietor, "Bring me the biggest ginger ale in the house!"

Matters came to a head in mid-April; there were daily and nightly sessions in Dallas, at the Stock Exchange, at Lasker's suite, finally at the S.E.C. offices in Washington. Perot did not carry out his threat to withdraw; the negotiations succeeded. In the last week of April an agreement was reached that would stick: Perot and his colleagues to lend $55 million, in exchange this time for at least 80 percent control of F. I. du Pont; and the Stock Exchange, through assessment of its members, to indemnify Perot against resulting losses up to the sum of $15 million.

For the reader who has been numbed by the size of the sums tossed around, and the surrealistic ease with which they escalated, let a single figure serve as summary and conclusion: over two years, it would eventually appear, the errors and miscalculations in the account books of F. I. du Pont had amounted to somewhere in the neighborhood of $100 million.

8

How had it all come about? Why hadn't it been prevented? Why, for example, had the required capital-to-debt ratio not been set lower than 1:20, and why was the ruinous ninety-day capital withdrawal rule allowed to stand? As a matter of fact, the Stock Exchange had required 1:15 until 1953, and had relaxed the requirement that year to ease the need for new capital brought about by vast postwar expansion of the national securities business. When the 1970 crisis came, it was too late for reform. Tightening the requirement then was out of the question because such a move would simply have thrown many additional firms into violation. As to the ninety-day withdrawal rule, it was there because it had always been there—because it had the powerful sanction of tradition, backed by the shared assumption that the gentlemen who provided the money for Wall Street's passage would not, in a crisis, choose to play the role of rats leaving a fleet of sinking ships. (The term for withdrawal notice was finally changed to six months in October 1970; in 1972, it was made eighteen months.) In sum, the problem was that the spirit abroad in the land at the time, the spirit that allowed conglomerates to buy profits with convenient mergers and mutual funds to write false assets with letter stock, spread to the core institutions of Wall Street, the huge old brokerage houses; and so the old rules that had been intended to govern men of caution, probity, and responsibility were suddenly failing to govern men caught in an obsession with greed.

But Wall Street was saved now, and the go-go years were about over. The Perot deal went through, and F.I. du Pont continued operations under the briskly competent management of Morton H. Meyerson, a young Perot lieutenant. "My objective is for du Pont to become the most respected firm in the securities business," said Perot, in the sober pear-shaped tones of many Wall Streeters before him, and it was at least possible that he would reach his objective. Lasker, Rohatyn, and their colleagues could begin to catch up on their sleep, and on their private business affairs. Albert H. Gordon, chairman of Kidder, Peabody, wrote to Lasker, "If you had once lost your nerve, we would have gone down with all hands lost." Surely no one could deny that Lasker had kept his nerve, done what of all things in the world he could do best: as a conservative, he had superbly filled the role of conservator.

Perot had come out probably the largest single investor in Wall Street and certainly the biggest man in its looming automated future; for all his outback ways a man of complexity and paradox: an idealist and yet a pragmatist, a passionate believer and yet conceivably a bit of a faker, and in Wall Street an Early American—such a leader as Wall Street might have had in 1870 —called to answer a Late American problem in 1970. In the nineteen sixties, finance capitalism as practiced in America had once again, through its own folly, dug itself an almost inescapable grave and then dug itself right out—had once again survived, but just barely. The architects of its survival, men like Lasker, Rohatyn, and Perot, had shown courage, persistence, and self-sacrifice amounting almost to heroism. The question remained, Was the heroism in a good cause? Was the old system that could produce "creative" accounting, manipulation of stock prices, victimization of naïve investors, and mind-boggling messes in brokerage firms really worth saving? There are those, a few of them in Wall Street itself, who thought and still think not—who believe that Hayden, Stone, Goodbody, and du Pont should have been allowed to go under so that the resulting bloodbath would cleanse Wall Street and bring about a government takeover to humble Wall Street's pride and set it on the path of righteousness. It goes without saying that those people do not include Lasker, Rohatyn, or Perot—and that, when all was said and done, in the 1970 crisis it was they rather than their opponents who had the vitality and the faith to win the day. How long the day would remain won was another matter.

And so this chronicle ends, as it began, with Henry Ross Perot, the extraordinary man who, metaphorically speaking, won the money game and used his winnings to buy Wall Street.

CHAPTER XIV

The
Go-Go
Years

1

Some epitaphs for the go-go years:

In mid-October 1970, the week before Gramco Management suspended redemptions and sales of its collapsed offshore-fund, Director Pierre Salinger sat perched on the desk in his London office and said amiably to a reporter, "The offshore business is a dead duck." Gramco stock, which had once sold at 38, was then available for 1½.

In June 1972, a block of preferred shares of Bernie Cornfeld's (more properly, formerly Bernie Cornfeld's) Investors Overseas Services changed hands in Geneva at one cent a share.

Between the end of 1968 and October 1, 1970, the assets of the twenty-eight largest hedge funds declined by 70 percent, or about $750 million. (Theoretically, hedge funds alone among financial institutions were ideally structured to survive a market crash or even to profit from one. But only theoretically. Structure is not genius; even for the exclusive hedge funds, genius turned out to have been a rising market. In practice, their managers, as carried away by the go-go spirit as anyone else, had simply forgotten to hedge in time. One of the most heralded of them had had the spectacular bad luck—or bad judgment—to begin large-scale short selling on May 27, 1970, the very day the market turned around and made a record gain.) Among the heavy losers in one such fund, which closed down in 1971, were Laurence Tisch, head of Loews Corporation; Leon Levy, partner in Oppenheimer and Company; Eliot Hyman, former boss of Warner Brothers Seven Arts; and Dan Lufkin, co-founder of Donaldson, Lufkin and Jenrette. The dumb money could take bitter comfort in the company it had among the smartest of the smart money—or former money.

A study of mutual funds by Irwin Friend, Jean Crockett, and Marshall Blume of the faculty of the Wharton School of Finance and Commerce, published in August 1970 by the Twentieth Century Fund, resulted in the startling conclusion that "equally weighted or unweighted investment in New York Stock Exchange stocks would have resulted in a higher rate of return than that achieved by mutual funds in the 1960–1968 period as a whole." More simply stated, the pin-the-tail-on-the-donkey system of stock selection would, according to the authors' figures, have worked better than the system of putting one's trust in expert portfolio management.

If that conclusion suggested that gunslinger performance had been a fantasy born of mass hysteria, an item in *Forbes* magazine in early 1971 suggested that corporate profit performance—presumably the bedrock beneath the boom—had been another. By *Forbes*'s method of reckoning, Saul Steinberg's Leasco, the king of all the go-go stocks, over the years of its stock-market glory had not earned any aggregate net profit at all.

2

Reform follows public crises as remorse follows private ones. Before the dust had settled on the 1969–1970 Wall Street crisis —indeed, before its last phase was over—reform began. In December 1970, Congress passed and President Nixon signed into law a bill creating a Securities Investor Protection Corporation, "Sipic" for short—a federally chartered membership corporation, its funds provided by the securities business, which would henceforth protect customers against losses when their brokers went broke, up to $50,000 per customer. Every customer hurt by a brokerage failure over the years 1969–1970 was eventually going to end up whole again, the Stock Exchange now announced—even the unlucky clients of Plohn, First Devonshire, and Robinson, apparently left to their fate back in August. The Exchange's temporary abandonment of them now appeared to have been part of the bargaining to get the Sipic bill passed. But what with lawsuits and the law's delays, it would take time. In midsummer, 1971, some eighteen thousand customers of liquidated firms were still waiting for their securities and money. By the end of 1972, virtually everyone had been made whole.

Just as in the nineteen thirties, the Stock Exchange set about reforming itself internally. In March 1972, its members voted to reorganize its governing structure along more democratic lines by replacing the old thirty-three-man heavily insider-dominated board with a new board comprising twenty-one members, ten of them from outside Wall Street, and a new salaried chairman to supercede the traditionally unpaid, nominally part-time chairman of the past, such as Lasker. In the spirit of reform, the new board, at its maiden meeting in July, selected as its first paid chairman James J. Needham, not a Wall Streeter but an accountant and S.E.C. man. The first new "public" representatives to be elected to the board were mostly rich industrialists scarcely likely to share the point of view of the small investor, suggesting that the job of reform was not done yet. Still, the change unmistakably represented progress.

And whose recommendations served as model for the new, more democratic structure at 11 Wall Street? None other than those of William McChesney Martin, Jr., the very same man who in 1937, as a precocious, serious-minded young broker just past thirty, had served as secretary of the committee proposing democratizing reform of the Stock Exchange structure, and the following year had become the Exchange's first president under the new structure, in the wake of the Whitney scandal. It must have been with a weird sense of experiencing a recurring dream that Martin, called out of retirement at Lasker's urgent request in December 1970, for the second time in his life spent half a year studying the question of how to transform the New York Stock Exchange from a club serving its members to a marketplace serving the public.

The final irony, then: history repeating itself not only as to pattern of events but, in one crucial instance, as to identity of protagonist. But if Wall Street's nineteen sixties were in many ways a replay of its nineteen twenties—refuting the optimism of those who believe that reform can make social history into a permanent growth situation rather than a cyclical stock—its go-go years were also utterly characteristic of the larger trends of their own time, reflecting and projecting all the lights and shadows of a troubled, confused, frightening decade the precise like of which had never been seen before and surely will not be seen again. Consider, for example, the subtle shift in the aspirations of the moneymakers who have dominated the various stages of this chronicle. Edward M. Gilbert, at the beginning of the decade, was a throwback to the vanished American style, originally canonized in the nineteen twenties, of personal and social irresponsibility elevated to the status of principle. Gerald Tsai—reaching his apogee in 1964 and 1965, the period of calm between the storms of John Kennedy's assassination and the upheavals of 1967 and after—aspired to and largely achieved a more rational American dream dating back to more stable times, that of the poor immigrant using his wits to make good in the land of the free. Saul Steinberg in 1968 and 1969 was the financial world's version of a figure familiar in the larger national scene at that moment, the young and brash outsider setting out to join the insiders by overthrowing them—and, like other contemporaneous American rebels, ending up largely gaining his objective by the ironical means of being defeated and then admitting his mistake. Bernard Cornfeld, typifying a conflicting and simultaneous national tendency, wrote satire with his life instead of his pen, made his life an exaggerated version of the manners and morals of his society; not deigning to aspire to join the Establishment, he aspired to thumb his nose at it as conspicuously as possible—as indeed he did. Finally, the two figures who dominated Wall Street at the decade's end, Lasker and Perot, dutifully reflected a national turn toward the more conservative and conventional forms of social responsibility. Unabashedly loving their country because it had provided such a complaisant arena for their personal ambitions, they set out to do what they could to reciprocate—Lasker by throwing his heart and soul and mind into the saving of the New York Stock Exchange, Perot by throwing huge sums of his own money into the same enterprise, and, in his futile attempt to rescue American prisoners in North Vietnam, riding off in all directions like a modern Don Quixote with a Boeing 707 as his Rosinante.

Manners and fashions change, but the wish to become rich remains constant; and the styles and motives of the greatest money-seekers reflect those changes as delicately as do those of great lovers.

3

What of the customer, the little investor, Wall Street's "consumer"? Was he fleeced as calculatedly and ruthlessly in the nineteen sixties as he had been in the nineteen twenties? Did the conglomerates and the performance funds treat him with no more consideration than had the market pools and investment trusts of old? Or did he, like the victim of a confidence game, have largely himself to blame?

To begin with, there can be little question that, by and large, he was a big loser in the nineteen sixties market. The Stock Exchange had the bad luck to release the results of its latest national stockholder census in July 1970, right at the bottom of the market collapse. As we have seen, the count came to about 31 million, more than one in every four of the nation's adults. This represented a 53.3 percent increase since 1965, when the census figure had been just over 20 million. The conclusion is inescapable that almost 11 million persons invested in the stock market for the first time between 1965, when the Dow stood just under 1,000, and mid-1970, when it stood at around 650. Exactly how much of the $300 billion overall paper loss in the 1969–1970 crash was suffered by those 11 million new investors is incalculable, but it may safely be assumed that as of July 1970, when the Exchange distributed its newest evidence of the arrival of people's capitalism, people's capitalism had left at least 10 million American investors, or one-third of all American investors, poorer than it had found them, and poorer by an aggregate sum of many billions of dollars.

The man or woman of the nineteen sixties who—in quest of a third car or a Caribbean vacation, or to pay a private-school bill, or merely to try to stay even with inflation—invested in Ling-Temco-Vought, or Leasco, or the Mates Fund, or even National Student Marketing Corporation, had one measurable advantage over the unfortunate who in 1929 had taken an equally disastrous flyer in Radio or Shenandoah or Alleghany. Thanks to the Securities Acts and the S.E.C., the nineteen sixties investor was technically protected from corporate deception by federal requirements of full disclosure. But the key word, of course, is "technically." If he had fully understood the abstruse implications of merger accounting, he might not have invested in Ling-Temco-Vought or Leasco; if he had grasped the significance of up-valuation of letter stock in a fund portfolio, he would probably not have invested in the Mates Fund; if he had read and understood the footnotes to the 1969 annual report of National Student Marketing, he would almost certainly not have entrusted his savings to that particular venture. The question, then, is whether or not an amateur investor, with affairs of his own to attend to and limited time and attention to give to the ins and outs of the stock market, might reasonably be expected to have had such understanding. Was he not entitled to rely on the investment skill and integrity of his broker and his mutual-fund manager—especially when their judgment was so often confirmed by that of the greatest professional investing institutions, the national banks, the huge mutual and pension funds, the insurance companies and foundations? In sum, had the game of stock investing really been made fair for the amateur as against the professional?

Indeed it had not—not when the nation's most sophisticated corporate financiers and their accountants were constantly at work finding new instruments of deception barely within the law; not when supposedly cool-headed fund managers had become fanatical votaries at the altar of instant performance; not when brokers' devotion to their customers' interest was constantly being compromised by private professional deals or the pressure to produce commissions; and not when the style-setting leaders of professional investing were plunging as greedily and recklessly as any amateur. Full disclosure in the nineteen sixties market was largely a failure, giving the small investor the semblance of protection without the substance. And that failure raised the question of just how much full disclosure can ever accomplish. Rules can be tightened, as many were during the decade and more will be in the future; but as surely as night follows day, the tricksters of Wall Street and its financial tributaries will be ever busy topping the new rules with new tricks, and there is no reason to doubt that the respectable institutions will again play Pied Piper by catching the quick-money fever the next time it is epidemic. As Lasker said in 1972, "I can feel it coming, S.E.C. or not, a whole new round of disastrous speculation, with all the familiar stages in order— blue-chip boom, then a fad for secondary issues, then an over-the-counter play, then another garbage market in new issues, and finally the inevitable crash. I don't know when it will come, but I can feel it coming, and, damn it, I don't know what to do about it."

Thus, in the nature of things, the amateur investor remains and probably will remain at a certain disadvantage in relation to the professional. Perhaps his best protection lies in knowledge of that fact itself.

4

All that notwithstanding, Wall Street is changing in a democratic direction, and will surely change more: the public will be better represented in the councils of the New York Stock Exchange (perhaps tied in with the Amex and the smaller regional exchanges), the commissions on more and more trades will be determined by free-market negotiation rather than by fiat of the securities industry, mutual-fund charges and operations will be better regulated. But perhaps the biggest change currently in the wind is not strictly financial, but rather social and cultural.

After it graduated, around the beginning of this century, from being chiefly an arena for the depredations of robber barons and the manipulations of sharp traders in railroad bonds, Wall Street became not only the most important financial center in the world but also a national institution. In the nineteen twenties it was in a real sense what Wall Streeters always cringed to hear it called, a private club—and not just any private club but probably the most important and interesting one in the country, a creator and reflector of national manners and a school for national leaders. In the nineteen sixties, despite declining aristocratic character and political influence, it was still those things, playing out week by week and month by month its concentrated and heightened version of the larger national drama. But after the convulsion with which the decade and that particular act in the drama ended, its days in the old role seemed to be numbered. Wall Street as a social context is apparently doomed not by reform but by mechanization. Already in the early nineteen seventies, a significant proportion of stock trading is being conducted not face to face on a floor under a skylight but between men sitting in front of closed-circuit television screens in offices hundreds or thousands of miles apart. There is a growing movement, forced by Wall Street's increasingly obvious inability to handle a vastly expanded national securities business, to abolish stock certificates and replace them with entries in computer memory units. The head of the nation's biggest brokerage firm—Regan of Merrill Lynch—predicted in 1972 that "by 1980 Wall Street will have lost lots of its distinctive flavor. . . . The Street will be the scene of a lot less colorful action than we have witnessed in the past few years. . . . Early to go, I imagine, will be that decorative piece of paper [the stock certificate]. . . . When all the electronic gear is in place, will we still need a New York Stock Exchange? Probably not in its present form."

Good-bye, then, to the private club. The twin forces that hold Wall Street together as a social unit are the stock certificate, the use of which calls for geographical unity because it must be quickly and easily conveyed from seller to buyer, and the stock-exchange floor, which gives stock trading a visible focal point. If the certificate and the floor go, Wall Street will have moved a long way toward transforming itself into an impersonal national slot machine—presumably fairer to the investor but of much less interest as a microcosm of America. The private-club aspect, however deplorable from the standpoint of equity and democracy, is necessary to the social ambiance; the wishes of a reformer and those of a social historian must be at odds. If the private club goes, with it, perhaps, will go that tendency of Wall Street's of which I have spoken: to be a stage for high, pure moral melodrama on the themes of possession, domination, and belonging. This may be, conceivably, one of the last books to be written about "Wall Street" in its own time.

Notes
on Sources

Since little formal history has yet been written about United States
financial life in the nineteen sixties, I have necessarily relied chiefly
on business and government publications, contemporaneous newspaper and magazine articles, and, above all, the personal accounts of
those involved either as observers or as participants, among them:
Louis S. Auchincloss, William L. Cary, Manuel F. Cohen, Orval
DuBois, Russell Goings, Jr., Walter Guzzardi, Jr., H. Erich Heine-
mann, the Rev. Francis C. Huntington, David S. Jackson, Eliot Jane-
way, Edward C. Johnson II, Edward C. Johnson III, Alfred Winslow
Jones, Gilbert E. Kaplan, Kenneth Langone, Bernard J. Lasker,
Thomas Marquez, the Rev. John W. Moody, Osgood Nichols, Henry
Ross Perot, William S. Renchard, Felix G. Rohatyn, M. J. Rossant,
Eugene H. Rotberg, William R. Salomon, Ralph S. Saul, Andrew
Segal, Lee J. Seidler, Saul P. Steinberg, Gerald Tsai, Jr., Thomas O.
Waage, and John Westergaard.

I owe thanks to all of these persons, and to others who wished not
to be identified.

CHAPTER I

Surprisingly little has been published about Henry Ross Perot's career prior to his 1970 involvement in Wall Street affairs. See Arthur M. Louis, "The Fastest Richest Texan Ever," *Fortune*, November 1968; and "H. Ross Perot: America's First Welfare Billionaire," *Ramparts*, November 1971.

The story of Trinity Church's role in the May 1970 riot is well told in *The Trinity Parish Newsletter*, May–June 1970.

CHAPTER II

The reform of the American Stock Exchange is reconstructed (apart from interviews) largely from Amex and S.E.C. documents, along with newspaper accounts in *The New York Times*, *The New York Herald-Tribune*, and *The Wall Street Journal*. See especially the *Herald-Tribune*, June 25, 1961; "Interim Report of the Special Committee for Study of American Stock Exchange," December 21, 1961; and the *S.E.C. Staff Report on the American Stock Exchange*, January 1962.

On Birrell and Guterma: T. A. Wise, *The Insiders* (New York, 1962).

CHAPTER III

On Edward M. Gilbert: *Time*, June 22, 1962; *Life*, June 29, 1962; *The Saturday Evening Post*, October 19, 1963. A remarkable and detailed account of Gilbert in Nevada in May 1962, and subsequently in Rio, is contained in an article by M. J. Rossant, *The New York Times*, June 24, 1962. I am grateful to several other persons who provided information on Gilbert's career and personality.

CHAPTER IV

Cary tells his own story of his S.E.C. chairmanship, and gives his views on federal regulation, in William L. Cary, *Politics and the Regulatory Agencies* (New York, 1967). See also Louis M. Kohlmeier, Jr., *The Regulators* (New York, 1969), and *American Bar Association Journal*, March 1963, in which Cary's "private club" speech is reprinted.

The basic document is *Report of Special Study of the Securities Markets of the S.E.C.* (Washington, 1963).

CHAPTER V

On Zeckendorf's downtown real-estate operations: William Zeckendorf with Edward McCreary, *Zeckendorf* (New York, 1970).

On the early feminist brokerage firm of Woodhull, Claflin and Company: Johanna Johnston, *Mrs. Satan* (New York, 1967).

On Bart Lytton: *The New York Times*, June 30, 1969.

On Atlantic Acceptance Corporation, Ltd.: the complete story is told in *Report of the Royal Commission Appointed to Inquire into the Failure of Atlantic Acceptance Corporation* (four volumes; Toronto, 1969). A brief and sound early account, by M. J. Rossant, appeared in *The New York Times*, November 14, 1965.

CHAPTER VI

The rise of Gerald Tsai is described in Gilbert Edmund Kaplan and Chris Welles, *The Money Managers* (New York, 1969). See also *Business Week*, February 2, 1965, and *Newsweek*, May 9, 1966 and May 13, 1968.

An account of Alfred Winslow Jones and the hedge-fund business appears in *The Money Managers*.

CHAPTER VII

The literature on conglomerates, unlike that on most aspects of nineteen sixties finance, is already voluminous. The basic source, up to now, is *Investigation of Conglomerate Corporations: Hearings Before the Antitrust Subcommittee of the Committee on the Judiciary, House of Representatives, Ninety-first Congress* (seven volumes; Washington, 1970), along with a summary volume, *Investigation of Conglomerate Corporations: A Report by the Staff of the Antitrust Subcommittee* (Washington, 1971). A useful book for the general reader is *The Conglomerate Commotion*, by the editors of *Fortune* (New York, 1970). A detailed account of the career of James Ling is to be found in Stanley H. Brown, *Ling: The Rise, Fall, and Return of a Texas Titan* (New York, 1972). Among particularly enlightening magazine and newspaper articles are "Litton's Shattered Image," *Forbes*, December 1, 1969; "Meshulam Riklis: What Makes Rapid Run," *Forbes*, March 15, 1971; and "Affinity for Tennis Turned a Mansion Into a Showplace" (on Eugene V. Klein), *The New York Times*, September 6, 1971.

On accountants and accounting: *The Insiders* (cited under Chapter

II); "The Accountants Are Changing the Rules," by Arthur M. Louis, *Fortune*, June 1968; and "A Comparison of the Economic and Social Status of the Accounting Profession in Great Britain and the United States of America," by Lee J. Seidler, *The Accountant's Magazine*, September 1969.

CHAPTER VIII

On back-office snarls: Hurd Baruch, *Wall Street: Security Risk* (Washington, 1971), a sound and thorough study by an S.E.C. official; Christopher Elias, *Fleecing the Lambs* (Chicago, 1971), which is biased and unreliable but nevertheless useful and suggestive; "The Back Office: An Inside View of Wall Street's New Ball Game," by John W. Faison (The Wall Street Ministry, New York; pamphlet); *The New York Times*, 1968 and 1969, especially an article by Marilyn Bender, January 9, 1972. The question of Mafia connections in Wall Street is dealt with in the *Times*, November 26, 1969.

CHAPTER IX

On the youth boom in money management, see *The Institutional Investor*, October 1968; *Business Week*, March 15 and May 3, 1969; *Forbes*, January 15, 1969.

Abbie Hoffman's 1967 exploit at the Stock Exchange is described in his *Revolution for the Hell of It* (New York, 1968).

Trinity Church's community programs are described in "New Hope for the Wall Street Ghetto," by Mary Cole Hanna, *Sign* magazine, August 1969, and *The New York Times*, June 5, 1969.

CHAPTER X

Extensive documentation of the Leasco-Reliance merger and the Leasco-Chemical encounter are contained in *Investigation of Conglomerate Corporations*, Volume 2, and in the *Report by the Staff*. Among the more enlightening of many articles that have been published about Saul P. Steinberg are "Fast Money Power," by Chris Welles, in Clay Felker, ed., *The Power Game* (New York, 1969), and "Steinberg's Complaint," *Forbes*, May 15, 1969.

CHAPTER XI

On the offshore business as a whole, see *Business Week*, March 22, 1969, and *The New York Times*, October 12, 1970; on Gramco in particular, *The Sunday Times* of London, October 11, 1970.

On Cornfeld and I.O.S.: Godfrey Hodgson, Bruce Page, and Charles Raw, *"Do You Sincerely Want to Be Rich?"* (New York, 1971), in which the story is told in exhaustive detail; and Bert Cantor, *The Bernie Cornfeld Story* (New York, 1970), in which it is told with gossip and *brio*.

On Parvin-Dohrmann: *S.E.C.* vs. *Parvin-Dorhmann et. al.*, initiated October 16, 1969, in the U.S. District Court for the Southern District of New York. A good popular account is contained in John F. Lawrence and Paul E. Steiger, *The Seventies Crash and How to Survive It* (New York, 1970).

National Student Marketing Corporation: Andrew Tobias, *The Funny Money Game* (Chicago, 1971), and "How Cortes Randell Drained the Fountain of Youth," by Rush Loving, Jr., *Fortune*, April 1970.

On institutional investing and its effect on the securities markets, with comments on offshore funds, hedge funds, and letter stock: *Institutional Investor Study Report of the Securities and Exchange Commission: Summary Volume* (Washington, 1971). However, this long-awaited study must be rated a disappointment.

The full text of the famous Nixon letter on the securities industry is reprinted in *The New York Times*, October 2, 1968.

Statistics on concentration of capital are derived from *Investigation of Conglomerate Corporations: A Report by the Staff*.

CHAPTER XII

The allusions to the events of 1929 are drawn from J. K. Galbraith, *The Great Crash, 1929* (Boston, 1961), and from John Brooks, *Once in Golconda: a True Drama of Wall Street 1920–1938* (New York, 1969).

Donald T. Regan's account of the White House dinner of May 27, 1970, is contained in his *A View from the Street* (New York, 1972). The menu on that occasion, and other engaging details, come from an article by Terry Robards in *The New York Times*, May 31, 1970. Galbraith's article drawing parallels between 1929 and 1970 appeared in the *Times* on May 3, 1970.

On the economic dimension of the 1969–1970 crash, relative to that of 1929, see "The Great Crash in Growth Stocks," by Max Shapiro, *Dun's Review*, January 1971.

The action of the Federal Reserve in the Penn Central bankruptcy is described in *Perspective '70: Economic Highlights of the Year* (pamphlet; the Federal Reserve Bank of New York, 1971), and in *Business Week*, October 24, 1970.

CHAPTER XIII

There are a number of well-researched early accounts of various aspects of the 1970 Wall Street capital crisis. These include "Wall Street on the Ropes," by Carol J. Loomis, *Fortune*, December 1970; "The Unbelievable Last Months of Hayden Stone," by Mrs. Loomis, *Fortune*, January 1971; "Ross Perot Moves in on Wall Street," by Arthur M. Louis, *Fortune*, July 1971; and articles by Terry Robards in *The New York Times*, December 17, 23, and 31, 1970, and March 28, 1971. See also Baruch, *Wall Street: Security Risk*.

Background material on the du Pont family is drawn from William H. A. Carr, *The du Ponts of Delaware* (New York, 1964).

The November 1970 dispute over Haack's Economics Club speech is described in *The New York Times*, November 22, 1970.

CHAPTER XIV

Irwin Friend, Marshall Blume, and Jean Crockett, *Mutual Funds and Other Institutional Investors* (New York, 1970).

Collapse of the hedge funds: *Fortune*, May 1971, and Robert Metz in *The New York Times*, March 16, 1972.

Leasco's unprofitability: *Forbes*, January 15, 1971.

William McChesney Martin, Jr., "The Securities Markets: A Report, With Recommendations, Submitted to the Board of Governors of the New York Stock Exchange, August 5, 1971."

Index